VOLUME 2

LIFE OF CHRIST

God's Word *for the* **Biblically-Inept**™ SERIES

Robert C. Girard

STARBURST PUBLISHERS®

P. O. Box 4123, Lancaster, Pennsylvania 17604

CARTOONS BY
Reverend Fun
(Dennis "Max" Hengeveld)
Dennis is a graphic de-
signer for Gospel Films and
the author of *Has
Anybody Seen My Locust?*
His cartoons can
be seen worldwide at
www.reverendfun.com.

To schedule author appearances, write:
Author Appearances
Starburst Publishers
P.O. Box 4123
Lancaster, Pennsylvania 17604
(717) 293-0939

www.starburstpublishers.com

CREDITS:
Cover design by David Marty Design
Text design and composition by John Reinhardt Book Design
Illustrations by Melissa A. Burkhart and Bruce Burkhart
Cartoons by Dennis "Max" Hengeveld

Unless otherwise noted, or paraphrased by the author, all Scripture quotations are from the New International Version of The Holy Bible.

Scripture taken from the HOLY BIBLE: NEW INTERNATIONAL VERSION® (NIV®). Copyright © 1973, 1978, 1984 by International Bible Society. Used by permission of Zondervan Publishing House. The "NIV" and "New International Version" trademarks are registered in the United States Patent and Trademark Office by International Bible Society.

Reverend Fun cartoons ©Copyright Gospel Films Incorporated.

To the best of its ability, Starburst Publishers® has strived to find the source of all material. If there has been an oversight, please contact us, and we will make any correction deemed necessary in future printings. We also declare that to the best of our knowledge all material (quoted or not) contained herein is accurate, and we shall not be held liable for the same.

First Printing, September 2000

ISBN: 1-892016-39-7
Library of Congress Number 99-67256

Printed in the United States of America

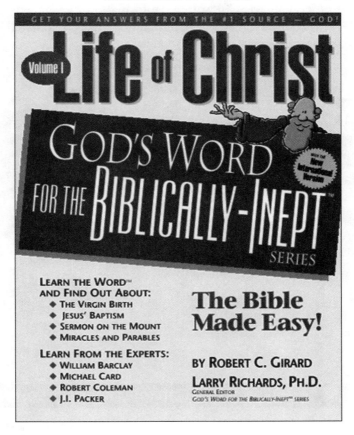

READ THIS PAGE BEFORE YOU READ THIS BOOK . . .

Welcome to the *God's Word for the Biblically-Inept*™ series. If you find reading the Bible overwhelming, baffling, and frustrating, then this Revolutionary Commentary™ is for you!

Each page of the series is organized for easy reading with icons, sidebars, and bullets to make the Bible's message easy to understand. *God's Word for the Biblically-Inept*™ series includes opinions and insights from Bible experts of all kinds, so you get various opinions on Bible teachings—not just one!

There are more *God's Word for the Biblically-Inept*™ titles on the way. The following is a list of available books. (See the following page for ordering information.) We have assigned each title an abbreviated **title code**. This code along with page numbers is incorporated in the text **throughout the series**, allowing easy reference from one title to another.

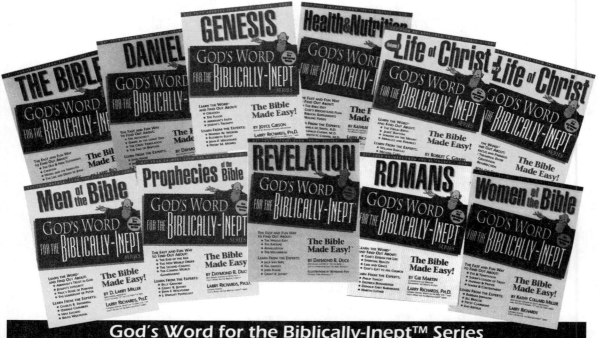

God's Word for the Biblically-Inept™ Series

CHAPTERS AT A GLANCE

CHAPTERS AT A GLANCE

PART THREE: The Price of Redemption

PART FOUR: Sonrise

ILLUSTRATIONS

INTRODUCTION

Welcome to *Life of Christ, Volume 2—God's Word for the Biblically-Inept™*. This is another REVOLUTIONARY COMMENTARY™ designed to uncomplicate the Bible. You will have fun as you discover what's in this amazing book that has had such an enormous influence on the culture in which we live. I intend to change your outlook on the Bible forever. You *will* Learn the Word™.

To Gain Your Confidence

Life of Christ, Volume 2—God's Word for the Biblically-Inept™ is designed to make the Bible user-friendly. I've taken a sound educational approach. I've also put a lot of effort into keeping things simple while allowing you to participate in an exciting adventure of enlightenment and joy when you discover what the Bible is all <u>about</u>. My wife, Audrey, worked with me to keep my writing clear and understandable. She was "first responder" on the scene to rescue me from being complicated. In addition to doing valuable research, she has been my best friend and most honest critic.

> The best source of information needed to understand the Bible is the Bible itself—"the *real* thing." That's why I often use other Bible references to shed light on Bible statements I'm trying to explain. The Bible is its own best commentary.

What Is The Bible?

The Bible is a collection of 66 books organized in two sections: an "Old" Testament of 39 books and a "New" Testament of 27 books. The Old Testament was written by different authors and poets, mostly of Hebrew heritage, between 1400 and 400 **B.C.** It deals with events before the birth of Jesus Christ that mostly center on the nation of Israel. The New Testament was written in 60 years between 40 and 100 **A.D.** It tells about the birth, life, teachings, death, and resurrection of a historical person named Jesus, and about the movement begun by the people who believed Jesus was the Son of God.

CHAPTER HIGHLIGHTS

(Chapter Highlights)

Let's Get Started

(Let's Get Started)

Matthew 16:16 Simon Peter answered, "You are the Christ."

(Verse of Scripture)

☞ GO TO:

John 15:11 (about)

(Go To)

Remember This . . .

(Remember This)

B.C.: *Before Christ*

A.D.: *Latin phrase anno domini, meaning "in the year of our Lord"*

(What?)

THE BIG PICTURE 🔍

Luke 10:30–35 Jesus told a story about a traveler who got robbed.

(The Big Picture)

EARLY CHURCH LIFE:

(Early Church Life)

KEY Outline:

True Faith

Have one God

Love God

Love others

(Key Outline)

KINGDOM
👑
OF GOD

(Kingdom of God)

Many years after the Bible was written, scholars divided its books into chapters and verses to make it easier to locate stories and teachings. Thus John 3:16 indicates the third chapter of the book written by John and the 16th verse of that chapter.

Why Study The Bible?

First, even though the Bible was written a long time ago by ordinary people, it is a special book. It is special because God is its source. The writers of the Bible claim over 2,600 times that they are speaking or writing God's words. Millions of people over thousands of years have believed them.

Second, the Bible is the best-selling book in history, and for good reason. It offers answers to the questions we wonder about. How did the world begin? What is my purpose in life? What makes people act the way they do? What will happen to me when I die? To help us understand the answers to those questions, God gave us the Bible. Many, many people have found relief and comfort in its pages.

Third, even people who don't believe the Bible owe it to themselves to find out what's in it. The Bible's stories and images have shaped Western society. The moral code in the Bible has been used as the source of most of our laws. Everyone who wants to be fully educated needs to have some knowledge of this influential book.

The Life Of Jesus Christ

The person whose story is told in the New Testament is Jesus, also known as "Christ," "Jesus Christ," "the Lord Jesus Christ," and "Jesus of Nazareth." If the stories and teachings of Jesus recorded in the New Testament are true (and millions of Christians worldwide stake their lives on the belief that they are!), then Jesus was the most unusual person who ever lived. The study of his life and accomplishments is one of the most important pursuits in which anyone can engage.

We tell this amazing story in two volumes. *Life of Christ, Volume 1,* begins before Jesus is born, describes what we know about his childhood, and details his ministry and teachings, including many of his parables. *Life of Christ, Volume 2,* begins with the events described in Matthew 16 and discusses Jesus' later ministry, crucifixion, and resurrection.

The Early Years

Jesus was the firstborn son of a young Jewish woman named Mary from the crossroads town of Nazareth, Galilee. An unmarried virgin, she conceived Jesus through the miraculous overshadowing of the **Holy Spirit**. She and her fiance, a God-fearing Jew named Joseph, were told by the angel Gabriel that Mary's boy-child was God's Son, the **Messiah-Savior**, <u>Immanuel</u> ("God with us"), sent from the heavenly world according to centuries-old promises God had made through the Old Testament **prophets**. Jesus was born in Bethlehem, Judea, and grew to manhood in Nazareth.

The Teaching Years

When he was 30 years old, Jesus began to preach. In the **synagogues** of Galilee, he announced that he was the one God sent to liberate people, give them new sight, and show them God's love and forgiveness. Jesus described a set of values and a lifestyle totally contradictory to typical human thinking and attitudes. He made **repentance**, humility, teachability, giving of oneself, hunger for righteousness, reconciliation, nonviolence, faithfulness, and forgiveness the measure of true success, prosperity, and happiness. He attacked religious **hypocrisy** and judgmentalism as enemies of true spirituality.

The Gathering Crowds

Jesus' unique personality, claims, and teachings led to national and family division. People from all walks of life were attracted to him, put their faith in him, and their lives were changed. Most who followed were from the disadvantaged, oppressed segments of Jewish society—the poor, sick, crippled, mentally ill, hungry, weak, and powerless. He healed, fed, and accepted them all. He performed many miracles to meet their needs and to demonstrate his authenticity.

The crowds coming to see and hear him became so huge, and the opposition to his message became so determined and constant, he could no longer preach in the synagogues but had to take his ministry out of doors. Out in the countryside his audiences came to number in the tens of thousands. While attracted to him, nearly all struggled with his refusal to live up to widely held, inaccurate, supernationalistic messianic expectations based on faulty interpretations of Old Testament prophecies.

The kingdom Jesus was putting together was not the political-military force the listeners had been taught to expect. And he insisted the authentic kingdom of God could not come to them until they recognized him as king of their hearts and Lord of their daily lives and actions. Jesus wanted his followers to look to him to supply not only their material but also their spiritual needs.

Holy Spirit: *the Spirit of God*

Messiah: *Christ, the Anointed, Sent-One*

Savior: *Rescuer*

☞ **GO TO:**

Isaiah 7:14; Matthew 1:22–23 (Immanuel)

prophets: *men and women speaking God's message*

synagogues: *Jewish houses of worship*

repentance: *sorrow for sin and willingness to change*

hypocrisy: *playing a part; pretense to impress people*

Dig Deeper

(Dig Deeper)

Who's Who

(Who's Who)

The members of the religious establishment (Bible scholars and clergy) saw in Jesus a threat to their positions of power and influence. Most chose to align themselves against him. He exposed and condemned their hypocrisy, **legalism**, and pride. Their disapproval and persistent slander quickly evolved into organized opposition and a conspiracy to assassinate him.

legalism: religion based on strict rules and ceremonies

His Disciples

apostles: "sent-ones," ambassadors, representatives, messengers

disciples: pupils, learners, seekers

From those who were responsive, Jesus called 12 as **apostles** and began training them for leadership in his movement. (For a chart listing their names with brief biographies, see appendix D.) They believed in him and remained loyal even while other **disciples** turned away. *"To whom shall we go?"* they said. *"You have the words of eternal life. We believe and know that you are the Holy One of God"* (John 6:68–69). Even so, they continued to struggle with the same messianic inaccuracies as the rest of the people. That's where we begin the story found in this volume.

☞ **GO TO:**

John 1:32–34 (descended)

Just The Facts, Ma'am

The approach taken in this commentary is to present the facts of Jesus' story as the New Testament writers recorded them and to provide a simple explanation of those facts where necessary. When facts from the culture and history of Jesus' times can help us understand more clearly the significance of some event or report or teaching, I will share those facts, too. My goal is to present a picture of Jesus accurately and simply, consistent with the way the New Testament pictures him.

Something to Ponder

(Something to Ponder)

Not everything Jesus did or said is recorded in the Bible. One New Testament writer insists that if everything were told, *"the whole world would not have room for the books that would have to be written"* (John 21:25). So many thousands were touched and changed by his life, and his was a life Bible writers insist began before time (John 1:1) and will continue forever (Isaiah 9:6–7).

The Four Gospels

gospels: biblical stories of good news

The four **gospels**—Matthew, Mark, Luke, and John—represent four pictures (angles, perspectives) of the same person—Jesus Christ. The four New Testament versions of the life of Christ were written by three Jewish men and one Greek. None includes a byline identifying the author. But from earliest times, the church has attributed the four to Matthew, Mark, Luke, and John.

These accounts do not pretend to be objective. These men are convinced that the Jesus about whom they write is exactly what he claimed—Son of God, Savior, Messiah, King. They are not writing to encourage speculation and further research about who Jesus is. They know who he is. And each aims to help readers know Jesus of Nazareth. The contents of their books are not inventions to spark a Christ-legend. Each is carefully composed from eyewitness testimony and well-researched fact.

Matthew's Life Of Christ

AUTHOR: MATTHEW: Also known as Levi. A <u>tax collector</u> who worked for the Roman government before Jesus invited him to join his team. As one of **<u>the 12</u>** he spent three years with Jesus and was appointed by him as his first **apostle**. He was an <u>eyewitness</u> to most of the events of which he writes.

TARGET: The Jewish people. To prove Jesus was the promised **Messiah**, Matthew carefully documents Jesus' fulfillment of Old Testament prophecies.

DATE: Written between 50–70 A.D., no way to tell exactly. Early Christians considered Matthew's to be the first of the four authoritative accounts of Jesus' life.

Papias: Matthew collected the sayings of Jesus in the Hebrew tongue.[1]

Mark's Life Of Christ

AUTHOR: JOHN MARK: Also called "John" or "Mark." <u>Companion to Paul</u>, <u>Barnabas</u>, and <u>Peter</u>. Mark was an eyewitness in a limited sense. He was personally acquainted with Jesus and present at key points in the story he tells (see Mark 14:51–52). Peter was Mark's major source of information.

TARGET: Primarily Romans and others unfamiliar with the Old Testament or biblical **theology**. Pictures Jesus as a man of action and authority—the kind of man who would appeal to the pragmatic, militaristic Romans.

DATE: Probably written near the time of Peter's **martyrdom** in Rome, 68 A.D.

☞ **GO TO:**

Luke 5:27–28 (tax collector)

Matthew 10:3 (the 12)

1 Corinthians 15:3–8; Acts 1:8; 2:32; 5:32; 10:39 (eyewitness)

the 12: *original group of disciples who became apostles*

apostle: *ambassador, one sent on a mission*

Messiah: *Hebrew for Christ, God-sent deliverer*

What Others are Saying:

(What Others are Saying)

☞ **GO TO:**

Acts 12:25; Philemon 24 (Companion to Paul)

Acts 15:39 (Barnabas)

1 Peter 5:13 (Peter)

theology: *study of God*

martyrdom: *killed for being a Christian*

What Others are Saying:

Papias: Mark, having become the interpreter of Peter, wrote down accurately, though not indeed in order, whatever he remembered of the things said or done by Christ.[2]

Luke's Life Of Christ

☞ **GO TO:**

Acts 13:2–3, 5; 15:40–16:2, 10
(missionary team)

Luke 1:3
(thorough research)

Acts 23:23–24; 24:27
(Caesarea)

Acts 28:30–31
(house arrest)

AUTHOR:

LUKE: A well-educated Greek that Paul calls *"our dear friend Luke, the doctor"* (Colossians 4:14). Authored both the third gospel and Acts. His use of medical language indicates the writing of a physician (and his writing was readable!). He was Paul's companion, even in jail. Luke was not an eyewitness. He probably first heard the story from Paul and his <u>missionary team</u>. He wrote his Life of Christ after <u>thorough research,</u> mostly done in <u>Caesarea</u> where Paul was imprisoned for two years.

TARGET:

Greeks and other Gentiles, like himself. His Life of Christ focuses on Jesus' relationships with all sorts of people—especially women, the poor, and oppressed.

DATE:

Written between 58 A.D., while Paul was in jail in Caesarea, and 63 A.D., when Paul was under <u>house arrest</u> in Rome.

What Others are Saying:

William Barclay: The gospel according to St. Luke has been called the loveliest book in the world. . . . It would not be far wrong to say that the third Gospel is the best Life of Christ ever written.[3]

John's Life Of Christ

☞ **GO TO:**

Matthew 4:21–22
(fishing business)

AUTHOR:

JOHN: An "insider"—one of the 12 who was with Jesus for three years. When Jesus called him, John was a partner in a <u>fishing business</u> on the Sea of Galilee with his brother James and their father, Zebedee. Like the other Life-of-Christ authors in the New Testament, John never identifies himself by name. He calls himself *"the disciple whom Jesus loved"* (John 21:20–24).

TARGET:

The whole world. The heartbeat of his writing may be summed up in a sentence called "the golden text of the Bible"—John 3:16: Because God loves the world of human beings, he gave his Son so that whoever puts their faith in him might escape spiritual disaster and live forever!

DATE: John was the last of the original apostles to write—between 75–100 A.D.

☞ **Check It Out:**

John 2:12–22

(Check It Out)

Clement of Alexandria: John . . . being urged by friends and inspired by the Spirit, composed a spiritual gospel.[4]

What Others are Saying:

The Gospel Quartet In Harmony

This commentary will use all four gospels—Matthew, Mark, Luke, and John—to tell the story. The first three are called **synoptic** gospels. That is, while each author has distinctive purposes in mind, all three take the same basic approach to telling the story. John marches to a slightly different drumbeat. He focuses more on Christ as a person and the teachings and signs that prove Jesus is the Son of God. The first three report many of the same incidents. A few are reported by all four. My approach will be to collect the facts from all four and focus on the events of Jesus' life in chronological order (which is not always easy to figure out). Watch for the Gospel Quartet in Harmony icon, which tells when and where an event is reported by more than one writer.

synoptic: summary, tell the story in similar fashion

GOSPEL QUARTET IN HARMONY

Matthew 16:24–27
Mark 8:34–38
Luke 9:23–26

(Gospel Quartet in Harmony)

The Original Language Of The Good News

Archaeological discoveries and evidence from the New Testament show the **Jews** were trilingual:

1. Aramaic had once been the language of the aristocracy, but by Jesus' time it had filtered down to the lower classes and was used in daily conversation.

2. Hebrew was the language of religious life at synagogues and the Temple and was also used in daily conversation.

3. Greek, like English today, was the universal language spoken all over the world. Alexander the Great (who preceded the Romans in conquest of the area) had invented a language called *koine* (koy-nay) or "common" Greek. As his empire spread, Alexander instituted the use of koine Greek from Europe to Asia. Most Jews were fluent in it. It was the language for interaction with Roman authorities and trade with foreigners. Palestinian Jews also spoke and wrote Greek in their communication with each other.

Jews: people of Hebrew descent

KEY POINT

When we acknowledge our guilt and trust Jesus as Savior, God forgives our sins freely and completely.

(Key Point)

Roman Empire: *Europe, Egypt, and the Middle East ruled by Caesars of Rome*

The Second Coming

(The Second Coming)

Study Questions

(Study Questions)

CHAPTER WRAP-UP

(Chapter Summary)

There is evidence Jesus was fluent in all three languages. The New Testament was originally written in common Greek so as to be read and understood by people all over the **Roman Empire**. By Jesus' time scholars believe much of the Old Testament had been copied onto papyrus scrolls. It is likely the gospel writers used papyrus as well.

Why Use The New International Version (NIV)?

Today English-speaking people have a wide range of Bible translations and paraphrases from which to choose. I used several in preparation of this book. In addition, I often looked at verses in the original language. At the same time I tried to write for the person who is new at finding his or her way around the Bible. That's why we use the New International Version (NIV) of the Bible. It is a scholarly translation that accurately expresses the original Scriptures in clear and contemporary English and, at the same time, faithfully communicates the thoughts of the original writers.

How To Use *The Life Of Christ—God's Word For The Biblically-Inept*™

Sit down with this book and your Bible.

- Start the book at chapter 1.
- As you work through each chapter, read the accompanying verses, or the CHECK IT OUT passages in your Bible.
- Use the sidebars loaded with icons and helpful information to give you a knowledge boost.
- Answer the Study Questions and review with the Chapter Wrap-Up.
- Then go on to the next chapter. It's simple!

This book contains a variety of special features that will help you learn. Here they are, with a brief explanation of each.

Sections and Icons	What's It For?
CHAPTER HIGHLIGHTS	the most prominent points of the chapter
GOSPEL QUARTET	all the places where this story is reported
Let's Get Started	a chapter warm-up
Verse of Scripture	what you came for—the Bible
THE BIG PICTURE	summarizes long passages
Commentary	my thoughts on what the verses mean
CHECK IT OUT:	Bible passages to look up
GO TO:	other Bible verses to help you better understand (underlined in text)

Sections and Icons	What's It For?
What?	*the meaning of a word (bold in text)*
KEY POINT	*major point of the chapter*
Key Outline	*mini-outline of information*
What Others are Saying:	*if you don't believe me, listen to the experts*
Illustrations	*a picture is worth a thousand words*
Time Lines	*shows how events fit in history*
Act of the Holy Spirit	*indicates God's personal intervention in people's lives identified as the work of the Holy Spirit*
Who's Who	*identifies key people*
Something to Ponder	*interesting points to get you thinking*
Remember This . . .	*don't forget this*
Dig Deeper	*find out more from the Bible*
Kingdom of God	*a taste of the kingdom; facts and teachings related to God's reign in persons and the community of faith*
Early Church Life	*practices and principles of the church in the first century*
The Second Coming	*facts and teachings relating to Christ's return*
Study Questions	*questions to get you discussing, studying, and digging deeper*
CHAPTER WRAP-UP	*the most prominent points revisited*

Jesus said the Spirit will *"guide"* us in discovery of *"all truth"* (John 16:13). It helps to read and study the Bible with an open heart, expecting God to light up your life in some surprising and enriching ways.

Remember This . . .

A Word About Words

There are several interchangeable terms: Scripture, Scriptures, Holy Scriptures, Word, Word of God, God's Word, Gospel. All these mean the same thing and come under the broad heading called the Bible. I may use each of these terms at various times.

The word "Lord" in the Old Testament refers to Yahweh, the God of Israel. In the New Testament it refers to Jesus Christ, God's Son.

The Ultimate Purpose Of A "Life Of Christ"

ACT OF THE HOLY SPIRIT

Real faith is a miracle from the Holy Spirit

(Act of the Holy Spirit)

The Bible was never given by God as an end in itself. And knowing what the Bible says and means is not all there is to being an authentic God-worshiper. The Bible is a means to an end. The end and goal of learning God's Word is to know God. The reason for learning about Jesus Christ is that by knowing him we can know his Father, God.

When we maintain an openness about Jesus of Nazareth, God rewards us with understanding. Many types of people can profit from reading about Jesus:

believers: Christians, followers of Christ

unbelievers: don't yet trust Christ as Savior

- New believers just beginning in their new way of life
- Untaught or untrained **believers**—new and old
- Seekers of God and truth who have not fully embraced him
- Respected **unbelievers**—friends, neighbors, relatives, business associates

Both volumes of *Life of Christ—God's Word for the Biblically-Inept*™ speak to such people.

Expect to be surprised and excited about the knowledge you are about to gain. No one who ever lived is as surprising and exciting as Jesus Christ.

Bible Quote: This is where you'll read a quote from the Bible.

James 1:5 If any of you lacks wisdom, he should ask God, who gives generously to all without finding fault, and it will be given to him.

Decisions, Decisions: In Or Out?

James, the brother of Jesus, is writing to the new believers who were scattered about the Roman world (see GWBI, pages 213–214) when they fled from persecution. James knows that godly wisdom is a great gift. He gives a simple plan to get it: if you need wisdom, ask for it. God will give it to us.

Up 'til now we've concentrated on finding the wind [for the] sails of your drifting marriage and overcoming marital prob[lems]. But you may be the reader who is shaking her head, thinking that I just don't understand what you're going through. You can't take the abuse any longer; you've forgiven the **infidelity** time after time; and in order for you and your children to survive, you see no alternative but divorce.

So let m[e]

husband [   ] your

get out a[   ] nues,

abuse sec[   ] ep the

ing to you; they are also harmful to your children's physical and emotional state.

When you feel you've depleted all of your options, continue to ask God for wisdom in order to have the knowledge to make the right decisions. Wise women seek God. God is the <u>source</u> of wisdom and wisdom is found in Christ and the Word.

Commentary: This is where you'll read commentary about the biblical quote.

"What?": When you see a word in bold, go to the sidebar for a definition.

infidelity: sexual unfaithfulness of a spouse

Go To: When you see a word or phrase that's underlined, go to the sidebar for a biblical cross-reference.

☞ **GO TO:**

Psalm 111:10 (source)

Remember This . . .

What Others are Saying:

Gary Chapman, Ph.D.: Is there hope for women who suffer physical abuse from their husbands? Does reality living offer any genuine hope? I believe the answer to those questions is yes.[8]

Give It Away

You don't have to be a farmer to understand what the Apostle Paul wrote to the Corinthian church (see illustration, page 143). A picture is worth a thousand words, and Paul is painting a masterpiece. He reminds us of what any smart farmer knows: in order to produce a bountiful harvest, he has to plan for it.

What Others Are Saying: This is where you'll read what an expert has to say about the subject at hand.

MEN OF POWER: LESSONS IN MIGHT AND MISSTEPS 9

127

Feature with icon in the sidebar: Thoughout the book you will see sections of text with corresponding icons in the sidebar. See the chart on pages xx–xxi for a description of all the features in this book.

Part One

TURN TOWARD THE CROSS

REVEREND FUN

Zacchaeus never knew how lucky he was that Jesus actually noticed him in his new feather coat.

1 ROAD TO MESSIAHSHIP AND DISCIPLESHIP

CHAPTER HIGHLIGHTS

- Church Rock
- The Rocky Road of Messiahship
- The Road of Discipleship
- The Splendor of the Son
- The Battle to Believe
- King of the Mountain

GOSPEL QUARTET IN HARMONY

Matthew 16:13–18:35
Mark 8:27–9:50
Luke 9:18–9:50

Let's Get Started

Always hanging around Jesus of Nazareth was the little knot of eager-beaver partisans New Testament writers refer to as *"the Twelve."* We call them the disciples or the apostles. The original 12 who were closest to Jesus were Peter, Andrew, James (son of Zebedee), John, Philip, Bartholomew (also called Nathanael), Matthew, James (Matthew's brother), Thomas, Simon, Thaddaeus, and Judas Iscariot. (For a brief biography of each one, see appendix D.)

Five of these men had been with the controversial Jesus most of the time since the day John the Baptist introduced him as *"the Lamb of God"* (John 1:35). That was the first time any of them had met Jesus. But that very first day they confessed to believing some amazing things about him:

- *"We've found the Messiah!"* Andrew told Peter (John 1:41).
- Philip told Nathanael he believed Jesus was *"the one Moses wrote about in the Law, and about whom the prophets also wrote"* (John 1:45).
- When Nathanael met Jesus he said, *"You are the Son of God; you are the King of Israel!"* (John 1:49).

Did they, at that early date, really know what they were saying? Or were they just parroting things their mentor, John the Baptist, had said? The full significance of the words did not really soak in

☞ **GO TO:**

Matthew 3:11–12;
John 1:15, 26–27,
29–34 (had said)

until they'd spent more than three years and had some amazing experiences with Jesus. But along the way, there were signs their faith was getting a tighter grip on their hearts.

Who's Who

JOHN THE BAPTIST—Son of Zechariah, a Jewish priest, and Elizabeth. His parents were past childbearing age when the angel Gabriel announced John's birth to his father, predicting John would be a great prophet who would turn many Israelites back to the Lord, restore family relationships, turn spiritually disobedient people to lives of righteousness, and prepare the nation for the arrival of the Messiah, called Christ (Luke 1:11–17). He lived in the desert and preached along the Jordan River. He introduced Jesus to the crowds who came to hear him as the *"Lamb of God who takes away the sin of the world"* (John 1:29). John and Jesus were cousins.

Check It Out:

Matthew 16:13–20

Mark 8:27–30

Luke 9:18–21

GO TO:

Mark 8:22–26 (healing)

Matthew 14:1–2 (suspicion)

Tetrarch: *ruler of a small province*

Archelaus: *Ethnarch (govenor) of Judea mentioned in Matthew 2:22*

Antipas: *Tetrarch of Galilee, ordered execution of John the Baptist*

Gentiles: *everyone who is not Jewish*

> **Matthew 16:13–16** When Jesus came to the region of Caesarea Philippi, he asked his disciples, "Who do people say the Son of Man is?"
>
> They replied, "Some say John the Baptist; others say Elijah; and still others, Jeremiah or one of the prophets."
>
> "But what about you?" he asked. "Who do you say I am?"
>
> Simon Peter answered, "You are the Christ, the Son of the living God."

Church Rock

From Bethsaida, where the two-stage <u>healing</u> of a blind man took place (GWLC, page 284), it was about 20 miles north along the Jordan River to Caesarea Philippi (see appendix A). This was the major city of the territory ruled by **Tetrarch** Herod Philip. As Herods go, especially compared to his brothers, **Archelaus** and **Antipas** (see illustration, page 5), Philip was a good guy—a just ruler. For one thing, he didn't share Antipas' <u>suspicion</u> toward Jesus.

The people of Caesarea Philippi were a mix of **Gentiles** and Jews, predominantly non-Jews. Crowds would be smaller and attract less attention there. Opposition from Jewish leaders would be minimal. It was not yet time for full-scale confrontation with them. The faith of the disciples needed refinement. Their understanding of their call needed sharpening.

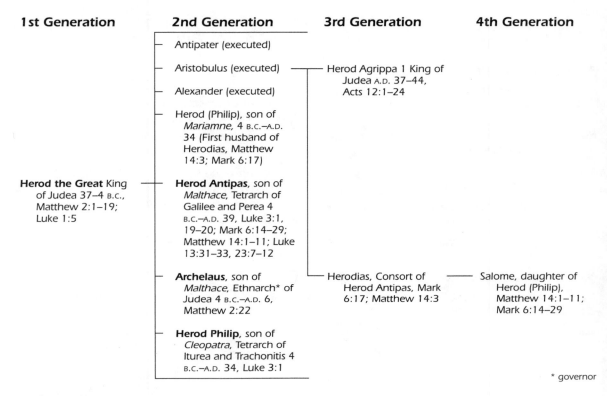

1st Generation	2nd Generation	3rd Generation	4th Generation
	Antipater (executed)		
	Aristobulus (executed)	Herod Agrippa 1 King of Judea A.D. 37–44, Acts 12:1–24	
	Alexander (executed)		
	Herod (Philip), son of *Mariamne*, 4 B.C.–A.D. 34 (First husband of Herodias, Matthew 14:3; Mark 6:17)		
Herod the Great King of Judea 37–4 B.C., Matthew 2:1–19; Luke 1:5	**Herod Antipas**, son of *Malthace*, Tetrarch of Galilee and Perea 4 B.C.–A.D. 39, Luke 3:1, 19–20; Mark 6:14–29; Matthew 14:1–11; Luke 13:31–33, 23:7–12		
	Archelaus, son of *Malthace*, Ethnarch* of Judea 4 B.C.–A.D. 6, Matthew 2:22	Herodias, Consort of Herod Antipas, Mark 6:17; Matthew 14:3	Salome, daughter of Herod (Philip), Matthew 14:1–11; Mark 6:14–29
	Herod Philip, son of *Cleopatra*, Tetrarch of Iturea and Trachonitis 4 B.C.–A.D. 34, Luke 3:1		

* governor

Herod's Family Tree

The Herod family tree shows all the Herods mentioned in the Gospels and how they were related to one another. Major leaders during Jesus' life are in bold. Wives of rulers are in italics.

THE HERODS—Herod Philip, Herod Archelaus, and Herod Antipas were sons of the first "Herod" (a family name which became a title), Herod the Great, under appointment by the **Roman Emperor**, ruled Galilee, Judea, Samaria, and other territories at the time of Christ's birth. Herod the Great died just a few months after Jesus was born and his territory was divided among his three sons.

"Who Am I?"

The idea that Jesus was not just your average preacher-guy had hit his people like gangbusters at various points in their travels with him. We can see the development of their concept of Christ by examining what they blurted out in those moments of astonishment.

Who's Who

Roman Emperor: *Caesar Augustus, head of the Roman Empire who ruled Israel during the time of Christ*

Dig Deeper

"Aftermath" of Miracles: Development of the Disciples' Faith in Jesus

After Jesus Did This	They Said	Scripture
After he cast a demon out of a man at Capernaum	"What is this? A new teaching—and with authority! He even gives orders to evil spirits and they obey him."	Mark 1:27
Peter, after the miracle of the big catch of fish on Lake Galilee	"Go away from me, Lord; I am a sinful man!"	Luke 5:8
After he forgave and healed the quadriplegic at his home in Capernaum	"We have never seen anything like this!"	Mark 2:12
After he raised a widow's son from the dead in the village of Nain	"A great prophet has appeared among us . . . God has come to help his people."	Luke 7:16
After he calmed the storm with a single command	"What kind of man is this? Even the winds and the waves obey him!"	Matthew 8:27
After he walked on the water	"Truly, you are the Son of God!"	Matthew 14:32
After he claimed to be the bread of life sent down from heaven	"You have the words of eternal life. We believe and know that you are the Holy One of God."	John 6:68–69

Not Your Father's Prophet

"Who do people say I am?" Jesus asked.

They listed some ideas floating around Galilee. "John the Baptist," said one.

"<u>Elijah</u>," volunteered another.

"An Old Testament prophet back from the dead," suggested another.

"Maybe <u>Jeremiah</u>," added another.

Fine. But it's never enough for a disciple to be able to tell you what others are saying about Jesus. Followers of Christ must ultimately speak for themselves.

"*Who do you say I am?*"

The question of Christian faith does not revolve primarily around **creeds** or doctrinal statements—"I know *what* I believe." It revolves around making personal connection with the central <u>person</u> of the Christian faith—"I know <u>whom</u> I have believed."

☞ **GO TO:**

1 Kings 17–19 (Elijah)

Jeremiah 1:1 (Jeremiah)

creeds: sets of fundamental beliefs, sometimes recited by worshipers

Remember This . . .

☞ **GO TO:**

1 Timothy 3:16 (person)

2 Timothy 1:2 (whom)

The Overpowering Secret Of Faith

Peter spoke first. Peter *always* spoke first. It was apparently a combination of a quick tongue and the ability to sense the consensus of the group, because nobody argued with him when he answered for them all: *"You are the Christ, the Son of the living God"* (Matthew 16:16).

"Christ"—"Christ" and "Messiah" are the same word in Greek and Hebrew. Both mean "**Anointed** One." Jesus is royalty—God's chosen Savior-King.

"Son of the living God"—Jesus claimed to be sent by God and that God was his Father. His followers came to recognize his special relationship with God as God's "one and only," God's Son and expression in a way no one else is God's Son and expression.

> **Matthew 16:17** "This was not **revealed** to you **by man**, but by my Father in heaven."

The Miracle Of Faith

Peter and others had said words before that sounded like these. What's the difference this time? This time Peter's statement of faith expressed a conviction planted deep in his heart, mind, and spirit by God himself. Such faith is a gift—even, we can say, a miracle—*the* miracle upon which the movement of Christ is founded.

> **Matthew 16:18–19** I tell you that you are Peter, and on this rock I will build my **church**, and the gates of **Hades** will not overcome it. I will give you the **keys** of the kingdom of heaven; whatever you bind on earth will be bound in heaven, and whatever you loose on earth will be loosed in heaven.

Network On The Rocks

This is Jesus' first recorded mention of the church. He was not referring to the development of an organization or institution, but to the new fellowship of people who believe in him—the new shape the Jesus movement would take—a new network of relationships with his committed followers at its core.

Some have thought Jesus was saying that Peter was the rock on which Jesus would build his church. In fact, the solid rock on which the church is built is none other than Jesus Christ himself.

KEY POINT

The faith issue: Who do *you* say Jesus is?

Anointed: "smeared with oil," symbol of authority to reign, minister, or prophesy

revealed: revelation; God's actions of self-disclosure

by man: teachers, reasoning, observation, testimony

☞ **GO TO:**

John 6:44–45, 63, 65 (by my Father)

church: Greek: ekklesia, "called out ones"

Hades: Greek: place of the dead; some translations say "hell"

keys: authority

☞ **GO TO:**

Acts 4:8–12; 1 Corinthians 3:11; Ephesians 2:19–22 (rock)

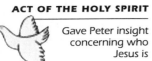

ACT OF THE HOLY SPIRIT

Gave Peter insight concerning who Jesus is

Something to Ponder

Dig Deeper

KEY Outline:

Revelation Process
  Other's words
  Observation
  Experience
  Insight
  Verbalize it

☞ **GO TO:**

2 Corinthians 10:3–5 (spiritual conquest)

spiritual conquest: not physical warfare but spiritual warfare

---

Peter and the other apostles are among the first stones laid on the foundation, but the foundation is Christ.

Christ is the living foundation on which Christianity rests. Without him, present and active in his people, there is no Christianity! With him present and active in people impelled by a Peter-style conviction of who he is, planted in their hearts by the Spirit of God, the living church becomes an aggressive, invading force, storming the gates of death and hell, freeing spiritual captives, and blocking the devil's destructive design.

Keys of the Kingdom

The Key to This	Scripture
The power of agreement, the power to discipline	Matthew 18:15–20
The power to forgive, the power to carry others' sins	John 20:21–23
The power of new life	Revelation 1:18
The power to seize opportunities	Revelation 3:7–8

EARLY CHURCH LIFE: The Rock is Jesus Christ, and he is the foundation of the church.

> **Matthew 16:20** Then he warned his disciples not to tell anyone that he was the Christ.

Keep This Under Your Hat!

They were convinced he was the Messiah. But as real as their conviction was, their understanding was deeply flawed. Their kingdom dreams did not factor in the cross. Jesus couldn't have them stirring up ill-timed hopes of a conqueror who would drive the Romans into the sea when God's timetable called first for **spiritual conquest** that required the Messiah's death! Unless they understood, their witness would only result in disillusioned converts.

> **Matthew 16:21** From that time on Jesus began to explain to his disciples that he must go to Jerusalem and suffer many things at the hands of the elders, chief priests and teachers of the law, and that he must be killed and on the third day be raised to life.

The Rocky Road Of Messiahship

The breakthrough to an irreversible conviction of Jesus' identity opened the way for the disciples to be taken deeper into the understanding of what he had been sent to do. They must share the secret of the difficult trajectory he was on. Messiah Road led straight to the cross! **Ahead** for him—and them—lay rejection, savage opposition, and death. Then . . . resurrection! But first, death.

The Destiny Of Saviorhood

Before they could tell the world of his messiahship, they had to own the necessity of his <u>saviorhood</u>. Jesus' turn toward the cross was calculated, deliberate. Matthew, Mark, and Luke each include the word *"must"* in their description of what he told them about his coming death. The original word for *"must"* is *dei*, meaning legally or morally binding. It's used 100 times in the New Testament to indicate necessity imposed by the will of God. Jesus believed rejection, death, and resurrection were his destiny.

Robert E. Coleman: His [Jesus'] life was ordered by his objective. Everything he did and said contributed to the ultimate purpose of his life. Not for one moment did Jesus lose sight of his goal. Nothing was haphazard about his life—no wasted energy, no idle words. He was on business for God. He lived, he died, and he rose again according to schedule. Like a general plotting his course of battle, the Son of God calculated to win. . . . Weighing every alternative and variable factor in human experience, he conceived a plan that would not fail.[1]

Say It Isn't So!

In Matthew's record, Peter, who'd just made the stunning confession of faith in Jesus' messiahship, took Jesus aside and started to scold him for talking about rejection and death. How negative! Such an idea was incompatible with Peter's concept of messiahship.

"Never, Lord!" he said. *"This shall never happen to you!"* (Matthew 16:22).

Jesus whirled around and stared at his disciples. He spoke sharply to Peter. "Get <u>out of my way</u>, Satan! You aren't looking at things from God's perspective, but from man's!" (Matthew 16:23, paraphrased). Jesus found his friend's suggestion as tempting as any the devil threw at him in the desert (see GWLC, pages 65–75). The thought of going to the cross was repulsive and, <u>if possible</u>, to be avoided. Yet, as Messiah, he knew it was the only way. They must come to know it too.

GOSPEL QUARTET IN HARMONY

Matthew 16:24–27
Mark 8:34–38
Luke 9:23–26

ahead: *the predicted events took place about a year later*

☞ **GO TO:**

Isaiah 53; Matthew 1:21 (saviorhood)

What Others are Saying:

KEY POINT

Temptation sometimes comes from our best friends.

☞ **GO TO:**

Matthew 4:10 (out of my way)

Luke 22:40–42 (if possible)

GOSPEL QUARTET IN HARMONY

Matthew 16:24–28
Mark 8:34–38; 9:1
Luke 9:23–27

☞ **GO TO:**

Luke 9:23;
1 Corinthians 15:30–
32 (daily)

*self-denial: disown,
renounce one's own plans
and priorities to commit
to the will of God*

**What Others
are Saying:**

*crucifixion: identification
with Jesus*

*six days: between above
teaching and this event*

☞ **GO TO:**

Mark 6:46; Luke 6:12;
22:39–41; John 6:15
(places to pray)

Joshua 11:17; 12:1;
Psalm 89:12; Song of
Solomon 4:8
(history and poetry)

*Mt. Hermon: 9,400-foot
mountain north of the
Sea of Galilee*

> **Matthew 16:24–26** Then Jesus said to his disciples, "If anyone would come after me, he must deny himself and take up his cross and follow me. For whoever wants to save his life will lose it, but whoever loses his life for me will find it. What good will it be for a man if he gains the whole world, yet forfeits his soul? Or what can a man give in exchange for his soul?"

The Road Of Discipleship

These words were for everyone—disciples and people thinking about becoming disciples. The call to discipleship has no fine print requiring a magnifying glass to read. Followers of Jesus must know what they are getting into. Suffering and death in the course of doing God's will was his destiny as Messiah. It was also the destiny of anyone who joined him. The "must" of the cross applies as surely to followers as to their Leader. Follow Jesus and you find yourself picking up your cross <u>daily</u> and marching beside him up the road of **self-denial** and **crucifixion**, willing to face rejection, sufferings, and death.

J. B. Phillips: Then Jesus said to his disciples, "If anyone wants to follow in my footsteps he must give up all right to himself, take up his cross and follow me."[2]

> **Matthew 17:1–3** After **six days** Jesus took with him Peter, James and John the brother of James, and led them up a high mountain by themselves. There he was transfigured before them. His face shone like the sun, and his clothes became white as the light. Just then there appeared before them Moses and Elijah, talking with Jesus.

The Splendor Of The Son

Jesus loved to climb mountains. They were among his favorite <u>places to pray</u>. Fourteen miles from the city of Caesarea Philippi was **Mt. Hermon** (see appendix A), one of the highest mountains mentioned in biblical <u>history and poetry</u>. It can be seen from the Dead Sea, 100 miles away. The whole Jordan Valley is visible from its summit.

Jesus took Peter, James, and John up this mountain to pray (Luke 9:28). They must have spent the night on the mountain. It would have taken all day to reach the top, and Luke says the disciples were overcome with sleep.

While Jesus prayed, his face and clothing began to <u>glow</u>. This is described as being **transfigured**.

Two men they intuitively recognized as Moses and Elijah appeared and talked with Jesus. Moses (see GWMB, pages 71–89) had led the Israelites out of slavery in Egypt to Mount Sinai where God gave the Ten Commandments to his people. Elijah (see GWMB, pages 130–140) was a prophet sent by God to confront a wicked king and idol worshipers in a contest to call fire from heaven.

Luke, in his account, tells what the two historical faith heroes talked about: *"They spoke about his **departure**, which he was about to bring to fulfillment at Jerusalem"* (Luke 9:31).

Figuring Out The Transfiguration

It's not easy to figure exactly what happened at the transfiguration or what it accomplished. Among its possible purposes and effects were these.

For the disciples:
- To visually <u>confirm</u> that Jesus was all they had come to believe he was
- To encourage them after the demanding revelations about the cost of discipleship
- To teach that cross bearing does not diminish Christ's majesty or that of his followers
- To affirm the <u>supremacy</u> of Christ over Old Testament Law and Prophets

For Jesus:
- To personally <u>reaffirm</u> God's approval of him and the direction he was headed
- To refocus the purpose of his mission and the glory that would follow
- To encourage and strengthen him for the ordeal ahead

Supremacy Of The Son

The bright-as-sun light roused the sleeping disciples (Luke 9:32). Their eyes popped open to the dazzling sight of Jesus like they'd never seen him before, with Moses and Elijah basking in his radiance. Surrounded by sunlight-power radiance, a 40-watt bulb went on over Peter's inventive head! He had an idea whose bril-

**GOSPEL QUARTET
IN HARMONY**

Matthew 17:1–9
Mark 9:2–10
Luke 9:28–36

☞ **GO TO:**

Exodus 34:29–35
(glow)

John 16:7 (departure)

transfigured: *changed in form*

departure: *coming events—confrontation with authorities, death on the cross, resurrection, ascension*

☞ **GO TO:**

2 Peter 1:16–17
(confirm)

John 1:16–18;
Colossians 1:18;
Hebrews 1:1–4; 3:3–6
(supremacy)

Matthew 17:5; Luke
3:22; John 12:28
(reaffirm)

KEY Outline:

Transfiguration
Visual confirmation
Encouragement
Christ's supremacy
God's approval
Mission clarification
Strength for suffering

shelters: temporary huts
used at the Feast of
Tabernacles

☞ **GO TO:**

Exodus 40:34–38;
2 Chronicles 5:13–6:2
(cloud)

**Something
to Ponder**

KEY Outline:

**Christ's Revelation of
God**
Superior to
 • Moses
 • OT prophets

**What Others
are Saying:**

KEY POINT

Pay attention to Jesus'
words.

liance he was sure matched the brilliance of the vision he was seeing.

"Master, this is wonderful! Let's stay here. Let me slap together three **shelters**—*"one for you, one for Moses, and one for Elijah"* (Luke 9:33). Three "shrines" for the three greats! What a brainstorm! Luke perceptively adds, Peter *"did not know what he was saying!"*

> **Luke 9:34–35** While [Peter] was speaking, a <u>cloud</u> appeared and enveloped them, and they were afraid. . . . A voice came from the cloud, saying "This is my Son, whom I have chosen; listen to him."

Listen Up And Calm Down

Matthew tells that at the sound of the voice Peter, James, and John, terrified, fell to the ground, face down. As they lay there, scared to death to look, Jesus touched them and told them to get up and not to be afraid (Matthew 17:6–7). When they got courage enough for a peek, *"Jesus was alone."*

As you think about the transfiguration of Christ, here are some points for the three and thee and me to ponder.

Inappropriate responses to fresh breakthroughs in understanding of Christ may include (1) building shrines, (2) stopping too long at the place where the spiritual breakthrough occurred, (3) putting our own ideas ahead of what Jesus says and teaches, and (4) terror.

Appropriate responses most certainly include (1) recognizing that Jesus is God's Son and the revelation of God through him is superior to the Old Testament Law (represented by Moses) and the prophets (represented by Elijah), (2) giving Jesus' words and teachings greater authority than the ideas of men, and (3) getting up and going, following Jesus by applying the new insights to daily life.

Jerome: Do not set up tents equally for the Lord and his servants. "This is my beloved Son; hear him," my Son, not Moses or Elijah. They are servants; this is the Son. This is my son, of my nature, of my substance, abiding in me, and he is all that I am. . . . They, too, indeed are dear to me, but he is my beloved; hear him therefore. They proclaim and teach him, but you, hear him. He is the Lord and master, they are companions in service.[3]

Oswald Chambers: If Jesus Christ had gone to heaven from the Mount of Transfiguration we might have worshiped him, but we would have had no power to live the kind of life he lived. But Jesus did not come to show us what a holy life was like: He came to make us holy by means of his death.[4]

No Bragging Allowed

Again, Jesus told the three not to tell anyone what they had seen, until after his resurrection (Matthew 17:9). It would be a hard secret to keep. The difficulty of keeping this mountaintop experience to themselves may have contributed to some of the incidents that took place after they came down from the mountain—incidents that might have been triggered by <u>spiritual pride</u>.

The Battle To Believe

Peter, James, and John came down from their mountaintop experience with their feet barely touching the ground.

I can see them now—assuming the stance of the Timid Lion in the Wizard of Oz, busting with bravado, scaring off everything he was scared of by pretending to punch out some imaginary opponent: "Bring 'em on! We've been on the mountain with Jesus, Moses, and Elijah! We've seen and heard stuff nobody else has. We can take on all comers! They're no match for the likes of us!"

> **Matthew 17:38–40** A man in the crowd called out, "Teacher, I beg you to look at my son, for he is my only child. A spirit seizes him and he suddenly screams; it throws him into convulsions so that he foams at the mouth. It scarcely ever leaves him and is destroying him. I begged your disciples to drive it out, but they could not."

You Can't Win 'Em All!

Uh oh! The very next day at the bottom of the hill, the disciples faced a challenge that showed their limitations, what spiritual wimps they were, and how much they still needed to learn in order to be effective.

The scene was chaotic (Mark 9:14–18). Even though Jesus had given them <u>authority</u> to deal with evil spirits and they had some success in doing so, the nine apostles waiting in the valley were unable to deal with this one. The cupboard of their faith and power

What Others are Saying:

☞ **GO TO:**

Mark 9:33–42; Matthew 20:20–21 (spiritual pride)

KEY POINT

Bragging about spiritual experiences spoils their true splendor.

GOSPEL QUARTET IN HARMONY

Matthew 17:14–21
Mark 9:14–29
Luke 9:37–43

☞ **GO TO:**

Matthew 10:1, 8; Luke 9:1 (authority)

histrionics: deliberate acting

spirit: evil spirit, demon

sacrifice: "fasting" (Matthew 17:21, NIV margin)

KEY Outline:

Dealing with Demons
Care
Believe
Sacrifice
Pray

GOSPEL QUARTET IN HARMONY

Matthew 17:22–23
Mark 9:30–32
Luke 9:43–45

What Others are Saying:

---

was bare (Matthew 17:17). And the distraught father of the deaf, mute, epileptic, self-destructive boy wasn't sure what he believed (Mark 9:24). Into this helpless crowd stepped Jesus.

The young Messiah took control and, in spite of the atmosphere of embarrassment, doubt, and panic, he *"rebuked the demon."* With some last gasp violent **histrionics**, the **spirit** left the boy at peace (Mark 9:26).

The 12 men destined to be God's men of faith and power learned something of their limitations and dependence on Jesus for power to do their work. They also learned something about dealing with demons. Later, in private, Jesus told them that people can be set free from some kinds of evil spirits only through a process involving prayer and **sacrifice** on the part of spiritual helpers (Mark 9:28–29).

> **Luke 9:42–43** But Jesus rebuked the evil spirit, healed the boy and gave him back to his father. And they were all amazed at the greatness of God.

No Time For Oohs And Aahs

As the relieved man and his son strode off together, everyone marveled at the miracle. Jesus had a way of doing his work that left people talking about *"the greatness of God."* He had no time to revel in the victory. His eyes were on the cross—the end of the road he was traveling. He repeated the prediction of his approaching rejection, death, and resurrection. But his disciples simply could not grasp the reality of it.

William Barclay: It would have been so easy to take the way of popular success; it was Jesus' greatness that he rejected it and chose the cross. He would not himself shirk that cross to which he called others.[5]

> **Matthew 17:24** After Jesus and his disciples arrived in Capernaum, the collectors of the two-drachma tax came to Peter and asked, "Doesn't your teacher pay the temple tax?"

From Mountain Dew To Revenue

Talk about coming back to earth after a mountaintop experience! Leaving the heady world of the transfiguration on Mt. Hermon's summit, Jesus and his men returned to Capernaum just in time to become embroiled in the down and dirty world of taxes.

The temple tax collectors were in town.

They collared Peter and asked about *"the **temple tax**."* There's a pretty good chance the questioners, part of the anti-Jesus religious establishment, were hoping the answer would be "no." This would give them something else for which to accuse Jesus.

temple tax: *half shekel annually (two days wages), required of Jewish males over 19*

Aware of the emptiness of the young kingdom community's common purse, Peter took the matter to Jesus.

He turned it into a teaching opportunity, giving Peter two things: (1) freedom from the obligation of the outdated religious system being replaced with personal relationship with God through Christ, on the basis of faith, and (2) God's supply of something to give.

At Jesus' instructions, Peter went to the sea and threw in a hook and line. A fish grabbed the bait, and Peter reeled it in. In the fish's mouth were four drachmas—enough to pay both Jesus' and Peter's temple tax.

KINGDOM OF GOD

Calling them sons of the kingdom Jesus indicated his followers were free from obligation to pay the temple tax. The **Temple** was part of the outdated religious system. In the new system the Temple would be obsolete. On the other hand, sons of the kingdom were also free to pay the temple tax if they chose to, out of love for Jewish contemporaries who might otherwise be offended.

Temple: *the Jewish center of worship located in Jerusalem*

Three things are important: (1) In God's economy, money always plays second fiddle to peace between people (see Matthew 5:40–42; Luke 6:30, 34–35; 1 Corinthians 6:7–8); (2) When financial shortages occur, believers should ask, "What is God trying to teach us?"; and (3) God intends to supply what is needed so his followers can be generous givers (see 2 Corinthians 9:8–11).

Remember This . . .

> **Mark 9:33** When he was in the house, he asked them, "What were you arguing about on the road?" But they kept quiet because on the way they had argued about who was the greatest. Sitting down, Jesus called the Twelve and said, "If anyone wants to be first, he must be the very last, and the servant of all."

KEY POINT

Children of the kingdom sometimes limit their own freedom in order to demonstrate love.

Matthew 18:1–14
Mark 9:33–50
Luke 9:46–50

King Of The Mountain

A really childish game of "king of the mountain" erupted among the 12 on the road to Capernaum.

It may be that the "privileged three," fresh from Mt. Hermon's lofty heights, exuded a superior (dare I say "holier than thou"?) attitude because of their unique experience. The other nine, licking fresh wounds from failure with the epileptic boy, were wearing their feelings on their sleeves.

Wounded egos reacted to spiritual arrogance with jealousy and defensiveness. What resulted was that manly mix of bragging, putdowns, and spiritual "can you top this?" that religious people engage in when their egos are threatened or they're struggling to gain position in the "pecking order."

> **Matthew 18:2–3** "I tell you the truth, unless you change and become like little children, you will never enter the kingdom of heaven. Therefore, whoever humbles himself like this child is the greatest in the kingdom of heaven."

How To Be Great In The Kingdom

Spiritual pride, jealousy, and competition are not attitudes that make good witnesses for Christ. Jesus' ideas of greatness, like so many of his ideas, turn the world upside down!

It's no surprise to read that he brought a little child and put him in the middle of that puffing circle of burly fishermen, tax collectors, and **Zealots**. (Tradition says the child was Peter's son, who grew to be Ignatius of Antioch, influential Christian writer and martyr in the early second century A.D.)

Their set jaws visibly relaxed at the presence of the wee one. Jesus used the child as an object lesson to teach future leaders of the church five principles of authentic spiritual excellence.

Zealots: right-wing political party committed to the overthrow of Roman occupation forces

1 *Greatness is childlikeness.* Christ's kingdom is ultimately experienced by people humble enough to see themselves as weak, vulnerable, dependent, and trusting, like little children.

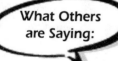

What Others are Saying:

Peter Marshall: We ask thee to give to each of us that childlike faith, that simplicity of mind which is willing to lay aside all egotism and conceit, which recognizes vanity for what it is—an empty show, which knows that we are incapable of thinking the thoughts of God, which is willing to be humble again.[6]

2 *Greatness is servanthood.* *"If anyone wants to be first, he must be the very last, and the servant of all"* (Mark 9:35). The word Jesus used for *"servant"* is the Greek *diakonos*, "helper" or "minister." The focus is on the needs the servant can meet. "Christians should serve one another, being sensitive to needs and willing to meet them."[7]

3 *Greatness welcomes children.* *"And whoever welcomes a little child like this in my name welcomes me"* (Matthew 18:5). Jesus once became angry when his disciples welcomed adults and community bigwigs for heavy discussions with him, while shooing away parents who wanted him to touch their kids (Mark 10:13–14). Children are vital to the kingdom community. Their presence provides a model of the vulnerability that characterizes all Christians.

4 *Greatness is inclusive rather than exclusive.* The Jews used the word *child* in two ways: (1) literally, to mean "a little child"; and (2) figuratively, a student of a particular teacher or **rabbi** was referred to as the teacher's <u>child</u>. A child by this definition was "a beginner in the faith."[8] Great-souled people are able to freely embrace the "little guy" who doesn't make a big splash and who's just learning to follow Christ.

John reported that he and the others had seen a man who was not part of their inner circle driving out demons in Jesus' name (Mark 9:38–40). They told the man to stop *"because he is not one of us."* Jesus surprised them: "Don't stop him. He's on our side. Nobody can do a miracle in my name and then turn around and badmouth me!"

To nail the point home, he added that the smallest act of kindness done in his name (such as giving someone a drink of water) will be rewarded (Mark 9:41).

John A. Martin: John must have thought that the disciples' own greatness was diminished if others who were not of the Twelve could also cast out demons. Jesus' reply . . . suggested that the Twelve were not to see themselves as God's exclusive representatives. Rather they should have rejoiced that the power of God was being manifested on earth by others as well.[9]

Christians are still confused about this. One who doesn't fit our comfortable religious mold, or isn't part of our liturgical, doctrinal, organizational, or experiential circle, we may

KEY POINT

The kingdom is built, not by powerful leaders, but by self-sacrificing servants.

rabbi: Jewish teacher

☞ **GO TO:**

1 Corinthians 4:14–15; 3 John 4 (child)

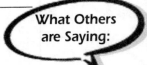
What Others are Saying:

Something to Ponder

try to drive off, rather than draw our circle of acceptance big enough to take in all of Jesus' friends. Exclusionist attitudes are a hindrance, not only to our own spiritual progress, but to the "little guy" whose progress is blocked by our rejection. Jesus warns us to rid ourselves of such prideful, self-righteous attitudes before they destroy us and others (Matthew 18:6–14; Mark 9:42–50).

5 *Greatness forgives and restores wanderers.* Question: What if someone strayed from the "straight and narrow"? What should another Christian's attitude be toward the wanderer? Answer: The Christian's attitude should be the attitude of God. He is not willing that any be lost, and will do all he can to restore them. He is happy when they return (Matthew 18:10–14).

☞ **GO TO:**

Matthew 5:44–48;
   Luke 6:35–36;
   1 John 4:7–12, 16–21
   (attitude of God)

2 Peter 3:9 (not willing)

Galatians 6:1–2
   (restore)

Luke 15:7, 10 (happy)

KEY POINT

Forgiveness never stops.

☞ **GO TO:**

Matthew 5:7; 6:14–15;
   James 2:13 (forgive)

> **Matthew 18:21–22** Then Peter came to Jesus and asked, "Lord, how many times shall I forgive my brother when he sins against me? Up to seven times?" Jesus answered, "I tell you, not seven times, but seventy-seven times."

The New Math Of Forgiveness

Rabbis taught one should not forgive more than three times. Peter was ready to go way beyond that. Seven times was plenty in Peter's mind.

Some versions read Jesus answered "seventy times seven," but the point is the same. Jesus' answer showed that there is no end to the amount of forgiveness one should extend to another. The parable with which Jesus followed this mind-boggling statement teaches at least two major things about forgiveness:

- We must forgive in order to be forgiven.
- The person who refuses to forgive will suffer because of his unforgiveness.

What Others are Saying:

attribute: *quality, characteristic*

Gayle Erwin: Maybe Jesus was telling us that our heart for forgiving should exceed someone's ability to sin against us.[10]

Oswald Chambers: I have no right to say that I believe in forgiveness as an **attribute** of God if in my own heart I cherish an unforgiving temper. The forgiveness of God is the test by which I myself am judged.[11]

Christine Poehls:

> When I forgive I say, "I'll not be judge of what you've done to me."
> I can forgive because the penalty was paid on Calvary.
> When I forgive I say, "I loose the chains that hold this hurt to me."
> As I forgive I'm passing on the mercy that was granted me.[12]

Study Questions

1. Where did Peter get the insight expressed in his confession (Matthew 16:16)? What did Jesus say would not be able to stand against the church founded on this truth?

2. What did Jesus call Peter when Peter tried to get him to stop talking about his death (Matthew 16:23)? What did he say was wrong with Peter's perspective?

3. What three things did Jesus say would be involved for people who came along with him (Mark 8:34)? How has becoming Jesus' companion affected your personal lifestyle? Values and priorities? Relationships?

4. What two Old Testament characters appeared with Jesus on the Mount of Transfiguration (Matthew 9:2–8)? Name two possible reasons for this experience for the disciples? For Jesus?

5. How many times did Jesus tell Peter he ought to forgive someone who wronged him (Matthew 18:22)? What did he mean?

CHAPTER WRAP-UP

- Jesus asked his 12 disciples who they thought he was. Peter, answering for the rest, said he was the Christ, the Son of God. Jesus told Peter this insight had come to him from God and that his church would be built on the reality he had just confessed. (Matthew 16:13–20)

- Then Jesus revealed to his men that his personal destiny, toward which he was soon to head, involved rejection and execution by the authorities, after which he would rise from the dead. (Matthew 16:21–23)

- For his disciples, the road ahead also held self-denial, a personal cross each would carry every day, and following the same basic trail (destiny) he was on. (Matthew 16:24–26)

- Jesus took three of his disciples with him to the top of a high mountain where he was visibly changed before them, becoming as radiant as the sun. Appearing with him were Elijah and

Moses, talking with him about the ordeal ahead for him. (Matthew 17:1–8)

- Coming down the mountain, Jesus and the three were met by a desperate father with a demon-possessed son, whom Jesus' disciples had been unable to help. After chiding them all for their lack of faith, he cast the demon out and taught them that self-denial and prayer were often the only way to set people free from such evil spirits. (Mark 9:14–29)

- A childish argument developed among the 12 as to which was most important in the kingdom. Using a little child as an example, Jesus taught them the nature of true greatness, climaxing with an important message about forgiveness. (Matthew 18:1–35)

2 FEAST OF SPIRIT AND LIGHT

CHAPTER HIGHLIGHTS

- Back Road to Jerusalem
- Festival Troublemaker
- River of the Spirit
- Power and Light
- Unbelieving Believers

Let's Get Started

Widely divergent groups in Israel who found their positions of influence threatened by the presence and preaching of Jesus of Nazareth began to find each other in a weird fraternity of hostility.

They could not have agreed on theology or political philosophy. In fact, at times they plotted each other's assassinations.

But their hate for this man was so intense it made them willing to temporarily lay aside their hate for each other, to cooperate on the project of ridding the nation of him!

They might have accomplished their diabolical quest sooner had Jesus not so carefully orchestrated the timing and intensity of both the people's commitment to make him king and his enemies' commitment to see him dead.

This he did by spending most of his time in Galilee, away from the Jerusalem power center (John 7:1). In addition, he took well-timed trips outside the country (Mark 7:24–30) and into areas of mixed Gentile and Jewish population.

His enemies were sparse there and the crowds smaller, so he attracted less attention (Mark 7:31; 8:27).

It was in those off-the-beaten-path locales where Jesus began to tell his friends about the necessity of his rejection and death at the hands of the anti-Jesus conspiracy (Mark 8:31; 9:31). At this talk of blood and death, many of his disciples recoiled and cooled in their enthusiasm. His numbers dropped off temporarily (John 6:66).

GOSPEL QUARTET IN HARMONY

Matthew 8:19–22
Luke 9:51–62
John 7–8

At the same time, though, the faith of the 12 broke through to bedrock. Though they did not understand his prophecies of rejection and death, they renewed their commitment to go with him, whatever the cost (John 6:68–69; Matthew 16:16–18).

After six months of skirting the limelight, Jesus, like a skilled deep-sea fisherman playing his catch, made several strategic forays into Judea and Jerusalem. He would go in for a while, then back off to a distance, letting his prey run with the hook, preparing for the final moment when the prophecies of his sacrifice and triumph (see GWPB, page 66) would be fulfilled.

> **John 7:2–3, 5** But when the Jewish Feast of Tabernacles was near, Jesus' brothers said to him, "You ought to leave here and go to Judea, so that your disciples may see the miracles you do. . . ." For even his own brothers did not believe in him.

Back Road To Jerusalem

In late September the time for the **Feast of Tabernacles** approached. This was one of Israel's most popular festivals (see GWHN, pages 223–224), a happy family celebration, combining all the discomfort and merriment of an eight-day picnic! The crowds would be huge.

<u>Jesus' brothers</u> thought he was a couple of bricks short of a load! They may have believed he could perform miracles, but it is likely they were mocking him a little when they said, "If you want people to know who you are, you ought to go to the feast and do something really big and impressive" (John 7:3–4).

> **John 7:6–8** Therefore Jesus told them, "The right time for me has not yet come; for you any time is right. The world cannot hate you, but it hates me because I testify that what it does is evil. You go to the Feast. I am not yet going up to this Feast, because for me the right time has not yet come."

Good Politics: Being In The Right Place At The Right Time

Jesus' brothers were not incorrect in their assumption that anyone who wants to make a public impact must go public (John

GOSPEL QUARTET IN HARMONY

John 7:2–10
Matthew 8:19–22
Luke 9:51–62

☞ **GO TO:**

Exodus 23:16;
Leviticus 23:34, 39
(Feast of Tabernacles)

Mark 3:21, 31–32; 6:3
(Jesus' brothers)

Feast of Tabernacles:
the greatest of Hebrew feasts, lasting seven days

ACT OF THE HOLY SPIRIT

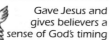

Gave Jesus and gives believers a sense of God's timing

7:4). Before the festival ended, Jesus arrived and became highly visible. But he was coming from an entirely different place than his brothers (and I don't mean Galilee!). They understood the power of public relations but knew nothing of the leadership of the Holy Spirit.

There were deep differences in their perspectives.

1. Jesus' brothers did not believe he was the Messiah (verse 5). Jesus knew he was.

2. Jesus' brothers were not committed to God's timing and direction, only to what seemed convenient or politically expedient (verse 6). He was concerned with both **God's timing** and the most **advantageous time** to go public.

3. The world did not hate Jesus' brothers. Their lives did not challenge its wickedness. But Jesus' teachings, life, works, and character were a living rebuke against society's spiritual rottenness. The hatred he would face in Jerusalem called for action based on different principles.

"I won't go just yet," he told them (verse 8).

> **John 7:10** However, after his brothers had left for the Feast, he went also, not publicly, but in secret.

Sneaking In Under The Fence

Jesus' brothers headed for Jerusalem with the mass of Galilean pilgrims to arrive for the beginning of the festivities—in time to put together the temporary **shelters** made of branches (tabernacles, booths, tents) from which the feast took its name.

After most people were on their way, Jesus and his men hit the road secretly. They went through Samaria on less traveled roads (Luke 9:51), aiming to arrive halfway through the feast (John 7:14). They would enter the **Holy City** quietly, without attracting attention.

> **Luke 9:52–54** And he sent messengers on ahead, who went into a Samaritan village to get things ready for him; but the people there did not welcome him, because he was heading for Jerusalem. When the disciples James and John saw this, they asked, "Lord, do you want us to call fire down from heaven to destroy them?"

☞ **GO TO:**

Luke 9:51; John 2:4; 7:30; 8:20; 12:27 (God's timing)

John 7:6, 8 (advantageous time)

God's timing: Greek: hora, *"hour," "time"; "the destined hour of God"*[1]

advantageous time: Greek: kairos, *"time"; the best time to do something*

KEY Outline:

Time to Act
God's timing
  ▪ Spirit led
Advantageous time
  ▪ common sense

shelters: built to provide shade from the sun and a view of the stars at night; reminders of Israel's nomadic history

Holy City: Jerusalem

GO TO:

John 4 (welcomed)

1 Kings 18:37–39;
2 Kings 1:10, 12
(call fire down)

 **Who's Who**

KEY POINT

Jesus came to save
people, not to destroy
them.

**Something
to Ponder**

 GO TO:

John 3:17; Acts 10:38
(destroy)

"Burn Down This Town!"

The animosity between Samaritans and Jews is legendary. Previously, Jesus was <u>welcomed</u> in Samaria (see GWLC, pages 134–135, 139).

This time, however, he was on his way to Jerusalem, to a religious festival from which Samaritans were excluded. The **response** was drastically different. A couple of disciples were sent ahead to a Samaritan town to make arrangements to stop for the night and, possibly, to preach. Because they could see he was on his way to Jerusalem, the townspeople refused to welcome him.

James and John were enraged. *"Lord, do you want us to <u>call fire down</u> from heaven to destroy them?"* (Wow! Those two were really "feelin' their oats!") This may have been the place where Jesus gave them the nickname "Sons of Thunder" (Mark 3:17). He *"turned and rebuked them,"* and went on to a more receptive village.

SAMARITANS—People living in the territory between Judea and Galilee. After King Solomon's death, 10 Israelite tribes seceded and called themselves "Israel," or the Northern Kingdom. Two southern tribes, Judah and Benjamin, were known as "Judah," or the Southern Kingdom. When the Assyrians conquered the Northern Kingdom (2 Kings 17), they carried most Jews off to other parts of the Assyrian Empire and replaced them with foreigners from other conquered nations. This created a mixed race—part Jew, part Gentile—and led to a corrupt form of religion centering at Mount Gerizim rather than Jerusalem. Samaritans and "pure" Jews developed deep hatred for each other.

Some old manuscripts of Luke's gospel quote Jesus as saying to James and John, *"You don't know what kind of spirit you are of; for the Son of Man did not come to <u>destroy</u> men's lives, but to save them"* (Luke 9:55–56). How often have Christians forgotten this! Crusades, inquisitions, wars, terrorism, imprisonments, persecutions, and political pressures have all been used at times to try to force people to submit to Christianity or to a particular interpretation of it!

> **Luke 9:57–62** As they were walking along the road, a man said to him, "I will follow you wherever you go."
> Jesus replied, "Foxes have holes and birds of the air have nests, but the Son of Man has no place to lay his head."

He said to another man, "Follow me."

But the man replied, "Lord, first let me go and bury my father."

Jesus said to him, "Let the dead bury their dead, but you go and proclaim the kingdom of God."

Still another said, "I will follow you, Lord; but first let me go back and say goodbye to my family."

Jesus replied, "No one who puts his hand to the plow and looks back is fit for service in the kingdom of God."

The High Price Of Traveling With Jesus

As Jesus moved toward hostile territory, he confronted three kinds of issues on the minds of his followers.

1. *The issue of status and security* (Luke 9:58). A man who was a **scribe** (see illustration, page 26) or a lawyer, according to Matthew 8:19, announced his intent to follow Jesus. Not many scribes did this. Lawyers were highly respected and materially secure. This man's decision would be costly. Jesus reminded him of the cost. After that, there is no record that the man followed Jesus.

2. *The issue of family* (Luke 9:60). The second man may have been one of the 12. Jesus called him to "preach the kingdom of God"—the same words he used in commissioning the 12 for their mission in Galilee (Luke 9:2). As danger loomed ahead, the man was having second thoughts. "I must first bury my father," he said. This phrase is still used in the Middle East to say, "I have to take care of my obligations to my parents until my father dies."

   "Let the dead bury their own dead," Jesus replied. He knew he only had a few months left with his followers. If this potential apostle failed to follow immediately, he would miss the greatest opportunity of his life.

3. *Issues of breaking with the past* (verse 62). A third man used a similar argument to delay his response to Christ's call. Jesus heard in it a reluctance to make a clean break with the past. The plowman who is always looking back over his shoulder can never cut a straight furrow. Jesus called for a clear-cut and decisive choice.

scribe: *expert and teacher of the Law of Moses and Jewish traditions*

Scribe

A scribe was a person who recorded and preserved important documents, including the Old Testament Scriptures. He was an expert and teacher of the Law.

What Others are Saying:

KEY Outline:

Cost to Follow Jesus

*Lose status or security
Leave family
   responsibilities
Break with the past*

deceives: *a capital offense (Deuteronomy 13:1–5)*

Jews: *Jewish leaders, not rank-and-file Jewish people*

Leon Morris: The Jews counted proper burial as most important; to leave a father unburied was something scandalous. . . . The duty of burial took precedence over the study of the law, the Temple service, the killing of the Passover sacrifice (and) the observance of circumcision. But the demands of the kingdom are more urgent still.[2]

Oswald Chambers: The one mark of discipleship is the mastership of Jesus—his right to me from the crown of my head to the sole of my foot.[3]

> **John 7:11–13** Now at the Feast the Jews were watching for him and asking, "Where is that man?" Among the crowds there was widespread whispering about him. Some said, "He is a good man." Others replied, "No, he **deceives** the people." But no one would say anything publicly about him for fear of the **Jews**.

Festival Troublemaker

Even before he and his men slipped unnoticed into the city, Jesus was the talk of the festival crowds. No one was neutral about him.

The Boiling Pot of Attitudes toward Jesus at the Feast of Tabernacles

John 7–8

Enemies:	The Jews (7:11, 13, 15, 35; 8:22, 48, 52, 57)
	The **Pharisees** (7:32, 47; 8:13)
	The chief priests and the Pharisees (7:32, 45–52)
	The teachers of the Law and the Pharisees (8:3)
Friendly/mildly friendly:	The crowd (7:12, 20, 31–32)
	The people (7:40–41, 43)
	This mob (7:49)
	Nicodemus (7:50)
	Many who put their faith in him (8:30)
Undecided:	The crowds (7:12–13)
	The people of Jerusalem (7:25)
	The temple guards (7:32, 45–46)
	The Jews who had believed him (8:31)

Dig Deeper

Pharisees: *religious leaders who strictly observed Jewish laws and traditions*

> **John 7:15–16** The Jews were amazed and asked, "How did this man get such learning without having studied?" Jesus answered, "My teaching is not my own. It comes from him who sent me."

The Revealer Of "Secret Knowledge"

Midpoint in the festivities Jesus joined the crowds in the temple area and began to teach. John doesn't tell us what he said, only that whatever it was the leaders and people found it astonishing. In speaking he combined a complete grasp of Scripture with fresh authority.

The Jews' question was not about literacy. Most Jewish men could read and write. Their question rose from two facts:

1. According to the rules, only a scholar who had been tutored by an accredited rabbi had the right to teach the Scriptures or interpret the Jewish law.
2. The "secret knowledge" required to be able to interpret the Scriptures could only come from study of "sacred books" to which only scholars had access, because they were written in Hebrew rather than Aramaic, the language of the people.

☞ **GO TO:**

Matthew 7:28–29; Mark 1:22; Luke 4:32 (authority)

KEY Outline:

License to Teach
Tutored by rabbi
Knowledge of sacred books

Jesus was an "uneducated" carpenter who had never studied under a recognized rabbi. Yet he possessed the "secret knowledge." The "scholars" were scandalized!

> **John 7:16–18** Jesus answered, "My teaching is not my own. It comes from him who sent me. If anyone chooses to do God's will, he will find out whether my teaching comes from God or whether I speak on my own. He who speaks on his own does so to gain honor for himself, but he who works for the honor of the one who sent him is a man of truth; there is nothing false about him."

Who Was Jesus' "Rabbi"?

☞ GO TO:

John 12:49; 14:10
(teacher)

His answer to their question was that God was his <u>teacher</u>.

He did not claim to be self-taught—that would be grounds for discreditation. He never claimed to be the originator of the ideas he shared. His words came from his Father in heaven.

Jesus proposed a simple, practical test to prove the authenticity of his teaching: Practice what I teach—*"choose to do God's will"*—and you will know *"my teaching comes from God."*

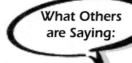

What Others are Saying:

KEY POINT

Jesus' mentor was God the Father.

Dan McCartney and Charles Clayton: Implicit in this pursuit of biblical understanding is the commitment to obey God's will. Study is not merely for the purpose of savoring doctrine in the abstract. The industrious searching for biblical truth, the daily meditation on the Word, and the striving for sound interpretation are useful only if driven by a desire to please the Lord, to submit to his wishes.[4]

> **John 7:19–20** "Has not Moses given you the law? Yet not one of you keeps the law. Why are you trying to kill me?"
> "You are demon-possessed," the crowd answered. "Who is trying to kill you?"

☞ Check It Out:

John 7:19–31

Assassins In The Crowd

Addressing the Jewish leaders, Jesus pressed the point: If they were practicing God's will even as it was revealed in the Law of Moses, they wouldn't be conspiring at that very moment to kill him. Instead they would <u>believe and welcome</u> him.

☞ GO TO:

John 5:45–47 (believed and welcomed)

Most people listening were unaware of the leaders' plot. They wrote off Jesus' suggestion as the absurd ravings of a deranged person (verse 20).

Jesus knew where the conspiracy started. *"I did one miracle, and you are all astonished"* (John 7:21). The leaders had been incensed over his healing of the paralyzed man at the Pool of Bethesda on the Sabbath and over his general defiance of man-made Sabbath rules (John 5:8–16).

The **Pharisees** and **chief priests** decided it was time to shut Jesus up. They dispatched a squad of temple police to arrest him (John 7:32). Most likely their instructions were to watch for a strategic moment to make the arrest so as not to create a riot. A riot would get the Roman troops involved—the last thing the leaders wanted.

While waiting for the right moment, the officers heard what Jesus was saying. In fact, they apparently listened to him for several days before reporting back to their superiors.

> **John 7:37–39** On the last and greatest day of the Feast, Jesus stood and said in a loud voice, "If anyone is thirsty, let him come to me and drink. Whoever believes in me, as the Scripture has said, streams of living water will flow from within him." By this he meant the Spirit, whom those who believed in him were later to receive. Up to that time the Spirit had not been given, since Jesus had not yet been glorified.

River Of The Spirit

One of the high points each day at the Feast of Tabernacles was a procession through the streets of Jerusalem to the Pool of Siloam (see illustration, page 30).

At the pool a priest filled a golden pitcher with water. When the procession returned to the Temple, the water was poured into a silver funnel leading to the base of the altar of burnt offering while the congregation chanted the **Hallel** and shook branches of palm and other trees toward the altar. When the singing ended there was a moment of silence as the priests prepared the sacrifices.[5]

It was probably during that moment of silence the voice of Jesus was heard inviting thirsty people to come to him and drink, promising everyone who believed in him *streams of living water* flowing within them.[6]

The Bible historian, John, comments that this living river is the Holy Spirit who would be given to everyone who **believes** in Jesus.

Pharisees: group committed to strict adherence to religious laws and traditions taught by the scribes

chief priests: Jewish clergy who controlled the Temple and religious life

☞ **GO TO:**

Mark 14:1–2 (strategic moment)

Hallel: Psalms 113–118

believes: trusts Jesus as the One sent from God, Savior, Lord, eternal life-giver

☞ **GO TO:**

Leviticus 23:40 (branches)

John 4:14 (living water)

John 14:15–23; 16:7–15; Acts 1:8; 2:38–39 (everyone)

Pool of Siloam

The Pool of Siloam was at the mouth of the tunnel King Hezekiah built to bring water into Jerusalem from the Spring of Gihon, outside the walls.

Something to Ponder

dogma: doctrine, formal religious or moral teaching

What Others are Saying:

☞ **GO TO:**

John 14:15–21 (presence)

More than any other reality connected with being a follower of Christ, the Holy Spirit, which Jesus described as *"streams of living water"* flowing *"from within,"* raises Christianity above mere "religion" and makes it an exciting adventure. Christ's <u>presence</u> in his followers' lives, in the person of the Holy Spirit, makes the Christian faith more than tedious religious activity or lifeless **dogma**. With the Holy Spirit the challenging teachings of Jesus become "mission possible."

Billy Graham: God does not want us to come to Christ by faith, and then lead a life of defeat, discouragement, and dissension. Rather, he wants to "fulfill every desire for goodness and the work of faith with power; in order that the name of our Lord Jesus Christ may be glorified in you" (2 Thessalonians 1:11–12, *New American Standard Bible*). *To the great gift of forgiveness God adds also the great gift of the Holy Spirit.* He is the source of power who meets our need to escape from the miserable weakness that grips us. He gives us the power to be truly good. . . .

If you believe in Jesus Christ, a power is available to you that can change your life, even in such intimate areas as your marriage, your family relationships, and every other relationship. Also, God offers power that can change a tired church into a vital, growing body, power that can revitalize Christendom.[7]

KEY POINT

Holy Spirit is an inner life stream for all who trust Christ.

> **John 7:45** Finally the temple guards went back to the chief priests and Pharisees, who asked them, "Why didn't you bring him in?"

The Tragedy Of The Unconvinced

The officers sent to arrest Jesus returned to their superiors empty-handed.

"No one ever spoke the way this man does." These were not exactly the words the chief priests and Pharisees wanted to hear. Jesus had slipped through their fingers again.

"Has any of the rulers of the Pharisees believed in him? No!"

Well, er, uh . . . One lone, hesitant voice, dared to ask, *"Does our law condemn anyone without first hearing him to find out what he is doing?"* It was the voice of the Pharisee Nicodemus, who, about two years before, had met with Jesus secretly (see GWLC, pages 111–116).

☞ **Check It Out:**

John 7:45–52

☞ **GO TO:**

John 3 (Nicodemus)

Who's Who

NICODEMUS—A leading teacher among the Pharisees and a member of the ruling Jewish Council, who first showed an interest in Jesus after Jesus' first cleansing of the Temple (John 2:12–16). He came to Jesus after dark. Jesus told him he needed to be born again (John 3:3, 5). After Jesus' death, Nicodemus joined Joseph of Arimathea in burying Jesus in Joseph's Garden Tomb.

Edwin A. Blum: Even though Nicodemus was a respected member of the nation (John 3:10), he was insulted by the other members of the Sanhedrin. Their prejudice and hatred against Jesus was already strong enough to overthrow reason.[8]

What Others are Saying:

Power And Light

Each night at the Feast of Tabernacles four huge lamp stands blazed in the temple court of women. All night long, led by the priests, the gathered nation danced and sang praises to God by the leaping torchlight.

The purpose of this feast of unbridled joy was to celebrate the Lord's leadership of the Israelites, during their wanderings through

☞ **Check It Out:**

John 7:53–8:20

☞ **GO TO:**

Exodus 13:20–22;
14:19–20; 40:36–38
(cloud and fire)

the wilderness, with the pillar of cloud and fire—reminders of his presence, protection, and spiritual illumination.

The incident that follows illustrates the difference the light of God's grace (in this case visible in the person of Jesus Christ) can make in a very bad situation.

The Case Of The Controversial Fragment

The oldest and best **Greek manuscripts** of John's gospel do not contain the first 11 verses of John 8. It probably was not part of the book in its original form.

The early Christian theologian Augustine thought the story ought to be removed on grounds that Jesus' readiness to forgive the adulterous woman might encourage Christian wives to sin. Not a good argument, St. Augustine!

Even if it was written by someone other than John and inserted later, it is consistent with everything we know about Jesus. There's no reason to doubt it really happened.

It illustrates beautifully the incredible grace of God we see in Jesus. And it may very well have happened in precisely the context in which it appears.

Greek manuscripts:
copies of New Testament
books, handwritten in
Greek by copyists, used to
make our English
translations (the originals
have been lost)

> **John 8:2–6** At dawn he appeared again in the temple courts, where all the people gathered around him, and he sat down to teach them. The teachers of the law and the Pharisees brought in a woman caught in adultery. They made her stand before the group and said to Jesus, "Teacher, this woman was caught in the act of adultery. In the Law Moses commanded us to stone such women. Now what do you say?" They were using this question as a trap, in order to have a basis for accusing him.

adultery: sex with one
who is not one's wife or
husband

stone: the condemned
was crushed by rocks in a
pit outside the city

executed: no execution
was permitted without
the Roman governor's
okay

Kicking And Screaming Into The Light

In their commitment to destroy Jesus, the religious leaders hatched scheme after scheme to embarrass or entrap him in front of the people. Most backfired. But they kept trying. In this incident they thought they'd snare him in a catch-22 and get him in trouble with both Jewish and Roman law.

They brought a woman who had committed **adultery**. *"Moses commanded us to* **stone** *such women. Now what do you say?"* the woman's accusers asked. Actually, the Law demanded that both the man and woman be **executed**. Where was the man? He was as

☞ **GO TO:**

Acts 7:57–60 (stone)

guilty as she. The adulterer probably was part of the conspiracy and his escape had been arranged.

The leaders were not really concerned about what was right. Their only concern was getting Jesus into a legal dilemma from which he could not escape.

- If he agreed she should be stoned he would compromise his own way of life and his teaching of **grace** and forgiveness, and sacrifice his reputation as a <u>friend of sinners</u>.

- If he said she should not be stoned, they could accuse him of ignoring the demands of Moses' Law.

Adultery was a capital offense among the Jews (Deuteronomy 22):

- For adultery with a married woman, the penalty was death for both the man and woman (Deuteronomy 22:22).

- For adultery involving a girl or woman engaged to another man, if she was a consenting partner (failed to scream for help) the penalty was death by stoning for both (verses 23–24).

- For adultery with an engaged girl or woman where no one was near enough to hear her screams, punishment for the rapist was the same as for a murderer (verses 25–27).

- For adultery with an unmarried, unengaged virgin, the man must pay her dowry and marry her (verses 28–29).

grace: God's loving-kindness toward sinners

☞ **GO TO:**

Luke 5:20; 7:48; John 3:17 (grace)

Matthew 11:19; Luke 5:31–32; 15:1–2 (friend of sinners)

Remember This . . .

William Barclay: It is extremely unlikely that the scribes and the Pharisees even knew this woman's name. To them she was nothing but a case of shameless adultery that could now be used as an instrument to suit their purposes.[9]

What Others are Saying:

> **John 8:7** "If any one of you is without sin, let him be the first to throw a stone at her."

Sinners In The Spotlight

Jesus was seated in the temple court teaching when the woman was dragged before him. Sitting there he bent down and wrote on the dusty pavement with his finger. The arrogant religionists repeated their question. He looked up at them and hit them with an exploding word grenade.

KEY Outline:

Adultery
Capital offense
Man and woman share guilt
Forgivable

wrote: Greek: "write," "draw," or "write down a record against someone"

KEY Outline:

Theories

Jesus wrote

- doodles to cool his anger
- Bible verse
- accusers' sins
- adulterers' names

☞ **GO TO:**

Luke 5:20; 7:47–48; 23:34; Romans 5:8 (before they asked)

☞ **Check It Out:**

John 12–20

Dig Deeper

He stooped down and again **wrote** on the ground. Nobody knows what he wrote. There are plenty of theories:

- He was doodling to cool his anger or to buy time to think.
- He wrote a passage from the Old Testament.
- He listed the sins of the woman's accusers.
- He wrote the name of the leaders who had themselves committed adultery.
- He wrote what he said in verse 7 about the person who hasn't sinned throwing the first stone.

The men who had arranged this disgusting spectacle found themselves exposed and left, confronted by their own guilt.

Lone Star State

Soon everyone was gone but Jesus and the woman standing before him. There is no record that she confessed her sin or promised to stop. Even so, Jesus told her that he did not condemn her—meaning he forgave her.

It was not the first time he forgave someone <u>before they asked</u> for it. It would not be the last.

When Jesus said to the woman, "I don't condemn you," that did not make her innocent. It did make her forgiven. The next step was up to her. Forgiven—her record cleansed of her sin— she was now ready for a new start: *"Go now and leave your life of sin,"* he urged (John 8:11).

Celebration Of The Light

The nightly festivities in the court of women were carefully prepared to separate men and women.

Principles for Dealing with People Who Fail

Scripture	Principle
Matthew 7:1–5; Luke 6:41–42	Only the person who is dealing honestly with his or her own faults is in a position to judge others
Luke 6:37; Romans 8:1	In dealing with offenders, the attitude of choice is "no condemnation"
Matthew 18:15; 1 Corinthians 5:5; Galatians 6:1	Salvation and restoration is top priority when dealing with erring people
Matthew 18:21–23	Forgiveness is never to be withheld—no matter what the offender has done or how many times he or she has done it
Luke 17:3; Ephesians 4:15; James 5:19–20	Along with forgiveness, the offender needs encouragement—sometimes confrontation—to give up the sin

Four priests kept four golden bowls filled with oil that fueled great, blazing, multiarmed golden lamp stands (see illustration below). Trained dancers—men chosen for good works and commitment to Judaism—danced through the night with torches in their hands, singing psalms of praise to the Lord. A **Levite** orchestra came down the steps into the courtyard and accompanied the singing and dancing with trumpets, cymbals, lyres, and harps.

At a high point in the night's sacred jubilation, two priests with trumpets descended the steps, blowing their horns. The congregation fell silent. Turning toward the Temple the priests shouted, "We belong to **Yahweh**, and our eyes are directed to Yahweh!" The people repeated the shout again and again. Focus was on God, Israel's light, source of salvation, hope, and joy.

> **John 8:12** "I am the light of the world! Whoever follows me will never walk in darkness, but will have the light of life!"

The Light Of The World

It may have been in the moment of silence, when the orchestra and the singing stopped, the dancers paused, seconds after the trumpet blasts on the stairs, as the people listened for the proclamation of the priests, that Jesus' voice pierced the smoke-filled air with his statement.

This was Jesus' second *"I am"* declaration reported by John. It was an outright claim of Godhood. In the context of the festival he was claiming to Israel and the world to be everything symbolized by the blazing candelabra.

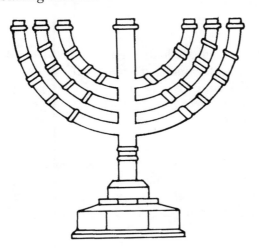

ACT OF THE HOLY SPIRIT

Convicts us of personal sin

Levite: *descendants of Jacob's son Levi who assisted in temple worship*

Yahweh: *Hebrew name by which God introduced himself to Moses*

KEY POINT

Forgiving people before they ask for forgiveness is God's plan for changing sinners.

KEY POINT

God is the Light of Israel.

The Menorah

The Menorah is a multiarmed lamp stand. At the Feast of Tabernacles, four huge versions of this lamp stand illuminated the temple court of women during the nightly festival of light.

Dig Deeper

What Jesus Claimed by Saying, "I Am the Light of the World"

Jesus Claimed to Be	Scripture
The pillar of fire and cloud that led Israel to freedom	Exodus 13:20–22
Israel's protector and guide	Psalm 23; Matthew 23:37; John 10:11
Source of spiritual illumination	John 1:4–5; 3:19–21; 1 John 1:7
Revealer of God among men	John 1:14, 18; 8:19; 14:7–11; 1 John 1:1–3
Messiah whose glory the celebration anticipated	Luke 9:28–36; 2 Peter 1:16–17
Object of worship, praise, singing, and celebration	John 9:38; 20:28
The one to follow	Matthew 4:18–22; Mark 8:34; Luke 9:57–62

☞ **GO TO:**

Matthew 9:34; 12:24, 38–39; John 6:30–31 (ignorant)

Matthew 23:25–28 (appearances)

John 5:31–46 (witnesses)

John 14:10–11 (behind)

Something to Ponder

The Impenetrable Darkness

The response of the Pharisees to Jesus' "*I am*" assertions was to demand witnesses to back up his claims. His own witness was not enough, they said (John 8:13).

His response was to tell them that they had no real authority to pass judgment on his claims. He cited two reasons:

1. They were purposely <u>ignorant</u> of where he came from (verse 14). All his miracles and gracious teachings had failed to convince them.

2. They judged by human standards, outward <u>appearances</u> (verse 15). When they looked at Jesus they saw only a man who was disturbing their status quo.

Jesus also insisted he had all the <u>witnesses</u> he needed: The Father in heaven stood <u>behind</u> everything he said about himself (verses 16–18).

It was and is impossible to persuade closed-minded people to believe Jesus' testimony about himself. A point comes when reason and argument have gone as far as they can go, and the person must make a decision to accept Jesus' claims on the basis of faith.

> **John 8:28** So Jesus said, "When you have lifted up the Son of Man, then you will know that I am the one I claim to be and that I do nothing on my own but speak just what the Father has taught me."

Unbelieving Believers

"Who are you?" the people asked. Jesus' answer amounted to, "I am who I claim to be." Besides being the light of the world, Jesus was the Son of God (John 8:16, 18, 23), the bearer of God's message (verses 26, 28), the one who pleases God in everything (verse 29), and the one who has God with him (verse 29).

At first glance, the next statement is cause for celebration: *"Even as he spoke, many put their faith in him"* (verse 30).

Some who believed at that moment were part of the religious elite ("the Jews," verse 31). The word translated "believed" indicates they <u>really believed</u>.

But something was missing. Three sentences later, John reports that some of these "believers" debated with Jesus about his suggestion that they needed to be set free (verses 32–33). Their resistance against what he was saying became so intense that Jesus called them children of the devil (verse 44)!

And before the conversation ended some of these "believers" picked up stones from the temple pavement to throw at him (verse 59)! How is this possible?

The key to understanding what happened here is in what Jesus said to those who believed: *"If you hold to my teachings, you are really my disciples"* (John 8:31).

> The original Greek word for "hold to" indicates a settled determination to live in and by the teachings of Christ. Intellectual assent that Jesus was who he claimed to be was not enough to make these "believers" real disciples of Christ.
>
> Real disciples are those who determine to allow Jesus' teachings to reshape their thinking, values, priorities, attitudes and behavior. Those who follow intellectual conviction with actions that acknowledge Jesus as Leader *"will know the truth, and the truth will set them free!"* (John 8:32).

Oswald Chambers: Obedience to Jesus Christ is essential. . . . In the early stages we have the notion that the Christian life is one of freedom, and so it is, but freedom for one thing only—freedom to obey our Master.[10]

☞ **Check It Out:**

John 8:21–59

KEY Outline:

Jesus' Claims
Light of world
Son of God
Sent by God
Revealer of God
God's messenger
Pleases God
God is with him

☞ **GO TO:**

John 1:12; 3:16; 4:39; 5:24; 6:69
(really believed)

Something to Ponder

What Others are Saying:

Dig Deeper

KEY Outline:

Evidence of True Faith

Believe Christ's teachings

Live by Christ's teachings

Light in the Bible

Natural: sunlight	Genesis 1:16
Artificial: lamplight	Matthew 25:1
Figurative: the nature of God	1 Timothy 6:16
Spiritual holiness	Isaiah 5:20; Romans 13:12
Spiritual insight	Psalm 119:105; John 3:19–21; Ephesians 5:14
Honesty before God and others	1 John 1:5–10
God is light	1 John 1:5
Christ, the light of the world	John 8:12

Study Questions

1. Identify the three differences between Jesus and his brothers.
2. What answer did Jesus give in Luke 9 when James and John suggested they might call down fire on a rejecting Samaritan village?
3. According to John 7:16, who gave Jesus the things he taught and gave him the right to teach? How did Jesus suggest a person might know for sure his teachings came from God?
4. On the last day of the feast what did Jesus promise to the people who put their faith in him?
5. List three of the five principles of Jesus for dealing with people who fail.
6. Jesus accepts us "as is" and refuses to condemn us. Does knowing that free you to change, or reinforce your bad behavior? How?

CHAPTER WRAP-UP

- As the Feast of Tabernacles approached, Jesus' skeptical brothers advised him to go to Jerusalem and "go public." He followed God's timing, not theirs. He left at a different time. On the way a Samaritan town refused to let him stay overnight. (Luke 9:52–56; John 7:1–10)

- Halfway through the feast, Jesus arrived and began to preach. The crowd was split—some for him, some against, some confused. Temple police were dispatched to arrest him. (John 7:11–36)

- On the last day of the feast, Jesus announced that anyone who believed on him would have a river of living water flowing inside—he spoke of the Holy Spirit. Temple police returned to the high priests empty-handed. They hadn't arrested Jesus. They'd gotten caught up in his teachings. (John 7:37–53)

- A woman caught in the act of adultery was brought to Jesus for judgment. He forgave her and forced her accusers to face up to their own sins. (John 8:1–11)

- At the same festival, Jesus introduced himself as "The light of the world." People were forced to make a decision about who he was. Many believed he was telling the truth—he was everything he claimed to be. Still they rejected him; some even tried to stone him. (John 8:12–59)

3 BRIGHT SONLIGHT, DARK SHADOWS

CHAPTER HIGHLIGHTS

- Witness of the Lambs
- Private Lessons
- The Incredible Shrinking Hypocrite
- Critical Admonitions for Disciples

Let's Get Started

The clock was ticking. Jesus <u>knew</u> his days were numbered. Only about six months remained before the final conflict with his enemies, which would climax in his crucifixion.

He and the 12 had saturated Galilee (see appendix A) with the basic message of the kingdom. He had saved Judea and the territories east of the Jordan River for a final campaign; he knew that the more public exposure he had in Jerusalem, the center of ecclesiastical and political power, the more quickly the opposition would intensify.

Timing was important. The ultimate crisis must not come too soon. All Israel must hear the message of the kingdom's nearness before Jesus presented himself in Jerusalem as the **Passover Lamb** on April 15, 29 A.D.[1] (To learn more about the Passover, see GWBI, page 28.)

> **Luke 10:1–3** After this the Lord appointed seventy-two others and sent them two by two ahead of him to every town and place where he was about to go. He told them, "The harvest is plentiful, but the workers are few. Ask the Lord of the harvest, therefore, to send out workers into his harvest field. Go! I am sending you out like lambs among wolves."

GOSPEL QUARTET IN HARMONY

Luke 10:1–13:21
John 9:1–10:39

☞ GO TO:

Matthew 16:21; Luke 9:44 (knew)

Passover Lamb: *lamb sacrificed at the Passover Feast to free people from sin's slavery*

Sanhedrin: the ruling council and supreme court of Israel

☞ **GO TO:**

Matthew 10; Luke 9:1–
9 (crusade)

judgment: "Woe" an expression of regret, like "Alas!"

☞ **GO TO:**

Matthew 10:14–15;
Luke 10:10–15
(more severe)

KEY POINT

The more you know, the more responsibility you have.

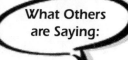
What Others
are Saying:

Witness Of The Lambs

With only a few months to go, Jesus commissioned a second wave of advance witnesses—72—to prepare the way for his arrival in cities and towns of Judea and Perea (see appendix A). Some translations say there were 70, not 72, who were sent. The difference is due to a copyist's error. Whatever amount, the number corresponds to elders assisting Moses (Numbers 11:16–27) or the number of men in the **Sanhedrin**.

The instructions given this second, larger team are essentially the same as those given the 12 for their <u>crusade</u> in Galilee, including the warning that they are being sent *"like lambs among wolves."* The Judean response could be expected to be even more "wolf-like" than what had faced Galilee campaigners.

More Light, Greater Responsibility, Heavier Judgment

The warnings of **judgment** on cities that might reject the witness of the 72 were <u>more severe</u> than for rejecting the 12. By the time the 72 were sent, the towns Jesus mentioned—Korazin, Bethsaida, and Capernaum (see appendix A) in verses 13–15—had more exposure to Jesus and his message, more time to consider their response, and thus bore more responsibility for their negative choices.

- *Korazin:* Jesus did convincing miracles there (Matthew 11:21).
- *Bethsaida:* the feeding of the 5,000 took place near there (Luke 9:10–17).
- *Capernaum:* Jesus' adopted "hometown"; he did wonder-works there; they were amazed at his authority (Luke 4:31–41); he preached the Sermon on the Mount near there (Matthew 5–7).

In spite of their opportunities, the people of these towns failed to follow through on what they'd seen and heard, placing themselves in danger of judgment (Luke 10:12, 15).

Today the location of Korazin can't be found. The site of Capernaum is deserted. Even its rubble is difficult to locate.

Leon Morris: In rejecting the preachers they were not simply rejecting a couple of poor itinerants, but the very kingdom of God, and that has serious consequences. The people have drawn down judgment on themselves.[2]

> **Luke 10:17–20** The seventy-two returned with joy and said, "Lord, even the demons submit to us in your name." He replied, "I saw Satan fall like lightning from heaven. I have given you authority to trample on snakes and scorpions and to overcome all the power of the enemy; nothing will harm you. However, do not rejoice that the spirits submit to you, but rejoice that your names are written in heaven."

Debriefing

Thirty-six teams of excited campaigners returned from their mission, high on success and adventure. Their message had not been rejected. Troubled people had been liberated. Demons cowered when team members confronted them using Jesus' delegated authority!

Jesus' response, *"I saw Satan fall like lightning from heaven"* (Luke 10:18), was like saying, "When you guys were out there preaching the kingdom message, confronting demons, and healing sick people, I saw the devil falling in defeat before you!"

It was a high point for him. It showed his teaching had taken root in them. Their process of preparation was exactly where it had to be if the church and kingdom were to be established on schedule. He had given them authority to stomp on <u>serpents</u>, and they did!

In his post-campaign debriefing Jesus put their heady sense of invincibility into perspective. "Your power to command devils, exciting as it is, is nothing compared to simply knowing your names are **written in heaven**" (verse 20 and see GWRV, pages 302–303).

 Jesus' kingdom people share his authority to stomp on the devil-serpent (Satan) and his cohorts.

> **Luke 10:21** At that time Jesus, **full of joy** through the Holy Spirit, said, "I praise you, Father, Lord of heaven and earth, because you have hidden these things from the wise and learned, and revealed them to little children."

KEY POINT

Being certain of eternal life is more cause for joy than is being able to control demons.

☞ **GO TO:**

Genesis 3:1; 2 Corinthians 11:3 (serpents)

Exodus 32:32; Daniel 12:1; Hebrews 12:23; Revelation 3:5 (written in heaven)

---

written in heaven: *"the Book of Life," God's record of those who have eternal life*

full of joy: *Greek meaning, "to leap for joy"*

Brighter Than The Brainy

Jesus broke into prayer, joyfully praising his Father for the fresh spiritual understanding his disciples were experiencing as they returned from their mission.

By doing God's will they had become even more convinced than ever that Jesus and his teachings were from God! The Bible's word for what had happened to them is **revelation**.

revelation: God's self-disclosure

Compared to the world's sophisticated scholars, this group of simple Galileans and other relatively uneducated people were *"little children."* Yet they were making spiritual discoveries the educated and clever missed in the smoke screen of their pride.

Their discoveries were these:

- The power of faith in Jesus' name to put down evil (verse 17)
- The protection faith in Jesus gives in the work and the war against evil (verse 19)

These insights were gifts <u>from God</u> (verse 21), and prepared the disciples for the following additional revelations:

☞ **GO TO:**

Matthew 16:17; John 6:44 (from God)

- The wide range of Jesus' authority (verse 22)
- The unique father-son relationship between God and Jesus (verse 22)
- The role of Jesus as the Revealer of God in the world (verse 22)

The ordinary Christian believer is able to understand truths the brilliant and powerful long to see but cannot unless they recognize they are "ordinary" believers, admit spiritual ignorance, become *"little children,"* humbly put their faith in Jesus, and seek to do God's will.

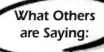

What Others are Saying:

John Wesley: Give me one hundred preachers who fear nothing but sin, and desire nothing but God, and I care not a straw whether they be clergymen or laymen, such alone will shake the gates of hell and set up the kingdom of heaven on earth.[3]

> **Luke 10:25** On one occasion an expert in the law stood up to test Jesus. "Teacher," he asked, "What must I do to inherit eternal life?"

Private Lessons

The words with which Luke introduced this story, *"On one occasion,"* hints that it may not have taken place immediately after the return of the 72, but was inserted here as an example of the worldly wise person who has trouble seeing God's simple truth.

An expert in Jewish law pretended to be searching for the answer to life's great question: *"What must I do to inherit eternal life?"* But the lawyer's question was a dead giveaway, revealing that he believed he could be saved by his deeds.

Jesus saw through the ruse and did not give the man a direct answer. Instead, he asked the lawyer three questions to make him face the issue for himself. First, Jesus asked, "What does your reading of the Law tell you about how to have eternal life?" (Luke 10:26).

Every serious Jew could be expected to know by heart the answer to this legal question: *"Love God . . . love your neighbor."*

"Do this and live," Jesus responded.

"Who is my neighbor?" the lawyer asked, squirming to wriggle out of the limelight.

THE BIG PICTURE 🔍

> **Luke 10:30–35** Jesus told this story: A traveler on his way to Jericho was beaten, robbed, and left for dead. A priest walked by and ignored him. Then a Levite passed by and also ignored him. But when a Samaritan saw the victim, he helped him, took him to an inn, and paid the staff to look after him until he was well.

The Good Samaritan

In answer to the lawyer's question about his neighbor, Jesus told the now-famous parable of the Good Samaritan.

In Jesus' story, the despised outlander was the hero. After the religious people refused to get involved, the Samaritan rescued the beat-up robbery victim, transported him to safety, cared for him, and paid the bills!

Jesus then asked his second question: Which of the three in the story—priest, Levite, or Samaritan—proved to be the robbery victim's neighbor (verse 36)?

"The one who had mercy on him," the lawyer answered.

Correctamundo! Jesus said, *"Go and do likewise."*

Jesus' third question was never asked aloud. The lawyer was left to ask himself, "To whom am I a neighbor?"

KEY Outline:

God's Secrets Revealed to Believers

Jesus' power
Jesus' protection
Jesus' authority
Jesus' divine Sonship
Jesus, God's Revealer

☞ **GO TO:**

Deuteronomy 6:5 (love God)

Leviticus 19:18 (love your neighbor)

The Israelites of Jesus' day typically thought the ancient Love-thy-neighbor command applied only to fellow Jews. It never entered their heads that neighbor loving might include all human beings, regardless of racial or religious background.

It was an idea that was essential to Jesus' followers, who would soon be sent into the whole world with the Good News.

"Good Sam"
Characters
Traveler (victim)
Bandits (danger)
Priest/Levite (religious)
Samaritan (outsider)

Remember
This . . .

Samaritans were outsiders. They crossed the borders to do business (which would explain this Samaritan's travel down the Jericho Road), but Samaritans and Jews maintained a mutual animosity for one another.

Bandits were a danger every time one ventured out on the roads of Israel. For mutual protection, people traveled in groups.

The priest and Levite represented the clergy of Israel—the spiritual leaders, guardians of faith, caretakers of the Temple.

What Others
are Saying:

☞ **GO TO:**

1 John 4:20 (neighbor)

KEY POINT

Loving one's neighbor is part of loving God and includes strangers and aliens.

KEY Outline:

"Good Sam"
Questions
What must I do?
What does the Bible say?
Who is my neighbor?
To whom am I a neighbor?

Leon Morris: The lawyer wanted a rule or a set of rules that he could keep and so merit eternal life. Jesus is telling him that eternal life is not a matter of keeping rules at all. To live in love is to live the life of the kingdom of God. . . . Our attitude toward God determines the rest. If we really love him we love our <u>neighbor</u> too.[4]

> **Luke 10:39–40** [Martha] had a sister called Mary who sat at the Lord's feet listening to what he said. But Martha was distracted by all the preparations that had to be made. She came to [Jesus] and asked, "Lord, don't you care that my sister has left me to do all the work by myself? Tell her to help me!"

The Flip Side Of Good Samaritanism

Jesus took care to keep his teachings in balance. This incident demonstrated the flip side of "Good Samaritanism."

In the little village of Bethany, just five miles from Jerusalem, lived a family that was very dear to Jesus—and he to them—Mary, Martha, and Lazarus (two sisters and their brother).

The personalities of the sisters were quite different. And they expressed their deep love for Jesus in completely different ways.

When he came to their house, Mary would sit on the floor near him and hang on every word he spoke. Martha was no less glad to see him, but her style was to fuss and clean and prepare meals.

There is a place for both expressions of love.

In all her busyness, however, Martha revealed mixed motives that threatened to make her "loving" labors less than loving. She complained to Jesus that Mary was not helping with the housework. Actually, she went further than that: She blamed Jesus for not caring that she had to do all the work while her sister lollygagged with him!

Whoops!

Jesus gently adjusted Martha's priorities. *"Mary has chosen what is better, and it will not be taken away from her"* (Luke 10:41–42).

There was an important message in this for the newly returned campaigners. Effective Christian work requires laying aside "practical" work from time to time in order to refuel, spiritually.

Believers who fail to keep their personal relationship with Jesus Christ "hot" can easily slip into a <u>lukewarm</u> religion that is lifeless and tasteless.

___

Roy Irving: We can become so involved in the work of the Lord that we neglect the Lord of the work.[5]

> **Luke 11:1** One day Jesus was praying in a certain place. When he finished, one of his disciples said to him, "Lord, teach us to pray, just as John taught his disciples."

Practical Principles Of Powerful Praying

Jewish rabbis customarily taught their students a prayer to pray.

John the Baptist had taught such a prayer to his people.

In the <u>Sermon on the Mount</u> (see GWLC, pages 189, 197) Jesus gave his earlier disciples a pattern for prayer, which Christians recite as the <u>Lord's Prayer</u>.

Since then additional disciples had joined his ranks. One of them observed Jesus praying and asked to be taught how to pray. Jesus' response was to repeat the model prayer.

The point, as with the Matthew 6 version of it, is not to provide a little religious ritual that can be rattled off at the drop of a hymnbook. The point is to capsulize in digestible form the principles of effective prayer.

KEY POINT

Practical work is good, but it is no substitute for listening to Christ's words.

☞ **GO TO:**

Revelation 2:4; 3:14–20 (lukewarm)

Something to Ponder

What Others are Saying:

☞ **Check It Out:**

Luke 11:1–13

☞ **GO TO:**

Matthew 5:1–48; 6:1–34; 7:1–29; Luke 6:20–49; 11:1 (Sermon on the Mount)

Matthew 6:9–13 (Lord's Prayer)

☞ **GO TO:**

Romans 8:15; Galatians
4:6 (Daddy)

Exodus 16:11–21
(daily bread)

Matthew 5:23; 6:14–
15; Mark 11:25;
Luke 17:3–4
(relational healing)

1 Corinthians 10:13
(not into temptation)

Matthew 6:8
(already knows)

James 1:13 (never)

Romans 10:10
(hear ourselves)

☞ **Check It Out:**

Luke 11:5–13

KEY Outline:

Lord's Prayer
Model, not ritual
Agree with God
Not inform him
For us, not him

- Approach God as <u>Daddy</u> (*"Father"*). This word is used 250 times in the New Testament for "God"; in Aramaic it is, *Abba*, and translated "Daddy."
- Put God and his glory first (*"hallowed be your name"*).
- Long for God's rule (*"your kingdom come"*).
- Depend on God for daily needs (*"give us our <u>daily bread</u>"*).
- Be committed to <u>relational healing</u> (*"forgive us our sins for we also forgive everyone who sins against us"*).
- Seek help for the battle (*"lead us <u>not into temptation</u>"*).

Why Pray?

Prayer is not a matter of informing God. He <u>already knows</u> what we need. Nor is it a matter of convincing God to do what he ought to do. He'll <u>never</u> do anything else. Prayer is not for God; it's for us. Prayer brings our hearts, minds, and wills into harmony with God's. We need to <u>hear ourselves</u> say those things. (For more on prayer, see WBFW, pages 20–22.)

> **Luke 11:9** "So I say to you: Ask and it will be given to you; seek and you will find; knock and the door will be opened to you."

Shameless Prayer

Jesus told a story about a host who was unprepared for his guests to teach that successful praying revolves around two important factors:

1. The brashness of the pray-er (verses 5–8)
2. The goodness of God (verses 9–13)

It was not unusual in those days for people to travel in the evening to avoid the intense midday heat. For a guest to arrive at midnight was fairly common. Hospitality was a sacred trust.

When the unexpected guest arrived, the family bread (see GWHN, page 30)—baked fresh each morning—had been eaten. In order to fulfill his obligation to common courtesy, the host needed to borrow some bread from a neighbor.

The neighbor was reluctant to disturb his whole family, light a lamp, and unbar the door just to loan his unprepared friend a couple of loaves of bread. So he refused. But his brash friend kept bangin' on the door. So the neighbor got up and gave him what he wanted, not because he was a friend, but to get him to stop pounding on the door! The shamelessness and brashness of the man got the response.

Of course, God who listens to our prayers is far more willing to give us what we need than that sleepy, irritated neighbor. This is Jesus' point with his "ask, seek, and knock" promises (verses 9–10).

He made the same point about God's generosity by contrasting it with the nasty father who gives his child a snake when he's hungry for fish or a scorpion when he asks for an egg (verses 11–13).

There are two more messages here about prayer:

1. Too much politeness can get in the way of prayer by hiding the raw, desperate sense of urgent need.

2. Our Father God is more willing than our earthly fathers to give us what we need—especially when what we need is his own enabling presence.

Tony Evans: God is not saying, "Ask for whatever you want." Instead, he is saying, "Ask for what is good." When you ask for good things, our heavenly Father will surely approve—and he will never substitute something harmful. If you have prayed for something you desire with all your heart and have not received it, it is because this desire is either not good or not good *for now.* God is either saying, "No" or "Wait."[6]

What Others are Saying:

> **Luke 11:14–15** Jesus was driving out a demon that was mute. When the demon left, the man who had been mute spoke, and the crowd was amazed. But some of them said, "By Beelzebub, the prince of demons, he is driving out demons."

The Incredible Shrinking Hypocrite

Somewhere in Judea, Jesus drove out a mute spirit. The demon left; the liberated man spoke. In Galilee, the coalition of Jesus' enemies spread the groundless slander saying he performed his miracles by the power of *"Beelzebub, the prince of demons."* He soon discovered the coalition's lie was being believed and spread by some ordinary people in the crowds. He answered with the same arguments with which he had countered this lie the first time around. And then he told a story with a warning.

☞ **Check It Out:**

Luke 11:14–13:21

☞ **GO TO:**

Matthew 12:22–50; Mark 3:20–35; Luke 8:19–21 (in Galilee)

Beelzebub: Lord of Flies or Prince of Dung, the devil

> **Luke 10:24–26** "When an evil spirit comes out of a man, it goes through arid places seeking rest and does not find it. Then it says, "I will return to the house I left." When it arrives, it finds the house swept clean and put in order. Then it goes and takes seven other spirits more wicked than itself, and they go in and live there. And the final condition of that man is worse than the first."

The Politics Of Personal Destruction . . . Again

For the delivered mute, Jesus' words stressed the urgency of filling his life with a holy presence to replace the departed evil presence. He needed to fill his life with God.

For Jesus' enemies, the invasion of devils pictured the danger of substituting man-made cleansing rituals (Luke 10:25) for allegiance to the Lord himself.

Remember This . . .

> A good house for demons is one that is empty of God and in which a cleansing ritual has been substituted for commitment to the Lord.

> **Luke 11:27–28** A woman in the crowd called out, "Blessed is the mother who gave you birth and nursed you." He replied, "Blessed rather are those who hear the word of God and obey it."

The Saccharine Song Of Stupefying Sentimentalism

A woman in the crowd couldn't resist saying how wonderful it must be to have a son like Jesus!

It was true. What a <u>wonderful thing</u> it was to be Jesus' mother! Jesus was the promised son (Messiah) every Jewish mother dreamed her firstborn son might be.

In typical fashion, Jesus redirected her enthusiasm.

☞ **GO TO:**

Luke 1:28, 42–45 (wonderful thing)

Something to Ponder

> Religious sentimentalism is never a substitute for listening carefully to the Word of God and obeying it.

> Emotionalism, enthusiasm, and sentiment can easily become just another form of hypocrisy, a cover-up to keep from dealing with life's tough realities and the challenging instructions of the Word of God.

William Barclay: The moment of emotion is a fine thing; but the greatest thing is a life of obedience in the routine thing of everyday. No amount of fine feeling can take the place of faithful doing.[7]

What Others are Saying:

Albert Barnes: Jesus admits . . . that it was an honor to be his mother, but he says that the chief happiness, the highest honor, was to obey the word of God. Compared to this, all earthly distinctions and honors are as nothing. Man's greatest dignity is in keeping the holy commandments of God, and in being prepared for heaven.[8]

> **Luke 11:29** As the crowds increased, Jesus said, "This is a wicked generation. It asks for a miraculous sign, but none will be given it except the sign of Jonah."

Spiritual Astigmatism

Many in the Judean crowds were withholding acceptance of Jesus, waiting for some extraordinary demonstration of power as proof of his messiahship.

Everywhere Jesus had gone for three years, he had left behind paralytics carrying their beds, blind people trashing their white canes, deaf people hearing, mute people speaking, sick people back in the workforce, mentally ill people functioning normally, epileptics without seizures, dead people walking, calmed storms, footprints on the water, and 9,000 people still talking about how they'd eaten till they were ready to bust on food he created on the spot.

The names of people who'd experienced a miracle at his word or the touch of his hands could fill the phone book of a medium-sized city. Signs were all over the place.

But the jaded Judeans and their **myopic** mentors still hounded him for *"a sign!"*

What were they waiting for? Another Moses <u>parting</u> the Red Sea? Another Joshua commanding the <u>sun</u> to stand still? Yes, Christ could have done those things. Didn't he work with God in the <u>creation</u> of the universe?

The hard, cold fact is that even if he parted the sea or stopped the sun (again!), some people still would refuse to believe. When they could not deny a miracle, they dismissed it as the work of the devil! (Luke 11:15). They'd find a way to ignore anything he did to prove he was Messiah.

☞ **Check It Out:**

Luke 11:29–36

myopic: nearsighted

☞ **GO TO:**

Exodus 14:21 (parting)

Joshua 10:12–13 (sun)

John 1:1–3 (creation)

One Sign Left To Read

What if he'd rise from the dead?

"No sign will be given this generation '*except the sign of Jonah*,'" he said. What was the sign of Jonah? It was two things:

1. *Jonah himself* (verse 30). Confronted by the prophet *himself*, the <u>Ninevites repented</u> (see GWBI, pages 88–90). Standing before the skeptical Judeans at the very moment was the greatest sign that could possibly be given—Jesus himself. To demand a sign after they'd seen him was appalling evidence of deliberate spiritual blindness.

2. *Resurrection from the dead* (Matthew 12:40). In another setting Jesus explained that as Jonah spent three days in the belly of the <u>big fish</u>, he (Jesus) would spend three days buried in the earth. Then he would rise from the dead. Even when it happened, most would still <u>refuse to believe</u>.

"Doing Lunch" With The Enemy

A Pharisee invited Jesus to "do lunch" (Luke 11:37). Jesus knew the rules. But in order to take the conversation quickly where he wanted it to go, he deliberately broke the first rule for eating with a Pharisee: He went in and **reclined** at the table without first doing the hand-washing ritual.

This procedure had nothing to do with cleanliness. It was a ceremony to remove "defilement" from contact with sinful people, an arrogant statement of self-righteousness and spiritual superiority.

His host was surprised at Jesus' neglect. Jesus knew what he and the others were thinking. He attacked their spiritual duplicity. He accused them of being *"full of greed and wickedness"* (verses 39–41).

In effect he said: "If you Pharisees were as concerned about the persons you are on the inside as you are about this **foolish** external practice, you'd actually be clean!" (verses 39–42).

Then, having set the tone for the table conversation, Jesus pronounced six "**woes**" on them for their hypocrisy (verses 42–52). A corresponding Old Testament word for "<u>woe</u>" means "wasting away" and "leanness." He warned them that their pseudo-sanctimony had shrunken and shriveled their souls!

☞ **GO TO:**

Jonah 3:5–10 (Ninevites repented)

Jonah 1:17 (big fish)

Matthew 28:11–15 (refuse to believe)

☞ **Check It Out:**

Luke 11:37–54

reclined: *meals were served to guests lying on couches around a low table*

KEY POINT

The double-barreled sign of messiahship was Jesus himself and his future resurrection.

---

foolish: *Greek means froth, foam; silliness*

woes: *cry of grief, "Alas!"; Jesus grieves for the disaster of hypocrisy*

☞ **GO TO:**

Isaiah 24:16 (woe)

Six Calamities of Hypocrisy

1. Slavishly doing the impersonal, formal, institutional aspects of religion while neglecting personal aspects of fair treatment of others and love for God (Luke 11:42)

2. Seeking honor and recognition from people instead of leaving the rewards of spirituality to God (Luke 11:43)

3. Hiding your own spiritual deadness, while infecting others with it (Luke 11:44)

4. Expecting others to live by moral and spiritual standards you are not willing or able to live by, and judging rather than helping them when they fail (Luke 11:46)

5. Honoring dead saints, while inwardly rebelling against the things they stood for (Luke 11:47–51)

6. Hindering others from discovering the truth by substituting religious rules and rituals for real knowledge of and relationship with God (Luke 11:52)

Dig Deeper

> **Luke 11:52** "Woe to you experts in the law, because you have taken away the key to knowledge. You yourselves have not entered, and you have hindered those who were entering."

Hypocrisy Steals The Key Of Knowledge

This was the last straw! When Jesus left the luncheon and his remarks were reported to the other Pharisees and Bible scholars, their anger intensified. From then on he was besieged with almost constant attempts to get him to say something that could be turned against him.

What Others are Saying:

Robert L. Thomas and Stanley N. Gundry: The key to the knowledge of God was the Old Testament, the true meaning of which they had hidden by their erroneous interpretations and man-made traditions.[9]

> **Luke 12:1–5** Meanwhile, when a crowd of many thousands had gathered, so that they were trampling on one another, Jesus began to speak first to his disciples, saying: "Be on your guard against the yeast of the Pharisees, which is hypocrisy!"

Critical Admonitions For Disciples

After his latest attack on the hypocrisy of the religious establishment, and with Judean crowds even larger than those in Galilee, Jesus took his disciples aside for some vital counsel.

Admonition 1: Guard Against Hypocrisy

Yeast is a fungus. When mixed with flour and water, it gives off a gas that changes its environment and spreads throughout whatever it is in. In the New Testament, yeast is used three ways:

- To picture the way the kingdom of God spreads—from a small beginning, gradually working its way until it influences the entire culture (Luke 13:21)
- To picture how sin spreads in a church when members' sins are not confronted and dealt with (1 Corinthians 5:6–8)
- To warn that if Jesus' disciples permit even a little hypocrisy, it can undermine their relationship with God as surely as it undermined the Pharisees' relationship with God (Luke 12:1)

Popularity can create pressure to put on a good show and keep the truth about ourselves concealed. But all efforts at self-concealment are futile. Ultimately the realities of our lives will be exposed (verses 2–3).

> **Luke 12:4–5** "I tell you, my friends, do not be afraid of those who kill the body and after that can do no more. But I show you whom you should fear: Fear him who, after the killing of the body, has power to throw you into hell. Yes, I tell you fear him."

Admonition 2: Don't Waste Your Fear

Religious hypocrites, especially in leadership, have power to intimidate people. Their weapons have historically included threats of rejection, guilt, shame, oppression, expulsion, and death.

Believers in every generation, including ours, have paid with their lives for taking a stand against spiritual falsehood and duplicity.

Christ's followers are encouraged not to waste their fear on people who can kill the body and do no more. Death is <u>not the worst</u> thing that can happen to a Christian. The one to fear is the one who, after killing the body can throw a person into <u>hell</u>. The

KEY Outline:

Yeast Pictures

Spread of the kingdom
Spread of sin
Influence of hypocrisy

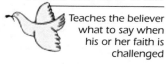

ACT OF THE HOLY SPIRIT

Teaches the believer what to say when his or her faith is challenged

☞ **GO TO:**

2 Timothy 4:6–8
(not the worst)

Matthew 5:22, 29–30; 10:28; 18:9; Mark 9:43–47; Luke 12:5 (hell)

Greek word for "hell" in this passage is *gehenna*, the word Greeks used for the perpetually burning garbage dump near Jerusalem. It was a metaphor for eternal punishment.

Who can send a person's soul to hell? Not the devil. He is <u>strictly limited</u> as to what he can do to us. Beyond the power we allow him to have over us in this life the devil has no power over us at all! Certainly not the hypocrites trying to force us to conform to their standards. Who then?

God alone has authority to send people to heaven or hell. "***Fear him.***" For the follower of Jesus fear of God is not <u>terror of punishment</u>, but a combination of respect for God's goodness and justice with acknowledgment of our proneness to sin. Who is this we are to *fear*?

- The One who <u>never forgets</u> **sparrows** sold in the market (verse 6)

- The One who knows the **number of hairs** on your head (verse7)

- The One who values his people <u>above all</u> other creatures (verse 7)

EARLY CHURCH LIFE: Early church members were persecuted for telling the truth about their faith.

Tim Stafford: Jesus predicted that his followers would suffer the same troubles he did, and never was a prediction more thoroughly fulfilled. The early years of the church were played out against a background of official and unofficial harassment, of arrest, imprisonment, torture and death. Every Christian lived and breathed this atmosphere.[10]

The God who never forgets a near-worthless sparrow is most certainly not going to forget you!

"*Don't be afraid; you are worth more than many sparrows!*" (Luke 12:7).

That being the case the believer can . . .

- openly acknowledge his or her relationship with Jesus Christ (Luke 12:8–9)

- always know that he is forgiven (verse 10)

- trust the Holy Spirit to give answers for those who demand we defend our faith (verses 11–12)

☞ **GO TO:**

Job 1:12; 2:6 (strictly limited)

Romans 8:1 (terror of punishment)

Isaiah 49:15–16 (never forgets)

Matthew 6:26, 28–29 (above all)

fear: respect for God's authority to determine one's eternal destiny

sparrows: small, edible bird; five sold for two pennies; nearly worthless

What Others are Saying:

number of hairs: literally, a blonde has about 145,000 hairs; a dark-haired person, 120,000; and a redhead, 90,000

Remember This . . .

It is a foregone conclusion that Jesus' followers will be defending their faith. Allegiance and obedience to him put his people in places where opposition from the powers that be must be expected. For all such occasions, Jesus gives this encouraging assurance—the Holy Spirit will teach us what to say.

**What Others
are Saying:**

Julian of Norwich:

He said not, Thou shall not be tempested,
Thou shall not be travailed,
Thou shall not be afflicted,
But he said, Thou shall not be overcome.[11]

Study Questions

1. When the 72 returned from their preaching mission what were they most excited about? What did Jesus say they should be most excited about? What was he most excited about?
2. What two "loves" fulfill the two greatest Old Testament commandments? In the story, what did the Good Samaritan do that showed that he loved his neighbor?
3. Around what two factors does successful praying revolve, according to Luke 11:5–13?
4. How can religious sentimentality become a form of hypocrisy? Who is more blessed than Jesus' mother?
5. Which of the six "Calamities of Hypocrisy" do you most easily fall into?

CHAPTER WRAP-UP

- About six months before the climactic events at Jerusalem leading to his crucifixion and resurrection, Jesus sent a second wave of 72 disciples to the towns of Judea and Perea to prepare them for his personal arrival to preach the kingdom message there. (Luke 10:1–24)

- Jesus told the story of the Good Samaritan to show his followers their love should include people who were different from them. He corrected an obsessive housekeeper's priorities. He taught the importance of shameless praying. (Luke 10:25–11:13)

- After the resurfacing of the slander that his miracles were the work of the devil, Jesus attacked hypocrisy, climaxing with a luncheon at the home of a Pharisee where he named six calamities of hypocrisy in the lives of the Pharisees and legal experts. (Luke 11:14–53)

- He warned his disciples against hypocrisy. He predicted they would be arrested and forced to defend themselves before secular and religious authorities, but not to fear—God would never forget them, and the Holy Spirit would teach them what to say. (Luke 12:1–12)

4 SEEING WITH NEW EYES

GOSPEL QUARTET IN HARMONY

Luke 12:13–13:21
John 9

Let's Get Started

When the third New Testament historian, Luke, describes the crowds that came to see Jesus in Judea during his final six months of ministry he uses the Greek word *myrias* (Luke 12:2). The word means audiences numbered in the "tens of thousands."

The spiritually starved, sick, and curious thronged him in the capital province in even greater numbers than in Galilee.

In private conversation, question-and-answer sessions, story and lecture, warning and promise, he taught them principle upon principle of the kingdom of God. Friends, enemies, and honest seekers found him ready to engage them in unique learning experiences.

The Jews used a word for preaching that fit Jesus' style well—*charaz*— "stringing pearls."[1] In the Jewish definition, the "pearls" need not be closely connected with each other. In Jesus' teaching and preaching, one "string" held the "pearls" together: the lifestyle, values, priorities, and future of the kingdom.

> **Luke 12:13–15** Someone in the crowd said to him, "Teacher, tell my brother to divide the inheritance with me." Jesus replied, "Man, who appointed me a judge or an arbiter between you?" Then he said to them, "Watch out! Be on your guard against all kinds of greed; a man's life does not consist in the abundance of his possessions."

covetousness: excessive desire for wealth and possessions

☞ **GO TO:**

Exodus 20:17;
Colossians 3:5–6
(greed)

KEY POINT

Greed is not good. It's deadly to the spirit.

☞ **Check It Out:**

Luke 12:16–21

☞ **GO TO:**

Deuteronomy 8:18;
1 Corinthians 3:7;
James 1:17 (gift)

Treasure Hunt

Jesus refused to get involved in the dispute. There were magistrates for that. He spoke to the deeper issue behind the man's request, the problem of **covetousness** or greed.

"Watch out! Be on your guard," is the language of war, of violent action to defend against a dangerous foe.

The insidious enemy that must be confronted along many fronts and driven off with its slimy tail between its ugly legs is the silly game we all know as "keeping up with the Joneses." Gotta have what they have—if possible, *before* they get it!

"Watch out!" Jesus said, "Fight it off!"

> **Luke 12:16–17** The ground of a certain rich man produced a good crop. He thought to himself, "What shall I do? I have no place to store my crops."

Fool's Gold

Jesus told a story. What this successful farmer decided to do was tear down his too-small barns and build bigger ones, store his wealth, and live it up for the rest of his life . . . which, as it turned out, ended *"that very night!"* (Luke 12:20).

"This is how it will be with anyone who stores up things for himself but is not rich toward God," Jesus concluded (verse 21).

Wealth was not the farmer's problem. Good crops are a gift from God. The point swirls around the farmer's question, *"What shall I do?"* The choices he made and the priorities those choices revealed caused God to call the farmer a "fool" (verse 20).

1. The farmer's choices were totally selfish. The words *I, me, my,* and *myself* occur 11 times in verses 17–19 (NIV). This guy wasn't concerned about wise use of his wealth or God's will or anybody but numero uno.

2. He gave no thought to eternity. His number was up the very night he was laying out his self-indulgent plans. In a few hours, he would be ordered, "Go directly to the grave! Do not pass Go; do not collect $200!"

The man operated on the misconception that he was in control of his life. Actually, everything but his choices was beyond his control. The growth of his crops, the timing of his death, the ultimate disposition of his property, and the future destiny of his soul—all were in the hands of God.

A man, or woman, is *"rich toward God"* if he can thank God for his success and wealth but hold both loosely, and if he can care about others, focus on eternity, and trust his future to God.

Radical Investment Strategy

Turning to his disciples, Jesus went deeper into the issue of money and possessions.

1. *Don't worry* (Luke 12:22–28). If true richness isn't found in material abundance, neither is it found in "the simple 'bear' necessities," as Balou the bear sings in Disney's *Jungle Book*. *"Life is more than food, and the body more than clothes"* (verse 23). Jesus reminded them of **ravens** (verse 24) and **lilies** (verse 27). It's silly to think of birds stockpiling food or plants worrying about having nothing to wear. It's just as silly for people who trust God to worry about food, clothing, physical stature, or the length of life.

2. *Seek God's kingdom* (Luke 12:29–34). Unlike the *"pagan world,"* the people of God set their hearts on the "community of God," the kingdom. To seek the kingdom (verse 31) is to pour one's energy into doing God's will and watching out for the well-being of fellow kingdom citizens, leaving the supply of personal necessities to a generous God (verses 31–32).

3. *Radical investment* (Luke 12:33). The no-anxiety lifestyle makes possible a liberal, giving spirit that moves the kingdom toward its goals. Jesus told his followers to sell what they had and give to needy people. The original disciples took him literally.

EARLY CHURCH LIFE: Early Christians took material as well as spiritual responsibility for each other.

KINGDOM OF GOD | Jesus described two radically different ways of handling wealth. His kingdom people use their money differently from people who are not of his kingdom.

People in the World	People in God's Kingdom
self-indulgent	self-giving
forget God	depend on God
priorities that don't prepare them for eternity	priorities the world considers foolish
this world is all there is	this is only the beginning of life
wealth is for self-gratification	wealth is for investing in others

Remember This . . .

☞ **Check It Out:**

Luke 12:22–34

☞ **GO TO:**

Matthew 6:24–34 (don't worry)

Leviticus 11:15 (ravens)

Matthew 5–7; Luke 6 (seek God's kingdom)

Acts 2:44–45; 4:32–37 (literally)

ravens: *unclean birds, according to Old Testament Law—God cares for them*

lilies: *crocus, gladiolus, anemone, iris, wildflowers that grow in Palestine*

pagan: *anyone who does not believe in Christ*

Remember
This . . .

KEY Outline:

Worry-Free Living
Remember
- ravens and lilies
- God's generosity

Seek the kingdom
- God's will
- each other's good
- community of faith
- God's supply

Be generous

☞ **Check It Out:**

Luke 12:35–13:9

☞ **GO TO:**

Matthew 5:14–16;
25:1–13
(lamps burning)

John 7:38–39; Romans
8:5–9; Ephesians
5:15–20 (filled)

filled with the Spirit:
*controlled by and
responsive to Christ*

According to Jesus, there's more to life than scratching to make ends meet or working ourselves into the ground to put together a portfolio for future security. There's the kingdom, the city of God, the community of people who recognize the rule of God and the debt of love they owe one another.

> **Luke 12:35–37** "Be dressed ready for service and keep your lamps burning, like men waiting for their master to return from a wedding banquet, so that when he comes and knocks they can immediately open the door for him. It will be good for those servants whose master finds them watching when he comes."

Matters Of Life And Death

At this point Jesus added a new dimension to his teaching. During the weeks leading to the end of his earthly life he would talk a lot about something Christians call "the Second Coming of Christ" (see GWDN, pages 35–36).

A powerful motive for faithfulness and service is the need to be ready when Jesus returns.

The Second
Coming

How to Be Prepared for the Lord's Return

The story Jesus told urged his followers to have three bases covered at all times:

1. *Be dressed ready for service* (Luke 12:35). Literally, "Let your loins be girded." His listeners understood this to mean, "Be ready and working." A man doing a strenuous job would gather his robe close to his body and tuck it up under his belt, and he would say his loins were girded.

2. *Keep your <u>lamps burning</u>* (verse 35). A lamp was a cotton wick floating in a dish of oil (see illustration, page 63). To keep the light shining, the wick had to be trimmed and the oil replenished. This pictures the need to be continually faithful and **filled with the Spirit**.

3. *Be watching . . . ready* (verses 37–38, 40). Be awake, alert, attentive, vigilant . . . all the time. Christ will return when it's least expected (verse 40).

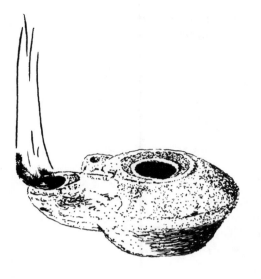
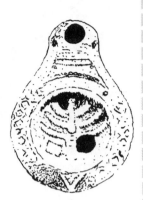

Oil Lamp

Small cups or deep oil-filled saucers with one or more wicks were kept burning at night in Hebrew homes.

KEY Outline:

Ready for Christ's Return

Working

Spirit-filled

Alert

steward: *one who cares for another's property or business*

The Universal Principle Of Accountability

Peter wanted to know if this story was for disciples only or for everybody (Luke 12:41). Jesus let Peter draw his own conclusions and told another story (verses 41–46).

In Jesus' parable, the master of the house was away and the exact time of his return was unknown. Jesus drew two possible finishes for the story:

1. The master returns and finds his **steward** carrying out his responsibilities and rewards him by trusting him with greater responsibilities (verses 43–44). (People wealthy enough to have several household servants usually placed one, the "steward," in charge.)

2. The master is delayed. The steward interprets the delay as an opportunity to mistreat people he's responsible for. The master shows up unexpectedly and tears the unreliable manager limb from limb! (verses 45–46).

The Second Coming

The point of Jesus' story was this: When Christ returns, his servants will be <u>held accountable</u> for their handling of spiritual responsibilities, and especially their treatment of their fellow servants. We will give an account for our actions.

☞ **GO TO:**

1 Corinthians 3:12–15;
2 Corinthians 5:10
(held accountable)

> **Luke 12:47–48** That servant who knows his master's will and does not get ready or does not do what his master wants will be beaten with many blows. But the one who does not know and does things deserving punishment will be beaten with few blows. From everyone who has been given much, much will be demanded; and from the one who has been entrusted with much, much more will be asked.

Ignorance Is No Excuse

When Christ returns, rewards and discipline will be dished out in direct proportion to what each of us has done with what we've known. Ignorance is no excuse.

The truth is, there is no such thing as absolute spiritual ignorance—everyone has the basic "<u>light</u>" available in (1) the created <u>universe</u> and (2) our <u>conscience</u>.

Judgment will be less harsh for those who know less, but all are accountable for what they know.

☞ **GO TO:**

John 1:4–5, 9; Titus 2:11 (light)

Psalm 19:1–4; Romans 1:18–20 (universe)

Romans 2:14–15 (conscience)

> **Luke 13:1–3** Now there were some present at that time who told Jesus about the Galileans whose blood Pilate had mixed with their sacrifices. Jesus answered, "Do you think that these Galileans were worse sinners than all the other Galileans because they suffered this way? I tell you, no! But unless you repent, you too will all perish."

Repent Or Perish

As Jesus spoke of judgment, some people recalled an incident they thought illustrated God's judgment.

They may have been referring to an episode, documented by Jewish historians Josephus and Philo, in which crowds gathered in the temple area to protest the Roman governor's confiscation of temple money ("holy money") to reconstruct Jerusalem's water works.

Governor Pilate had sent soldiers wearing robes over their battle gear to infiltrate the gathering. At a prearranged signal, the legionnaires were to disperse the crowd. Things got out of hand and many Jews were killed.

Galileans were a volatile people, known for political dissent and hatred of the Romans. It was likely many of them would have joined such a protest. And many would have been killed.

"Do you think these Galileans were killed because they were worse sinners?"

Jesus knew that was exactly what some of them were thinking. Most Jews believed suffering comes to people as a direct result of their sin. It's that theological error that the Old Testament book of Job was written to correct (see GWBI, pages 72–73).

"And how about those 18 men killed when the tower of Siloam collapsed? Was it because they were more guilty than anyone else in Jerusalem?" Jesus pressed the issue, reminding them of another tragedy they knew about (Luke 13:4).

To both scenarios he answered emphatically, *"I tell you, no! But unless you repent, you too will perish"* (verses 3 and 5).

It's Not What You Think

When disaster strikes—hurricane, earthquake, famine, war, epidemic—many people assume it's a direct result of the sin of those suffering.

It is true that the Bible teaches that God uses natural and man-caused disasters for purposes of judgment and discipline. But it is seldom that simple.

Jesus offers three important insights to clarify that teaching:

1. Suffering does not indicate the sufferers are worse sinners than others. All of us are sinners.
2. Death is a certainty for everyone. It often strikes suddenly and unexpectedly.
3. Repentance—willingness to be changed, to adopt God-like values, attitudes, and lifestyle, to reorient your life around Jesus Christ—is *the* way to prepare for death.

Aleksandr Solzhenitsyn: On the whole, you know, I have become convinced that there is no punishment that comes to us in this life on earth which is undeserved. Superficially, it can have nothing to do with what we are guilty of in actual fact, but if you go over your life with a fine-tooth comb and ponder it deeply, you will always be able to hunt down that transgression of yours for which you have now received the blow.[2]

☞ **GO TO:**

Job 4:7
(theological error)

KEY POINT

It is an error to believe that all suffering is in direct proportion to the suffering person's sin.

☞ **GO TO:**

Deuteronomy 28;
Ezekiel 5:5–17; 18:4
(God uses)

Romans 3:23 (all)

Hebrews 9:27
(certainty)

What Others are Saying:

KEY POINT

Death is sure. Repentance is preparation.

> **Luke 13:6–9** Then he told this parable: "A man had a fig tree, planted in his vineyard, and he went to look for fruit on it, but did not find any. So he said to the man who took care of the vineyard, 'For three years now I've been coming to look for fruit on this fig tree and haven't found any. Cut it down! Why should it use up the soil?' 'Sir,' the man replied, 'leave it alone for one more year, and I'll dig around it and fertilize it. If it bears fruit next year, fine! If not, then cut it down.'"

The Parable Of The Fruitless Fig

The epilogue to this discussion came in the form of a quickie tale about a feckless fig tree that produced nary a fig in three years!

"Fell that futile, fruitless fig to fuel my fire!" ordered the frustrated farmer.

"Give me one more year with it," protested the patient pruner. "I'll dig it and dung it. Perchance it will produce. If it fails, I'll finish it."

The parable makes several points related to God's judgment and the need for repentance:

- True repentance is demonstrated by visible fruit—change, action (Luke 3:8, 10–14).
- Spiritual fruitlessness invites disaster (Luke 13:7).
- Delayed calamity does not mean God approves of the way we are living (Romans 2:4). God, in patient love, often delays judgment to give time to repent (2 Peter 3:9).
- God's patience has limits—we can wait too long to change (Luke 13:9).

KINGDOM OF GOD This parable certainly had a relevant message for anyone who was putting off the decision to follow Christ. Beyond that, many scholars think its message was especially for Israel.

With Jesus present, the nation was at a spiritual crossroad.

If they rejected him and failed to follow him into the kingdom, they would find time running out for them as a nation.

After his death, resurrection, and the establishment of the church, Israel would have only about 40 years to produce the fruit of repentance. Then, unless there was a national spiritual turnaround, the end would come.

It came in 70 A.D. when Jerusalem was destroyed by the armies of Emperor Titus. After that, the Jews were a people without a homeland until 1948.

KEY Outline:

Fig Tree

Repentance bears fruit
Fruitlessness is disaster
Delayed judgment
    equals God's
    patience
Patience has limits

> **John 9:1–5** As he went along, he saw a man blind from birth. His disciples asked him, "Rabbi, who sinned, this man or his parents, that he was born blind?"
>
> "Neither this man nor his parents sinned," said Jesus, "but this happened so that the work of God might be displayed in his life. As long as it is day, we must do the work of him who sent me. Night is coming, when no one can work. While I am in the world, I am the light of the world."

Eye-Opening Experience

At the <u>Feast of Tabernacles</u> Jesus declared himself to be "the light of the world" (John 8:12). The arguments that followed demonstrated how his light shone into the darkness of Jewish legalism and opposition, and the <u>futile</u> attempts of the dark to extinguish his light.

Three months later, he returned to Jerusalem for the **Feast of Dedication**. Arriving before the festival, he and his disciples strolled through the temple area. There they met a blind beggar.

Whodunit?

This blind man had never seen the light of day.

The sight of him brought up a puzzling theological question from Jesus' **compadres**: Whose fault is it? "**Who sinned**, *this man or his parents, that he was born blind?*" (John 9:2).

The belief was deeply embedded in their culture that a righteous person would have health, prosperity, and God's blessing. If these things were missing . . . somebody blew it!

<u>Sometimes</u> disaster *is* the direct result of sin. Usually, however, there are other <u>factors</u> involved. For example, Job's troubles came not because of his sin, but because God <u>trusted</u> him.

Jesus' response to the question was that this man's trouble had nothing to do with who sinned. A more important dynamic was at work.

The blind man's struggle provided opportunity for the work of God to be displayed in his life (verse 3). The work of God was why Jesus was in the world (verses 4–5). What was this work of God? To be *"the light of the world"* (verse 5).

In fact Jesus and this blind beggar, who never would have thought himself suitable for such a destiny, were coworkers in the work of <u>lighting up</u> the world around them.

☞ **GO TO:**

Leviticus 23:33–43;
   Numbers 29:12–40;
   John 7–8
   (Feast of Tabernacles)

John 1:5 (futile)

John 10:22
   (Feast of Dedication)

Feast of Dedication:
Hanukkah or Feast of Lights

compadres: *friends*

who sinned: *rabbis discussed whether an unborn child could sin in the womb*

☞ **GO TO:**

Luke 13:1–5
   (who sinned)

2 Samuel 12:10–15;
   1 Corinthians 11:
   27–32 (sometimes)

Romans 5:3–5; 8:17–
   18, 35–39;
   2 Corinthians 4:8–10;
   12:7–10 (factors)

Job 1:8–12, 22; 2:3
   (trusted)

Matthew 6:14;
   Philippians 2:15
   (lighting up)

Dan McCartney and Charles Clayton: The most obedient Christian may also be one who suffers. Health, healing, freedom, security, and wealth are not ours by right, and the greatest saint may be deprived of them *under God's sovereignty.*[3]

> **John 9:6–7** Having said this, [Jesus] spit on the ground, made some mud with the saliva, and put it on the man's eyes. "Go," he told him, "wash in the Pool of Siloam." So the man went and washed and came home seeing!

☞ **GO TO:**

Mark 7:33; 8:23 (spit)

2 Kings 20:20;
2 Chronicles 32:2–8;
Isaiah 22:9–11
(Pool of Siloam)

2 Kings 5:10–14
(washed)

"Here's Mud In Your Eye!"

Jesus <u>spit</u>.

Stirring in a little Jerusalem street dirt, he made mud. He put a glob of the gooey grime on each of the man's sightless eyes.

"*Go wash,*" Jesus said, sending him to the <u>Pool of Siloam</u>. The word *Siloam* means "sent." The man went, <u>washed</u>, and "*came home seeing*" . . . for the first time in his life!

We are tempted to take pride in being useful in God's work. It may help keep things in perspective if we remember that three times Jesus used spit![4]

Remember
This . . .

KEY POINT

Christ was in the world to do "the work of God."

> **John 9:8–12** His neighbors and those who had formerly seen him begging asked, "Isn't this the same man who used to sit and beg?" Some claimed that he was.
> Others said, "No, he only looks like him."
> But he himself insisted, "I am the man."
> "How then were your eyes opened?" they demanded.
> He replied, "The man they call Jesus made some mud and put it on my eyes. He told me to go to Siloam and wash. So I went and washed, and then I could see."
> "Where is this man?" they asked him. "I don't know," he said.

KEY Outline:

Steps to a Miracle
Jesus spit
Mud in the eye
Wash in the pool
Go home seeing

Talk Of The Neighborhood

A delightful confusion broke out among the neighbors when the blind beggar showed up on the street where he lived, *seeing.*

A second "whodunit?" question (or "*How*dunit?"—John 9:10) quickly turned attention from the no-longer-blind man to the one who gave him his eyes: "*The man they call Jesus.*"

He'd never seen Jesus. He only knew what others said. As the story unfolds, we can observe the progress of the man's perception of his benefactor. At this point he saw him as a good, caring *"man."*

> **John 9:14–16** Now the day on which Jesus had made the mud and opened the man's eyes was a Sabbath. Therefore the Pharisees also asked him how he had received his sight. "He put mud on my eyes," the man replied, "and I washed, and now I see."
>
> Some of the Pharisees said, "This man is not from God, for he does not keep the Sabbath."
>
> But others asked, "How can a sinner do such miraculous signs?" So they were divided.

Sabbath Squad To The Rescue!

The unsuspecting neighbors immediately took the man to the Pharisees. There's no indication they were trying to get him in trouble. They assumed religious leaders, steeped in theology, could put this event into perspective.

They did not know they were delivering him into a swarm of killer bees disguised as men of God.[5]

The Pharisees' immediate response was to declare that the miracle worker could not be a man of God because he broke the Sabbath! How so?

- Jesus mixed saliva and dirt to make mud—work!—a Sabbath no-no.
- Jesus put the mud on the man's eyes, healing him—no healing was allowed on the Sabbath unless necessary to save a life.

None seemed to care that the beggar's ordeal was over. The great sin of religious legalists was (and is) that they care more for their institutions and traditions than for people! When they asked the man his opinion of Jesus, he answered, *"He is a prophet"* (John 9:17).

> **John 9:18–21** The Jews still did not believe that he had been blind and had received his sight until they sent for the man's parents. "Is this your son?" they asked. "Is this the one you say was born blind? How is it that now he can see?"
>
> "We know he is our son," the parents answered, "and

KEY Outline:

Broken Sabbath Rules
Mixed mud
Plastered the man's eyes
Bathed in the pool
*Healed conditions
    that weren't
    life-threatening*

**Something
to Ponder**

> we know he was born blind. But how he can see now, or who opened his eyes, we don't know. Ask him. He is of age; he will speak for himself."

The Third Degree—Round Two

The parents of the no-longer-blind man were brought in. They confirmed the healed man was their son and that he had been blind from birth. Asked if they knew how it was possible he could now see, though, they "pled the Fifth," refusing to answer on grounds of possible self-incrimination.

They feared an **official edict** by the religious leaders: *"Anyone who acknowledged that Jesus was the Christ would be **put out of the synagogue**"* (John 9:22). Religious leaders could have either (1) permanently excluded them and gave public notice that they were accursed, cut off from friends, relatives, and God; or (2) temporarily excluded them.

*"He is **of age**,"* the parents said, *"ask him"* (verses 21, 23).

> **John 9:24–25** A second time they summoned the man who had been blind. "Give glory to God," they said. "We know this man is a sinner."
>
> He replied, "Whether he is a sinner or not, I don't know. One thing I do know. I was blind but now I see!"

The Third Degree—Round Three

The inquisition again focused on this man, who was now seeing for the first time.

"Give glory to God," the inquisitors said. But they really had no interest in God's glory. What they meant was: "Confess your sin and agree that we are right—Jesus *is a sinner*!" (Condemned criminals were challenged with those words to confess and prepare to die.)

Instead of doing what they meant, though, the man did what they said: He gave glory to God. He stuck with his story.

The leaders pressed the man to repeat his story, hoping he'd contradict himself (John 9:26).

The irony hit its peak when the witness assumed the role of inquisitor: *"Why do you want to hear it again? Do you want to become his disciples, too?"* (verse 27). (The seeing man now sees himself as disciple of the healer.)

He'd touched their hot button! All pretext of politeness and orderly investigation were suddenly out the window, and bitter-

---

official edict: *first official attack against Christian believers*

put out of the synagogue: *excommunicated*

of age: *13 or older*

☞ **GO TO:**

Joshua 7:19 ("Give glory to God")

ness boiled over like a mini-**Kilauea**. Insults turned the air blue (verses 28–29).

> **John 9:31–32** "We know that God does not listen to sinners. He <u>listens to the godly</u> man who does his will. **Nobody** has ever heard of opening the eyes of a man born blind. If this man were not from God, he could do nothing."

Out With It

Under attack for a stranger he barely knew, the man became more courageous and insightful. He expressed shock at their unbelief.

To him it was not amazing someone should believe in Jesus—what was amazing was that anyone should fail to believe in the face of the evidence (verses 30–33)! The man's perception of Jesus sharpened: He is definitely *"from God."*

The Pharisees tore the lid off their theological prejudice and threw the man's blindness into his face: The fact he'd been blind proved he was a sinner. *"And they threw him out"* (verse 34).

George R. Beasley-Murray: The outraged Pharisees refuse the instruction of the healed man in words which, without realizing it, condemn their stratagem to deny the miracle: "You were born in utter sin!" Then the man *was* born blind! And Jesus *did* open his eyes! But they reject the man, the miracle, and the One through whom God wrought it. In so doing they reject the shining of the Light upon them, and plunge further into their darkness.[6]

Confess Faith in Christ: Expect Persecution

These New Testament passages tell believers to expect persecution.

Matthew 5:11–12
Matthew 10:32–33
Mark 8:37
Luke 6:22–23
Luke 12: 8–9

Luke 21:12–19
John 15:18–21
Acts 9:15–16
1 Peter 2:20–23

When You See The Son, Believe Or Go Blind!

When Jesus heard the newly seeing man had been thrown out of the Temple, he went looking for him. After Jesus had identified himself (after all, the man had never seen him before!), the healed man did three things (John 9:38):

Kilauea: volcano on the island of Hawaii

☞ **GO TO:**

Job 27:8–9; Psalm 34:15; 66:18; 145:18–19; Proverbs 15:29 (listens to the godly)

nobody: *Old Testament records no incident of a blind person receiving sight*

What Others are Saying:

Dig Deeper

☞ **Check It Out:**

John 9:35–41

worshiped: Greek word indicates the man prostrated himself and kissed Jesus' feet

Dig Deeper

Development of the No-Longer-Blind Man's Perception of Christ

Step 1: Saw Jesus as a good *man* (John 9:11)

Step 2: Saw Jesus as a prophet (John 9:17)

Step 3: Saw Jesus as a man sent from God—God's messenger (John 9:31–33)

Step 4: Saw Jesus as Son of Man—Messiah (John 9:35–38)

Step 5: Saw Jesus as worthy of worship (John 9:38)

KEY POINT

When believers are in trouble, Jesus comes to encourage them.

> **John 9:39–41** Jesus said, "For judgment I have come into this world, so that the blind will see and those who see will become blind."
>
> Some Pharisees who were with him heard him say this and asked, "What? Are we blind too?"
>
> Jesus said, "If you were blind, you would not be guilty of sin; but now that you claim you can see, your guilt remains."

Worse Than Being Born Blind

To the shock of those who heard it, Jesus insisted that, as light of the world, he served two paradoxical functions: (1) to open blind eyes, and (2) to blind "seeing" eyes!

The Pharisees knew he was talking about them.

"Surely you are not suggesting *we* are blind! We, the enlightened minds of Israel, who have studied the Scriptures and know the historic traditions backwards and forwards."

KEY POINT

Jesus' light opens blind eyes and blinds eyes that refuse to see.

"You are not blind," Jesus agreed. "If you were really unable to see, you wouldn't be guilty. The darkness in which you grope is far worse than what this blind man lived in. You choose darkness, in the face of light you clearly see! You are guilty!"

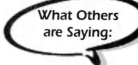

What Others are Saying:

George R. Beasley-Murray: The blind are in darkness, and therefore lost; the Lord comes to . . . enable them to "see" and to receive the salvation of God. The picture includes all humankind, but it assumes a distinction between those who are blind and know it and want to see, and those who do not acknowledge it and reject the revelation that would lead them into light. Jesus comes to give sight to the former and to condemn the latter to their darkness."[7]

Study Questions

1. Place a mark on the line below to show where you see yourself between the extremes.
   Frugal to a fault_____Spendthrift generosity
   Now place a mark to show where you see Jesus (according to Luke 12:13–34).
2. Identify two things that made the rich farmer's choices foolish. (Luke 12:16–21)
3. Identify three things that are part of the investment strategy Jesus taught.
4. Identify three things to do to be ready for the Second Coming of Christ.
5. When people suggested that some Galileans killed by Pilate may have been suffering from God's judgment because they were terrible sinners, what was Jesus' response? What did he mean?
6. What did the Pharisees care most about—their traditions or making people well?

CHAPTER WRAP-UP

- Jesus warned the people to guard against greed, then turned the world's concept of wealth, security, and investment priorities upside down. (Luke 12:13–34)

- Like a jeweler stringing pearls, he warned them to be ready for his return and to pay attention to the signs of the times. (Luke 12:35–48)

- He sought to correct people's thinking about the causes of calamity, and warned them to repent in preparation for the certainty of death. (Luke 13:1–9)

- In Jerusalem Jesus healed a man who had been born blind. The man witnessed to his neighbors, was interrogated by the Pharisees, and excommunicated from the Temple. Jesus met him, and he confessed faith in Jesus as Messiah. (John 9)

5 SHEPHERD LORD

CHAPTER HIGHLIGHTS

- The Good Shepherd
- The Hanukkah Challenge
- Heartbreak Hotel
- The Notoriety of God

Let's Get Started

When the Jesus of Nazareth blip first appeared on the radar screen of first-century Israel and he entered the "race" for national leadership, he found plenty of competition waiting to challenge his right to lead.

- The Romans, the Herods, and Pontius Pilate dominated the political scene.
- The High Priests and **Sadducees** ran Israel's official religious life, and controlled most of the money.
- The scribes (experts in the Law of Moses) and their most zealous disciples, the Pharisees, wielded heavy influence over Israelite life and thinking.
- Superpatriot Zealots engaged in terrorism, assassination, and all forms of anti-Roman, anti-establishment political and clandestine activities. Historian Josephus reports 10,000 revolutionary uprisings in Judea in the first century.
- The **Essenes** attracted a significant minority to their desert enclaves, lived austere lives of self-denial, studying and copying Scriptures and preparing for the Messiah. This group became famous in the mid-twentieth century with the discovery of the Dead Sea Scrolls (Scripture and other writings), which Essenes preserved in caves 2,000 years ago.
- A succession of pseudo "christs"—charismatic religio-political opportunists and con men—who appeared from

GOSPEL QUARTET IN HARMONY

Luke 13:22–15:32
John 10

Sadducees: *wealthy leaders opposed to Pharisees, and who denied the afterlife, angels, and spirits*

Essenes: *sect that believed in simple, communal living*

☞ **GO TO:**

Luke 21:8; Acts 5:36–37; 21:38
(pseudo "christs")

time to time, claiming to be the Messiah, led hundreds to disaster.

Jesus understood from the start that he had been sent by God to lead Israel into God's kingdom. The terms *King, Master, Rabbi, Teacher*, and *Lord* were all applied to him by his followers.

But one of his own favorite ways of describing his leadership was to call himself "Shepherd." In fact shepherds and sheep are mentioned more than 600 times in the Bible.

☞ **GO TO:**

John 1:29–35
(introduced)

Matthew 9:35–36
(without a shepherd)

compassion: *feeling others' pain and acting to ease it*

After John the Baptist <u>introduced</u> Jesus and he began to preach in Galilee, people came from everywhere with their diseases, sicknesses, mental and spiritual maladies and handicaps, suffering under poverty and oppression of all kinds—harassed and helpless. And *"he had* **compassion** *on them, because they were,"* he thought, *"like sheep <u>without a shepherd</u>."*

> **John 10:1–3** "I tell you the truth, the man who does not enter the sheep pen by the gate, but climbs in by some other way, is a thief and a robber. The man who enters by the gate is the shepherd of his sheep. The watchman opens the gate for him, and the sheep listen to his voice. He calls his own sheep by name and leads them out."

☞ **Check It Out:**

John 10:1–12

The Good Shepherd

Jesus had just come from a tense <u>conversation</u> with the Pharisees (self-proclaimed spiritual shepherds). They had spent much negative energy denying a miracle (Jesus giving sight to a man born blind). They threatened with expulsion and censure any who dared to say they believed in Jesus, and threw the former blind man out of the Temple simply for telling the truth.

☞ **GO TO:**

John 9:39–41
(conversation)

Legalism, distrust, prejudice, disdain for people, hatred, intimidation, and threats—these were the tools of their "leadership" style! With all this it would have been hard to wriggle out of Jesus' clear inference in the first verses of John 10 that they were not true shepherds at all, but thieves and robbers.

Life In The Flock

sheepfold: *a cave or corral-type enclosure*

In the lands of the Bible, sheep are kept in a **sheepfold** at night. Several flocks may occupy the same sheepfold. The fold has only one entrance. Often the pens have no door. To protect the flock once it is inside, the shepherd sleeps in the entrance. To get at the sheep, an animal or human intruder must literally "go through" the shepherd, or scale the **wall**.

What Do The Sheep-And-Shepherd Symbols Mean?

In Jesus' shepherd-and-flock allegory, the identity of the symbols is easily recognized.

- The sheepfold is the kingdom of God.
- The sheep are God's people.
- The <u>shepherd</u> is Jesus (also spiritual leaders).
- The **thief** and **robber** (John 10:1) are leaders who exploit the flock for selfish purposes, victimizing rather than protecting and nurturing. The thief's goals—to *"steal and kill and destroy"* (verse 10)—fit well the goals of the <u>devil</u>.
- The stranger (verse 5) is any false leader.
- The **gate** or door (verses 7–10) is Jesus. He is the sole access to the safety of God's kingdom: the gateway to "life . . . **to the full**" (verse 10).
- The **hired hand** (verses 12–13) is one who <u>doesn't really care</u> about the sheep.
- The <u>wolf</u> (verse 12) is any enemy seeking to harm God's people.
- The other sheep (verse 16) are Gentiles soon to be included in God's flock.

Phillip Keller: When our Lord, who referred to himself as the Good Shepherd spoke these parables, he saw the overall picture of the unique relationship between himself and his followers—between himself and those who had come under his good hand for the management of their lives.[1]

> **John 10:4** "When he has brought out all his own, he goes on ahead of them, and his sheep follow him because they do not recognize a stranger's voice."

Recognizing The Shepherd's Voice

In the West sheep and shepherds only make contact when the flock is moved from one pasture to another or at lambing and shearing seasons. Using sheepdogs, horses, or all-terrain vehicles, shepherds *drive* the sheep from one place to another.

wall: *often built of stone and topped with briars*

☞ **GO TO:**

Psalm 23 (shepherd)

1 Peter 5:8 (devil)

John 14:6; Ephesians 2:18; Hebrews 10:20 (gate)

John 7:45–52 (doesn't really care)

Matthew 10:16; Luke 10:3; Acts 20:29 (wolf)

What Others are Saying:

thief: *original word emphasizes trickery and deceit*

robber: *original word indicates violence in commission of the crime*

gate: *the shepherd*

to the full: *abundant, overflowing, extraordinary*

hired hand: *anyone doing his work for pay*

In Bible lands shepherds and sheep share a more interwoven relationship.

In first-century sheep care, several flocks spent the night in a single fold. The shepherds arrived in the morning, and each gathered his flock by calling the names of individuals or using a distinctive vocal sound his flock recognized.

A Mid-Eastern shepherd would speak to his flock in a singsong voice, a strange language of animal-like sounds. When they heard his voice, the sheep followed him out to that day's pasture.

Most sheep in Israel were not killed for food, but kept for shearing. So shepherd and sheep developed a relationship, a mutual fondness. The shepherd had a special name for each member of his flock. They trusted him.

He did not move them by driving them, but by walking in front of them, talking to them. The shepherd's voice and physical leadership gave the sheep a sense of security, and they followed wherever he led.

The voice of a stranger creates alarm. The sheep stop grazing and lift their heads. If they hear the strange call again, they are likely to scatter and run. The stranger's voice signals danger.

Jesus assures his "flock" that, in spite of the threat of "thieves and robbers," God's sheep are able to distinguish the true Shepherd's voice from the voices of false shepherds. The Scriptures assure that if they will use the <u>spiritual discernment</u> available to them through the Holy Spirit living in them, they need not be led astray.

☞ **GO TO:**

1 John 2:20–27
(spiritual discernment)

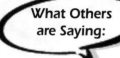

What Others are Saying:

Phillip Keller: Over a period of time sheep come to associate the sound of the shepherd's voice with special benefits. . . . His voice is used to announce his presence; he is there. It is to allay their fears and timidity. Or it is to call them to himself so they can be examined and counted carefully. He wants to make sure they are all well, fit and flourishing. Sometimes the voice is used to announce that fresh feed is being supplied, or salt, or minerals, or water. He might call them up to lead them into fresh pastures or into some shelter from an approaching storm. But always the master's call conveys to the sheep a positive assurance that he cares for them and is acting in their best interests.[2]

KEY Outline:

Shepherd's Voice
Distinctive
Familiar
Trusted, obeyed
Comforting, secure
Positive assurance

> **John 10:12** "The hired hand is not the shepherd who owns the sheep. So when he sees the wolf coming, he abandons the sheep and runs away. Then the wolf attacks the flock and scatters it."

How To Tell A Real Shepherd From A Mercenary

To Jesus' listeners, the concept of the "hired hand" was not totally negative. The term was also applied to fishermen who worked for wages (Mark 1:20).

The problem was that the hired shepherd was not the owner, did not know the flock, and lacked the owner's emotional attachment to it.

The difference becomes apparent when the flock is under attack. The true shepherd is willing to lay his life on the line to protect his sheep, whereas the man putting in his time did not share that level of concern.

The mercenary sheepherder was a picture of many of that day's religious leaders.

Priests, lawyers, and Pharisees were notorious for using their power to make a <u>profit</u>. They showed more concern for keeping themselves in positions of public honor and authority than for supporting the people's spiritual development.

Men and women who choose religious leadership as a profession because of economic, social, and personal advantages soon discover the profit motive isn't enough to keep them making the personal sacrifices the health and safety of God's flock <u>demands</u>. When the chips are down, the profit motive isn't enough to make a person willing to risk his or her life, as is sometimes necessary in other countries.

References to God as Shepherd and His People as His Flock

Psalm 23:1	Psalm 77:20	Psalm 79:13
Psalm 80:1	Psalm 95:7	Psalm 100:3
Isaiah 40:11	Jeremiah 23:1–4	Ezekiel 34:2
Ezekiel 34:15–16	Matthew 9:36	Matthew 18:12
Mark 6:34	Mark 14:27	Luke 12:32
Luke 15:4	1 Peter 2:25	Hebrews 13:20

> **John 10:17–18** "The reason my Father loves me is that I lay down my life—only to take it up again. No one takes it from me, but I lay it down of my own accord. I have authority to lay it down and authority to take it up again. This command I received from my Father."

KEY Outline:

Hired Shepherd
Non-owner
Unfamiliar
Lacks attachment
Unwilling to risk

Something to Ponder

☞ **GO TO:**

John 2:14–16; Luke 16:14 (profit)

1 Peter 5:1–4 (demands)

Dig Deeper

Jesus' "Good Shep-
herd" claim is a claim
to be the Messiah.

☞ **GO TO:**

Romans 5:7 (lay down)

Luke 23:46; John 19:30
(when to die)

**Something
to Ponder**

**What Others
are Saying:**

☞ **Check It Out:**

John 10:19–30

Solomon's Colonnade:
covered porch, east side
of Temple, built by
Solomon

surrounded: original
word indicates a hostile
crowd

☞ **GO TO:**

Acts 5:12 (Solomon's
Colonnade)

**Remember
This . . .**

The Shepherd's Choice

By calling himself the Good Shepherd, Jesus inferred that he was
the promised Messiah. However, he took the claim beyond what
most Jews, including his disciples, expected of the Messiah—he
said he would lay down his life for his sheep (verses 11, 15).

But more.

Heroes in war, men protecting their families, mothers protecting their children will <u>lay down</u> their lives for something they
care about. But no ordinary human being can take his life back
after sacrificing it.

Jesus claimed he had authority over his life. He would decide <u>when to die</u>. By authority given to him by his Father in
heaven, he would rise from the dead! A shepherd who can
overcome death can overcome anything!

Octavius Winslow: Who delivered up Jesus to die? Not Judas,
for money; not Pilate, for fear; not the Jews, for envy—but the
Father, for love![3]

The Hanukkah Challenge

As usual, the reaction of Jesus' listeners was divided.

Some wrote him off: "He's a stark, raving madman!"

Others could not dismiss him so easily: *"These are not the sayings of a man possessed by a demon. Can a demon open the eyes of
the blind?"* (John 10:19–21).

The healing of the blind man (John 9) and the teaching about
the Good Shepherd (John 10:1–18) evidently took place just before the Feast of Dedication.

One day at the feast Jesus was walking in the covered area called
Solomon's Colonnade, probably because it was raining, as it often did during this winter festival. The religious leaders **surrounded** him demanding he state openly whether or not he
claimed to be Messiah.

Jesus' claims require everyone to make a decision: Is he crazy,
or is he what he claims? There is no middle ground.

> **John 10:25** Jesus answered, "I did tell you, but you do
> not believe. The miracles I do in my Father's name speak
> for me."

Why Didn't Jesus Come Right Out And Say, "I Am The Messiah!"?

Jesus had made amazing claims.

- Privately to the Samaritan woman: *"I . . . am the (Messiah)"* (John 4:25–26)
- Publicly in Capernaum: *"I am the bread of life"* (John 6:35)
- Privately to the 12: He affirmed Peter's confession that Jesus was *"the Christ (Messiah), the Son of the living God"* (Matthew 16:16–18)
- Publicly in Jerusalem: *"Whoever believes in me . . . streams of living water (the Holy Spirit) will flow from within him"* (John 7:37–39)
- Publicly in Jerusalem: *"I am the Light of the world"* (John 8:12)
- Publicly in Jerusalem: *"I am the gate (to salvation)"* (John 10:9)
- Publicly in Jerusalem: *"I am the good shepherd (of God's flock)"* (John 10:11)

Why did he not state flatly, publicly, that he was the Messiah?

 Most Jewish people had mistaken ideas of what Messiah would be and do.

When they asked, "Are you the Messiah?" they were asking if he had come to set up a political-military kingdom to liberate Israel from Roman rule.

If he said openly that he was the Messiah, it could have sent off a chain of political events that could only end in disaster.

But Jesus never denied his messiahship, and whenever the title was applied to him by *believing* followers ready to accept the truth, he <u>affirmed</u> it.

 **EARLY CHURCH LIFE:** Jesus had been sent by God, not to muster an army of military or political revolutionaries, but to call out from the world a group of *spiritual* revolutionaries, renewed in spirit and character, which could conquer the world with God's love and forgiveness. The original word for *church* means "the called out ones."

KEY Outline:

Why Veil His Claims?
Wrong expectations
No political agenda
Said it plainly
- statements
- miracles

☞ **GO TO:**

John 1:41, 49
(affirmed)

> **John 10:26–28** "But you do not believe because you are not my sheep. My sheep listen to my voice; I know them, and they follow me. I give them eternal life, and they shall never perish; no one can snatch them out of my hand."

The Unvarnished Truth

Until this confrontation Jesus had veiled his claims when talking to his enemies. Now, suddenly, he tore the lid off—but still did it in words carefully chosen to give his opponents little that would stand up in court.

He pointed to past statements in which he had claimed messiahship. He reminded them that his miracles spoke eloquently of his relationship with God.

"But you do not believe because you are not my sheep!" (verse 26).

The marks of Jesus' sheep include these:

- They listen to his voice (verse 27).
- They follow him (verse 27).
- They have assurance of eternal life (verse 28).
- Nobody can ever snatch them away from Jesus or his Father (verses 28–29).

Then he said those words that drove them crazy: *"I and the Father are one"* (verse 30).

What Others are Saying:

Tim Stafford: In Jesus' life we may see God. Yet the choice to see remains with us. On any given day we may choose *not* to see God in Jesus. We may, without even sensing our deep and calamitous rebellion, ignore him, act as though he is merely a picture on the wall. I do so often for the simple reason that I have not yet been totally changed by the power of his glory. His Holy Spirit, however, is changing me, teaching me to recognize God in Jesus.[4]

> **John 10:31–32** Again the Jews picked up stones to stone him, but Jesus said to them, "I have shown you many great miracles from the Father. For which of these do you stone me?"

Rolling Stones And Men As Gods

The Jewish leaders correctly understood him to be claiming to be of one substance with and equal to God. They had pressed for a direct answer. He gave it to them.

They grabbed stones from the temple pavement to kill him right then and there for the crime of blasphemy, treating God with contempt. *"You, a mere man, claim to be God!"* they screamed.

Jesus reminded them of a verse from the Old Testament in which Moses calls Israel's judges "gods" (verse 34) because they carried out godlike responsibilities.

He argued that if the Bible identifies mere human beings exercising leadership and judgment with godlikeness, then, considering the overwhelming evidence of his miracles, he certainly had the right to claim to be God's Son (John 10:35–38).

Reasoning with them was pointless. They were not his sheep.

They grabbed for him. He slipped away (verse 39) and headed for John the Baptist's old stompin' grounds east of the Jordan River.

Receptive people found him there and confessed faith in him (verses 40–42).

Larry (Lawrence O.) Richards: Christ's argument was that if Scripture calls mere mortals who receive the divine Word by the courtesy title "gods," he himself, "whom the Father set apart as his very own and sent into the world," had a far greater right to claim deity. Jesus is God, and his miracles corroborate his claim.[5]

> **Luke 13:23–25a** Someone asked him, "Lord, are only a few people going to be saved?"
>
> He said to them, "Make every effort to enter through the narrow door, because many, I tell you, will try to enter and will not be able to. Once the owner of the house gets up and closes the door, you will stand outside knocking and pleading, 'Sir, open the door for us.'"

Heartbreak Hotel

After an unspecified hiatus in the desert, Jesus preached his way back toward Jerusalem.

A favorite pastime for the rabbis and other religious types with time on their hands was to argue about how many or few would be **saved**. Prevailing belief was that, except for a few really gross sinners, all Jews would be saved and all non-Jews **lost**.

☞ **GO TO:**

Deuteronomy 1:17; Psalm 82:6–7 ("gods")

KEY POINT

Jesus' enemies clearly understood his claim to be God's Son.

What Others are Saying:

☞ **GO TO:**

Proverbs 28:18; Isaiah 45:22; John 3:16–17; Acts 4:12 (saved)

Ezekiel 34:15–16; Matthew 10:6; Luke 19:9–10; John 10:28 (lost)

saved: *rescued from sin's eternal consequences*

lost: *perishing, separated from God because of unforgiven sin*

> **Luke 13:25b–27** "But he will answer, 'I don't know you or where you come from.'
>
> "Then you will say, 'We ate and drank with you, and you taught in our streets.'
>
> "But he will reply, 'I don't know you or where you come from. Away from me, all you evildoers!'"

Access Denied

Jesus' response upset some cherished apple carts. (Surprise! Surprise!) Not everyone who thinks they know the password will receive access to heaven.

- The way to salvation is <u>narrow</u> (Luke 13:24).
- Salvation requires effort (verse 24). Salvation is by faith, <u>not works</u>, but self-denial and a cross are involved (Mark 8:34). The Greek word for "effort" originally described competing in the Olympic Games. Our English word *agony* is derived from the Greek word for "effort."
- Salvation is a <u>limited-time</u> offer (verse 25). If death slams the door before you get in, you miss the party!
- Mere exposure to Jesus saves no one (verse 26). Exposure must lead to personal experience with him—you and Jesus "knowing" one another in an intimate, personal relationship (verses 25, 27).
- Salvation is not automatic for any group (verses 28–30). Jesus shocked his Jewish listeners by suggesting that people from everywhere (Gentiles) will be in the kingdom with the greats of Israel. But unless they came through him, many of his listeners would be <u>outside</u> looking in!

GO TO:

Matthew 7:13–23; John 14:6; Acts 4:12; 1 Corinthians 3:11 (narrow)

Ephesians 2:8–10 (not works)

Isaiah 55:6–7; 2 Peter 3:9 (limited-time)

Matthew 8:11–12 (outside)

What Others are Saying:

KEY Outline:

Salvation
Narrow way
Self-denial/a cross
Limited-time offer
Knowing Jesus
Offered to all

William Barclay: Jesus taught that the only aristocracy in the kingdom of God is the aristocracy of faith. Jesus Christ is not the possession of any one race of men; Jesus Christ is the possession of every man in every race in whose heart there is faith.[6]

> **Luke 13:31–35** At that time some Pharisees came to Jesus and said to him, "Leave this place and go somewhere else. Herod wants to kill you."
>
> He replied, "Go tell that fox, 'I will drive out demons and heal people today and tomorrow, and on the third day I will reach my goal.' In any case, I must keep

going today and tomorrow and the next day—for surely no prophet can die outside Jerusalem!

"O Jerusalem, Jerusalem, you who kill the prophets and stone those sent to you, how often I have longed to gather your children together, as a hen gathers her chicks under her wings, but you were not willing! Look, your house is left to you desolate. I tell you, you will not see me again until you say, 'Blessed is he who comes in the name of the Lord.'"

Cracks In The Pharisee Wall

At that point a rather strange and touching thing happened. Some Pharisees (of all people!) warned Jesus of death threats against him by **Herod** and suggested he "get out of Dodge City" to save his neck.

They may have been trying to scare him to keep him away from Jerusalem at Passover time, when support for him could build among the festival crowds.

The fact that Jesus did not expose any hypocrisy on their parts, indicates, though, that they may actually have been concerned for his safety. If they were honestly trying to protect him, they did so at the risk of censure by fellow Pharisees. If so, it comes as a surprise to discover that not all Pharisees were hostile to Jesus.

Later we discover that some Pharisees ultimately <u>declared themselves</u> for him openly.

Jesus' response was to shrug off Herod's threats and determine more firmly to go to Jerusalem, knowing he was walking into the jaws of death.

☞ **GO TO:**

Luke 9:7–9; 23:6–11 (Herod)

John 7:50–51; 19:38–40; Acts 15:5 (declared themselves)

Herod: Herod Antipas, Tetrarch of Galilee

Seven Classes of Pharisees[7]

The Jews of Jesus' day divided the Pharisees into seven groups they referred to by tongue-in-cheek terms:

1. **The Shoulder Pharisees** wore their good deeds on their shoulders so everyone could see them.
2. **The Wait-a-Little Pharisees** consistently put off good deeds until tomorrow.
3. **The Bruised Pharisees**, to keep from being seen talking to a woman in public, covered their eyes whenever they met a woman on the street—which often caused them to run into walls and get hurt.
4. **The Hump-Backed Pharisees** walked bent over in a show of false humility.
5. **The Ever-Reckoning Pharisees** were always adding up their good deeds to see if they outweighed their bad deeds.
6. **The Fearing Pharisees** were always terrified of being objects of God's wrath.
7. **The God-Loving Pharisees** lived faithful lives of genuine service to God and people. The Pharisees who warned Jesus of Herod's threats may have been from this group.

KEY POINT

People who can't
return the favor
should be included in
our parties and
dinners.

watched carefully:
original word means
"sinister espionage"

dropsy: edema: excess
accumulation of body
fluids in connective tissue;
painful swelling

☞ **GO TO:**

John 8:3
(purposely paraded)

Luke 18:4, 14; Matthew
23:12; James 4:6, 10;
1 Peter 5:6 (principle)

**What Others
are Saying:**

> **Luke 14:1–2, 7** One Sabbath, when Jesus went to eat
> in the house of a prominent Pharisee, he was being care-
> fully watched. There in front of him was a man suffer-
> ing from dropsy. . . . When he noticed how the guests
> picked places of honor at the table, he told them this
> parable.

Under Surveillance By The Sabbath Squad

A prominent Pharisee invited Jesus to a Sabbath luncheon where
arrangements had been made to use the young Messiah's well-
known compassion to entrap him into breaking the law. (If food
was prepared on Friday, rules allowed entertaining guests on the
Sabbath.)

Among the guests, Pharisees and experts in Jewish law, were
spies who **watched** him **carefully**. Also there, probably purposely
paraded in to provide bait for the trap, was a man with **dropsy**.

There was no way Jesus was going to be in the same room with
a hurting person and not act out of love to meet the person's need—
no matter what day of the week it was!

His enemies depended on his love to spring the trap.

It did. In an in-your-face confrontation with the manipulation
and callousness the situation represented, Jesus healed the man . . .
on the Sabbath.

Jesus was not trapped. In fact, he orchestrated the meal from
hors d'oeuvres to dessert.

In a tone tinged with sarcasm, he exposed as silly and childish
the egocentric jockeying by these "important" men for the best
positions at the dinner table (Luke 14:7–11).

The principle is stated many times in Scripture: Self-exaltation
leads to humiliation, but true humility leads, in the end, to true
exaltation (verse 11).

Jesus advised the host and his cronies that if they wanted to
throw a real gala, their guest list shouldn't be limited to people
who can reciprocate, but should include *"the poor, the crippled, the
lame,"* and *"the blind"* (verses 12–14).

Ronald J. Sider: Jesus . . . did not mean to forbid parties with
friends and relatives. But he certainly did mean that we ought to
entertain the poor and disadvantaged (who cannot reciprocate) at
least as often—and perhaps a lot more often. . . . The Bible specifically commands believers to imitate God's special concern for the
poor and oppressed.[8]

Leon Morris: The way to get to the top is to start at the bottom.[9]

KINGDOM OF GOD

Jesus topped off the dessert menu with a yarn crafted to further put the religious "superstars" in their place (Luke 14:15–24). The story went like this:

Well in advance, according to Mid-Eastern custom, guests were invited to a great banquet. According to custom, a follow-up invitation was sent to let them know the banquet was ready. But, at that late moment, the invited guests began to make excuses as to why they could/would not come.

In justified anger, the host sent his servants into the "**streets** and **alleys**" to find guests to replace the excuse-makers. *"Not one of those men who were invited will get a taste of my banquet!"* said the angry host (verse 24). Jesus' point: Most of the guests first invited into the kingdom of God (the people of Israel) will refuse the invitation, so God will turn to the outcasts (Gentiles).

The "nobodies" in the world's eyes will be treated by the host (the Lord) as honored guests at the kingdom party.

streets: *well-traveled routes*

alleys: *narrow paths between the homes of the poor*

KEY Outline:

> **Luke 15:1–2** Now the tax collectors and "sinners" were all gathering around to hear him. But the Pharisees and the teachers of the law muttered, "This man welcomes sinners and eats with them."

Jesus Censured
Religious hypocrisy
Self-exaltation
Self-serving guest list
Spiritual excuse-making

The Notoriety Of God

The things Jesus was saying to the religious leaders (Luke 13:13, 21) told Israel's "lost souls" that Jesus was their friend.

As a result, everywhere he went he was surrounded by synagogue dropouts, prostitutes, and people with occupations considered contrary to the Law.

"One must not associate with an ungodly man," wrote one of the respected teachers. The Pharisees avoided such people like the plague. A popular Pharisee teaching was that the sight of one of these sinners being destroyed brought joy to the heart of God!

No wonder the Pharisees didn't understand Jesus!

He associated with such people. In fact, he was often seen *eating with them!* Eating together implied acceptance. His reputation for going to dinner with such people became part of the <u>mud</u> with which his enemies smeared his name.

The way Jesus represented the heavenly Father in the stories he told in response to the religionists' criticism was enough, in the Pharisees' opinion, to smear *God's* reputation with the same mud.

☞ **Check It Out:**

Luke 15

KEY POINT

Eating together implies acceptance.

☞ **GO TO:**

Luke 5:31; 7:34 (mud)

> **Luke 15:3–7** Then Jesus told them this parable: "Suppose one of you has a hundred sheep and loses one of them. Does he not leave the ninety-nine in the open country and go after the lost sheep until he finds it? And when he finds it, he joyfully puts it on his shoulders and goes home. Then he calls his friends and neighbors together and says, 'Rejoice with me; I have found my lost sheep.' I tell you that in the same way there will be more rejoicing in heaven over one sinner who repents than over ninety-nine **righteous** persons who do not need to repent."

righteous: doctrinally correct, separated, holier-than-thou

Lost And Found: The 100th Sheep

Jesus told three stories about losing and finding prized things.

Back to the shepherd theme (verses 3–7). Shepherds were second-class citizens, but sheep were vital to the economy and religion—the source of wool and leather, thousands of temple sacrifices, and the main course at banquets.

☞ **GO TO:**

John 10
  (shepherd theme)

- The shepherd represents God.
- The lost sheep represents the helplessness of people separated from God by sin.
- Leaving the flock in the open field to search for the lost one (a good shepherd would never do this except in extreme emergency) represents God's urgency.
- Jewish teachers taught that God would receive repentant sinners. But the idea that God actively pursues sinners was revolutionary to the first-century Jewish mind.

KEY POINT

God gets a kick out of welcoming sinners.

> **Luke 15:8–10** "Or suppose a woman has ten silver coins and loses one. Does she not light a lamp, sweep the house and search carefully until she finds it? And when she finds it, she calls her friends and neighbors together and says, 'Rejoice with me; I have found my lost coin.' In the same way, I tell you, there is rejoicing in the presence of the angels of God over one sinner who repents."

☞ **GO TO:**

Exodus 22:17; Genesis 29:18 (dowry)

dowry: groom's gift to bride's father; father's gift to the bride

Lost And Found: The 10th Coin

The missing coin (verses 8–10) was probably part of the woman's **dowry**. A dowry coin (see illustration, page 89) would have been prized because it symbolized her worth as a person, individuality, and rights as a woman.

The dowry signified she was a partner in the marriage, not just a servant—a person in her own right, not just her husband's wife. Her sense of dignity was wrapped up in this coin. And should something happen to her husband or the marriage, the gift would be used to assure her independence.

What this tells us about God is that the lost are precious to God for reasons relating to who he is, his character as the Creator who wants to live with his creatures in a continuing personal relationship.

> **Luke 15:11–12** Jesus continued, "There was a man who had two sons. The younger one said to his father, 'Father, give me my share of the estate.' So he divided his property between them."

Lost And Found: The Second Son

A father could pass his property to his heirs in one of two ways: (1) after his death by means of a last will and testament, or (2) while he was still alive by gifts given to his heirs. (Usually these gifts were in the form of property.)

Exceptions could be made. In this case, the younger son asked for cash. Liquid assets in hand, the younger son left those confining "little-town blues" for the Big Apple (Luke 15:13, *"a distant country"*).

There, he blew it all! Wealth, opportunity, self-respect, youth, his future—down the tubes! When he hit bottom, he hit it hard. Twin crises slammed him as he harvested his crop of wild oats: (1) his cash flow dried up! and (2) his adopted country ran out of food!

The only employment he could find was a low-down, poverty-level job not covered by the minimum wage and well **below the dignity** of a son of Israel—feeding pigs!

KEY Outline:

Why People Get Lost
Three pictures
- sheep (no sense of right/wrong)
- coin (victims of circumstances)
- son (deliberate choices)

below the dignity:
"Cursed is he who feeds swine!" (ancient Jewish axiom)

☞ **GO TO:**

Hebrews 9:16–17 (will)

Leviticus 11:7 (pigs)

Dowry Coins

In New Testament times fathers often gave a string of silver coins to their daughters at the time of their marriage. The coins were worn as a headdress or necklace and were highly prized as symbols of the woman's worth as a person, and of her independence.

> **Luke 15:17–19** "When he came to his senses, he said, 'How many of my father's hired men have food to spare, and here I am starving to death! I will set out and go back to my father and say to him: Father, I have sinned against heaven and against you. I am no longer worthy to be called your son; make me like one of your hired men.'"

The View From The Bottom

From that vantage point—he'd hit bottom—with failure staring him in the face, his arrogance buried in pigpen muck, the young man *"came to his senses."* At this "critical threshold," far from home and keeping company with swine, this young Jew evaluated his life.

With nowhere to go but up, it was not hard to make "up" the direction of choice. The foolish young man did three smart things to turn his life around:

1. He faced up to the spiritual issues in his life (Luke 15:17).
2. He decided to go back and face the music (verses 18–19).
3. He acted on his decision (verses 20–21).
   - He returned to the place the relationship had broken down—*"to his father."*
   - He admitted he'd "sinned to <u>high heaven</u>!"
   - He confessed his sin against his father—he'd broken the <u>sixth commandment.</u>
   - He confessed his need for **grace**—he no longer deserved to be called *son.*

☞ **GO TO:**

Ezra 9:6
 (high heaven)

Exodus 20:12
 (sixth commandment)

grace: undeserved favor

> **Luke 15:20** But while he was still a long way off, his father saw him and was filled with compassion for him; he ran to his son, threw his arms around him and kissed him!

Parable Of The Forgiving Father

This story is known as the parable of the prodigal son, but the father's response is the main focus. It probably ought to be renamed the parable of the forgiving father.

This father demonstrates how God responds to sinners who turn to him:

1. God longs for sinners to return to him (Luke 15:20).
2. God has compassion on sinners who are on their way to him (verse 20).
3. God is ready to forgive (verse 20).
4. God accepts, as sons and daughters not servants, sinners who come to him (verses 20, 22–24). Jesus' description of the father's enthusiastic, loving acceptance was a rebuke to self-righteous hypocrites who objected to Jesus eating with and accepting sinners.
5. The list of the father's expressions of love and welcome is impressive:
   - kisses—demonstrate unbroken affection
   - best robe—symbol of position and honor
   - ring—symbol of authority
   - shoes—symbol of a son not a slave (slaves wore no shoes)
   - barbecued calf—sign the father saw the homecoming as a most special occasion
   - celebration—sign of the father's joy (see verses 7, 10)
   - announcement: *"my son was dead and is alive"* (verse 24)—restored relationship

There is no hint that the young man's sin or the heartache he caused was ever held over his head to punish or keep him doing right. Jesus meant his listeners to understand God does <u>not remember</u> forgiven sin.

Oswald Chambers: We would feel much happier in our backslidden condition if we knew that our backsliding had altered God, but we know that immediately we come back we will find him exactly the same . . . . If God would only be angry with us and demand an apology, it would be a gratification to us; when we have done wrong we like to be lashed for it. God never lashes.[10]

Donald Grey Barnhouse, *to a man who told him, "I've confessed my sin 100 times":* Ah! That's your problem. You see, the last 99 times you came to confess, God had to say, "What sin?" He <u>forgave</u> and <u>forgot</u> your sin the first time you confessed![11]

KEY Outline:

God's Response to Repentant Sinners

Yearning
Loving
Forgiving
Accepting as children

☞ **GO TO:**

Hebrews 10:17 (not remember)

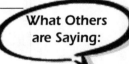
What Others are Saying:

☞ **GO TO:**

1 John 1:9 (forgave)

Hebrews 10:17 (forgot)

> **Luke 15:28** The older brother became angry and refused to go in. So the father went out and pleaded with him.

☞ **Check It Out:**

Luke 15:25–32

The Party Pooper

To say the elder brother was not happy with his brother's return is to put it mildly.

He came in from the field caked with dust, his hands calloused from hard work. When he heard the laughter, smelled the barbecued meat, and was told what the hullabaloo was about, he was filled with rage. His bitterness, envy, and lack of forgiveness hung over the scene like killer smog.

The father loved the elder son, too. He came out to him, just as he had for the young wanderer (verse 28). The elder brother exploded in a torrent of resentment.

1. He saw all his years of "faithful" work as drudging "slavery" (verse 29).
2. He felt he was unappreciated and poorly treated (verse 29).
3. He refused to accept the prodigal as brother, calling him *"this son of yours"* (verse 30).
4. He amplified the prodigal's sins. He was first to accuse the younger son of wasting his father's inheritance on *"prostitutes"* (verse 30).

KEY Outline:

The Elder Brother
 Faithfulness a drudgery
 "I get no respect"
 "Your son," not "my brother"
 Magnified prodigal's sins

The elder brother in Jesus' story represented the Pharisees and their attitudes toward the needy people with whom Jesus spent time.

The father's response to the elder's tirade reveals God's gracious attitude toward even his hypocritical children. He called him *"my son"* (verse 31), expressed appreciation for his faithfulness, affirmed his place in the family, and assured him that the prodigal's return would not affect his <u>rights</u> as the eldest son (verse 31). The father also refused to acknowledge the rift between the brothers—he called the prodigal *"your brother"* (verse 32), and urged his eldest to join the party.

☞ **GO TO:**

Deuteronomy 21:15–17 (rights)

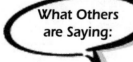

What Others are Saying:

John Killinger: In the end, the son who had stayed home proved to be more lost to the father's heart than the one who had wandered off.[12]

Study Questions

1. Explain the meaning of the following symbols in Jesus' shepherd-and-flock allegory: (a) sheepfold, (b) sheep, (c) shepherd, (d) thief, (e) gate, and (f) wolf.

2. As the ultimate Shepherd of his sheep, Jesus said he would choose when to lay down his life. What else did he say he had the authority to do?

3. What do the stories of the lost sheep, lost coin, and prodigal son teach us about God's attitude toward wayward people who turn to him? How did the elder brother react to the prodigal's return?

4. With whom do you personally identify in this story and why? The prodigal, the father, or the elder brother?

5. How do you respond to the idea that following Jesus is like coming to God's party? (Why?) (a) Denial: There's no party in this life. (b) Party pooper: Sorry, I'm too busy to celebrate. (c) Party animal: I'm ready; let's party! or (d) Wallflower: I'm at the party, but I can't dance.

CHAPTER WRAP-UP

- In a society where sheep were extremely important to the economy and religious life, Jesus introduced himself as the Good Shepherd and promised to lay down his life for his sheep, then to take his life back by rising from the dead. (John 10:1–18)

- At Hanukkah in Jerusalem, Jesus' enemies demanded that he declare himself openly—was he the Messiah? He reminded them of how he had already made messianic claims and proven their validity by doing miracles. (John 10:22–25)

- Jesus' enemies did not believe his claims, he said, because they were not his true sheep. If they were they would recognize his voice and enjoy assurance of their salvation. (John 10:25–39)

- A question about the number of people who will be saved led to Jesus' teaching about the narrowness of the way of salvation. A parable about excuse-making invited guests underscores the truth that the kingdom of God will include a lot of people the Jews of his day did not expect to be included—namely Gentiles. (Luke 13:22–14:24)

- Criticized for welcoming and celebrating with known sinners and irreligious people, Jesus told three stories (the lost sheep, lost coin, and Prodigal Son) to show how God rejoices when sinners return to him and how freely he offers them his grace. (Luke 15)

6 YOUR MONEY OR YOUR LIFE

CHAPTER HIGHLIGHTS

- The Real Rich Man
- Life-Giving Friend
- The Resurrection and the Life
- Assassins' Plot

Let's Get Started

Jesus taught that welcoming repentant sinners makes God deliriously happy. But he also carefully showed his followers a clear road map to real change in their lives.

After all, the prostitutes he forgave (Luke 7:36–50; John 8:3–11) were not paragons of feminine virtue! The tax collectors he accepted and ate with (Luke 5:27–32; 15:1) were not heroes! They were greedy, conniving, white-collar thieves.

Their newfound friend, Jesus, could no more leave these promiscuous women and two-bit shysters in their dishonest lifestyles than he could pussyfoot around the hypocrisies of the Pharisees. So after correcting misconceptions about God's attitude toward sinners (he doesn't hate them—he welcomes them) and **flaying** the Pharisees for their insensitivity (Luke 15), he aimed his legendary story guns at his fresh recruits.

The Real Rich Man

Jesus challenged his rookie disciples to take another attitude than they had been taking toward wealth and poverty, marriage and **fidelity**, heaven and hell, life and death, and faith.

> **Luke 16:1–2** Jesus told his disciples: "There was a rich man whose manager was accused of wasting his possessions. So he called him in and asked him, 'What is this I hear about you? Give an account of your management, because you cannot be manager any longer.'

GOSPEL QUARTET IN HARMONY

Luke 16:1–31
John 11

---

flaying: harshly criticizing

☞ **Check It Out:**

Luke 16:1–15

fidelity: marital faithfulness

> "The manager said to himself, 'What shall I do now? My master is taking away my job. I'm not strong enough to dig, and I'm ashamed to beg— I know what I'll do so that, when I lose my job here, people will welcome me into their houses.'"

Shrewd Investing

The first story Jesus told is unusual because there isn't a good guy in the whole motley cast of characters!

A middle manager mishandled his head honcho's financial affairs to his own dishonest advantage. The boss caught him with his hand in the till and terminated his employment.

Digging ditches was no option for the old embezzler—he was too out of shape. Begging was embarrassing. So he hatched a brilliant scheme to assure that when the boss gave him the gate he wouldn't wind up on the street.

He knew who owed his boss money. He went to the debtors one by one and offered to accept a drastically reduced amount in exchange for "paid-in-full" receipts. The olive grower got out of his debt for 50 cents on the dollar. The sharecropper got a paid-in-full receipt worth 1,000 bushels of wheat for the price of 800.

With a grand conspiracy between manager and debtors, a few altered entries in the records, and the shredding of a couple of strategic memos, the manager bought a couple of cronies who would do him a big favor he'd need once he was canned.

The boss, who prided himself in being a shrewd businessman, was so impressed with the manager's cleverness, he applauded, even though it cost him 500 gallons of olive oil and 200 bushels of wheat! What impressed him was not the cost of the swindle, but its creativity.

Jesus used this parable to say to his newly converted tax men: "Now that you've gone straight, you must put your infamous creativity to work devising ways to build up the kingdom of God!" (Luke 16:8).

 KINGDOM OF GOD Invest your cash and other assets in people, especially fellow Christians. The friendships you build will be your source of supply when you're in a tight spot (Luke 16:9).

View your material possessions as a trust you are handling for God (verse 10). All we own in this life is, in reality, his property— we are managers working for him.

Invest what you have in a way that makes you rich in things <u>of the Spirit</u> (i.e., love, joy, peace, generosity, etc.; see verse 11). Spiritual advancement hinges on how you handle your present opportunities.

Use what you have been given—much or little—in God's service, not as slaves of the **money-god** (verse 13).

Oswald Chambers: Never compromise with the spirit of mammon. . . . Mammon is the system of civilized life which organizes itself without any consideration of God.[1]

John Killinger: If we love God, we will use our money for spiritual purposes. But if we love money, we cannot use God to further our business situations. He will not be a party to our selfish designs.[2]

> **Luke 16:14–15** The Pharisees, who loved money, heard all this and were sneering at Jesus. He said to them, "You are the ones who justify yourselves in the eyes of men, but God knows your hearts. What is highly valued among men is detestable in God's sight."

Slaves Of The Money-God

Two reasons are given for the Pharisees' contempt for the financial management style Jesus taught:

- They loved (were greedy for) money (Luke 16:14). Most were wealthy.
- They used that fact to *"justify themselves in the eyes of men"* (verse 15) by teaching that material success was evidence of God's approval.

So, for their benefit and that of his friends, Jesus added a sobering assertion: *"What is highly valued among men is **detestable** in God's sight"* (verse 15).

If we value wealth for itself, hoarding rather than sharing it in creative ways that serve the Lord's purposes, our possessions will turn our hearts from God.

☞ **GO TO:**

Galatians 5:22–25 (of the Spirit)

What Others are Saying:

money-god: Greek: Mammon, *the evil spirit of material wealth*

KEY Outline:

Creative Use of Wealth

Care for people
Make kingdom friends
View wealth as trust
Invest in spiritual things
Love God with it
Value what God loves

detestable: Greek: *"abominable"*; OT equivalent describes God's hatred of immorality and idolatry

Remember This . . .

Lawrence O. (Larry) Richards: Either the love of money will drive out love for God as the central motivation of our life, or love for God will drive out love for money.[3]

Mother Teresa: I think people are so preoccupied with material difficulties. In the industrial world where people are supposed to have so much, I find that many people, while dressed up, are really, really poor. By having nothing we will be able to give everything—through the freedom of poverty.[4]

Law and the Prophets:
Old Testament Scriptures

John: the Baptist

> **Luke 16:16–18** The **Law and the Prophets** were proclaimed until **John**. Since that time, the good news of the kingdom of God is being preached, and everyone is forcing his way into it. It is easier for heaven and earth to disappear than for the least stroke of a pen to drop out of the Law.
>
> Anyone who divorces his wife and marries another woman commits adultery, and the man who marries a divorced woman commits adultery.

Storming The Kingdom

The style of life Jesus teaches in this chapter is one of intense commitment to godly values and a totally new way of life.

If in order to live the way Jesus teaches we must <u>violently</u> say "No" to ourselves and the old way of life, if we must bulldoze through inner and outer challenges to the new way, running roughshod over the barriers our own sin-plagued nature throws up to keep Christ's life from emerging—then, even though it is painful, Jesus calls us to be that committed to his new way.

No Holiness Made Easy

The moral commandments and gracious principles of *"the Law and the Prophets"* are not replaced. *"The good news of the kingdom of God"* is not "holiness made easy." The ancient principles come alive in Jesus' followers, as they walk with him in the <u>Spirit</u> and in <u>love</u>.

KINGDOM OF GOD

One moral principle carried over into the life of the kingdom community is faithfulness to marriage commitments.

Jesus chose this as an example, in part at least, because it was

☞ **GO TO:**

Matthew 5:29–30; Mark 9:43–47 (violently)

KEY POINT

To gain the kingdom with its lofty values and relationships we must be willing to say "No" to ourselves.

☞ **GO TO:**

Romans 8:1–4; 13:8–10; 2 Corinthians 5:14–15; Galatians 5:6 (Spirit . . . love)

an area in which the Pharisees and first-century Jewish culture had departed from the spirit of Old Testament Law. Jesus consistently opposed the family-destroying trend of easy divorce.

The Holy Spirit gives those who trust him power to keep their promises. Forgiveness is available to those who fail, and divorce does not disqualify a person for citizenship in the kingdom community.

Lifelong marriage, however, is clearly what <u>Jesus taught</u>. Keeping a marriage together may require self-denial and sacrificial love. But who, listening to him and watching his lifestyle, can conclude anything but that these are completely consistent with everything Jesus stands for?

☞ **GO TO:**

Matthew 19:3–12;
Mark 10:3–12
(Jesus taught)

> **Luke 16:19–21** There was a rich man who was dressed in purple and fine linen and lived in luxury every day. At his gate was laid a beggar named Lazarus, covered with sores and longing to eat what fell from the rich man's table. Even the dogs came and licked his sores.

The Topsy-Turvy Tale Of A Poor Rich Man And A Rich Poor Man

Chances are this is a story that really happened. In no other parable did Jesus reveal his characters' names. The poor man in this tale was named **Lazarus**. Jesus did not name the rich man, but tradition calls him **Dives**.

While some pretty dire details about hell are revealed in this story, it does not really answer the question of why some people go there when they die and why others go to heaven. It does not tell us all we need to know in order to be <u>saved</u>. Other parts of the Bible reveal that people are given eternal life if they put their faith in Christ. If they don't, they perish. But that's not the issue Jesus is dealing with here.

This saga, like the rest of Jesus' teachings in Luke 16, relates to the handling of material possessions, but it doesn't suggest there is any connection between a person's financial status and his eternal destiny. No one goes to hell simply because he is rich. And no one goes to heaven simply because he is poor. Rich and poor have nothing to do with a person's eternal destiny.

☞ **Check It Out:**

Luke 16:19–31

Lazarus: name means "God help him"

Dives: (pronounced: die-vees) Latin for "rich man"

☞ **GO TO:**

John 3:16; Romans 10:9–10; 1 John 5:11, 20; Romans 16:31 (saved)

Who's Who

DIVES, THE RICH MAN: Well-dressed man (Luke 16:19) who wore "purple"—expensive cloth dyed with an expensive dye obtained from rare shellfish—and "fine linen." He lived in luxury every day (verse 19). In the original language of the New Testament the phrase indicates he enjoyed one feast after another. He was not ready to die (verse 23).

Who's Who

LAZARUS, THE BEGGAR: A sick man—covered with sores—too weak to chase away the street dogs that came and licked his oozing ulcers (Luke 16:20–21) and competed with him for table scraps. He was hungry—waiting at the rich man's gate for the garbage to be thrown out so he could eat (verse 21). He was ready to die (verse 22).

> **Luke 16:22** The time came when the beggar died and the angels carried him to Abraham's side. The rich man also died and was buried.

A Tale Of Two Destinies

In this life, all the good things came to the rich man, while poor Lazarus got stiffed, ate garbage, suffered the torment that goes with being too broke to buy decent food or get medical help.

But death is the great leveler—after they died, there was a great switcheroo: Lazarus left the street for a wonderful place called "**Abraham's side**" and got the good things; Dives went straight from his sumptuous earthly life to **hell** (verses 22–24).

Abraham's side: "paradise," a holding area for the righteous dead awaiting resurrection

hell: Greek: Hades

What Others are Saying:

Charles Swindoll: When Lazarus, the believer, died, his body was probably tossed in the local dump, the refuse pile. Chances are good he didn't even receive a decent burial. But his soul and spirit were taken immediately into the presence of the Lord, called here "Abraham's side." When we read, "The rich man died and was buried," we can be sure his burial was one of great pomp and elaborate ceremony. So much for his body. It is his eternal soul that interests us. We find him "in hell." . . .[5]

All You Ever Wanted to Know about Hell but Were Afraid to Ask[6]

Dig Deeper

The basic first-century Jewish idea:

The Greek word translated "hell" (Luke 16:23) is *Hades*, place of the dead. Jews of Jesus' time believed both righteous and unrighteous dead went, at death, into a "holding area" to await final judgment. This area was divided into two parts separated by an uncrossable chasm. The righteous side was called *"paradise"* (Luke 23:43) or "Abraham's bosom" (Luke 16:22). The unrighteous side was called "Gehenna," the place of punishment.

New Testament words for hell (the place of punishment):

- *Abaddon:* "destruction" (Revelation 9:11)
- *Abyss:* "bottomless" or "deep" (Luke 8:31; Romans 10:7; Revelation 9:11)
- *Gehenna:* "Valley of Hinnon," the perpetually burning garbage dump outside Jerusalem, once a place babies were burned as sacrifices to pagan gods; it became a metaphor for final punishment (Matthew 5:22, 29, 30; 23:15–33; Mark 9:43–49; Luke 12:5; James 3:6)
- *Hades:* "realm of the dead" named for a Greek god (Matthew 16:18; Revelation 1:18; 6:8; 20:13)
- *Lake of fire:* (Revelation 19:20; 20:10, 14, 15), "for the devil and his angels" (Matthew 25:41)
- *Tartaros:* "place of eternal punishment" in Greek mythology (2 Peter 2:4)

What hell is like according to Luke 16:23–31:

- A conscious experience (verse 23)
- Torment (verses 23, 27), thirst (verse 24), agony (verses 24, 25), fire (verse 24), regret (verse 28)
- Paradise can be seen from there, but never experienced (verses 23, 26)
- No escape, destinies are fixed in this life and cannot be changed in the next (verse 26)

Words like *thirst* and *fire* should be taken figuratively. The torments are real but not physical—the body has been buried or disposed of (verse 22). The afterlife is in the spirit world.

How to avoid going to hell:

- Pay attention to *"Moses and the Prophets"*—the Word of God, written and preached (Luke 16:29, 31).
- Repent. Change your way of living (verses 30–31).

It's wrong to think
some are destined for
poverty while others
are destined for
luxury.

☞ **GO TO:**

Luke 10:38–42
(Mary, Martha)

John 12:1–8; Mark 14:9
(poured perfume)

John 9:2–3
(for God's glory)

John 7:39; 12:16, 23,
27–28, 31–32; 13:31;
17:1 (glorified)

John 10:40–42 (Perea)

☞ **Check It Out:**

John 11

Lazarus: *not the previous
beggar, but a wealthy
man*

love: *Greek: phileo,
"good friend"*

glorified: *Jesus used this
term to refer to the end of
his life—crucifixion, death,
burial, resurrection, and
ascension*

"Lucky Me! Too Bad About You."

The rich man's sin was not that he did nasty things to Lazarus. He
didn't chase him away from his gate. Nor did he refuse him first
crack at his garbage. He didn't kick him while he was down. All
he did was buy into the fatalistic idea that some people are meant
to be rich and others are meant to be poor.

He thought it was okay (even God's will, perhaps) for him to
live in luxury while Lazarus lived on the street and died of malnu-
trition and lack of medical care. Dives simply closed his eyes to
any suggestion that the beggar at his gate was his responsibility!

The tale has one main message: Nobody can love both God and
money (Luke 16:13–15). If a person loves God, he or she will
invest money and wealth in caring for others. According to Jesus
(Luke 6:36, 38; 12:32–34), love for God expresses itself in doing
something with our wealth to correct the injustices that go with
poverty. With wealth goes responsibility to care for the poor.

> **John 11:1–4** Now a man named **Lazarus** was sick. He
> was from Bethany, the village of <u>Mary</u> and her sister
> <u>Martha</u>. This Mary, whose brother Lazarus now lay sick,
> was the same one who <u>poured perfume</u> on the Lord
> and wiped his feet with her hair. So the sisters sent
> word to Jesus, "Lord, the one you **love** is sick."
> When he heard this, Jesus said, "This sickness will
> not end in death. No, it is <u>for God's glory</u> so that God's
> Son may be **glorified** through it."

Life-Giving Friend

When the message came about Lazarus' illness, Jesus was preaching in <u>Perea</u>, across the Jordan River, about 20 miles east of the
village of Bethany (see appendix A). When his 12 friends heard
him say Lazarus' illness would not end in death, they interpreted
it to mean the illness was temporary—Lazarus would recover.

Jesus, however, was looking beyond his friend's sickness and
death to the greatest miracle of his career (except for his own
resurrection), and he saw glory for God and himself.

The Mystery Of Waiting

The historian, John, reminds his readers that *"Jesus loved Martha
and her sister and Lazarus"* (John 11:5). The word for *"love"* here
is *agape*, Greek for the most perfect kind of love. The writer's point

seems to be: Don't misinterpret Jesus' next actions as a lack of love.

"When he heard that Lazarus was sick, he stayed where he was two more days" (verse 6). He didn't delay his departure to Bethany because he didn't care, but precisely because he cared so much!

Don't get the idea he was waiting for Lazarus to die. That would seem cruel and inconsistent with everything else we know about Jesus of Nazareth. The fact is, Lazarus was dead before the messenger ever found Jesus to deliver the message. Do the math:

1 day—time for the message-bearer to travel the 20 miles from Bethany to Perea

2 days—time Jesus and his men hung around Perea after the message came

1 day—time for Jesus to travel the 20 miles from Perea to Bethany

---

4 days—total time from dispatch of the messenger to Jesus' arrival at Bethany

Upon arrival, how long did they tell him Lazarus had been dead and in the grave? Four days (verse 17). In the first century, Jews buried the dead the same day they died. Rabbis taught that the grave should be visited for three days following burial to be sure the person was really dead. (One rabbi taught that the soul hung around for three days, hoping to return to the body; in three days it could tell by the color of the corpse's face it was really dead, then it would leave.)

Jesus, however, had a different <u>purpose</u> in his procrastination. He wanted there to be no doubt Lazarus was dead, so when he raised him from the dead there would be no doubt it was a miracle. The <u>effect</u> on the faith of his friends hinged on the official certification that Lazarus was dead.

> **John 11:7–8** Then he said to his disciples, "Let us go back to Judea."
> "But Rabbi," they said, "a short while ago the Jews tried to stone you, and yet you are going back there?"

Daylight March To Risk And Glory

At Jesus' words protests erupted from his men. Still fresh in their memories was the confrontation at Hanukkah, when the leaders tried to stone Jesus for his claim to be one with God (John 10:30–31).

KEY POINT

God often does special things for us that can only happen if we are willing to wait.

☞ **GO TO:**

Psalm 37:7–8; Isaiah 40:31; Acts 1:4–5; Romans 8:18–25 (purpose)

Romans 5:1–5; 1 Peter 1:6–8 (effect)

☞ **Check It Out:**

John 11:7–16

Twelve hours: *every day was divided into 12 hours no matter the season or length*

"*Are there not* **twelve hours** *of daylight?*" he answered. "*A man who walks by day will not stumble, for he sees by this world's light. It is when he walks by night that he stumbles, for he has no light*" (John 11:9–10).

It was one of those "Jesus-isms," figures of speech that kept his followers scrambling to understand. What he meant was something like, "God has given me a certain amount of time in which to do what I was sent to do. I've always 'walked in daylight.' That is, I've followed the Father's plan and timetable. What is ahead is the most crucial part of my work. I won't stop walking in the light now."

He also meant to assure his friends they did not have to be afraid to go with him into dangerous territory—"As long as you have me (the Light) you won't stumble."

☞ **GO TO:**

John 8:12 (the Light)

KEY POINT

There is no good time to stop walking in the bright daylight of God's will.

KINGDOM OF GOD

Jesus was also giving his future apostles a principle to shape their own approach to work in the kingdom after he was gone.

1. Each day offers a limited number of hours of opportunity to do what we are called to do. Everyone has to live and work within those time limits. Nobody, for example, has more than seven days a week. No one is expected to do more than he or she can do in the allotted time. Whatever time we are given, it is enough to accomplish what God has in mind for us. There is no need to rush or be anxious. It is important to wisely use the time God gives.

2. It is important to walk in the light during time we are given. God is light (1 John 1:5). Christ is the light of the world (John 8:12). Walking in the light means following God's instructions and living by his plan and timetable. This is how we keep from **stumbling**. Those who live and work in the dark—without God's light—will stumble because they don't have enough light to walk safely.

☞ **GO TO:**

Ephesians 5:15–21 (use the time)

1 John 1:7; John 3:19–21 (walk)

Luke 8:52; Acts 7:60; 1 Corinthians 11:30; 15:17–18 (asleep)

stumbling: *failure, entrapment*

asleep: *Bible often speaks of believers' death as "falling asleep"*

> **John 11:11–14** "Our friend Lazarus has fallen **asleep**; but I am going there to wake him up."
>
> His disciples replied, "Lord, if he sleeps, he will get better." Jesus had been speaking of his death, but his disciples thought he meant natural sleep.
>
> So then he told them plainly, "Lazarus is dead."

The Ultimate Nap

His disciples thought he meant, "He's sleeping"—a sign he was on the mend. Not so. Jesus restated it clearly: *"Lazarus is dead."* For the believer in Christ, death is merely a pause, a moment of sleep, from which we <u>immediately awake</u> in the presence of the Lord.

☞ **GO TO:**

Luke 16:22–23; 23:43;
  2 Corinthians 5:8;
  Philippians 1:21–23
  (immediately awake)

What Others are Saying:

Leon Morris: In the New Testament death for the believer is characteristically spoken of as "sleep." . . . Few things illustrate more graphically the difference the coming of Christ made than this. Throughout the ancient world the fear of death was universal. Death was a grim adversary that all men feared and no man could defeat. But Christ's resurrection altered all that for his followers. For them death no longer was a hateful foe. Its sting was drawn (1 Corinthians 15:55). . . . Death is no more now than sleep.[7]

KEY POINT

Believers' death is the ultimate nap and is often called "sleep."

> **John 11:16** Then Thomas (called Didymus) said to the rest of the disciples, "Let us also go, that we may die with him."

The Resurrection And The Life

With a visible shrug of resignation, the 12 men close to Jesus fell in behind him, headed back into hostile territory. Thomas (sometimes called "<u>doubting Thomas</u>") was the first to confess his "faith" that they were all headed for death! But, bless his pessimistic little heart, he was the first in line to volunteer.

As they approached Bethany, word of Jesus' arrival reached Mary and Martha (see GWWB, pages 257–269). It was the fourth day after Lazarus' death, the day professional mourners, flute players, and hired wailing women really hit the crescendo in their funereal racket. Martha went out to meet Jesus.

Mary was too overcome with grief. She **stayed** in the house where the mournful chaos harmonized with her heart-wrenching pain.

After the body was taken out of the house, chairs and couches were reversed; mourners sat on the floor or on low stools to grieve.[8]

☞ **Check It Out:**

John 11:16–44

☞ **GO TO:**

John 20:25
  (doubting Thomas)

stayed: literally, "she sat"

> **John 11:21** "Lord," Martha said to Jesus, "if only you had been here, my brother would not have died. But I know that even now God will give you whatever you ask."

The Evolution Of Resurrection Faith

Martha was aware that Lazarus had died before the message of his illness could reach Jesus. Her "if only," sometimes interpreted as <u>scolding</u>, was more likely an expression of grief and regret, mingled with enough faith to think that, if he had been present, he could have kept her brother alive.

In a flash of impulse, she spoke her wildest dream. But immediately she probably told herself to forget it. Might Jesus raise her brother from the dead? He'd <u>done it before</u> for others.

"Your brother will rise again," Jesus assured her.

Martha believed in the future, <u>end-time resurrection</u>. Serious Jews did. *"I know he will rise again in the resurrection at the last day"* (verse 24).

> **John 11:25–26** Jesus said to her, "I am the resurrection and the life. He who believes in me will live, even though he dies; and whoever lives and believes in me will never die."

The Bedrock Of Believing

This is one of the most startling statements Jesus ever made.

He was taking Martha from where her faith was to the bedrock foundation on which her faith was built.

Resurrection hope is more than a mist-shrouded future event we can only imagine, a subject for professors of biblical **eschatology** to wrangle about. Resurrection is entirely wrapped up in a living person.

The *"**resurrection** and the **life**"* was standing in front of Martha, talking with her, at that very moment! Her friend Jesus.

This is an awesome claim. It is not the kind of statement that could be made by a man who was merely an ordinary man. It puts him in another category. Either he is a liar, or he is more than appears on the surface.

Jesus claimed not only to have the power to give life and raise the dead; he claimed to be the <u>source</u> of life. He meant that the existence of all forms of life was and is dependent on him and that he, personally, was and is the substance of life.

☞ **GO TO:**

Luke 10:40 (scolding)

Luke 7:14–15; 8:53–55 (done it before)

1 Corinthians 15; 1 Thessalonians 4:13–18; Revelation 20:4–6 (end-time resurrection)

---

eschatology: *science of future events, study of prophecy*

resurrection: *the power and promise to bring the dead to life*

life: *source and sustainer of all life, including life from the dead*

☞ **GO TO:**

John 1:3–4; 5:26; 14:6 (source)

He is the <u>fountainhead</u> of resurrection. If anyone rises from the dead, it will be because of him. And because of him, resurrection is a certainty!

Jesus further insisted that anyone who puts his or her personal faith in him is <u>alive</u>. It is impossible to kill such a person! Death is for dead people, not those who have eternal life. Consequently, eternal death is an impossibility for the person who trusts his or her life and destiny to Jesus.

Jesus was not saying the person who trusts in him will never have to face physical death. The context in which the statement is made makes that clear—Lazarus, a believer, had died. (And, poor guy, he would have to do it again!) Since Jesus made this claim, millions of other believers, including all the apostles, have died. What he was saying is that physical death is strictly under his control and is definitely temporary for the person who, by faith, has placed himself in Jesus' care.

When a believer's body succumbs to death, his or her spirit lives on—alive in God and alive to God, in intimate, uninterrupted fellowship and communication with Christ. Eternal death (the hellish torment of never ending separation from God) will never happen to the person who believes on Jesus Christ, because the moment a person trusts Jesus, he or she becomes the <u>possessor</u> of eternal life.

The Future Resurrection of the Dead

Find and read the following passages. Note what you can learn from each passage concerning the future resurrection.

Job 14:13–14	John 5:28–29
Job 19:25–27	John 11:25–26
Exodus 3:6; Matthew 22:31–32	John 20:17
Psalm 16:8–11	1 Corinthians 15:20–24
Psalm 49:14	1 Corinthians 15:35–58
Isaiah 26:19	Philippians 3:21
Daniel 12:2	1 Thessalonians 4:13–18
Matthew 17:23	Revelation 20:11–14
Luke 16:22–24	

> **John 11:26b–27** "Do you believe this?" [Jesus asked.] "Yes, Lord," she told him, "I believe that you are the Christ, the Son of God, who was to come into the world."

☞ **GO TO:**

John 5:21, 24–25, 28–29 (fountainhead)

John 5:24; 10:10; Romans 5:9–10; 1 Corinthians 15:22 (alive)

1 John 5:12–13 (possessor)

Dig Deeper

Getting Faith Out Where You Can Look At It

At the strategic moment when all appearances were to the contrary, and everyone around her was wailing their belief that the opposite was true, and her own mind grappled to understand what Jesus was saying, it was important for Martha to put her faith into <u>words</u>.

Martha sometimes gets a bad rap as a person fussing about secondary things, a compulsive housekeeper, a critic of her sister's more laid-back approach to faith. But, talking to Jesus at that difficult moment, she demonstrated she was a woman of genuine faith, carefully thought through.

The original word for *"I believe"* indicates Martha's faith in Jesus was no quick-draw, glib-lipped credo, but something "once given and permanently remaining."[9]

A better translation would be "I *have* believed." Her faith was not a vague, mushy abstraction—a thoughtless nod to "the man upstairs." It came from a place deep inside and was full of content. She knew what she believed and could state it in certain terms. Martha <u>believed</u>:

- Jesus was *"the Christ"* (Messiah) the Jews had been expecting.
- Jesus was *"the Son of God"*—the unique "One and Only" expression of God's own nature.
- Jesus was the One *"who was to come into the world"*—the Savior the prophets predicted God would send.

> **John 11:32** When Mary reached the place where Jesus was and saw him, she fell at his feet and said, "Lord, if you had been here, my brother would not have died."

Grave Sorrow

Mary was brought from her place of mourning to where Jesus and Martha had been talking.

The entourage of mourners trooped along with her, thinking she was going to her brother's tomb to continue the grieving process.

When she saw Jesus, the more emotional sister fell down at his feet and repeated the same "if only" lament her sister had verbalized earlier.

KEY Outline:

Martha's Faith Development

Sent for Jesus
"If only"
"Whatever you ask"
"He will rise"
"You are Christ, God's Son"
Let the stone be rolled away

> **John 11:33–37** When Jesus saw her weeping, and the Jews who had come along with her also weeping, he was **deeply moved** in spirit and **troubled**.
> "Where have you laid him?" he asked.
> "Come and see, Lord," they replied.
> Jesus **wept**.
> Then the Jews said, "See how he loved him!"
> But some of them said, "Could not he who <u>opened the eyes</u> of the blind man have kept this man from dying?"

deeply moved: literally, "snorted like a horse"; was indignant, angry, intensely displeased

troubled: Greek: inwardly distressed, troubled, disgusted

wept: literally, "shed tears"

☞ **GO TO:**

John 9 (opened the eyes)

Grave Rage

The meanings of the original words John, the author, uses in telling this story (see sidebar) reveal that, as he approached the cave where the body of Lazarus was buried, Jesus felt a very intense mix of sorrow and anger.

Anger? At the grave of his friend? We know he wasn't weeping for Lazarus (see verses 4 and 15). Why was he so angry he snorted like a horse?

Perhaps it was the unbelief represented in the hopeless wails of the professional mourners or the thought of death's destructive and unnecessary grip on humans or the tragedy of the human situation caused by humanity's sin, combined with the personal heartbreak suffered by his dear friends Mary and Martha.

Most likely, though, his rage was against the archenemy of God—the devil, the "thief" Jesus says comes against God's flock with no other purpose than to "kill, steal, and destroy" (see John 10:10).

B. B. Warfield: It is death that is the object of [Jesus'] wrath, and behind death, him who has the power of death and whom [Jesus] has come into the world to destroy. Tears of sympathy may fill his eyes, but this is incidental. His soul is held by rage: and he advances to the tomb, in Calvin's words . . . "as a champion who prepares for conflict." The raising of Lazarus thus becomes . . . a decisive instance and open symbol of Jesus' conquest of death and hell. . . . John . . . uncover[s] to us the heart of Jesus, as he wins for us our salvation. Not in cold unconcern, but in flaming wrath against the foe, Jesus smites on our behalf.[10]

Henri J. M. Nouwen: The one who sees unceasingly the limitless goodness of God came to the world, saw it broken to pieces

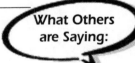

🔑 **KEY Outline:**

Jesus at Lazarus' Tomb
Angry
Troubled
Weeping
Praying
Conquered death

What Others are Saying:

by human sin, and was moved to compassion. The same eyes which see into the heart of God saw the suffering hearts of God's people and wept (John 11:35). These eyes which burn like flames of fire penetrating God's own interiority, also hold oceans of tears for the human sorrow. . . .[11]

> **John 11:39–40** "Take away the stone," he said.
> "But, Lord," said Martha, the sister of the dead man, "by this time there is a bad odor, for he has been there four days."
> Then Jesus said, "Did I not tell you that if you believed, you would see the glory of God?"

The Death Destroyer

At the tomb, Jesus again expressed his rage with a deep sigh (verse 38). *"Take away the stone," he said.* According to custom, a huge, flat stone had been rolled over the entrance to the **burial cave**.

At first, Martha recoiled from the prospect of death's unpleasant **odor**. Her brother's body would have begun to decompose by now. But Jesus assured her that if she trusted him she should not expect something horrible, but something wonderful (verse 40).

At Martha's nod, several men moved to the entrance of the tomb and rolled away the heavy stone.

Jesus prayed a simple prayer: (1) to assure that all the glory would go to his Father in heaven for the wonder that was about to take place, and (2) to assure that the people would see this miracle as a sign of Jesus' messiahship.

> **John 11:42–43** "Father, I thank you that you have heard me. I knew that you always hear me, but I said this for the benefit of the people standing here, that they may believe that you sent me." When he had said this, Jesus called in a loud voice, "Lazarus, come out."

Y'All Come!

In the words John originally wrote to describe this happening, the order Jesus shouted to the corpse in the tomb literally was: "Lazarus! Here! Outside!"

The mourners fell silent. Every eye was fixed on the dark opening of the grave cave. Nobody breathed.

Something moved inside the tomb. A few shuffling sounds. Then

burial cave: cave cut in a rock hillside; 6 feet long, 9 feet wide, 10 feet high, with shelves cut in the walls for several bodies

odor: Jews packed their dead with spices to counteract decomposition odors

KEY Outline:

Jesus' Joy
God's glory
Christ's glorification
Disciples' faith
Martha and Mary's faith
The peoples' faith
Leaders' ("Jews") faith

suddenly in the entrance of the cavern appeared a startled, struggling figure wrapped from head to foot in strips of white linen!

"Take off the grave clothes and let him go!" Jesus said. Lazarus, certified dead man, was living again!

Jesus' prayer for the faith of his friends' friends was answered: *"Many of the Jews who had come to visit Mary, and had seen what Jesus did, put their faith in him"* (John 11:45).

Something to Ponder

> Jesus promised that the time will come when all who are in their graves will hear his voice and come out (John 5:28–29).
>
> I have read that the late atheist Robert Ingersoll claimed, in public lectures, that Lazarus' resurrection was a fraud hatched between Jesus and Lazarus to deceive people. Lazarus, Ingersoll claimed, hid in the tomb so that when Jesus called his name, he could come out, and everyone would be convinced Jesus had raised him from the dead.
>
> At one of his lectures Ingersoll, in the course of describing this supposed scam, asked his audience, "Why did Jesus call Lazarus' name?" A Christian in the back of the room spoke up: "Because if my Lord had not specified Lazarus, the whole graveyard at Bethany would have risen!"

> **John 11:45–46** Therefore many of the Jews who had come to visit Mary, and had seen what Jesus did, put their faith in him. But some of them went to the Pharisees and told them what Jesus had done.

Assassins' Plot

Some who were there in Bethany comforting the sisters were Pharisee informers.

They went directly from Lazarus' resurrection party to the Pharisees in Jerusalem, just two miles away, and reported what Jesus had done and the effect it was having on the people. An emergency meeting of the Sanhedrin was called.

The deliberate blindness of people who refuse to believe even when they see irrefutable proof is astounding. The tattling witnesses and the Jewish religious leaders actually admitted to one another that Jesus was performing real miracles and that these miracles were "signs" (the word means "proofs," "evidence") that he was from God (John 11:47). In the face of the evidence, their concern was for their own positions of political and ecclesiastical power (verses 47–48).

Another astounding thing is the evidence God was at work even among these rebellious, self-motivated men. Though it was the last thing he intended, Caiaphas, the High Priest, one of Jesus' most committed enemies, spoke prophetic words the early Christians recognized as coming from God:

"You know nothing at all!" he said, *"You do not realize that it is better for you that one man die for the people than that the whole nation perish."* The New Testament historian adds this comment: *"He did not say this on his own, but as high priest that year he prophesied that Jesus would die for the Jewish nation, and not only for that nation but also for the scattered children of God, to bring them together and make them one"* (John 11:49–52).

Under Caiaphas' "inspired" leadership, the Sanhedrin officially agreed Jesus must die. Thus the specific plot which culminated in his crucifixion was born the day Lazarus lived again.

KEY POINT

God speaks even through his enemies.

☞ **GO TO:**

Numbers 22:21–35 (donkey)

What Others are Saying:

Larry (Lawrence O.) Richards: John points out that Caiaphas "did not say this on his own." It was an unwitting prophecy. . . . We need to remember that God is not limited. At one time he spoke even through a <u>donkey</u>![12]

Study Questions

1. Finish this statement of Jesus: "What is highly valued among men is ___."
   What did the Pharisees value most highly? (See Luke 16:15.)
   Who did Jesus say they were serving instead of God?
2. Identify three characteristics of hell revealed in the story of the rich man and Lazarus.
3. How long had Jesus' friend Lazarus been dead when Jesus raised him from the dead? In conversation with Lazarus' sister Martha, what did Jesus say could never happen? What did he mean?
4. Identify four things Martha believed about Jesus (John 11:22, 27). What did Jesus promise she would see if she believed?
5. If you had been there and saw Jesus crying, how would you have felt? (a) embarrassed: Grown men don't cry, (b) relieved: It's okay to cry, (c) awkward: Let's get on with it, (d) mad: You could have done something if you had gotten here earlier, and now all you can do is blubber, (e) comforted: He really cared,[13] or (f) other: _____ .

- With two parables Jesus taught the difference between the world's way of handling money and his followers' way. He called for creativity in investing in others, and for awareness that how we invest our possessions has eternal consequences. (John 16:1–31)

- Jesus' friend Lazarus died. He and his disciples returned to Bethany (two miles from Jerusalem), where Jesus raised Lazarus from the dead and announced, *"I am the resurrection and the life"* (John 11:25).

- Some Jewish leaders put their faith in Jesus when they saw Lazarus rise from the dead. Others reported it to the Pharisees. At an emergency meeting of the Sanhedrin the high priest unwittingly prophesied Jesus would be sacrificed for the people. Plans were made to arrest and kill Jesus. (John 11:45–53)

7 FINAL JOURNEY TO JERUSALEM

CHAPTER HIGHLIGHTS

- Walking Dead Men
- What Is This Kingdom of God?
- The Hotline of Prayer
- On Marriage and Children
- The Love of Money
- Leader as Servant
- While Passing through Jericho

GOSPEL QUARTET IN HARMONY

Matthew 19–20
Mark 10
Luke 17:11–19:28
John 11:54

Let's Get Started

As soon as the miracle of Lazarus of Bethany was reported to the leaders at Jerusalem they met to lay specific plans to end the young Nazarene's career (John 11:53). What else could they do? The choice was clear: Either embrace and endorse Jesus, or . . . assassinate him! Operation Assassination, Phase 1, was the official order calling for Jesus' immediate arrest (verse 57).

Always aware of his Father's timetable, Jesus quietly slipped out of Bethany and took his men to the Judean mountain village of Ephraim, about 15 miles north (see appendix A). This was the final retreat before the final march to the final Passover in the Holy City.

As the time approached for pilgrims to head toward Jerusalem and the Passover, Jesus and his men trekked northward through Samaria to Galilee (see appendix A), in time to join the throngs of Galilean travelers on their way south.

> **Luke 17:12–16** As he [Jesus] was going into a village, ten men who had leprosy met him. They stood at a distance and called out in a loud voice, "Jesus, Master, have pity on us!" When he saw them, he said, "Go, show yourselves to the priests." And as they went, they were cleansed. One of them, when he saw he was healed, came back, praising God in a loud voice. He threw himself at Jesus' feet and thanked him—and he was a Samaritan.

Walking Dead Men

leprosy: contagious skin disorders; Hansen's Disease

☞ **GO TO:**

Leviticus 13–14 (law)

As Jesus and his men were about to enter a village in the disputed territory along the border between Galilee and Samaria, a pitiful group of 10 men with **leprosy** met them. In compliance with the <u>law</u> concerning lepers, they remained outside of town, loudly calling attention to their condition. The law required lepers to cover their upper lip and cry "Unclean!" They also had to keep away from people. If the wind blew from the leper's direction, a distance of "100 paces" (50 yards) was maintained between the public and the leper.

Usually the leper's cry was to protect other people from entering their quarantine zone. In this case, it was a call for help: *"Jesus, Master, have pity on us!"*

Jesus immediately challenged them to act on their faith. According to Old Testament Law, healed lepers must show themselves to a priest who could certify their cure (Leviticus 14).

With the symptoms still visible, it took faith to go to the priest as Jesus ordered. *"As they went, they were cleansed"* (Luke 17:14)—the diseased flesh became healthy, the symptoms disappeared.

One-Man Praise Band

One of the 10, when he discovered his body was free of disease, broke ranks with the others and returned shouting praise to God at the top of his healed lungs! He threw himself down at Jesus' feet and thanked him. Luke notes, *"He was a Samaritan"* (Luke 17:16).

"Were not all ten cleansed?" Jesus asked, *"Where are the other nine? Was no one found to return and give praise to God except this foreigner?* Then to the man he said, *"Rise and go; your faith has made you well"* (verses 17–19).

Hidden in Jesus' statements are a couple of ideas worth noting:

1. Jesus used different words to describe what happened to the nine who did not thank him and what happened to the one who did.

   - The original word for the healing of nine (*"cleansed"*) simply means they were cleansed of leprosy, physically healed.

   - The original for the healing of the thankful one (*"made . . . well"*) means he was completely healed, fully restored—it's a biblical word for *salvation*.

2. Jews held a deep and abiding prejudice against Samaritans. Jesus delighted in showing Samaritans and foreigners in a <u>good light</u>.

☞ **GO TO:**

Matthew 15:21–28; Luke 7:2–9; 10:29–37; John 4:4–42 (good light)

Tim Stafford: Praise of God is fundamental to my relationship with him. It opens a channel of loving regard. When I bring my requests to God, I stand by him looking toward mutual concerns, but when I praise him my eyes are lifted in intimacy and warmth toward him. I look to his face.[1]

What Others are Saying:

Harry Emerson Fosdick: [Jesus] cared for persons one by one, and his concern about them and desire to help them were stopped by no economic, national or racial lines. . . . Jesus' thought of every soul as infinitely precious in the sight of God was one of his incontestable characteristics.[2]

KEY Outline:

Power of Faith and Gratitude
Body—healed
Spirit—saved

> **Luke 17:20–21** Once, having been asked by the Pharisees when the kingdom of God would come, Jesus replied, "The kingdom of God does not come with your careful observation, nor will people say, 'Here it is,' or 'There it is,' because the kingdom of God is within you."

What Is This Kingdom Of God?

Jesus had begun his public ministry three years earlier <u>announcing</u> arrival of the kingdom of God. People looking for him to establish a visible, earthly government were still looking.

The Pharisees, always out to embarrass him, pressed the issue, as if to say to Jesus, "You've said the kingdom of God is near. All right, Teacher, when is this kingdom of yours going to come?"

☞ **Check It Out:**

Luke 17:20–18:14

☞ **GO TO:**

Matthew 4:17; Mark 1:14–15; Luke 4:43 (announcing)

Matthew 13:33; Luke 13:20–21 (secret)

KINGDOM OF GOD

The Kingdom Here and Now

Jesus' answer said two things about the kingdom of God: (1) you can't find it by spying (*"careful observation"*) to find something to use against Christ (Luke 17:20), and (2) the kingdom is a <u>secret</u> within-you operation; don't expect it to appear in some familiar form in an identifiable geographical location with a flashing neon sign saying, "Welcome to God's kingdom!"

Far from helping to bring in the kingdom, Israel's rejection of its Messiah forced the kingdom-of-God movement "underground" in the hearts and minds of people, unrecognized and unblessed by the powers that be.

What Others are Saying:

Howard A. Snyder: The central battleground in the struggle between God's kingdom and Satan's counterfeit is people's minds and hearts. It is here where the clash of wills takes place. . . . Something strange and wonderful is happening in the world, and

KEY POINT

The kingdom of God is a spiritual reality happening within and among God's people.

KEY POINT

The kingdom is not built on Christ's visible presence but on the presence of his Spirit.

revealed: Greek: apokolypto, "disclosure"

☞ **GO TO:**

Matthew 24:5–11, 23–25; Mark 13:21–23; Luke 21:8–9
(false predictions)

Matthew 24:30; 26:64; 1 Timothy 6:14; Titus 2:13 (see him)

Genesis 6:1–12
(Noah's time)

Genesis 19:1–15, 24–29; Ezekiel 16:49–50
(Lot left)

Mark 8:34–38;
1 Corinthians 7:29–31; 1 John 2:15–17
(detachment)

the world does not know what it is. And it won't believe because it sees no great power—no armies or parliaments to impress it. But Christians know the kingdom of God has appeared in Jesus, is now present implicitly in the church, is at work secretly in the world and will come in true, creative, restoring and judging power when Jesus Christ returns to earth.[3]

> **Luke 17:24–25** For the Son of Man in his day will be like the lightning, which flashes and lights up the sky from one end to the other. But first he must suffer many things and be rejected by this generation.

The Kingdom To Come

Turning to his own people, Jesus talked of the future. In the near future they would remember the special days they had spent with him, man to man, and would ache to return to them. But his death, resurrection, and ascension would make that impossible.

The kingdom would not be built on Christ's visible presence (Luke 17:22). He took them still deeper into the future with his discussion of the *"day when the Son of Man is **revealed**"* (verse 30)—the time of Christ's second return.

The Second Coming

The Day the Kingdom Comes

The day of Christ's Second Coming will be like no other time.

- That day will be preceded by <u>false predictions</u> of his coming (Luke 17:23)—stay cool; don't be misled.

- That day the whole world will <u>see him</u> (verse 24).

- That day will be like <u>Noah's time</u>; people will be occupied with satisfying physical needs, and miss God's warning signals (verses 26–27).

- That day will be like the day <u>Lot left</u> Sodom when people were so busy with production quotas and institution building they failed to notice God's fire-and-brimstone judgment was about to break loose (verses 28–30).

- Survival in that day will depend on having developed an attitude of <u>detachment</u> from the things of this world—possessions, jobs, homes, even life itself (verses 31–33).

- That day will disrupt the most intimate of human relationships (verses 34–35).

"Where, Lord?" his disciples asked. He told them to watch for where the **carrion-eating birds** were flocking together. The judgments of which he spoke were going to fall wherever there is **spiritual death**. So <u>stay alive</u>!

William Barclay: The coming of Christ is certain, but its time is quite unknown. Speculation is vain. People will come with false prophecies and false predictions: but we must not leave our ordinary work to follow them. The best way that Christ can come upon a man is when he is faithfully and humbly and watchfully doing his duty.[4]

Unknown author: No man will foresee it, and all men will see it.[5]

The Hotline Of Prayer

Since the kingdom of God is *"within you"* and is built around the spiritual rather than visible presence of Jesus, the chief system for communication between kingdom citizens and their King is the hotline of prayer. On the road toward Jerusalem, Jesus told two stories to illustrate prayers that fulfill kingdom goals.

> **Luke 18:1–5** Then Jesus told his disciples a parable to show them that they should always pray and not give up. He said: "In a certain town there was a judge who neither feared God nor cared about men. And there was a widow in that town who kept coming to him with the plea, 'Grant me justice against my adversary.'
> "For some time he refused. But finally he said to himself, 'Even though I don't fear God or care about men, yet because this widow keeps bothering me, I will see that she gets justice, so that she won't eventually wear me out with her coming!'"

Prayer As A Fight For Justice

If a crooked, godless judge will grant justice when confronted with courage and persistence, God, who cares about people and loves righteousness and justice, eagerly waits for people to come to him for help! If the justice we pray for is delayed, we can be

---

carrion-eating birds: vultures, which consume dead animals

spiritual death: separation from God caused by independence from God

What Others are Saying:

☞ **GO TO:**

Revelation 3:1–3 (stay alive!)

☞ **Check It Out:**

Luke 18:1–14

KEY Outline:

Days of Christ's Return
False predictions
Business as usual
Unaware of impending judgment
All will see him
Survival depends on detachment

☞ **GO TO:**

2 Peter 3:8–9 (waiting)

Who's Who

Who's Who

justice: fair treatment, an honest verdict including restitution

KEY Outline:

Judge
Unjust
Unconcerned
Worn out

Widow
Powerless
Courageous
Persistent

God
Just
Concerned
Eager to help

justified: right with God; declared righteous or innocent

fast: skipping meals

tithe: 10 percent of income was given to the Temple

sure it is because he is <u>waiting</u> for people to repent and turn to him in faith (Luke 18:8).

THE JUDGE: An unjust man (verse 6), without fear of God or concern for people (verse 2). Both Herod and the Romans hired men to serve as magistrates. The people called these notoriously corrupt men "robber judges." A bribe could buy you a verdict. Poor people had little hope of justice.

THE WIDOW: A typical first-century widow, she had been left without resources for bribery. Only courage, persistence, and knowledge that her cause was right gave this woman clout. She nagged the judge for **justice** until he acted on her behalf.

> **Luke 18:10–14** "Two men went up to the temple to pray, one a Pharisee and the other a tax collector. The Pharisee stood up and prayed about himself: 'God, I thank you that I am not like other men—robbers, evil-doers, adulterers—or even like this tax collector. I fast twice a week and give a tenth of all I get.'
>
> "But the tax collector stood at a distance. He would not even look up to heaven, but beat his breast and said, 'God, have mercy on me, a sinner.'
>
> "I tell you that this man, rather than the other, went home justified before God. For everyone who exalts himself will be humbled, and he who humbles himself will be exalted."

Prayer As A Cry For Justification

The next story Jesus told was especially for *"some who were confident of their own righteousness and looked down on everybody else"* (Luke 18:9). Self-righteousness is a hard sin to deal with, because nobody ever feels guilty for being "righteous." And it's a dangerous sin because no one is ever "**justified**" (verse 14) by comparing himself or herself with others to see if they are as good as or better than someone else.

This Pharisee went way beyond the requirements of the Law:

- *Fasting.* The Law required one **fast** a year, on Yom Kippur. He fasted twice a week.
- *Tithing.* The Law required a **tithe** of grain, new wine,

flocks, and herds. He paid tithes on everything (Luke 11:42), even garden herbs (see illustration below).

What a guy! God was lucky to have him.

THE PHARISEE (Luke 18:11–12): As a superfollower of the Jewish religion, he prayed three times a day (9 A.M., noon, and 3 P.M.). In his prayer he spent most of the time comparing himself with several kinds of sinners—"*robbers, evildoers, adulterers . . . this tax collector.*" Thank God! He was not like any of those rascals.

THE TAX COLLECTOR (verse 13): A man of very questionable character. Associated (as the Pharisee's prayer reminded him) with robbers, evildoers, and adulterers. His body language screamed, "Guilty!"—he stood in back; he wouldn't even look up; he *"beat his breast"* (sign of sorrow). *"God, have **mercy** on me, a sinner!"*

Why was this admitted "bad guy" accepted by God, while the Pharisee wasn't?
  The Pharisee expected God to accept him based on how he compared with other people; the tax collector <u>compared</u> himself with God and knew he didn't have a chance without God's mercy.

William Barclay: No man who despises his fellowmen can pray. In prayer we do not lift ourselves above our fellow men. We re-

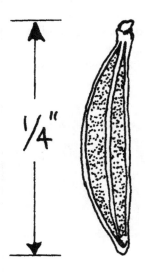

Who's Who

mercy: *God's compassionate response to sinners; pardon*

Who's Who

☞ **GO TO:**

Romans 3:23
(compared)

**Something
to Ponder**

**What Others
are Saying:**

Cummin Tithe

The herb, cummin or cumin, from a small plant in the parsley family, was tithed by legalistic Pharisees. The seeds inside were carefully counted in order to give God 10 percent.

member that we are one of a great army of sinning, suffering, sorrowing humanity, all kneeling before the throne of God's mercy.[6]

On Marriage And Children

A hot topic in that day as in ours was the question of divorce. No culture had ever held marriage in such high esteem as the Jews did. They took God's earliest commandment to *"be fruitful and increase in number"* (Genesis 1:28) very seriously. According to ancient teachings, to fail to be married and produce children was to "lessen the image of God on the earth."[7]

But the rabbis, official interpreters of the Old Testament Law, were all over the map on the subject of divorce.

- Rabbi Shammai and his followers taught that **adultery** was the only legitimate grounds for divorce.
- Rabbi Hillel, however, took a considerably more liberal view: "A man may divorce his wife even if she burned his soup."
- Rabbi Akiba held that a man had the right to divorce his wife "if he should find a woman fairer than his wife."

The Pharisees tried to get Jesus to take sides in the debate. They may have figured that, no matter which rabbi he sided with, he'd make somebody mad! Jesus refused to take the bait.

Instead he raised the marriage and divorce issue to a new level.

The Pharisees had asked what was "lawful." Jesus took them back behind the Law to the story of creation in the Book of Genesis.

Matthew 19:4–6 "Haven't you read," he replied, "that <u>at the beginning</u> the Creator 'made them male and female,' and said, 'For this reason a man will leave his father and mother and be united to his wife, and the two will become one flesh'? So they are no longer two, but one. Therefore what God has joined together, let man not separate."

GOSPEL QUARTET IN HARMONY

Matthew 19:1–12
Mark 10:1–12

KEY POINT

To get right with God we must compare ourselves with him, not other people.

adultery: sexual unfaithfulness to one's marriage partner

KEY Outline:

Two Pray-ers
Pharisee
- religious
- holier-than-thou
- comparing
- no answer

Tax collector
- admitted sinner
- deep grief
- desperate for grace
- forgiven

☞ GO TO:

Genesis 2:24
(at the beginning)

Jesus On Marriage

From the creation story Jesus drew these insights on marriage:

- *Man and woman.* God created marriage by making human beings *"male and female,"* giving them to each other and commissioning them to bear children (Matthew 19:4; Genesis 1:27–28; 2:22–23).

- *Monogamy.* God's original design called for **monogamous** marriage, like Adam's and Eve's—one man with one woman (Matthew 19:5; Genesis 2:24; GWGN, pages 31–34). **Polygamy** was permitted and existed among Jews even in the first century, but was never the Creator's ideal.

- *Oneness.* Marriage is a man and a woman—leaving all others to become *"**one flesh**"* (Matthew 19:5–6; Genesis 2:24). The two become "joined in such a way that they share everything in their journey of life together";[8] spiritually, emotionally, and physically; sexual union is "the ribbon that ties the marriage bundle together."

- *Permanence.* Marriage is intended to be permanent (Matthew 19:6; Malachi 2:13–16; WBFW, pages 94–104).

> **Matthew 19:8–9** Jesus replied, "Moses permitted you to divorce your wives because your hearts were hard. But it was not this way from the beginning. I tell you that anyone who divorces his wife, except for marital unfaithfulness, and marries another woman commits adultery."

Jesus On Divorce

The Pharisees were less than thrilled with his first answer, so they hit him up again: *"Why then did Moses command that a man give his wife a certificate of divorce and send her away?"* they argued. (A certificate of divorce was not an important court document; it was just a written notice by a husband saying, "She is not my wife, and I am not her husband.")

Jesus' response this time was clear:

- Divorce was never *commanded*, as the Pharisees erroneously said (Matthew 19:7). Divorce was *"permitted"* (Matthew 19:8; Deuteronomy 24:1).

- The reason God, through Moses, allowed divorce was because people's *"hearts were hard."* The Greek word for

monogamous: *one man married to one woman*

polygamy: *marriage to more than one partner*

one flesh: *man and woman joined together in body, mind, and emotions*

☞ **GO TO:**

Ephesians 5:21–33 (one flesh)

KEY Outline:

Marriage
Man and woman
Monogamy
Oneness
Permanence

☞ **GO TO:**

Deuteronomy 24:1–4 (Moses)

☞ **GO TO:**

Jeremiah 17:9; Romans
1:21–22, 28–32
(messed up)

Ezekiel 16; Hosea 2
(spiritual infidelity)

1 Corinthians 7:15
(desertion)

spiritual infidelity:
unfaithfulness to the
covenant (relationship)
with God

KEY POINT

The springboard
for right action
should not be hard-
heartedness, but
love.[9]

KEY Outline:

Jesus on Divorce
Not God's will
Permitted because
- hardness of heart
- marital
  unfaithfulness
- desertion

ACT OF THE HOLY SPIRIT

Provides the
spiritual energy to
make marriage work

accept: grasp, make
room in their thinking,
handle, "get it"

hard-hearted means obstinate, stubborn in opposing what
is right or reasonable, wrong-headed. (Let's face it! Sin has
royally <u>messed up</u> the human mind. Confused, stubborn
thinking and covenant-breaking actions distort relationships to the point where they become destructive instead
of supportive and healing.)

- Jesus took a stand against divorces of convenience. However, he made an exception for divorce in cases of *"marital
  unfaithfulness"* (Matthew 19:9). The Greek word is usually
  used for sexual promiscuity, but it can also be a metaphor
  for **spiritual infidelity**. Sex with a person who is not one's
  marriage partner shatters the marriage covenant, often
  beyond repair. Marital unfaithfulness can take other forms
  as well (such as <u>desertion</u>).

All forms of disloyalty to one's marriage vows come from hard-
heartedness, not love.

Jesus On Remarriage After Divorce

Among Jews it was assumed the divorced person, like one whose
spouse had died, would <u>remarry</u> (see Deuteronomy 24:2). Remarriage, like divorce, was not God's ideal, but his Law permitted it.

In his discussion with the Pharisees on the road to Jerusalem,
Jesus had this one thing to say about getting married after a divorce. If the divorce is not on valid grounds, neither is the remarriage. If the divorce is valid, remarriage is acceptable.

In his report of this incident, Mark (10:1–12) includes an insight Matthew fails to mention. In first-century Hebrew society, a
man could divorce his wife, but a woman could not divorce her
husband. If her husband decided to dump her, the best the woman
could hope for was to be given back the material assets she brought
into the marriage. Otherwise she had no say.

Jesus sweeps away this sexist inequality by addressing his remarks on divorce and remarriage to *both* men and women. According to Jesus the woman had equal rights with the man in
divorce and remarriage (Mark 10:11–12).

This was revolutionary. It turned that "men's world" upside
down! And it helps explain the shock expressed by his disciples.
Jesus' disciples commented (with shaking heads), *"If this is the
situation between a husband and wife, it is better not to marry"* (Matthew 19:10).

To which Jesus answered, *"Not everyone can **accept** this word
[about divorce and remarriage], but only those to whom it has been
given"* (verse 11).

People without access to the spiritual energy (see John 7:37–38; Acts 1:8; Philippians 2:13; 4:13) available through Christ can't be expected to live by his teachings. But those who believe and who have invited Christ to live in them have access to the power to do the right thing.

To people who have failed in marriage, or made bad choices in the past, the message of Jesus is hope and forgiveness, not condemnation. To see how he responds to divorced people, we need only remember how he responded to the multi-married-and-divorced woman at Jacob's well. He reached out to her with grace.

> **Matthew 19:12** For some are eunuchs because they were born that way; others were made that way by men; and others have renounced marriage because of the kingdom of heaven. The one who can accept this should accept it.

Jesus On Singleness

To the disciples' suggestion that it might be better to remain single than get married (Mathew 19:10), Jesus answered that some people are better equipped to do that than others. He used the term **eunuchs** to mean people who remain **celibate**.

He listed three reasons for celibacy:

1. Some are *"born that way"*—physically or psychologically unequipped for marriage.

2. Some are *"made that way"*—kings and queens sometimes chose men for royal service and had them castrated so they wouldn't be distracted from government duties by family responsibilities or so they could be trusted not to fool around with the king's harem.

3. Some *"have renounced marriage because of the kingdom of heaven,"* choosing to remain single in order to devote all their energies to God's service.

Most of us are better equipped to serve God as married people.

Gary M. Burge: Divorce is the tragic result of what becomes of humanity as it wrestles with sin and brokenness. Whenever a marriage fails, we should mourn it as tragic. But there should be no error so grave that it cannot be forgiven; no mistake beyond the reach of grace. Likewise, God is a God of renewal and restora-

Remember This . . .

Something to Ponder

☞ GO TO:

John 3:17–18;
Romans 8:1
(not condemnation)

John 4
(divorced woman)

KEY POINT

Men and women share equal rights and responsibilities in marriage, divorce, and remarriage.

eunuchs: *people unable to perform sexually*

celibate: *unmarried, abstaining from sexual intercourse*

☞ GO TO:

Acts 8:27–39
(royal service)

What Others are Saying:

tion. In some cases, this means restoring a marriage to its original partnership. In other cases . . . it means that remarriage is an opportunity for renewal and new hope.[10]

What Others are Saying:

William Barclay: Only by the help of Jesus Christ can a man develop the sympathy, the understanding, the forgiving spirit, the considerate love, which true marriage requires. Without the help of Jesus Christ these things are plainly impossible.[11]

> **Matthew 19:13–14** Then little children were brought to Jesus for him to place his hands on them and pray for them. But the disciples rebuked those who brought them. Jesus said, "Let the little children come to me, and do not hinder them, for the kingdom of heaven belongs to such as these."

GOSPEL QUARTET IN HARMONY

Matthew 19:13–15
Mark 10:13–16
Luke 18:15–17

Kids In The Kingdom

It is no accident that the story of parents bringing their children to Jesus follows hot on the heels of that heavy discussion of marriage and divorce.

The humility, honesty, dependence, and teachability of little children stands in refreshing contrast to the pride, infidelity, independence, and rigidity that destroy marriages. Jesus makes childlikeness the ideal for all his followers.

Children also provide a model for kingdom citizens in the way they relate to God. They approach him more directly and personally, as a friend and father.

Mark's telling of this story adds two emotional touches:

- When the disciples tried to shoo the kids away, Jesus got angry (Mark 10:14).

- He did not just do a ceremonial "laying on of hands"; Jesus picked these children up in his arms and held them (Mark 10:16).

KINGDOM OF GOD

Childlike Attitudes and Qualities Necessary for Kingdom Life[12]

Dependence	Humility	Ability to play
Openness	Vulnerability	Simplicity
Complete trust	Unworldliness	Powerlessness
Sense of wonder	Teachability	Curiosity
Joy in little things	Natural obedience	Capacity for easy forgiveness

> **Mark 10:17–21** As Jesus started on his way, a man ran up to him and fell on his knees before him. "Good teacher," he asked, "what must I do to inherit eternal life?"
>
> "Why do you call me good?" Jesus answered. "No one is good—except God alone. You know the commandments: 'Do not murder, do not commit adultery, do not steal, do not give false testimony, do not defraud, honor your father and mother.'"
>
> "Teacher," he declared, "all these I have kept since I was a boy."
>
> Jesus looked at him and loved him. "One thing you lack," he said. "Go, sell everything you have and <u>give</u> to the poor, and you will have treasure in heaven. Then come, follow me."

The Love Of Money

As Jesus started out on the next leg of his journey to Jerusalem, a **young ruler** ran to meet him. This young man was eager to know how to get eternal life.

Jesus reminded him that no Jewish teacher called another "good." The rabbis said, "There is nothing that is good, but the Law."

Then Jesus listed five of the <u>Ten Commandments</u>, focusing on human relationships (not attitudes toward God). The young man said he'd kept these all his life.

Jesus *"looked at him and loved him."* Then he struck the nerve issue standing between this man and God—his wealth (Mark 10:21).

What Jesus asked him to do would have been difficult even for a poor man! We can't help wondering why he made the way so tough for this man when he doesn't require the same level of abandonment from everyone.

Here may be some reasons:

1. Eternal life can only be obtained on the <u>basis of faith</u>— keeping commandments and being a good or successful citizen is not enough. To do what Jesus asked would require complete trust in Jesus.

2. To show the young man his failure to keep the first, most important commandment: *"You shall have no other gods before me"* (Exodus 20:3). The god this man served was not <u>Yahweh</u> but <u>Mammon</u>. (The young ruler's response

GO TO:

Deuteronomy 15:7–8, 11 (give)

GOSPEL QUARTET IN HARMONY

Matthew 19:16–30
Mark 10:17–31
Luke 18:18–30

young ruler: *civil rather than religious official; too young to be an elder*

GO TO:

Exodus 20 (Ten Commandments)

Ephesians 2:8–9 (basis of faith)

☞ GO TO:

Exodus 3:14 (Yahweh)

Luke 16:23 (Mammon)

Matthew 10:38; 16:24;
John 10:4, 27; 12:26
(called)

Matthew 4:19; 8:22;
9:9; Mark 2:14;
John 1:43
(direct command)

☞ GO TO:

Job 1:10; 42:10; Psalm
37:25 (approval)

KEY POINT

Wealth can be and
often is a hindrance to
entering fully into
kingdom community
life, which involves a
sharing attitude and
generosity.

**What Others
are Saying:**

showed he was unwilling to serve God if it meant giving up his money. See Mark 10:22.)

3. Another reason may be hidden in the command, *"Follow me"* (verse 21). All believers are <u>called</u> to follow Christ, but in the four gospels the <u>direct command</u>, *"Follow me,"* is nearly always associated with a call to apostleship. Did Jesus want this man to become his apostle?

> **Mark 10:24–25** "How hard it is for the rich to enter the kingdom of God! . . . It is easier for a camel to go through the eye of a needle than for a rich man to enter the kingdom of God."

Impossible For Man—Possible For God

The disciples were amazed at this statement. Nothing was more inconceivable to them than that wealth should be a hindrance to getting into the kingdom. Common Jewish belief was that wealth was a sign of God's <u>approval</u>, and that the man who was blessed with it must be a good man.

Some say there was a gate in the wall of Jerusalem designed for human passage. This gate was so small, a camel could only pass through on its knees, and then only if it carried nothing on its back (a picture of the rich man who must give up his trust in wealth in order to enter the kingdom).

One gospel writer, however, uses the Greek word for a literal tailor's needle here. Most think Jesus is drawing a hilarious mental cartoon—a camel trying to get through the eye of a tailor's needle—a ridiculous impossibility!

"Who then can be saved?" the disciples moaned (Mark 10:26).

"All things are possible with God," Jesus answered.

Even the rich can be saved and enter into the experience of the kingdom, through the grace of God and power available in him to make right choices about the place of wealth and how it should be handled.

Ronald J. Sider: Wealth and possessions are the most common idols of us rich Westerners. . . . We have become ensnared by unprecedented material luxury. . . . The standard of living is the god of twentieth-century America, and the ad man is its prophet.[13]

Dividends On Spiritual Investments

Impulsive Peter blurted out that he and the other apostles had left everything to follow Jesus—they had passed "through the needle's eye."

But Jesus responded that no one gives up anything to pursue the kingdom who does not gain far more than he gave—both in this life and in the *"age to come"*—even when he has sacrificed such all-important things as being with a <u>supportive family</u>, having a place to call home, and being free from *"persecutions"* (Mark 10:30)!

Jim Elliot, missionary to the Auca Indians of South America, just before his martyrdom: He is no fool who gives what he cannot keep to gain what he cannot lose.[14]

> **Matthew 19:30** But many who are first will be last, and many who are last will be first.

Not Too Late For Grace

Jesus felt a story comin' on.

Near the end of September, Israel's grape crop gets ripe. Fall rains will soon begin. The grapes must be picked or the crop will be ruined.

Early in the morning a farmer went to the marketplace where **day laborers** hung out, waiting to be hired. He hired all who were there, agreeing to pay them a **denarius** (see illustration, page 130) for a day's work. About 9 A.M. he returned and hired more men, promising to pay them whatever is right. He did the same at noon, at 3 P.M., and at 5 P.M., about an hour before sunset.

At **dusk** the foreman called the workers together and paid them, according to his boss's instructions. To the somewhat understandable consternation of the workers who'd been in the vineyard since dawn, all were paid the same (one denarius)—even if they'd only worked an hour (Matthew 20:9–10).

Even though they got what they'd agreed to work for, the guys who'd put in a full day ran up the "unfair flag." The boss's answer makes the parable's point: *"Don't I have the right to do what I want with my own money? Or are you envious because I am generous?"* (verse 15).

The farmer represents God. The point of the story is that God

---

GOSPEL QUARTET IN HARMONY

Matthew 19:27–30
Mark 10:28–31
Luke 18:28–30

age to come: *future destiny of believers, including eternal life*

What Others are Saying:

☞ **GO TO:**

Acts 2:43–47; 4:32–37; 5:1–11; 6:1–7 (supportive family)

☞ **Check It Out:**

Matthew 19:30; 20:1–16

day laborers: *like migrant farm workers; lowest on Israel's social and economic scale*

denarius: *standard daily wage for a farm laborer*

dusk: *Moses' Law required field workers be paid every day for work done that day*

☞ **GO TO:**

Deuteronomy 24:15 (dusk)

---

does not deal with us on the basis of what we deserve. If he did, none of us would have the ghost of a chance for eternal life.

Instead God deals with all of us on the basis of his generosity—whether we have served him for a lifetime or, like the <u>thief</u> crucified with Jesus, cried out to him with our dying breath.

☞ **GO TO:**

Luke 23:32–33, 39–43 (thief)

Something to Ponder

In a conversation with my wife, Audrey, an 83-year-old terminal cancer patient said, "I wish I had spent less time on the golf course and more time in church." Audrey reassured her that *when* in life she came to Christ was not important, only that she did. And then she shared with the elderly woman this story, Jesus' story of the farm workers who all received the same pay—even though some worked all day while others worked only the last hour.

What Others are Saying:

Manford George Gutzke: One of the first things to remember is that the benefits we receive from God through the Lord Jesus Christ are not wages. They are not earned by our efforts. Our relationship with God is not an employer-employee relationship. It is a father-son relationship. The father gives and the son serves. The son serves as he can, the father gives as he will.[15]

Robert L. Thomas and Stanley N. Gundry: Ultimately all rewards will issue from the sovereign grace of God who may, on the basis of his judgment of men's motives, grant richer rewards to those who have labored less.[16]

Denarius

A Denarius was a silver coin bearing the head of Tiberius Caesar on one side and the Roman personification of peace on the other. During Jesus' life, this coin was a day's wage for a workman.

Leader As Servant

On the road to Jerusalem, Jesus took the lead, a lonely figure, striding resolutely ahead of the 12 (Mark 10:32). The NIV says the disciples were *"astonished"* as they trudged along behind him. The closer they got to the Holy City, the more they struggled with a sense of impending disaster.

The Servant-Savior's Cup

Jesus again confided in them about the mistreatment, death, and resurrection waiting for him in Jerusalem.

In Luke's telling of the Jesus story, this is the <u>seventh time</u> he prophesied those events. It's the first time, however, that he predicted he would be turned over to the Gentiles.

His companions still did not understand what he was talking about, and would not, until after it happened (Luke 18:32–34).

THE BIG PICTURE

> **Matthew 20:20–28** The **mother of Zebedee's sons** came to Jesus and asked him to give her two sons places in his kingdom on his right hand and left. Jesus told her she didn't know what she was asking. He asked her sons, "Can you drink **the cup** I am going to drink?" They said they could. Jesus said to them, "You will indeed drink from my cup, but to sit at my right or left is not for me to grant. <u>These places</u> belong to those for whom they have been prepared by my Father."
>
> Then Jesus called the disciples together and taught them that leadership in his kingdom is different from in the world. Leaders must be servants, just as he came to serve and give his life for others.

The Servant-Leader's Cup

If you ever wondered where Jesus' two apostles James and John, sons of Zebedee, got the aggressive personalities that got them the nickname, <u>Sons of Thunder</u>, look no further!

Their mother had high hopes for her boys. This ambitious request and the anger that erupted among the other 10 apostles when they heard about it gave Jesus an opportunity to teach the leaders of his soon-to-be-born church some important principles of leadership.

GOSPEL QUARTET IN HARMONY

Matthew 20:17–28
Mark 10:32–34
Luke 18:31–34

astonished: amazed and bewildered

☞ **GO TO:**

Luke 5:35; 9:22, 43–45; 12:50; 13:32–33; 17:25; 18:31–34 (seventh time)

mother of Zebedee's sons: Salome, sister of Jesus' mother

the cup: self-sacrificing servanthood

☞ **GO TO:**

Revelation 4:6–10; 5:4–8 (these places)

GOSPEL QUARTET IN HARMONY

Matthew 20:20–28
Mark 10:35–45

☞ **GO TO:**

Mark 3:17 (Sons of Thunder)

KINGDOM OF GOD The request shows that even a few days before his crucifixion, Jesus' closest followers still did not understand the true nature of his kingdom. Leadership in the community of believers was to be utterly unlike anything observable in earthly society.

advance contingent: a foretaste, beachhead of the completed reality to come

☞ **GO TO:**

1 Corinthians 9:15–23; 2 Corinthians 2:17; 1 Timothy 6:6–11 (not their own)

Acts 19:27–31; 1 Peter 5:1–4 (care)

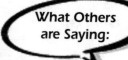

What Others are Saying:

self-aggrandizement: making oneself greater, putting oneself first

KEY Outline:

Servant Leaders
Invitation, not demand
Greatness is service
Christ is the model
Serve, not be served

EARLY CHURCH LIFE: According to Jesus' design, the authority structure of the church (the kingdom's advance contingent) is established on servanthood, not "leadership" (as that term is usually understood). Church leaders are, first and foremost, servants. They don't throw their weight around, pull rank, or demand that others serve them.

- Their greatness is measured by the quality of their serving (Matthew 20:26).
- They serve, <u>not their own</u> needs, but the needs of those in their <u>care</u> (verse 27).
- Their leadership is modeled after the self-giving servanthood of Jesus (verse 28).

Lawrence O. (Larry) Richards: When we think of *leadership* in Christ's terms, the normal connotations must be put behind us. Leadership in the church is not related to authority: Christ only is our "leader." . . . Leadership in the church is not related to **self-aggrandizement**: the leader is to be, like Christ, the servant of all. . . . For a man to wear the mantle of leadership humbly, and to lose himself in service to others, his *character* will be far more important than his accomplishments.[17]

Manford George Gutzke: In the world, the big man is the one who is in charge. He shows he is in charge by putting you in your place. But among the followers of Christ, the mark of greatness is humility and willingness to serve.[18]

While Passing Through Jericho

The throng of Galilean pilgrims crossed the Jordan River into Judea and passed through Jericho (see appendix A).

Jericho was known as the "City of Palms." Nearby was a great

132

GOD'S WORD FOR THE BIBLICALLY-INEPT

date palm forest. And the fragrance of balsam trees perfumed the air for miles around. Roman traders carried Jericho dates and balsam all over the world. Jericho was a place to get rich. The Herods' lavish estates lay nearby in the Jordan River Valley.

> **Mark 10:46–47** Then they came to Jericho. As Jesus and his disciples, together with a large crowd, were leaving the city, a blind man, Bartimaeus (that is, the Son of Timaeus), was sitting by the roadside begging. When he heard that it was Jesus of Nazareth, he began to shout, "Jesus, Son of David, have mercy on me!"

There's A Time To Be Quiet, And A Time To Scream!

On the Jericho Road, Jesus passed two blind men. Mark identifies one of them as Bartimaeus. He was probably the most vocal of the two, and became better known among early Christians. The other is only mentioned by Matthew (20:29–34).

When told Jesus was passing, Bartimaeus called to him for mercy.

"Be quiet!" the people near him said.

But blind Bart paid no attention; he just yelled louder! The original word used for this second shout describes "the instinctive shout of ungovernable emotion, a scream, almost an animal cry."

The result? Jesus stopped and healed blind Bart and his blind buddy.

There is a time to be quiet and polite. And there is a time to ignore protocol and let the desperation we feel be known in Dolby SurroundSound! Jesus, the blind-man <u>healer</u>, was passing, for heaven's sake! This might be blind Bart's only chance to see! His animal-like screams were a most eloquent form of prayer.

> **Luke 19:2–6** A man was there by the name of Zacchaeus; he was a chief tax collector and was wealthy. He wanted to see who Jesus was, but being a short man he could not, because of the crowd. So he ran ahead and climbed a sycamore-fig tree to see him, since Jesus was coming that way.
> When Jesus reached the spot, he looked up and said

KEY POINT

Blind Bart's prayer was not polite. It was a desperate scream that Jesus heard and answered.

GOSPEL QUARTET IN HARMONY

Matthew 20:29–34
Mark 10:46–52
Luke 18:35–43

Something to Ponder

☞ **GO TO:**

John 9 (healer)

> to him, "Zacchaeus, come down immediately. I must stay at your house today." So he came down at once and welcomed him gladly.

The Sinner-King Of Jericho

Of all the characters that crossed Jesus' path, few are more intriguing than Zacchaeus. He was a CEO of sinners. Hired sinners under him did his sinning for him!

He had everything money could buy. And a heart as empty as Mother Hubbard's cupboard. Spiritually, he was up a tree!

Desperately needy and hungry for a new life, the love-starved little man hoped for a glimpse of Jesus as he passed by. Too proud to scream for help like blind Bartimaeus, he'd just watch while the parade of hope passed by under his lonely tree-branch perch.

It was his great good fortune, however, that the route Jesus took brought the Life-Giver directly beneath the branches that masked the minute **miscreant**! Jesus looked up and ordered the surprised **sycamore**-sitter to slide down and make up the bed in the guestroom—Jesus would be staying the night!

Salvation of the lost, Jesus declared (verse 10), was not incidental to his mission; it was his mission. The tiny taxman climbed down from his roost, welcomed Jesus into his home and life and emerged from the encounter a changed man. *"Zacchaeus stood up and said to the Lord, 'Look, Lord! Here and now I give half of my possessions to the poor, and if I have cheated anybody out of anything, I will pay back four times the amount'"* (Luke 19:8).

ZACCHAEUS: A rich, runt of a man, small of stature and soul. A lackey of the Roman occupation forces. Leader in the outrageously corrupt tax-collection system. Among tax collectors he was *"chief"* (Luke 19:2). The contract to collect taxes in a local area was sold to the highest bidder, Zacchaeus. Once the object of Jesus' love, he became a changed man.

Big Lessons From A Little Man

From this incident with Zacchaeus we learn things about Christ:

- Christ can spot a hungry heart a mile away (Luke 19:5).
- Christ takes the initiative in locating sinners to save (verse 5).
- Christ values lost people (verse 5).
- Christ refuses to let man-made proprieties or public opinion get in the way of reaching a needy person (verse 7).

miscreant: villain, evildoer

sycamore: a type of mulberry, with spreading branches, easy to climb

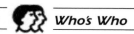 **Who's Who**

GOD'S WORD FOR THE BIBLICALLY-INEPT

We also learn things about how Zacchaeus found **salvation** (verses 4–8):

- He acted on his desire to see Jesus.
- He gladly <u>welcomed Jesus</u> into his home and life.
- He openly confessed his intent to live a new life.
- He let his encounter with Jesus change his attitude toward his possessions.
- He made **restitution** beyond the Law's requirements for wrongs done to others. (The Law said unintentional wrongs should be repaid at value plus 20 percent; a convicted thief repaid double.)

salvation: deliverance from power of sin, spiritual death, and Satan

restitution: repayment

☞ **GO TO:**

Revelation 3:20 (welcomed Jesus)

Exodus 22:4, 7–9; Leviticus 5:16; Numbers 5:7 (restitution)

Lawrence O. (Larry) Richards: The converted tax collector's sudden generosity is not the basis of his salvation, but rather is the chief indicator that he truly has been saved.[19]

What Others are Saying:

Taxes in First-Century Israel

Property taxes set by Romans	1% per year
Head tax for every person between ages 14 and 65	1 denarius per year
Customs duties collected at all provincial borders	2½%
Sales tax on firewood and produce collected at city gates	1%
Land rentals to the government or large landowners	40% of annual farm income
Head tax on all male Jews, paid at the Temple	½ shekel per year
Tithe, paid at the Temple	10% of net income

Plus: Taxes to Herod Archelaus

Taxes paid at major highway junctions

Whatever each tax collector could get away with adding to the citizens' tax bills

Study Questions

1. What type of prayer did Jesus encourage by his parable of the widow and the judge? By the one about the Pharisee and the tax collector? Which of the two comes closest to your own heart's desire right now?
2. Identify the four major insights Jesus gave on marriage.
3. Name seven childlike attitudes or qualities necessary for successful marriage and/or harmonious church life. Which is hardest and which is easiest for you? Why?

4. What did Jesus ask the rich young ruler to do to obtain eternal life? Why did he ask so much from him?
5. What does the Zacchaeus story tell us about Jesus? How did Zacchaeus demonstrate his readiness to receive the salvation Jesus offered? Where were you when you were first introduced to Jesus? (a) up a tree?, (b) out on a limb?, or (c) hiding, hoping he'd find you? Where are you now?

CHAPTER WRAP-UP

- On the border between Galilee and Samaria, 10 lepers cried for help. Jesus sent them to the priest to verify their healing. Only one—a Samaritan—returned to thank him. (Luke 17:11–19)
- When asked the location of the kingdom of God, Jesus answered that it is within people (and among them) and is not built around his physical presence but is built, rather, around his spiritual presence. (Luke 17:20–25)
- Using two parables, Jesus taught that prayer is a cry for justice or justification, and that it requires persistence, humility, and frank admission of desperate personal need. (Luke 18:1–14)
- A question from some Pharisees about divorce triggered an important teaching concerning marriage, divorce, remarriage, and singleness. He emphasized marriage rather than divorce. Hard-heartedness was the root cause of divorce, he said. (Matthew 19:1–12)
- A rich young ruler came asking how to obtain eternal life. Jesus told him to give away everything he owned and follow him. The man went away sadly. Jesus taught his disciples that it was difficult but not impossible for the rich to enter the kingdom. (Mark 10:17–31)
- At Jericho, Jesus encountered two desperate men—the physically blind beggar, Bartimaeus, and the spiritually blind tax collector, Zacchaeus. He healed the blind man and saved the taxman. (Luke 18:35–19:10)

Part Two

SIX DAYS TO GLORY

REVEREND FUN

You've been doing a great job serving others, but you gotta stop asking for tips.

8 PARADE!

GOSPEL QUARTET IN HARMONY

Matthew 21:1–22;
26:6–13
Mark 11:1–26; 14:3–9
Luke 19:11–48
John 11:55–12:50

☞ **GO TO:**

Luke 18:31–34; Mark
8:31–33
(unable to fit)

☞ **Check It Out:**

Luke 19:11–27

Let's Get Started

Even as Zacchaeus celebrated his new beginning, the man from Nazareth was looking down the road to Jerusalem, 17 miles away, where he knew he had a date with destiny.

God's clock was ticking. Time was running out.

But still his followers failed to grasp the true nature of his kingdom and the road he must follow to claim the throne. At least seven times, Jesus had told his friends about the events that would occur in Jerusalem—his rejection, suffering, death, and resurrection. But they were <u>unable to fit</u> the idea of the King's death into their understanding of his reign.

> **Luke 19:11** While they were listening to this, he went on to tell them a parable, because he was near Jerusalem and the people thought that the kingdom of God was going to appear at once.

All The King's Men

Jesus' disciples saw the crowds increasing. They heard the people talking.

Thousands would gather for the Passover. Many speculated that this celebration of Israel's liberation would be the ideal time to unveil the kingdom.

These people clung to the notion *"that the kingdom of God was going to appear at once."* Jesus told a story designed to chip away at their erroneous expectations.

mina: about 100 days'
wages

A nobleman had been appointed king. While the man was away
for his coronation, he turned his financial affairs over to 10 trusted
servants, giving each a **mina** to invest for him. Jesus added that
the man's *"subjects hated him and sent a delegation"* to try to pre-
vent his appointment (Luke 19:14).

When the newly appointed king returned, he called his 10 brokers to account for how they'd handled his money. One had earned
1,000 percent return (verse 16). Another had gained 500 percent
(verse 18). Both were given promotions in keeping with their success.

Then came the overscrupulous scaredy-cat who had stashed
the king's money in an old sock under his mattress (*"in a piece of
cloth,"* verses 20–21) because he thought the king was a **hard**
man.

hard: Greek: sour, harsh,
rigid, ungenerous, severe,
disagreeable

Many people picture Christ this way, as a cosmic killjoy who
takes the fun out of life.

Not only was this broker not rewarded for protecting the king's
money, it was taken away from him. He ended up with nothing to
show for his trouble but a reprimand!

As for those subjects who tried to keep him from reigning, the
king issued the order, *"Bring them here and kill them in front of me"*
(verse 27).

The interpretation revolves around four characters or groups:

- The nobleman pictures Christ.
- The imperial authority to whom he owed his appointment
  represents God the Father.
- The 10 servants trusted to care for his business represent
  Christ's disciples.
- The rebellious subjects determined to keep him off the
  throne represent Jesus' enemies.

KINGDOM OF GOD This story teaches several important things about
Christ's kingdom. Before Christ's reign could be fully
established on earth, he would go to his Father in
heaven.

The Second Coming Between the time Christ left the world to go to his
Father and his Second Coming there would be a
lengthy interval. While waiting for his return, his servants would be entrusted with resources for the work
he wanted them to do (Luke 19:13).

☞ **GO TO:**

John 15:5–7; Acts
   1:10–11 (go to)

Acts 1:8;
   1 Corinthians 12;
   Romans 12
   (resources)

Leslie F. Brandt: As God's children and his ministers and servants in a rebellious and disjointed world, you are the recipients of God-imparted gifts to be used toward the accomplishment of his purposes in the world. . . . The value or significance of these [resources] is not to be determined by the accolades of your peers, but the manner in which they are accepted and utilized for the glory of God.[1]

The Second Coming

Jesus knew that before and during his absence there would be <u>bitter opposition</u> to him.

In spite of opposition, Christ will assume the throne and <u>return</u> to earth. When this happens, those who oppose him will face judgment.

Upon his return, his servants will <u>account</u> for what they have done with what he gave them. <u>Opportunities</u> for greater kingdom service will be based on how the resources with which he left them were used.

Leon Morris: In the Christian life we do not stand still. We use our gifts and make progress or we lose what we have.[2]

Jesus' parable reminded the people of Jericho of an actual event they had seen unfold.

When Herod the Great died, his will divided his kingdom between his three sons—Antipas, Philip, and Archelaus. Archelaus was to be king of Judea subject to approval by the Emperor. He traveled to Rome to work out the arrangements.

The Judeans hated him. They sent a delegation to Rome to try to block the appointment. As a concession to the protestors, Caesar appointed Archelaus **tetrarch**, not king. To get even, Archelaus massacred 3,000 of his subjects at the first Passover after taking office.

His magnificent palace in the nearby Jordan River Valley was a reminder of the incident.

> **John 11:57** But the chief priests and Pharisees had given orders that if anyone found out where Jesus was, he should report it so that they might arrest him.

What Others are Saying:

☞ **GO TO:**

John 15:18–16:4 (bitter opposition)

Revelation 19:11–16 (return)

2 Corinthians 5:10 (account)

2 Timothy 4:7–8; Revelation 22:3–5 (opportunities)

What Others are Saying:

Remember This . . .

tetrarch: *means "fourth" or "ruler of a minor province"*

KEY Outline:

Parable of the Minas
Christ's return delayed
Use your gift
Expect opposition
Christ's return certain
Give account
Distorted view hinders servanthood
Gain or lose out

GOSPEL QUARTET IN HARMONY

Luke 19:28
John 11:55–12:1

☞ **GO TO:**

Leviticus 7:21; Numbers 9:6–13; 2 Chronicles 30:17–20
(ceremonial cleansing)

John 11 (raised Lazarus)

ceremonial cleansing: *required ritual before the feast*

Isn't he coming: *Greek: "Surely he won't come to the festival!"[3]*

sign: *proof he was the Messiah*

six days before: *Sabbath—sundown Friday to sundown Saturday*

KEY Outline:

Hit List
  Jesus of Nazareth
  Lazarus of Bethany

Arrest Warrant

Leaving Jericho for Jerusalem, Jesus again walked ahead (Luke 19:28). "All roads lead to Jerusalem," the saying went. The closer he came to the city, the larger the multitude around him grew as every side road emptied its flow of pilgrims onto the main thoroughfare.

Many planned to spend the week before Passover in **ceremonial cleansing** at the Temple (John 11:55).

Jesus was the main topic of conversation: *"What do you think? **Isn't he coming** to the Feast at all?"* (John 11:56).

The last time Jesus was near Jerusalem, at Bethany, he had <u>raised Lazarus</u> from the dead. As a direct result of that **sign**/miracle, Jesus' enemies in the Sanhedrin pushed through an official edict to arrest him. But whether they intended to help the authorities or not, everyone kept an eye peeled for a glimpse of the man who had the power to raise the dead.

The "outlaw" arrived at Bethany, two miles from Jerusalem, at the home of Lazarus, Martha, and Mary, **six days before** the Passover (John 12:1). Bethany would be his headquarters for the next few days.

Each day until Passover, he and his disciples would walk to the Temple (two miles west) and return at night (see illustration, page 143).

> **John 12:9–11** A large crowd found out that Jesus was there and came . . . because of him . . . and Lazarus, whom he had raised from the dead. So the chief priests made plans to kill Lazarus as well, for on account of him many of the Jews were going over to Jesus.

The Hit List

The streets of Bethany were filled with curiosity seekers, hoping for a glimpse of one or both "celebrities"—Jesus or Lazarus, the man alive from the dead, as Lazarus was living proof Jesus was the Messiah.

The number of people siding with the man religious leaders viewed as "public enemy number one" increased, while the number loyal to the leaders shrunk.

In desperation, the clergy added Lazarus to their list of people to be assassinated! For the man who had already died once, friendship with Christ suddenly became very costly.

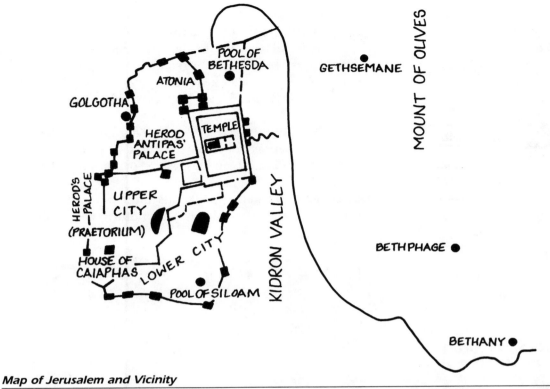

Map of Jerusalem and Vicinity

This map shows the route by which Jesus walked back and forth between Bethany and Jerusalem during the last week of his life.

> **John 12:3** Then Mary took about a pint of **pure nard**, an expensive perfume; she poured it on Jesus' feet and wiped his feet with her hair. And the house was filled with the fragrance of the perfume.

pure nard: precious imported oil from the Indian nard plant

GOSPEL QUARTET IN HARMONY

Matthew 26:6–13
Mark 14:3–9
John 12:2–8

☞ **GO TO:**

Luke 10:38–42
(usual role)

Priceless Worship

As Passover week began, a dinner in Jesus' honor was held in Bethany at the home of Simon the leper (Matthew and Mark supply the host's name).

Lazarus was there, alive and kicking, at the table with Jesus. His sister Martha, in her <u>usual role</u>, served the meal.

At some point in the party, Mary did an unusual thing: She brought an *"alabaster vial"* of perfume and emptied it on Jesus' head and feet as he reclined at the table.

It was an extravagant act. Some witnesses found such extrava-

costly: a year's wages,
300 denarii

spikenard: perfume from
roots of perennial nard
plant

Who's Who

☞ **GO TO:**

Luke 7:36–38
(with her hair)

**GOSPEL QUARTET
IN HARMONY**

Matthew 26:8–13
Mark 14:4–9
John 12:4–8

burial: "laying out the
corpse" for burial

☞ **GO TO:**

John 19:39–40 (burial)

Luke 4:18–19; Matthew
4:23–24; John
6:5–13
(nobody cared more)

Matthew 25:34–45
(care of the needy)

gance disturbing. Mary was concentrating on Jesus—dramatizing her love, gratitude, faith, and reverence.

As the **costly** oil ran over his feet, this highborn woman let down the tresses of her long hair (something Jewish women did not do in public), got on her knees behind him, and proceeded to wipe the excess **spikenard** from his feet <u>with her hair</u>.

SIMON THE LEPER: Gave a party in Jesus' honor. Either he currently had leprosy or had been cured of it. Possibly he was a relative of Lazarus and his sisters, perhaps their father.

EARLY CHURCH LIFE: Early Christians often reminded each other of Mary's spendthrift act of adoration for Christ.

> **John 12:4–6** Judas Iscariot . . . objected, "Why wasn't this perfume sold and the money given to the poor? . . . He did not say this because he cared about the poor but because he was a thief; as keeper of the money bag, he used to help himself to what was put into it.

The Priority Of Worship

Hiding behind a smoke screen of concern for the poor, Judas Iscariot protested the extravagance.

The truth was, he was a petty embezzler, pilfering the kingdom community's common purse of gifts given to support Jesus' ministry. Christ's response was to tell the self-motivated critic to stop harassing the worshiper.

Jesus insisted Mary was preparing him for "**burial**," which he knew would come within the week (verse 7). In John 19:40, the same word is used for the Jewish custom of wrapping the body with spices and linen. Nard was often one of the spices used.

<u>Nobody cared more</u> about the poor than Jesus, but Judas and the other critics within his own ranks (Mark 14:4) needed to understand two realities. First, he would be with them for only six more days—whatever they were going to do to express their love had to be done soon. Second, there would always be poor people to help; after he was gone, <u>care of the needy</u> would become a high priority expression of love to him (John 12:8).

Love-motivated social concern can be an authentic expression of <u>worship</u>. But social concern is no substitute for personal <u>devotion</u> to the Lord himself, devotion that sometimes can only be expressed in imprudent acts of adoration that seem irrational to those who have closed themselves off from the truth.

Sir Edwin Hoskyns: Mary consciously recognized the necessity of the death of Jesus, and also, recognizing that the hour had come, anticipated his burial by an act of intelligent devotion.[4]

Venerable Bede: We anoint the Lord's head when we cherish the glory of his divinity, along with that of his humanity, with the worthy sweetness of faith, hope and charity, [and] when we spread the praise of his name by living uprightly. We anoint the Lord's feet when we renew his poor by a word of consolation, so that they may not lose hope when they are under duress. We wipe [the feet of] these same ones with our hair when we share some of what is superfluous to us [to alleviate] the wants of the needy.[5]

> **Luke 19:35–38** They brought it to Jesus, threw their cloaks on the colt and put Jesus on it. As he went along, people spread their cloaks on the road. When he came near the place where the road goes down the Mount of Olives, the whole crowd of disciples began joyfully to praise God in loud voices for all the miracles they had seen:
> "Blessed is the king who comes in the name of the Lord!"
> "Peace in heaven and glory in the highest!"

The Victory Pageant

Next day, **Sunday**, Jesus led the way from Bethany to the Mount of Olives, about a half mile from Jerusalem. There he paused to put into operation plans for entrance into the city that would fulfill <u>Messianic prophecy</u>.

Two disciples were sent into Bethpage, a tiny village in the shadow of the city wall. They would find and borrow a never-before-ridden donkey colt. If, as they untied the colt the owners asked why, they were to answer with what may have been a prear-

Something to Ponder

What Others are Saying:

☞ **GO TO:**

Romans 12 (worship)

Deuteronomy 6:4; Luke 10:27 (devotion)

GOSPEL QUARTET IN HARMONY

Matthew 21:1–22
Mark 11:1–26
Luke 19:29–48
John 12:9–50

Sunday: now called "Palm Sunday"

☞ **GO TO:**

Isaiah 62:11; Zechariah 9:9; Matthew 21:5 (Messianic prophecy)

ranged password, *"The Lord needs it,"* and the owners would let them take it.

By the time the colt arrived, pilgrims were jamming the road. Exuberant disciples made a saddle of their outer cloaks and lifted Jesus onto the back of the animal.

Matthew mentions two animals, a donkey and a colt; both had been brought (21:2, 7). Jesus rode the colt, and the mother was led along so the colt would be at ease with its first rider.

Spontaneously, people <u>laid their cloaks</u> on the ground along with palm branches cut from nearby trees to form a multicolored royal carpet upon which Jesus rode in kingly triumph the last half mile into the city (John 12:13). Thousands waved <u>palm branches</u> and cheered loudly, a common practice for honoring a conqueror.

At last Jesus was doing what the <u>Galileans</u> had wanted him to do after the feeding of the 5,000. This time he accepted their acclamation of his royalty. He *was* the King of Israel!

Waving palm branches and shouting, "**Hosanna**!" was as natural for Jews as singing "God Bless America" is for Americans.

They had been practicing this for centuries. Every morning at the annual Feast of Tabernacles, this shout was part of chanting the *Hallel* (Psalm 113–118), with its high point at Psalm 118:25–26 when every man and boy in the Temple shook the family **lulab** and shouted these words:

> *"Hosanna! Hosanna! Hosanna!*
> *O Lord, grant us success.*
> *Blessed is he who comes in the name of the Lord.*
> *From the house of the Lords we bless you.*
> *The Lord is God,*
> *and he has made his light to shine upon us.*
> *With boughs in hand, join in the festal procession*
> *Up to the horns of the alter."*

KINGDOM OF GOD Some of the cheering Palm Sunday throng may have brought lulabs (branches) from home to wave like pom-poms at the ultimate pep rally.

Jesus knew most had misconceptions about what it meant for him to be king. Many expected a military conqueror. They would be disappointed.

He did one significant thing in this noisy parade to reshape

☞ **GO TO:**

2 Kings 9:13
   (laid their cloaks)

Revelation 7:9
   (palm branches)

John 6:14–15
   (Galileans)

Remember This . . .

☞ **GO TO:**

John 12:13; Psalm
   118:25 (Hosanna!)

Leviticus 23:40 (lulab)

Hosanna: Hebrew, *"Save us!"*

lulab: *a bunch of myrtle and willow tied to a palm branch*

KEY POINT

The greeting for King Jesus was, "Save us!"

their thinking—he rode in on the back of a young donkey, not a warhorse. The donkey ride was Jesus' claim to fulfill Zechariah's prophecy: *"See, your king comes to you, righteous and having salvation, gentle and riding on a donkey"* (Zechariah 9:9).

By this action he declared he was the kind of king the prophet described—righteous, saving, gentle, destroying the machinery of war, and bringing peace.

Puzzled Partisans

KINGDOM OF GOD

There was no way to stop this first-century ticker tape parade. Once the spontaneous carpet was laid and the cheering began, it took on a life of its own.

It had been building up in Jewish hearts for centuries. The longings of oppressed, multi-conquered people found focus for its mingled pain and hope in the young prophet from Nazareth. Trying to control the demonstration would be like trying to lasso a runaway freight train.

Even the 12 did not understand (1) that they were seeing the fulfillment of Zechariah's prophecy (see GWPB, pages 129–130), and (2) that Jesus was king of salvation and peace, not war and political victory (John 12:16).

Until they witnessed his death and resurrection (his *"glory"* John calls it) the true understanding of his kingship did not dawn on them.

Victory for Christ does not come through politics, military conquest, or worldly success. His kingdom, now as then, is established by <u>bearing the cross</u>.

> **Luke 19:39–40** Some of the Pharisees in the crowd said to Jesus, "Teacher, rebuke your disciples!"
> "I tell you," he replied, "if they keep quiet, the stones will cry out."

Fidgety Pharisees

Not everyone was thrilled. Many who watched the parade pour into the streets of Jerusalem were still asking, "Who is this?" (Matthew 21:10). The Pharisees demanded Jesus stop his supporters from shouting those unnerving Bible slogans!

"I tell you," he replied, *"if they keep quiet, the stones will cry out!"*

His kingship had to be proclaimed or the huge stones in the Temple walls would find voices. This was the day for the cosmos to acknowledge, "Jesus is King!"

Something to Ponder

☞ **GO TO:**

Matthew 16:24 (bearing the cross)

GOSPEL QUARTET IN HARMONY

Luke 19:39–40
John 12:19

Methodius of Philippi: Instead of our garments, let us spread our hearts before him.[6]

> **Luke 19:41–44** As he approached Jerusalem and saw the city, he wept over it and said, "If you, even you had only known on this day what would bring you peace—but now it is hidden from your eyes. The days will come upon you when your enemies will build an embankment against you and encircle you and hem you in on every side. They will dash you to the ground, you and the children within your walls. They will not leave one stone on another, because you did not recognize the time of God's coming to you."

KEY Outline:

Triumphal Entry Reactions

Disciples: "What's it all about?"

Pharisees: "Shut up!"

Jesus: "If only."

The Warrior

Jesus never forgot the realities to which this "victory march" was taking him.

He knew his enemies' hatred. His heart broke over their blindness. He saw the cross looming huge ahead.

As the borrowed donkey carried him through the city gate, Jesus **wept** and prophesied the city's destruction. Forty years later every tragic detail of his prophecy (verse 43) was fulfilled. In 70 A.D. Jerusalem was sacked, the Temple was reduced to rubble and burned by the armies of Emperor Titus, and 1,100,000 Jews were killed.[7]

It could have been averted had the city recognized his coming as the visitation of God (verse 44). So while multitudes of his supporters were high on happiness . . . Jesus grieved.

wept: Greek: "wailed," broke into sobs

Michael Card: How can we call it the "Triumphal Entry" when Jesus was still wiping tears from his eyes? . . . The disciples were singing. Jesus was weeping. . . . Jesus' first coming was characterized by misunderstanding. But there will be a Second. The misunderstood Messiah, who that day was a Lamb, will return as a Lion. . . . Jesus will not be wiping tears of sorrow from his eyes but most likely tears of joy and relief. And he will be wiping away our tears as well.[8]

Louis Paul Lehman: Jesus weeps over the sinning. He would meet their need, pardon their sin, forgive the past, assure them of heaven. He would—and he can: but they will not.[9]

> **Mark 11:11** Jesus entered Jerusalem and went to the temple. He looked around at everything, but since it was already late, he went out to Bethany with the Twelve.

Spring Cleaning In The House Of God

According to Mark's report, once inside the city wall, Jesus and the 12 toured the temple area and then returned to Bethany for the night.

> **Mark 11:12–14** The next day as they were leaving Bethany, Jesus was hungry. Seeing in the distance a fig tree in leaf, he went to find out if it had any fruit. When he reached it, he found nothing but leaves, because it was not the season for figs. Then he said to the tree, "May no one ever eat fruit from you again." And his disciples heard him say it.

The Curse Of Empty Promises

Next morning on the way back into Jerusalem, Jesus was hungry. He stopped at a lonely, leafy fig tree beside the road to see if there were any figs left from the year before.

Mark comments that this was not the season for figs (11:13), a fact Jesus well knew. But, the <u>fig tree</u> was a traditional symbol for the nation of Israel. The search for fruit he knew wasn't there was an attention-grabber for a **symbolic** teaching he wanted to share.

Finding *"nothing but leaves,"* Jesus spoke to the fruitless tree: *"May no one ever eat fruit from you again!"* (Mark 11:14). The tree shriveled up and died (Matthew 21:19).

He didn't explain the message. It appears to be a dramatized prophecy of Israel's spiritual situation: The nation had the history and the trappings (leaves) of religious ritual that promised a living faith. But in reality the faith of most citizens was dead and fruitless.

For centuries they'd said they expected the Messiah and would welcome him when he came, but when he came, the majority <u>rejected</u> him.

GOSPEL QUARTET IN HARMONY

Matthew 21:10–19
Mark 11:11–16
Luke 19:45–48

KEY POINT

The "leaves" of religion are no substitute for the "fruit" of real faith.

GOSPEL QUARTET IN HARMONY

Matthew 21:18–19
Mark 11:12–14

☞ **GO TO:**

Jeremiah 8:13; 29:17; Hosea 9:10, 16; Joel 1:7; Luke 13:6–9 (fig tree)

symbolic: *called "an enacted parable"*

☞ **GO TO:**

John 1:11 (rejected)

**GOSPEL QUARTET
IN HARMONY**

Matthew 21:1–13
Mark 11:15–18
Luke 19:45–48

☞ **GO TO:**

John 2:14–17 (same)

KEY Outline:

Reasons to Storm the Temple

Misuse
Exploitation
Exclusion
Distortion

The Redeemer's Wrath

For a man with a price on his head, Jesus took a big risk to reenter the city the next morning.

Right under the noses of the authorities who had ordered his arrest, he stormed into the Temple and single-handedly shut down the temple market, bodily ejecting entrepreneurs who were exploiting out-of-town worshipers.

He had begun his ministry with the same brash act (see GWLC, pages 107–109).

At least four things about the temple market lit Jesus' fuse:

1. Misuse of people's religious commitments to make personal profit.
2. Exploitation of pilgrims, especially the poor. Worshipers were forced to pay exorbitant exchange rates for the "proper" coinage for the temple tax. They were caught in a con game in which temple inspectors systematically disqualified sacrificial animals and birds bought outside the Temple, forcing worshipers to buy them inside at jacked up prices ("*robbers,*" Mark 11:17).
3. Systematic exclusion of Gentiles ("*the nations,*" verse 17) from the place set aside for them to pray. The market was in the "Court of Gentiles."
4. This monkey business distorted worshipers' picture of God and worship.

Predictably temple officials became more committed to kill Jesus. The only reason they didn't do it then and there was fear of political repercussions. *"They could not find a way to do it, because all the people hung on his words"* (Luke 19:48).

> **John 12:20–21** Now there were some Greeks among those who went up to worship at the Feast. They came to Philip, who was from Bethsaida in Galilee, with a request. "Sir," they said, "we would like to see Jesus."

Up With The Son!

It may have been Jesus driving the profiteers out of the Court of the Gentiles that made these **Greeks** eager to meet him.

They approached Philip, perhaps because he had a Greek name or because they were from the same town. Philip took them to Andrew (another with a Greek name). Together Andrew and Philip took the request to Jesus.

Jesus didn't respond directly (or perhaps he did but John did not report it). But he took the request as a signal that the <u>time</u> had come for his ministry to reach its climax. It was his time to be **glorified** and for his message to be taken to the world.

> **John 12:27–28a** "Now my heart is troubled, and what shall I say? 'Father, save me from this hour?' No, it was for this very reason I came to this hour. Father, glorify your name!"

One Life To Give

Jesus referred to his death by explaining how a kernel of wheat has to fall into the ground and die in order to multiply. "So I must give my life in order to produce many others who share my life and character. Here's the principle: A person who loves this earthly life too dearly will lose it, while the person who gives his or her life in service to God will never lose it" (John 12:23–26).

Jesus was human. He knew personal sacrifice would be involved. Part of him wanted to say, "Father, get me outta here! Rescue me from this hour!"

But, knowing that this is the time for which he was born, he said, "Father, use me to show the wonder of who you are!" John 12:28 says, *"Father, glorify your name!"* A person's name equals his or her reputation, character, and values. God's *"name"* is his essential nature and character.

Leon Morris: The way to fruitfulness lies through death. Unless the wheat falls into the ground and "dies" it will not bear. It is only through "death" that its potentiality for fruitfulness becomes actual. This is a general truth. But it refers particularly to our Lord himself.[10]

Greeks: Gentiles, not Greek-speaking Jews

☞ **GO TO:**

John 2:4; 7:30; 8:20 (time)

---

glorified: extolled, magnified, invested with majesty

KEY POINT

Lose your life in God and save it, or keep your life for yourself and lose it.

What Others are Saying:

> **John 12:28b** Then a voice came from heaven, "I have glorified it, and will glorify it again."

The Good Sonship Seal Of Approval

No sooner had Jesus' emotional prayer escaped his lips than the temple area shook with what sounded to the crowd like a clap of thunder.

Believing ears heard it as the <u>voice of God</u>.

God affirmed that everything Jesus was and did revealed his splendor, and promised that the wonders of God would continue to be revealed in Jesus (verse 30).

His disciples needed this assurance. Their faith would be severely tested in the days ahead.

☞ **GO TO:**

1 Samuel 3:1–14;
1 Kings 19:1–18;
Mark 1:11; 9:7; Acts
9:4–6 (voice of God)

> **John 12:31–33** "Now is the time for judgment on this world; now the prince of this world will be driven out. But I, when I am lifted up from the earth, will draw all men to myself." He said this to show the kind of death he was going to die.

The Magnetism Of The Cross

"The prince of this world" is Satan, God's enemy who <u>pulls the strings</u> of this world system. Jesus used the word *kosmos*, "world" to mean the structure and order of human society apart from and opposed to God. On his way to the cross, Jesus announced the time had come for the world to be judged (it <u>judged itself</u> by crucifying him), and for the evil prince's rule to be broken.

Jesus' phrase, *"<u>lifted up</u>,"* has double meaning: (1) It refers to Jesus being physically lifted up on the cross to die; and (2) it refers to the way people who put their faith in him lift him up in honor, worship, and gratitude for what he accomplished by his death.

People of all national and social backgrounds are attracted to the cross and to the person who gave his life there to <u>rescue sinners</u> from the consequences of their sins.

☞ **GO TO:**

Ephesians 6:12;
1 John 5:19
(pulls the strings)

John 3:18
(judged itself)

John 3:14; 8:28
(lifted up)

Romans 5:6–11;
Colossians 2:13–15
(rescue sinners)

*Remember
This . . .*

Since Jesus' sacrifice, no one is obligated to obey the devil. Many do. But real authority over people has been stripped from him by forgiveness. His doom is sealed (Revelation 20:10).

John Calvin: For in the cross of Christ, as in a splendid theatre, the incomparable goodness of God is set before the whole world. The glory of God shines, indeed, in all creatures on high and below, but never more brightly than in the cross.[11]

THE BIG PICTURE

> **John 12:34–50** Even after Jesus had done all those miraculous signs in their presence, the Jews still would not believe in him. Their unbelief fulfilled prophecies of Isaiah. Some people, even among the leaders, believed in him, but because of the Pharisees they would not confess their faith for fear they would be put out of the synagogue. These secret believers loved praise from men more than praise from God.
>
> Jesus said those who believe in him believe in the one who sent him. He said he did not come to judge, but that there is a judge for those who reject him. Jesus stated that he speaks what God wants him to say.

KEY Outline:

The Cross of Christ
Displays God's splendor
Judges the world
Casts out Satan
Draws people
- to rescue
- to worship

No Time To Ride The Fence

As Jesus talked of his death, people faced the decision to believe or reject him.

The idea of his death did not fit their messianic expectations (John 12:34).

He urged them to cut through the questions and put their faith in him based on the **light** they already had, because in a few days he would be gone. Then he slipped away, perhaps to avoid arrest.

Decisions were made that day: Some still refused to believe (verse 37). Others believed, even some <u>Sanhedrin</u> members. But they kept their faith to themselves for fear of being <u>expelled</u> from the synagogue (verses 42–43).

Knowing it was his last chance to personally present his claims, Jesus returned to the Temple to restate the life-and-death issues involved in accepting or rejecting him (verses 44–50):

- To believe in Jesus is to believe in God; to reject Jesus is to reject God (verse 44).
- When a person looks at Jesus, he sees God (verse 45).
- To believe in Jesus is to live in light; to reject him is to stay in the dark (verse 46).
- Jesus did not come to condemn the world, but to save it (verse 47).

light: spiritual insight, information

☞ **GO TO:**

John 11:47–53 (Sanhedrin)

John 9:34 (expelled)

KEY POINT

To welcome Jesus is to welcome God. To reject Jesus is to reject God.

• Judgment of the world will be based on what people do with Jesus' words—his teachings and claims—because Jesus' words are exactly what God told him to say (verses 48–50).

Study Questions

1. What misconception does Jesus seek to correct with the parable about the king and the men to whom he gave his money to invest? Who do the following characters represent: The king? The distant empire? The enemies? The servants? What resources do you think Jesus has given you to invest for him?

2. How did Jesus interpret Mary's anointing him with expensive oil?

3. For his triumphal entry into Jerusalem, why did Jesus choose to ride a donkey instead of a horse?

4. Identify four reasons why Jesus became so angry about the Temple market.

5. What did Jesus mean when he said he would be "lifted up"? What three things did he say his "lifting up" would accomplish?

6. Why did the leaders who believed keep it a secret? In your life, how does love for "praise from men" get in the way of openly confessing your faith in Christ?

CHAPTER WRAP-UP

- Jesus told a parable to teach his followers that there would be an interval of time between his death and his Second Coming, and that they would be accountable for their handling of resources he left with them to carry on his work. (Luke 19:11–27)

- By the time Jesus reached Bethany, the Sanhedrin had issued orders for his arrest. People wondered if he would show up for the Feast. Lazarus, whom he'd raised from the dead was added to the list of those to be killed so the leaders could stay in power. (John 11:55–57; 12:9–11)

- A dinner in Jesus' honor was held in Bethany with Lazarus and his sisters in charge. Mary demonstrated her love and reverence by anointing Jesus with an expensive perfume. Judas protested the "waste." Jesus accepted Mary's actions as preparation for his burial. (John 12:1–8)

- The next day Jesus rode on a young donkey in triumphal procession into Jerusalem while thousands of his disciples welcomed him as Israel's King. The Pharisees protested. He replied that the people had to cheer him, or else the stones of the Temple would cry out. (Luke 19:28–40)

- When some Greeks asked to see him, Jesus took it as a signal that the climax of his ministry was near. He would be "lifted up" on a cross before the week ended. He pressed people to decide for or against him, and insisted that to accept or reject him was to accept or reject God. (John 12:20–50)

9 AMBUSH!

CHAPTER HIGHLIGHTS

- The Awesome Power of Raw Faith
- A Minefield
- Reinventing Authority
- Exposé
- Twopenny Serenade

Let's Get Started

Tuesday morning of Passover week found Jesus and the 12 once again on the road from Bethany to Jerusalem and into the temple area, just inside the eastern wall.

Again they passed the fruitless fig tree that, the day before, he'd used to symbolize the barrenness of Israel's religious life. This time he used it to teach the power of faith.

In the temple area Jesus fielded a barrage of questions, and challenged the right of hypocritical religious and political leaders to lead.

The Awesome Power Of Raw Faith

As they passed the shriveled fig tree, Jesus used it to teach five things about the power of faith.

If they had faith (1) they could overcome the fruitlessness of dead religion, represented by the fig tree (Mark 11:23); (2) they could *"cast into the sea"* the forces of opposition or hindrances to their spiritual growth, represented by ***"this mountain"*** (verse 23); (3) their prayers would be answered (verse 24); (4) they would be <u>able to forgive</u> their enemies (verse 25); and (5) they would be assured of <u>God's forgiveness</u> (verses 25–26).

A Minefield

The powerful enemies of Jesus had issued the order for his arrest. Privately, they plotted his murder.

GOSPEL QUARTET IN HARMONY

Matthew 21:19–23:39
Mark 11:19–12:44
Luke 20:1–21:4

GOSPEL QUARTET IN HARMONY

Matthew 21:19–22
Mark 11:19–26

this mountain: *Mount of Olives*

☞ **GO TO:**

Luke 17:3–6
(able to forgive)

Matthew 6:14
(God's forgiveness)

ACT OF THE HOLY SPIRIT

Enables the many
facets of faith

☞ **GO TO:**

John 7:32, 45–46
(empty-handed)

Matthew 21:26, 46;
26:3–5; Luke 20:6
(political realities)

But their attempts to bring him in were repeatedly frustrated. At the Feast of Tabernacles the squad of temple cops they'd sent to nab him came back <u>empty-handed</u>, too impressed by the things he was saying to carry out their orders.

Several times, too, their intentions were thwarted by <u>political realities</u>: Crowds often became so enthusiastic about what Jesus was saying, to arrest him would have caused a riot. At any such disturbance, Roman troops with swords swinging would descend on the temple area to restore order and Jewish leaders would be called to explain their inability to keep the peace. They stood to lose their advantageous political positions.

Until they could catch Jesus away from the crowds, they were left with the mostly ineffective tactics of spreading slander and disrupting his teaching with squirrelly questions.

**chief priests and the
elders:** *Sanhedrin, city
fathers, "teachers of the
Law"*

> **Matthew 21:23–24** Jesus entered the temple courts, and while he was teaching, the **chief priests and the elders** of the people came to him. "By what authority are you doing these things?" they asked. "And who gave you this authority?"

**GOSPEL QUARTET
IN HARMONY**

Matthew 21:23–27
Mark 11:27–33
Luke 20:1–8

"Your Driver's License And Registration, Please"

The coalition of enemies came demanding that Jesus reveal his credentials.

If he claimed someone (other than they) authorized his actions, they could accuse him of illegally usurping the nation's and city's duly recognized authorities, and might even be able to get him in trouble with the Roman occupation government.

If he claimed the right to act as he did because of who he was (Son of God), they could charge him with blasphemy (a capital offense) because he was usurping God's authority.

Jesus caught them in their own snare. He silenced them instantly by asking a question he knew they would refuse to answer for fear of self-incrimination: *"I will also ask you a question. If you answer me, I will tell you by what authority I am doing these things. John's baptism—where did it come from? Was it from heaven, or from men?"* (Matthew 21:24–25).

The power brokers of Israel were caught between a rock and a hard place. If they said John was sent by God they would have to admit Jesus was the Messiah, because that's what <u>John taught</u>. If they said John's ministry and message were not from God, they

☞ **GO TO:**

John 1:26–35
(John taught)

would lose the people's support, because the people believed John was God's prophet.

The most brilliant thing they could think of to say was, *"We don't know."* (Well, duh!)

"Neither will I tell you by what authority I am doing these things," Jesus said.

William Barclay: If a man consults *expediency* rather than *principle,* his first question will be not, "What is the truth?" but, "What is it safe to say?" And again and again his worship of expediency will drive him to cowardly silence. . . . If a man knows the truth, he is under obligation to tell the truth, though the heavens should fall.[1]

Reinventing Authority

As the foiled coalition squirmed, Jesus told four stories that exploded like a multiple-warhead A-bomb, blasting the right of Israel's official leadership to lead the nation.

This was not vindictiveness. He <u>cried</u> for these men. But he could not walk softly at this point, because such men as these stole the faith of Israel! They persisted in painting such a distorted picture of God that the only possible result was spiritual disaster for an entire people!

> **Matthew 21:28–30** "What do you think? There was a man who had two sons. He went to the first and said, 'Son, go and work today in the vineyard.'
>
> "'I will not,' he answered, but later he changed his mind and went.
>
> "'Then the father went to the other son and said the same thing. He answered, 'I will, sir,' but he did not go."

My Two Sons

With his first story, Jesus exposed their political waffling: A farmer with two sons asked his sons to work in his vineyard. Both were rebellious. The first refused, then changed his mind and obeyed. The second thought he'd get his dad off his back by agreeing to go to work, but then didn't keep his word.

"Which of the two did what his father wanted?" Jesus asked (Matthew 21:31).

"The first," they answered.

KEY POINT

Those unwilling to accept are given no revelation of who Jesus is.

What Others are Saying:

☞ **Check It Out:**

Matthew 21:28–22:14

Mark 12:1–12

Luke 20:9–19

☞ **GO TO:**

Luke 13:34; 19:41–44; Matthew 23:37–39 (cried)

KEY POINT

Jesus attacked the religious leaders because they stole Israel's faith, distorted the picture of God, and were leading unsuspecting people to hell along with them.

KEY Outline:

Two Rebellious Sons

Said no, did yes
- repentant

Said yes, did no
- unrepentant

repented: *turned from their sins; changed*

What Others are Saying:

wall: *"hedge" of thorn bushes to keep out wild boars and thieves*

GOSPEL QUARTET IN HARMONY

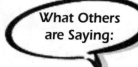

Matthew 21:33–41
Mark 12:1–9
Luke 20:9–16

☞ **GO TO:**

Isaiah 5:7 (vineyard)

vineyard: *OT symbol for nation of Israel*

prophets: *OT preachers and writers, John the Baptist*

Jesus revealed the identity of the sons. Number one son, who said "No" but then changed his mind, represented people the religious leaders despised most—tax collectors and prostitutes. Such "sinners" believed God's message and **repented**.

Number two son, who promised his father everything and gave him nothing, represented the leaders—who considered themselves spiritually superior to tax collectors and prostitutes. But it was humbug.

The sinners recognized God's authority. The leaders said they did, but didn't (verses 31–32). They had no business leading God's nation!

Lawrence O. (Larry) Richards: In the past we may have rejected God. But the door to sonship remains open. We can decide, now, to submit to him. And in submitting to him and claiming the promises God gives us in Christ, the worst of sinners can become a child of God.[2]

> **Matthew 21:33–34** "A landowner planted a vineyard. He put a **wall** around it, dug a winepress in it and built a watchtower. Then he rented the vineyard to some farmers and went away on a journey. When the harvest time approached, he sent his servants to the tenants to collect his fruit."

The Wretched Renters

At harvest time the property owner sent servants to collect his rent. The tenants brutalized them. So the landowner sent his son. Surely they would respect him. But the terrible tenants reasoned in their twisted minds that if they killed the son, they'd own the vineyard.

Jesus' listeners easily identified the characters: (1) The **vineyard** is Israel; (2) the owner of the vineyard is God; (3) the renters are the religious leaders entrusted with the vineyard's care; (4) the landlord's servants are the **prophets** Israel rejected and killed; and (5) the son is Jesus who would soon die at the hands of the leaders.

There's no happy ending. The wretched renters ended wretchedly. The landlord found others to work his vineyard.

God's work will be done. If those to whom he has trusted it fail to do what is right, he will do it through others. If Israel did not straighten up and fly right, God would accomplish his purposes through **another people** (1 Peter 2:9–10; Revelation 5:9–10).

Remember This . . .

another people: God's new nation, kingdom, church of Gentiles and Jews

> **Luke 20:16b–17** When the people heard this, they said, "May this never be!"
>
> Jesus looked directly at them and asked, "Then what is the meaning of that which is written: "'The stone the builders rejected has become the capstone'?"

The Rejected Rock

"May this never be!" cried the people (Luke 20:16).

Jesus looked them straight in the eye and reminded them of <u>a line</u> from the **Hallel**, about *"the stone the builders rejected"* becoming *"the <u>capstone</u>."* The original word indicates either (1) the "cornerstone," the first, most important stone in a building's foundation; or (2) the "capstone," the last stone placed at the top of the corner tying the building together and setting its shape (see illustration below).

Even though Israel rejected him, Jesus Christ is nonetheless the <u>beginning and end</u> of everything God is doing in the world!

GOSPEL QUARTET IN HARMONY

Matthew 21:42–46
Mark 12:10–12
Luke 20:17–19

☞ **GO TO:**

Psalm 118:22 (a line)

Acts 4:11; 1 Peter 2:7; Ephesians 2:20 (capstone)

Ephesians 1:9–10; Revelation 22:13 (beginning and end)

Hallel: Psalms 113–118, sung at the Feast of Tabernacles

Capstone

The capstone of an arched doorway—also called the keystone—held the structure together. It was the most important piece of the arch, and without it everything would crumble.

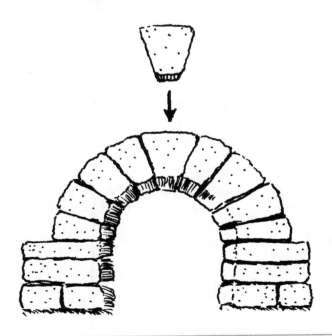

EARLY CHURCH LIFE: Psalm 118:22 is an important verse and *"the capstone"* an important metaphor early Christians used to explain who Jesus is.

> **Matthew 22:1–3** Jesus spoke to them again in parables, saying: "The kingdom of heaven is like a king who prepared a wedding banquet for his son. He sent his servants to those who had been invited to the banquet to tell them to come, but they refused to come.

The King Threw A Party And Nobody Came

Jesus' listeners were familiar with the etiquette involved in a banquet like the one in this parable.

The host hired an expensive cook who would have to return his fee if his cooking embarrassed the host. Guests were invited well in advance. A second invitation was delivered the day before the feast. Such banquets often began in the morning and lasted late into the night.

Some aspects of this tale of impoliteness, impatience, and indifference are exaggerated to stress the life-and-death issues Jesus had in mind. If the king seems to us to be overreacting and overly cruel, we only need remember that the "kings" Israel knew best were the late Herod the Great (murderer of the Bethlehem babies) and his son Archelaus (butcher of 3,000 Jews at a Passover Feast).

 **KINGDOM OF GOD** The parable makes two major points:

1. Israel was invited to celebrate arrival of God's Son and inauguration of the kingdom, but the general populace reacted with indifference (Matthew 22:5) or open <u>hostility</u> (verse 6). Both are rebellion. There would be serious <u>consequences</u> (verse 7). (It is estimated that two-thirds of first-century Jews rejected Christ, and only one-third believed.)

2. Since Israel and its leaders rejected the Messiah, the invitation would be offered to "<u>anyone</u>" (Matthew 22:9)— good or bad (verse 10). All that is required is that they put on the *"wedding clothes"* (verses 11–13)—that is, by putting their faith in Jesus, they become clothed (Romans 1:17; 3:22–24; 13:13–14) with his righteousness.

☞ **Check It Out:**

Matthew 22:1–14

KEY Outline:

Stone (Christ)
Rejected by builders
- leaders

Cornerstone/capstone
- beginning and end

Fall on it
- you're broken

Falls on you
- you're crushed

☞ **GO TO:**

Luke 4:28–29; John 7:30, 43–44; 8:59; 10:31, 39 (hostility)

Luke 13:34–35; 19:41–44 (consequences)

John 3:16; Acts 2:21; Romans 10:13 (anyone)

Sallie McFague: Jesus, in his friendship with outcasts and sinners, is a model of friendship with God. . . . The God of Jesus is the One who invites us to table to eat together as friends.[3]

What Others are Saying:

> **Matthew 22:15–17** Then the Pharisees went out and laid plans to trap him in his word. They sent their disciples to him along with the Herodians. "Teacher," they said, "we know you are a man of integrity and that you teach the way of God in accordance with the truth. You aren't swayed by men, because you pay no attention to who they are. Tell us then, what is your opinion? Is it right to pay **taxes** to **Caesar** or not?"

taxes: *poll tax, one denarius a year from ages 14 to 65*

Caesar: *Augustus; Emperor of Rome; symbol for civil authority*

The God-And-Politics Maneuver

With the chief priests and city fathers reeling from Jesus' four-barreled attack on their authority, the Pharisees decided it was their turn to outfox him.

Desperation shows in their decision to get their worst political enemies, the **Herodians**, involved in the hit-and-run assaults.

Popular enthusiasm for Jesus was running high, so they decided future attacks would be more subtle. In a sneak attack, they sent a team of rabbinical students and astute political liars to butter Jesus up, hoping flattery would get him to drop his guard (Matthew 22:16).

But Jesus saw through the flattery, as the truly humble usually do.

The question was carefully crafted *"to trap him in what he said."* If he said "Yes," the people could turn against him—some would die rather than pay Roman taxes. If he said "No," his enemies could report him to Pilate as a seditionist, and he would be arrested and executed by the Romans.

GOSPEL QUARTET IN HARMONY

Matthew 22:15–22
Mark 12:13–17
Luke 20:20–26

Herodians: *supporters of Roman occupation government*

> **Matthew 22:18–21** Jesus, knowing their evil intent, said, "You hypocrites, why are you trying to trap me? Show me the coin used for paying the tax." They brought him a denarius, and he asked them, "Whose portrait is this? And whose inscription?"
>
> "Caesar's," they replied.
>
> Then he said to them, "Give to Caesar what is Caesar's, and to God what is God's."

The Principle Of The Citizen-Christian

Jesus turned the trap into a chance to teach an important principle of Christian citizenship: If you accept the government's currency and use it, you are bound to accept the <u>government's right</u> to impose taxes. If you benefit from the state, you are obliged to pay your dues to the state. Taxation is a universal right that goes with rulership.

On the other hand, government's authority is limited. People bear God's image, which means they have duties to God that are more inescapable than their duties to the government.

 KINGDOM OF GOD The Christian's first loyalty is to God's kingdom. God, not the state, has the final word. At the same time, the state's ruling authorities are to be obeyed if they don't contradict Scripture.

☞ **GO TO:**

Romans 13:1–7
(government's right)

What Others are Saying:

Richard J. Mouw: The authority and mandate to govern, even in totalitarian societies, are given to human beings by God, so that no one may lightly dismiss the obligation to respect and obey political powers. But in modern democracies the power of national leaders is derived from the populace. . . . Democratic government grants Christians the right publicly to criticize, review, debate, and challenge current procedures and policies. Under these conditions, [Scripture] imposes on them the duty to make use of that right.[4]

Sadducees: aristocrats, high priests, ruling party; deny supernatural, angels

☞ **GO TO:**

Deuteronomy 25:5
(Moses)

Job 9:25–27; John
5:24–29;
1 Corinthians 15:12–
58; Revelation 20:4–5
(resurrection)

> **Matthew 22:23–28** That same day the **Sadducees**, who say there is no resurrection, came to him with a question. "Teacher," they said, "<u>Moses</u> told us that if a man dies without having children, his brother must marry the widow and have children of him. Now there were seven brothers among us. The first one married and died, and since he had no children, he left his wife to his brother. The same thing happened to the second and third brother, right on down to the seventh. Finally, the woman died. Now then, at the <u>resurrection</u>, whose wife will she be of the seven, since all of them were married to her?"

GOSPEL QUARTET IN HARMONY

Matthew 22:23–33
Mark 12:18–27
Luke 20:27–40

Resurrection Ridicule

The intent of this fabricated yarn was to make the resurrection look ridiculous. The resurrection will happen at the end of time when righteous and unrighteous dead will rise and face judgment, but the Sadducees didn't believe there would be a resurrection.

In the first place, Jesus told them, their ignorance of the Scriptures and the **power of God** were showing (Matthew 22:29). Life after resurrection will be totally different from anything experienced in this earthly life.

In Luke's report we learn that Jesus concentrated on the future life of the <u>righteous</u>, not the lost (Luke 20:35).

The Second Coming

Putting Matthew and Luke's reports together, Jesus told them four things about the resurrection world:

1. Marriage won't be necessary—it will be replaced by a new eternal relationship (Matthew 22:30).

2. Resurrected people will be **like the angels**—they will not be angels but will be immortal with spiritual bodies and other angel-like characteristics (Matthew 22:30).

3. It will be <u>impossible</u> for them to die (Luke 20:36).

4. They will be <u>known</u> as children of God because he is the God <u>of the living</u> not the dead (Luke 20:36).

> **Mark 12:28** One of the teachers of the law came and heard them debating. Noticing that Jesus had given them a good answer, he asked him, "Of all the commandments which is the most important?"

A Voice Of Reason In The Madness

Matthew's report makes this sound like another question concocted by the Pharisees to trap Jesus. Mark, however, gives the distinct impression that this lawyer was at least mildly approving of the way Jesus had handled the Sadducees on the subject of the resurrection (in which, by the way, Pharisees strongly believed).

Jesus' answer to the lawyer's question sums up the fundamentals of true Judaism and Christianity in three sentences:

- Monotheism: *"The Lord is one"* (Mark 12:29; Deuteronomy 6:4).

- Personal relationship with God: *"Love the Lord your God with all your heart and with all your soul and with all your mind and with all your strength"* (Mark 12:30; Deuteronomy 6:5).

power of God:
specifically, ability to raise the dead

☞ **GO TO:**

Romans 3:28; 4:3 (righteous)

like the angels: *Greek means "equal to angels"*

☞ **GO TO:**

Revelation 21:4 (impossible)

John 1:12–13; Romans 8:18–19 (known)

1 John 5:11–12 (of the living)

GOSPEL QUARTET IN HARMONY

Matthew 22:34–40
Mark 12:28–34

KEY POINT

Death can end physical existence but can never end a relationship to a God of love.

KEY Outline:

True Faith
Have one God
Love God
Love others

What Others are Saying:

GOSPEL QUARTET IN HARMONY

Matthew 22:41–23:39
Mark 12:35–40
Luke 20:41–47

☞ **GO TO:**

Matthew 16:13–16 (what)

John 1:14, 18; Philippians 2:5–8 (became flesh)

Luke 1:29–37; 2:4 (descendant)

What Others are Saying:

• Love for people: *"Love your neighbor as yourself"* (Mark 12:31; Leviticus 19:18).

The lawyer added that to do these things *"is more important than all burnt offerings and sacrifices"* (the formalities of religion). To which Jesus responded, *"You are not far from the kingdom of God"* (Mark 12:34).

It was the most enlightened thing to come out of the mouth of a Pharisee in a long time! He would not be the last whose heart opened to God through love.

Pierre Teilhard De Chardin: Some day, after we have mastered the winds, the waves, the tides and gravity, we will harness for God the energies of love and then for the second time in the history of the world man will have discovered fire.[5]

> **Mark 12:34b** And from then on no one dared ask him any more questions.

Exposé

His detractors had temporarily run out of gas. So in this rare moment when they had nothing to say, Jesus asked them the most crucial question anyone can answer:

"What do you think about Christ? Whose son is he?" (Matthew 22:42).
"The son of David," they replied.
"How is it then that David, speaking by the Spirit, calls him 'Lord'?" Jesus quoted the statement from the Old Testament (Matthew 22:44; Psalm 110:1).

In Jewish culture it would be appropriate for a son to call his father "Lord," but not the other way around. How can Christ be David's son and David's Lord at the same time?

The only answer is what Christians call the "Incarnation"—the miracle by which God <u>became flesh</u> in the person of Jesus Christ, whose human mother was a <u>descendant</u> of King David.

To accept the idea that Messiah was both Son of man and Son of God required a quantum leap in his listeners' concept of messiahship.

J. Dwight Pentecost: The fact that Messiah was David's son testified to Messiah's true humanity, but the fact that David called him "my Lord" testified to his true and undiminished deity, for "Lord" was a title for deity.[6]

William Barclay: There would be few that day who caught anything like all that Jesus meant. . . . They had the awed and the uncomfortable feeling that they had heard the voice of God, and for a moment, in this man Jesus, they glimpsed the very face of God.[7]

What Others are Saying:

> **Matthew 23:2–7** "The teachers of the law and the Pharisees sit in Moses' seat. So you must obey them and do everything they tell you. But do not do what they do, for they do not practice what they preach. They tie up heavy loads and put them on men's shoulders, but they themselves are not willing to lift a finger to move them.
>
> "Everything they do is done for men to see: They make their phylacteries wide and the tassels on their garments long; they love the place of honor at banquets and the most important seats in the synagogues; they love to be greeted in the marketplaces and to have men call them '**Rabbi**.'"

A Requiem For Hypocrisy

Jesus saves some of his biggest guns for attacks on <u>hypocrisy</u>. Again and again he opens fire on this sin.

From the amount of space given to the subject in the New Testament, it is hard to conclude anything but that Jesus classes spiritual arrogance and religious pretense among the most destructive and deadly of human transgressions—at least as far as the development of his kingdom fellowship is concerned.

In Matthew 23, he zeroes in on the problem of hypocrisy in spiritual leaders. The Pharisees gave every appearance of being spiritual. They believed they were superior in part because of their **phylacteries** (see illustration, page 169) and their **tassels**. People who teach, guide, or direct the spiritual life of others are not to be seen or to see themselves in any sense "above" or superior to either those they lead or their fellow leaders. He envisioned no hierarchy in the kingdom.

KINGDOM OF GOD When tempted to receive from others some elevated title (Matthew 23:8–10) or to be viewed by others in some elevated way, Christ's servant-leaders are to remember, *"You have only one Master and you are all brothers. . . . one is <u>your leader</u>,*[8] *the Christ"* (Matthew 23:8–10).

KEY POINT

Hypocrisy is possibly the deadliest sin.

Rabbi: teacher

☞ **GO TO:**

Matthew 6; Mark 7 (hypocrisy)

Exodus 13:9, 16; Deuteronomy 6:4–9; 11:13–21 (phylacteries)

Numbers 15:37–41; Deuteronomy 22:12 (tassels)

phylacteries: small boxes containing Bible verses, strapped to left wrist or forehead during prayers

tassels: fringe or cord attached to cloaks remind Jews of relationship with God

☞ **GO TO:**

Ephesians 1:22; 4:15; 5:23; Colossians 1:18; 2:19 (your leader)

What Others are Saying:

Dig Deeper

Dallas Willard: The hunger for titles and public awards in human life—indeed, in religious life—is quite astonishing. The bragging and exhibitionism . . . the almost routine puffing of credentials and resumes, and much that passes for normal as part of our "self-esteem" culture, are part of a life with no sense of our standing in the presence of God.[9]

What Is Hypocrisy?

Scripture	Definition of Hypocrisy	Solution
Matthew 23:3	Failure to practice what you preach.	Practice what you preach or shut up!
Matthew 23:4	Making rules for others that you don't intend to keep yourself.	Don't make rules for others unless you intend to keep them yourself.
Matthew 23:5	Being a religious show-off.	Stop trying to impress others with your religiousness or spirituality.
Matthew 23:6	Seeking places of honor in the synagogue or church.	Let God place you where he wants; don't settle for cheap substitutes for real honor (Luke 14:7–11).
Matthew 23:7–12	Demanding others notice your spiritual superiority; cherishing honors.	Satisfy yourself with the true greatness of humble servanthood.
Matthew 23:13	Making it difficult for others to find God.	Get out of the way; stop making rules; don't impose your ego on others.
Matthew 23:14–22	Misleading others into spiritual dishonesty and self-righteousness.	Lead people to God; let his Spirit change them (2 Corinthians 3:17–18).
Matthew 23:23–24	Majoring in minor issues ("gnats"/ useless rule keeping) while minoring in major issues ("camels"/personal, caring aspects of God's Law).	Get your priorities from God's word. Let his priorities become yours.
Matthew 23:25–28	A public image that masks hypocrisy and wickedness.	Deal with your inner sinfulness; let your "image" reflect the real you.
Matthew 23:29–36	Building monuments to dead heroes you'd oppose if they were alive.	Search your heart for the rejection, hatred, and violence that led to the martyr's death.

Other Scriptures with Jesus' Words about Hypocrisy:

Matthew 7:5	Matthew 6:5–6	Matthew 15:7–20	Matthew 24:45–49
Matthew 6:2–3	Matthew 6:16–18	Matthew 22:15–18	

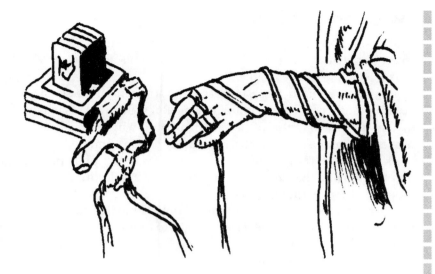

Phylacteries

Devout Pharisees strapped small boxes, called phylacteries, on their heads and left forearms during prayer. The boxes contained Scripture. Today Orthodox Jews still wear phylacteries.

Matthew 23:37–39 "O Jerusalem, Jerusalem, you who kill the prophets and stone those sent to you, how often I have longed to gather your children together as a hen gathers her chicks under her wings, but you were not willing. Look, your house is left to you desolate. For I tell you, you will not see me again until you say, 'Blessed is he who comes in the name of the Lord.'"

More Tears For Old Jerusalem

Jesus' requiem for the hypocrisy of Jerusalem and Israel's leaders does not end, as might be expected, with an angry tirade of epithets and vindictive judgments. It is, after all, a lament (a chant of woes). And it ends as a lament must end . . . with yearning tears!

Luke 21:1–4 As he looked up, Jesus saw the rich putting their gifts into the temple treasury. He also saw a poor widow put in two very small copper coins. "I tell you the truth, " he said, "this poor widow has put in more than all the others. All these people gave their gifts out of their wealth; but she out of her poverty put in all she had to live on."

Mark 12:40–44
Luke 20:47–21:4

two copper coins:
*quadrons or lepta, each
worth about 1/64 of a
denarius (day's wage)*

**Remember
This . . .**

**Something
to Ponder**

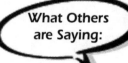

**What Others
are Saying:**

Twopenny Serenade

One of Jesus' stinging accusations of the hypocritical teachers of Israel was that, while they carried on their pious show, they *"devoured widows' houses"* (Luke 20:47).

The Law required these men to support themselves so their teaching could be offered without charge. But some teachers taught that supporting a rabbi was an act that could win you a place in heaven. Some misled disciples signed over their homes!

As he spoke, Jesus looked up and saw rich and poor people putting gifts into the temple treasury box. A nearly destitute widow dropped in **two copper coins**.

Her gift was a flyspeck on a football field compared to the gifts of the wealthy. But Jesus declared her gift to be greater than all the others. Rather than a percentage of their wealth, this poor woman gave everything she had to live on!

Jesus promised severe punishment to religious charlatans (Luke 20:47), but honored the sacrifice of sincere people who give to support what they understand to be the work of the Lord.

In dollars and cents, the gift of Mary of Bethany (John 12:3) who anointed the Lord with her expensive perfume (worth hundreds) and the twopenny gift of this widow (worth a fraction of a cent) don't even compare. In terms of love for God, they may be of equal worth.

John Chrysostom: [Jesus] paid no attention to the amount of the money. What he did heed was the wealth of her soul. If you calculate by the value of her money, her poverty is great. If you bring her intention into the light, you will see that her store of generosity defies description.[10]

Study Questions

1. In the story of the two brothers (Matthew 21:28–32), who do the two brothers represent? With which brother do you most identify?

2. Which group of Jesus' enemies joined the Pharisees for the trick question about paying taxes to Caesar? What item did Jesus use in answering this question? What principle did Jesus teach in his answer?

3. What four things did Jesus tell the Sadducees about the resurrection when they tried to make it look ridiculous?

4. Jesus hated hypocrisy. But when he finished exposing the hypocrites of Jerusalem, what happened (Matthew 23:37–38)? What does this reveal about Jesus' attitude toward hypocrites?

CHAPTER WRAP-UP

- Jesus used the fig tree he had shriveled to teach his disciples about the power of faith and forgiveness. (Matthew 21:19–22; Mark 11:19–20; Luke 17:3–6)

- During the last week of his earthly ministry, even though there was a price on his head, Jesus taught in the Temple. The religious and political leaders tried to trap him with questions. But, one by one, he turned the answers back on the questioners. (Luke 20:1–44)

- At the end of the debate, Jesus warned the people against following the example of the religious leaders, accusing them of failing to practice what they preach and turning Jewish religious life into an unbearable burden so they could maintain their positions of control. He gave a long lament over their hypocrisy, and wept for them and Jerusalem's rejection of him. (Matthew 23)

- Jesus accused the Pharisees of *"devouring widow's houses."* He used a widow's twopenny offering to teach that the value of giving is not the amount, but the heart of the giver and the level of sacrifice. (Luke 20:45–21:4)

10 FINAL HOUR PROPHECIES

CHAPTER HIGHLIGHTS
- The Fleeting Splendor of the Temple
- The Beginning of the End
- Jerusalem's Falling
- Signs of Christ's Return
- Ready or Not

Let's Get Started

During the last week of his earthly life Jesus talked more about the future than he ever had before. Some of what he said related to his disciples' near future, some to the distant future—"end-time events," signals of the Second Coming of Christ.

The Second Coming

Bible prophecy should be approached with a humble, teachable, flexible attitude. It is important to remember that Jesus clearly said no one would be able to predict the *"day or hour"* he would return (Matthew 24:36). And not even the most careful Bible scholar knows for sure what every symbol or sign means. The meanings become apparent as the prophecies are fulfilled and the actual events take place.

> **Luke 21:5–7** Some of his disciples were remarking about how the temple was adorned with beautiful stones and with gifts dedicated to God. But Jesus said, "As for what you see here, the time will come when not one stone will be left on another; every one of them will be thrown down."
>
> "Teacher," they asked, "when will these things happen? And what will be the sign that they are about to take place?"

GOSPEL QUARTET IN HARMONY

Matthew 24–25
Mark 13
Luke 21:5–36

**GOSPEL QUARTET
IN HARMONY**

Matthew 24:1–3

Mark 13:1–4

Luke 21:5–7

gifts: *from the rich and famous*

☞ **GO TO:**

1 Kings 5–7;
1 Chronicles 2–7
(Solomon)

Ezra 3–6; Haggai 1:1–
2:9 (70 years later)

☞ **GO TO:**

Luke 19:43–44 (before)

What Others
are Saying:

The Fleeting Splendor Of The Temple

It was late Tuesday of Jesus' final week. As he was leaving the temple area after a fast-paced day of controversy and confrontation with angry men determined to bring him down, his disciples commented on how beautiful and impressive the sacred buildings were with all the lavish **gifts** that decorated them.

The Temple held a cherished place in Jewish hearts. The Temple in which Jesus ministered had recently undergone a massive renovation project and was artistically more beautiful than any time since it was first constructed.

Here is a brief history:

- King <u>Solomon</u> built the first (in Jewish minds, the most magnificent) Temple in the 960s B.C. (see GWMB, pages 160–162). It was looted several times by enemies and finally destroyed by the Babylonians in 587 B.C.
- A smaller, less impressive Temple was built, <u>70 years later</u>, by Jews returned from Babylonian exile.
- Just before the birth of Jesus, Herod the Great launched a project to expand, refurbish, and beautify the second Temple. He commissioned a huge golden grapevine sculpture to embellish the entrance. The whole refurbishing project took 46 years and was completed after Herod's death.

While they were "ooh-ing and aah-ing," Jesus zapped his followers with a prophetic lightning bolt: This dazzling Temple would be destroyed so completely not one stone would be left on another (Matthew 24:2; Mark 13:2; Luke 21:6)! He'd said it <u>before</u>.

In stunned silence the disciples followed Jesus to the Mount of Olives, outside the city. There they broke the silence with three questions (Matthew 24:3):

- "When will the Temple be destroyed?"
- "What will be the sign of your coming?"
- "What will be the sign of the end of the age?"

As they sat among the ancient olive trees, Jesus gave them a telescopic glimpse into the future with a lengthy, detailed prophetic teaching.

Josephus: The outward face of the temple in its front wanted nothing that was likely to surprise either men's minds or their eyes, for it was covered over with plates of gold of great weight, and, at the first rising of the sun, reflected back a very fiery splendor, and made those who forced themselves to look upon it to turn their eyes away, just as they would have done at the sun's rays. But the temple appeared to strangers, when they were at a distance, like a mountain covered with snow, for, as to those parts of it that were not gilt, they were exceeding white.[1]

Larry (Lawrence O.) Richards: The years that stretch out toward the future will be marked by tension, disasters, wars, growing wickedness, and persecution for Jesus' followers. But these common disasters are only a foreshadowing of what is known in the Old Testament as the "day of the Lord," which Jesus describes here as a time of "great distress, unequaled from the beginning of the world until now—never to be equaled again" (Matthew 24:21).[2]

The Beginning Of The End

They asked for signs. Jesus told them to watch for these:

1 *A procession of deceivers* (Matthew 24:5; Mark 13:6; Luke 21:8). During the lifetimes of the apostles, **counterfeit christs** crossed the Israelite landscape like illusive desert dust devils, claiming to be the promised Messiah. Today the list of pretenders and false teachers is long and growing.

Beware of anyone who claims to be Christ or to have a special revelation that contradicts the teachings of the Bible. Put any person or group on your "suspect" list who has figured out exactly when Christ will return.

2 *Rumblings of wars and disasters* (Matthew 24:6–7; Mark 13:7–8; Luke 21:9–11). The period of history following Christ's resurrection was a time of great international unrest. Roman historian Tacitus said, "It was a time rich in disasters, horrible with battles, torn with seditions, savage even in peace."

Today, television and the internet bring live coverage of major disasters around the world while they are happening—hunger, disease, earthquakes, civil wars, tornadoes, hurricanes, tsunamis, and plane crashes.

Jesus encouraged his followers not to be frightened by such reports (Matthew 24:6). War and calamity are not necessarily signals of the end.

What Others are Saying:

GOSPEL QUARTET IN HARMONY

Matthew 24:4–26
Mark 13:5–23
Luke 21:8–1

counterfeit christs:
Theudas and Judas of Galilee (Acts 5:36–37); Dositheus and Menander

Remember This . . .

How to Identify a False Teacher

Dig Deeper

A False Teacher	Scripture from 1 Timothy
Engages in mystical speculations that titillate curiosity but do not promote devotion to God	1:4
Focuses on secondary issues, such as genealogies	1:4
Promotes controversies, questions designed to raise doubt	1:4
Promotes activities that do not develop faith and the doing of God's work	1:4
Pursues goals that lead to lovelessness, hate, prejudice	1:5
Acts and speaks from impure motives and actions	1:5
Promotes goals or teachings which violate your sense of right and wrong	1:5
Displays insincerity, spiritual and intellectual dishonesty	1:5
Engages in senseless talk	1:6
Is driven by selfish ambition	1:7
Lacks spiritual understanding	1:7
Departs from Christian belief and lifestyle	4:1
Follows pagan, non-Christian teachings	4:1
Is hypocritical, lying	4:2
Shows insensitivity of conscience, teachings that dull the sense of right and wrong	4:2
Presents a religion by rules and regulations, asceticism	4:3
Forbids marriage	4:3
Insists on arbitrary dietary restrictions	4:3
Disagrees with Jesus' teachings	6:3
Is arrogant	6:4
Has an argumentative, quarrelsome nature	6:4
Spreads envy, suspicion, gossip, divisiveness	6:5
Is motivated by greed and money	6:5

First Advent: Christmas, the birth of Christ

Second Advent: the Second Coming; Christ's return

The entire period between his **First Advent** and **Second Advent** will be characterized by distressing news of national and international conflict, wars, and catastrophes (Matthew 24:7–8; Luke 21:10–11).

When we hear such news, we are to remember that history is unfolding exactly as Jesus predicted, and will lead ultimately to his return.

GOD'S WORD FOR THE BIBLICALLY-INEPT

Oswald Chambers: "Do not panic." That is either the statement of a madman or of a Being who has power to put something into a man and keep him free from panic, even in the midst of the awful terror of war. The basis of panic is always *cowardice*. Our Lord teaches us to look things full in the face. He says—"When you hear of wars, don't be scared." It is the most natural thing in the world to be scared, and the clearest evidence that God's grace is at work in our hearts is when we do not get into panics.[3]

What Others are Saying:

3 *Persecution of Christ's followers* (Matthew 24:9–10; Mark 13:9–13; Luke 21:12–19). Jesus predicted that believers would face persecution. The nameless "they" (Luke 21:12) who harass followers of Christ and demand they answer for their identification with him include religious and secular authorities ("*synagogues . . . kings and governors*"). Association with Jesus can get you jail time (verse 12), betrayal by family and friends, and even death (verse 16) or worse. The unbelieving world <u>hates Christ</u>, and his followers often become the <u>target</u> of that hatred (verse 17).

☞ **GO TO:**

John 15:18–16:4 (hates Christ)

Matthew 5:10–12; Luke 6:22–23; Acts 5:17–18; Colossians 1:24 (target)

In every generation since Jesus spoke this prophecy, including the present, Christ's followers have paid in the currency of rejection, discrimination, suffering, torture, and death. But tucked into the persecution prophecy package are some priceless promises (Luke 21:13–19):

- Persecution will give Christians opportunities to share their faith (verse 13).
- Jesus' Spirit will be with them and give answers and wisdom (verses 14–15).
- Their enemies will hear what they say and be unable to refute it (verse 15).
- Even if it leads to **martyrdom,** the believer is safe—he or she will <u>never perish</u> (verses 18–19).

martyrdom: to be killed because of one's faith

EARLY CHURCH LIFE: During the first 250 years, the early Christians suffered 10 Imperial persecutions aimed at destroying Christianity.

☞ **GO TO:**

John 11:25–26 (never perish)

William Barclay: The man who walks with Christ may lose his life, but he can never lose his soul.[4]

What Others are Saying:

megatrends: major movements, directions in society

4 *Intensification of trouble and opportunity* (Matthew 24:9–26; Mark 13:14–23). As the present age moves toward its end (Matthew 24:14), several observable **megatrends** will develop which spell trouble for society and the church:

- Persecution will intensify (verse 9).
- Many will *"fall away"* from the Christian faith (verse 10).
- False prophets will emerge and increasing numbers of people will be misled by them (verse 11).
- Lawlessness and crime will be on the rise (verse 12).
- Love—for the Lord and other people—will <u>grow cold</u>; hate will flourish (verse 12).

☞ **GO TO:**

2 Timothy 3:1–5;
Revelation 2:4
(grow cold)

KINGDOM OF GOD

At the same time these disturbing trends are taking place, another very important movement will make its impact: *"the gospel of the kingdom shall be preached in the whole world for a witness to all nations"* (Matthew 24:14; Mark 13:10).

Many students of the Bible, including evangelist Billy Graham, believe this means that before all the prophecies of Jesus are fulfilled, people of every nation in the world will have the news of Jesus Christ in some form.

What Others are Saying:

C. Peter Wagner: In all of history, there has never been a more exciting time than this to be a Christian. A wave of world Christians is carrying the gospel to places it has never before reached. We are indeed in the springtime of missions.[5]

KEY Outline:

Signs of the End
Counterfeit christs
Wars and disasters
Persecution of Christians
Megatrends of trouble and opportunity

> **Luke 21:20–21, 23–24** "When you see Jerusalem surrounded by armies, you will know that its desolation is near. Then let those who are in Judea flee to the mountains, let those in the city get out, and let those who are in the country not enter the city. . . . There will be great distress in the land and wrath against this people. They will fall by the sword and will be taken as prisoners to all the nations. Jerusalem will be trampled on by the Gentiles until the times of the Gentiles are fulfilled."

Jerusalem's Falling

This section of Luke 21 speaks directly to the disciples' question, "When will the Temple be thrown down?" (verse 7).

Third-century Christian historian Eusebius tells of the tragic fall of the Holy City in **70 A.D.**

The Roman army under Emperor Titus surrounded Jerusalem with **siege works**, completely cutting off access in or out of the city. A million Jews who had crowded into the city for protection died of starvation and the slaughter that followed; 97,000 were taken prisoner.[6] The city was leveled.

Titus had given orders for his soldiers to spare the Temple, but their **rage** at the Jews was too intense. The looting and destruction got out of hand and the once-glorious Temple was reduced to burning <u>rubble</u>.

The large community of Christians living in Jerusalem were reminded by their prophets of Jesus' warning (Luke 21:21), and escaped to the mountains before the siege began. (Christians escaped to the Gentile town of Pella, east of the Jordan, where Herod Agrippa 2 gave them asylum.)

Following the destruction of Jerusalem, the Jews were <u>again uprooted</u> from their homeland and scattered among the nations, just as Jesus predicted (verse 24).

They would be a nation without a land for more than 1,900 years. For all those years Jerusalem and the Promised Land would be *"trampled on by the Gentiles."*

> **Matthew 24:3** As Jesus was sitting on the Mount of Olives, the disciples came to him privately. "Tell us," they said, "when will this happen, and what will be the sign of your coming and of the end of the age?"

Signs Of Christ's Return

Jesus had told his friends several times—directly or in story—that in the future, after his death and resurrection, he would <u>return</u> to judge the world and the church.

Tuesday evening before he died, among the olive trees, his disciples waited eagerly for the answer to their question: *"What will be the **sign** of your coming?"*

Jesus described four events, which would be developing at the time of his coming:

1 *Completion of the "times of the Gentiles"* (Luke 21:24). After its destruction, the Jewish nation would be gone, but Jerusalem and the Holy Land would be inhabited, dominated by Gentiles

70 A.D.: *less than 40 years after Jesus' prophecy*

siege works: *barricades*

rage: *"wrath," not God's but the Romans'*

☞ **GO TO:**

Matthew 23:38; 24:2; Luke 13:35; 19:44; 21:6 (rubble)

Genesis 46–47; 2 Kings 17; 24:10–25:12; 2 Chronicles 36:20 (again uprooted)

KEY POINT

Jesus' prophecies of Jerusalem's destruction were fulfilled in detail.

GOSPEL QUARTET IN HARMONY

Matthew 24:15–41
Mark 13:14–32
Luke 21:24–33

☞ **GO TO:**

Matthew 16:27; Mark 8:38; Luke 9:26; 12:37–40; 17:22–30 (return)

sign: *indication, signal*

time: most acceptable
span on God's timetable

until their "**time**" was up (see GWDN, pages 35–36). The end of
Gentile control would be an important milestone on the prophetic
calendar. After 1,900 years, in 1948 by edict of the United Nations, the Jews were reestablished in their homeland. In June 1967,
in the Six Day War, they recaptured Old Jerusalem. Though the
political dispute over Jerusalem continues, the Gentiles' time to
"trample" the city appears over.

2 *The sight of the "abomination that causes desolation" in the Temple*
(Matthew 24:15–26; Mark 13:14–23, and see GWRV, page 196–
198). This was predicted by the prophet Daniel (see GWDN, pages
255–256). The "abomination" is an act of sacrilege by a future
ruler who makes a treaty with Israel and tries to assume the place
of God. The "desolation" is the beginning of the great time of
trouble (see number 3, below). Daniel 11:36 describes this ruler
as a "king" who "will do as he pleases." The New Testament calls
him the "Antichrist," among other things. Two things must have
taken place before this: (1) The Jews must be back in the Promised Land (they are); and (2) the Temple must be rebuilt (plans
are ready; you can visit the architectural model in Israel).

☞ **GO TO:**

Daniel 8:13; 9:27;
11:31; 12:11
(abomination)

2 Thessalonians 2:3–11;
1 John 2:18–23; 4:3;
Revelation 13:11–18
(Antichrist)

3 *A time of great trouble* (Matthew 24:21–26; Mark 13:19–23;
Luke 21:25–26). "*A* **great distress***, unequaled from the beginning of the world until now—and never to be equaled again. If those
days had not been cut short, no one would survive, but for the sake of
the* **elect** *those days will be shortened*" (Matthew 24:21–22). This is
what students of prophecy call the Tribulation (see GWDN, page
319; GWRV, page 101).

distress: Greek:
tribulation, trouble,
emotional and spiritual
distress

elect: chosen people,
those who put their faith
in Jesus Christ

4 *Signs on the earth and in the sky* (Matthew 24:29; Mark 13:24–
25; Luke 21:25–26). The descriptions given may prophesy
celestial phenomena (meteors, comets, unusual weather patterns,
etc.), or sudden and violent national and international upheavals,
or both. In the Bible the "sea" is often a figure of speech for masses
of people. "*The roaring and tossing of the sea*" (Luke 21:25) could
be literal tidal waves, tsunamis, hurricanes, or violent demonstra-
tions and disturbing social changes. The darkening of the sun
and moon (Matthew 24:29) could result from the fires of war.
The mood of the times is described in Luke 21—mental distress,
perplexity, pressure (verse 25), fear, terror, astonishment, appre-
hension (verse 26) over what's coming on the world.

☞ **GO TO:**

Daniel 12:1; Revelation
6–18; Ezekiel 38–39
(great distress)

Romans 11:5–6; Titus
1:1–3; 1 Peter 1:1–2
(elect)

Isaiah 13:4–5
(upheavals)

Isaiah 13:6–8
(mental distress)

The Great Distress and the Day of the Lord

Old Testament images of the great distress (Tribulation/Day of the Lord) at history's end:

Deuteronomy 4:30	Daniel 12:1
Isaiah 2:12, 19	Joel 1:15
Isaiah 13:6–13	Joel 2:1–2, 11, 30–32
Isaiah 24:1–6, 19–21	Joel 3:14–16
Jeremiah 30:7	Amos 5:18–20
Ezekiel 13:5	Zephaniah 1:14–2:3
Ezekiel 30:2–5	Zechariah 14:1–21

Dig Deeper

Matthew 24:27–31 For as lightning that comes from the east is visible even in the west, so will be the coming of the **Son of Man**. Wherever there is a carcass, there the vultures will gather.

"Immediately after the distress of **those days**
   'the sun will be darkened,
   and the moon will not give its light;
the stars will fall from the sky,
   and the heavenly bodies will be shaken.'

"At that time the sign of the Son of Man will appear in the sky, and all the nations of the earth will mourn. They will see the Son of Man coming in the clouds of the sky, with power and great glory. And he will send his angels with a loud trumpet call, and they will gather his elect from the four winds, from one end of the heavens to the other."

Son of Man: *Jesus*

those days: *the time of great tribulation*

The Second Coming

Pow! Crash! A Blinding Flash! He Comes!

In his First Coming, Jesus came silently, in the womb of Mary, the girl from Nazareth. When he comes again it will be with all sorts of heavenly fireworks (Matthew 24:27–31):

- Lightning (Matthew 24:27; 1 Corinthians 15:52)
- Death and rotting corpses (Matthew 24:28; Ezekiel 39:11–13)
- Smoke, meteors, stars falling (Matthew 24:29; Revelation 1:12–14)
- Worldwide visibility (Matthew 24:30; Zechariah 12:10; Revelation 1:7) (television, internet coverage, or miracle?)

GOSPEL QUARTET IN HARMONY

Matthew 24:27, 30–31
Mark 13:26–27
Luke 21:27

- Shock and grief in all the nations (Matthew 24:30)
- Spectacular arrival on the clouds (Matthew 24:30; Daniel 7:13–14; Acts 1:10–11)
- Power and glory (Matthew 24:30; Matthew 26:64)
- Angels (Matthew 24:31; Revelation 19:8)
- Trumpet blasts (Matthew 24:31; 1 Corinthians 15:52; 1 Thessalonians 4:16; Revelation 8:6–13)

When Jesus comes, angels will be dispatched to gather the followers of Christ, living and dead, from every part of the universe (Matthew 24:31). Christians call this the "**Rapture**" of the church (see GWRV, pages 63–67).

Rapture: *Latin: rapio, meaning "to be caught up"*

☞ **GO TO:**

1 Thessalonians 4:15–17 (Rapture)

What Others are Saying:

KEY Outline:

"*Rapture*"
Jesus returns
Angels collect
Dead rise

Richard Kyle: If you're any kind of a sober, sincere Christian, you have to expect and believe that Jesus Christ is going to return physically at a particular time. The Bible doesn't give us many details about this, and so, unfortunately, the hope of Christ's return has become the fodder for the curious and for fanatics. But that doesn't change the essential biblical teaching: Christ will come again.[7]

Hal Lindsey: One out of every 25 verses in the New Testament is related to the second coming of Christ, and the survival of mankind as well as the fulfillment of hundreds of unconditional promises especially made to the believing remnant of the Jewish race are dependent on the second coming of Christ to this earth. As a matter of fact, in the Old Testament there were more than 300 prophecies regarding Christ's first coming (all of which were literally fulfilled), but more than 500 relating to his second coming.[8]

GOSPEL QUARTET IN HARMONY

Matthew 24:32–41
Mark 13:28–32
Luke 21:28–33

☞ **GO TO:**

Acts 1:7 (precisely)

> **Matthew 24:36, 42** "No one knows about that day or hour, not even the angels in heaven, nor the Son, but only the Father. . . . Therefore keep watch, because you do not know on what day your Lord will come."

Synchronize Your Watches! . . . Or Not

"*When will this happen?*" the disciples asked (Matthew 24:3).

Jesus did not tell them <u>precisely</u> when he would return. He gave them trends to watch so they'd know history was unfolding according to God's plan. He gave a few clues. He knew people would play amateur detective, and try to outguess God about the timing of the Second Coming, the great Tribulation, and the Rapture.

Jesus said even he didn't know when it would happen.

Some discreet detective work in Bible prophecy is a good thing if it leads to spiritual readiness and not just titillating speculation. But if you hear anyone saying he or she knows the date of Jesus' return, tune that person out—they're full of baloney! Only the heavenly Father knows.

Ready Or Not

"Jesus is coming soon!"

Survivalists take to the hills. Alarmists cry that the end is near. Hedonists say, "Eat, drink and be merry."

True believers pay attention to Jesus' warnings and instructions, keep themselves spiritually alert and alive, and eagerly anticipate his return (see GWRV, pages 325–327).

Lawrence O. (Larry) Richards: While interpretation of prophecy can be debated, there is no debate at all that we are to live as faithful servants of the Son of God. . . . personal commitment to readiness for Jesus' imminent return is far more important than being "right" about what form that return will take.[9]

Tim Stafford: Here and now we do not have Jesus as we want to have him. But rather than trying to do away with our uncomfortable unfulfillment, we should let ourselves feel most deeply what we miss. We should allow ourselves to dream of Jesus' full presence as we prepare for his coming.

The Second Coming is not the end of history; it is the fulfillment of history—a history we are now making. The King is coming. Let the kingdom prepare.[10]

Ten End-Time Exhortations from Luke 21[11]

1. Don't be deceived by false teachers (21:8).
2. Don't be frightened by disasters predicted to take place in the end times (21:9–11).
3. Don't be anxious when subjected to legal action because of your witness for Christ (21:12–15).
4. Do stand firm when betrayed by those dearest to you and when hated by all (21:16–19).

Remember This . . .

GOSPEL QUARTET IN HARMONY

Matthew 24:42–25:46
Mark 13:33–37
Luke 21:28–36

What Others are Saying:

Dig Deeper

5. Do be encouraged when the events associated with final judgment begin to take place (21:25–28).

6. Do recognize these events as evidence that God's kingdom is about to come in its fullness (21:29–31).

7. Do have confidence that during this time of tribulation Christ's words remain sure (21:32–33).

8. Don't be distracted by drugs and alcohol or by becoming weighed down with the cares of life (21:34).

9. Do watch and pray, so when Christ comes you may win his endorsement for your faithfulness (21:36).

10. Stand tall and look for emancipation (21:28).

A Six-Pack Of Preparedness Parables

Jesus told a batch of parables to show his hearers how important it was to be prepared.

1 *The Boss's Long Trip* (Mark 13:33–37). Christians waiting for Christ's return are like employees left in charge of the business while their boss is away. They don't know when he will return. The best way to be ready is simply to live and work so that it doesn't matter when he returns. He can come whenever he comes—they're ready 'cause they're doing what they should be doing . . . every day.

What Others are Saying:

Oswald Chambers: The only way to wait for the Second Coming is to watch that you do what you should do so that *when* he comes is a matter of indifference. It is the attitude of a child, certain that God knows what he is about. When the Lord does come it will be as natural as breathing.[12]

☞ **GO TO:**

Luke 12:39; 1 Thessalonians 5:2, 4; 1 Peter 3:10; Revelation 3:3; 16:15 (night burglar)

2 *The Night Burglar* (Matthew 24:42–44). No self-respecting second-story man calls on his cell phone to let you know when he's gonna burglarize your house. If he did, his crime spree would end with one break-in, because you'd have the cops waiting when he came. Jesus will return at a time least expected. We'd best be ready all the time.

3 *The Two Servants* (Matthew 24:45–51). Servant #1 faithfully carries out responsibilities the boss left with him. When the boss comes back, #1 is ready, even though he didn't know when to expect him. He's rewarded for a job well done. Servant #2 decides there's no hurry (*"My master is staying away a long time"*).

He puts off doing what he should be doing, mistreats his fellow servants, and wastes his time drinking with his cronies at the local pub. He plans to get around to fixing things later, before the boss returns. He's wrong. Unexpectedly the boss comes back, drags the procrastinator out of the pub and cuts him to pieces! The man is assigned *"a place with the hypocrites"* (verse 51). Because that's what an unfaithful servant is.

4 *The 10 Bridesmaids* (Matthew 25:1–13). Jewish weddings were joyful celebrations. The bride and friends waited at her home for the groom to come and take her to his home. As they waited, messengers repeatedly announced the bridegroom was coming. Everyone rushed out to meet him, only to discover it was a false alarm. So all went back inside. Finally about midnight, the groom and his friends arrived. Together, the two groups of friends and most of the townspeople noisily proceeded to escort the couple, lamps blazing, to the groom's home, taking the longest route so the most people could express their good wishes.

☞ **GO TO:**

Jeremiah 7:34
(joyful celebrations)

The bridesmaids—10 friends of the bride—are the focus of Jesus' story. Each had a lamp. Five brought extra oil to last through the long wait. Five brought lamps but no oil, thinking perhaps they could obtain it after they arrived. It was a tragic miscalculation. When the call came at midnight that the bridegroom was coming, the bridesmaids trimmed their lamps to go meet him. In the long wait, however, the five without extra oil had fallen asleep and their lamps were going out. When they woke up they asked their five counterparts to share oil with them, but the wise young ladies only had enough to supply their own lamps. (Oil may represent the Holy Spirit and lamps the state of each one's relationship with God—either full of (under control of) the Spirit or living on yesterday's experience with God).

While the shortsighted girls hurried to find an oil merchant in the middle of the night, the bridegroom arrived . . . for real. The procession went off to his house. The five wise bridesmaids went in and enjoyed the festivities. By the time the other five returned, the door was shut. They were left out in the cold. They missed everything!

The Second Coming

The story has one point: *"Therefore, keep watch, because you do not know the day or the hour"* (Matthew 25:13). What are you doing to prepare for his coming?

What Others are Saying:

☞ **GO TO:**

Luke 19:11–27
(familiar ring)

---

2 Peter 3:8–9, 15
(long time)

---

talents: *58 to 80 pounds of silver per talent—value: $1,000 or more*

KEY POINT

The time till Christ returns is best spent serving the Lord.

☞ **GO TO:**

Revelation 20:11–15
(judge)

Matthew 13:24–30,
36–43, 47–50;
24:40–41 (separate)

Luke 18:13–14;
Romans 3:21–26
(righteous)

---

righteous: *believers, justified in God's sight, experiencing forgiveness*

stranger: *alien, of a different nationality, race, culture, or social status*

William Barclay: There is no knell so laden with the tears of regret as the sound of the words, *too late.*[13]

Oswald Chambers: The parable of the ten virgins reveals that it is fatal from our Lord's standpoint to live this life without preparation for the life to come.[14]

5 *The Investment Challenge* (Matthew 25:14–30). The situation has a <u>familiar ring</u>. The boss departs on a long trip. (What else is new?) Jesus wanted his disciples to accept the reality of a long interval before he would set up an earthly kingdom—so he repeats it.

The master leaves three men in charge of his investments, according to their abilities. One is given five **talents** of silver ($5,000); the second, two ($2,000); the third, one ($1,000). They are to use their gifts to make money for their employer.

When he returned, an accounting took place. The first two were commended because both had doubled their money. The third had dug a hole in the ground and buried the money.

Needless to say the boss was not pleased. *"You wicked, lazy servant!"* he said (among other unpleasant things), took the $1,000 from him, and gave it to the one who had $10,000.

The point is, Christ will be gone a <u>long time</u> but he will return as promised. The interval is not to be spent dreaming of that future day or merely protecting the status quo. But the time is for serving the Lord, using what he has given you to advance his kingdom.

6 *The King's Disguise* (Matthew 25:31–46). When Jesus returns *all the nations* will stand before him as <u>judge</u>. Judge Jesus will <u>separate</u> the **righteous** from the unrighteous (verses 32–33, 37, 41). As he does, a startling thing will take place in that cosmic court scene. At some point the Shepherd-Judge will reveal something neither the good guys nor bad guys seemed to realize: While they were going about their daily lives, he was walking among them in disguise. At that moment the King will take off his mask: *"I was hungry . . . I was thirsty . . . I was a **stranger** . . . I needed clothes . . . I was sick . . . I was in prison"* (Matthew 24:35–36).

A wave of astonishment will sweep the courtroom. The Shepherd–Judge will say to the righteous, *"You fed me . . . you gave me a drink . . . you invited me in . . . you clothed me . . . you looked after me . . . you came to visit me* [in prison].*"

"Lord, when . . . ?" the righteous will reply, shaking their heads in amazement.

---

186   GOD'S WORD FOR THE BIBLICALLY-INEPT

The King will say, *"Whatever you did for one of the least of these brothers of mine, you did for me"* (verse 40).

KINGDOM OF GOD This story reveals that Jesus Christ personally and intensely <u>identifies</u> with and cares about needy, hungry, thirsty, lonely, naked, sick, and imprisoned people.

The Bible teaches that we <u>cannot be saved</u> by good works. But giving high priority to <u>caring</u> for such people is an important aspect of life in God's kingdom community, a powerful expression of genuine righteousness, and an important part of *"seeking <u>first</u> the kingdom of God."*

Scholars discuss who Christ's brothers are (Matthew 25:40)—fellow Christian believers? Or anyone weak, poor, or powerless?

His followers are certainly his brothers, but the early church took the view that Jesus' care included not only Christians but also *all* needy people.

As a result, a third-century pagan official wrote that the Christians were feeding more people in the city of Rome than the Roman government was!

EARLY CHURCH LIFE: The early Christians took economic as well as spiritual responsibility for one another. And when they met people in need, they shared what they had with them.

Ronald J. Sider: If Jesus' saying in Matthew 25:40 is awesome, its parallel is terrifying. "Truly I say to you, as you did it not to one of the least of these, you did it not to me" (verse 45). What does that mean in a world where millions die each year while rich Christians live in affluence? What does it mean to see the Lord of the universe lying by the roadside starving and walk by on the other side? We cannot know. We can only pledge, in fear and trembling, not to kill him again.[15]

Study Questions

1. To what three questions from his disciples did Jesus' Mount of Olives teachings give the answers?
2. How did Jesus say his disciples should *not* react when they hear of wars and disasters in the world? Why?
3. What four promises did Jesus give to Christians facing persecu-

---

☞ **GO TO:**

Proverbs 14:31; 19:17; Luke 4:18–19; Matthew 18:5; Acts 9:5 (identifies)

Romans 4:1–6; Galatians 2:16; Ephesians 2:8–9; 2 Timothy 1:9 (cannot be saved)

Something to Ponder

☞ **GO TO:**

Luke 12:32–34; Acts 2:42–47; 4:31–35; 11:28–30; Romans 12:13 (caring)

Matthew 6:33 (first)

What Others are Saying:

KEY POINT

What you do for needy people, you do for Jesus.

tion? How have you experienced God's faithfulness during times of pressure or persecution?

4. What were Christians told to do when they saw the armies surrounding Jerusalem?

5. Identify four or more of the nine "fireworks" Jesus says will accompany his Second Coming?

6. In the story of the Shepherd-King separating the sheep from the goats, list the six actions Jesus says will be used as a basis for judgment. In these six situations where do you feel best equipped to serve most naturally? In which of these six situations do you have the most trouble reaching out?

CHAPTER WRAP-UP

- Jesus' disciples were impressed by the magnificence of the Temple in Jerusalem. His response was to tell them the time was coming when the Temple would be destroyed. (Luke 21:5–7)

- In a lengthy prophetic teaching he spoke of war, disaster, earthquakes, and other disturbances, and told them not to fear when they saw these things; they were signs that God's plan was unfolding as he promised. He also promised them persecution. (Matthew 24:4–14; Luke 21:8–18)

- He told them what to watch for and what to do when they saw the armies encircling Jerusalem poised for its destruction. (Luke 21:20–24)

- Jesus taught there would be a great time of worldwide distress, such as has never been experienced by mankind before. The Antichrist would be revealed. The heavens would be shaken. There would be national and international unrest. (Matthew 24:15–25; Luke 21:25–28)

- He promised to come like lightning, visible throughout the world. His angels would gather his followers to be with him. He would come when least expected. They must be ready at all times. (Matthew 24:26–42)

- He told six stories about being ready, emphasizing the unexpectedness of his return, the need for faithfulness, the need to be alert and watching, the need to invest what he has given us in his work, and the need to care for people he identifies as his "brothers"—the poor and powerless. (Matthew 24:42–25:46)

11 COUNTDOWN TO GLORY

Let's Get Started

The final week of Jesus' earthly life moved closer to its climax. Few of the pilgrims gathered for the feast really knew this would be the most important Passover in Israel's history.

The <u>twin feasts</u> of Passover and Unleavened Bread were Israel's equivalent to Independence Day in the United States. Passover was the 15th of Nisan, first month of the Jewish calendar. The Feast of Unleavened Bread began the next day and lasted a week.

Every Jewish male within 15 miles of Jerusalem was required to attend. Families came along.

Jews all over the world kept Passover with the dream of celebrating in Jerusalem at least once in a lifetime. They still express that yearning in the wistful prayer: "Next year in Jerusalem!"

Weeks in advance, the entire nation focused on preparations. Roads and bridges were repaired. Tombs were whitewashed so no pilgrim would accidentally step on one and be disqualified from participation because of <u>ceremonial uncleanness</u>. The exciting story of the <u>first Passover</u> was told and retold, and its meaning explained in every synagogue.

Two days before Passover, a tradition in every home was for children and adults to light lamps and join in a happy search throughout the house for **leaven**, and then to destroy every trace they found.

> **Matthew 26:2** "As you know, the Passover is two days away—and the Son of Man will be handed over to be crucified."

CHAPTER HIGHLIGHTS

- The Price of Treachery
- The Last Meal
- Last Will and Testament
- Power Secrets
- Let's Get to Work!
- No Rose Garden
- Face to Face versus Spirit to Spirit

GOSPEL QUARTET IN HARMONY

Matthew 26:1–29
Mark 14:1–25
Luke 21:37–22:38
John 13:1–16:15

☞ GO TO:

Numbers 28:16–25 (twin feasts)

Numbers 19:16–22 (ceremonial uncleanness)

Exodus 12 (first Passover)

Exodus 12:17–20; 1 Corinthians 5:6–8 (leaven)

leaven: yeast, a symbol for sin

GOSPEL QUARTET IN HARMONY

Matthew 26:1–5, 14–16

Mark 14:1–2, 10–11

Luke 21:37–22:6

The Price Of Treachery

Two days before Passover, two groups were talking about the death of Christ. Jesus, spending the night with his men on the Mount of Olives, reminded them of what was ahead. Meanwhile, at the palace of the high priest inside the city, religious and civil leaders met to lay out a strategy to arrest and kill Jesus (Matthew 26:3–4).

The greatest challenge in their sordid business was to catch him alone, segregated from sympathetic festival crowds. If they seized him while he taught at the Temple, the leaders risked setting off a riot (verse 6), which would bring the Roman authorities down on their heads.

Judas made it easy.

> **Matthew 26:14–16** Then one of the Twelve—the one called Judas Iscariot—went to the chief priests and asked, "What are you willing to give me if I hand him over to you?" So they counted out for him thirty silver coins. From then on Judas watched for an opportunity to hand him over.

The Mind Of A Traitor

What sort of confused thinking turned a man <u>chosen</u> to be Christ's ambassador into his betrayer for a mere **30 silver coins**? Not much information is given. Consider these factors:

1. *Judas was disillusioned with Christ's plans for the kingdom.* He failed to see the kingdom of God as a spiritual community. When Mary <u>anointed</u> Jesus with expensive perfume, Judas was upset. The perfume could have been *"sold and the money given to the poor"* (John 12:4–5). Apparently he saw the kingdom as an uprising of the oppressed against the injustices of their oppressors. He missed the point that Jesus' primary mission was to rescue sinners. Judas had not signed on for that sort of kingdom.

2. *Judas <u>loved money</u> more than God* (Matthew 26:14–15). He was a petty embezzler (John 12:6). His outwardly noble social concern was corrupted by a hypocritical, greedy heart.

3. *Judas opened himself to <u>control by Satan</u>* (Luke 22:3). Disappointment with Jesus' leadership coupled with his own greed made Judas vulnerable to the diabolical suggestion to sell his mentor out to his enemies.

☞ **GO TO:**

Luke 6:12–16 (chosen)

Zechariah 6:12 (30 silver coins)

John 12:3–8 (anointed)

Matthew 6:24; Luke 16:13–15; 18:22–25 (loved money)

John 13:2; Luke 22:3 (control by Satan)

30 silver coins: *30 shekels, the price of a slave (Exodus 21:32)*

Luke 22:15–16 "I have **eagerly desired** to eat this Pass-over with you before I suffer. For I tell you, I will not eat it again until it <u>finds fulfillment</u> in the kingdom of God."

The Last Meal

Thursday of Passover week, during the daylight hours, preparations were made for Jesus and his 12 closest friends to eat the Passover meal in a borrowed upper room in Jerusalem.

During feasts, Jerusalemites opened their homes to out-of-town feast goers. An upper room was a box-shaped room atop a flat-roofed house, accessed by outside stairs.

After sunset the 13 friends gathered. Jesus began by sharing the intensity of his feelings.

Jesus did not hide his true feelings. J. B. Phillips translates the beginning of the above verse this way: *"With all my heart I have longed to eat this meal with you."* Compassion was natural for him, even for his enemies. He wept openly and expressed anger more than once.

He loved these men. For three years they'd been through everything together. Now he was up against the greatest challenge of his life. *"You are those who have stood by me in my trials,"* he said (Luke 22:28).

His psychological stress was tremendous. He would express his deepest emotions in unforgettable words.

eagerly desired: Greek: intense, irregular or violent desire, passion

☞ **GO TO:**

Matthew 18:20; Acts 2:4, 38–39, 42–47; 1 Corinthians 11:23–26 (finds fulfillment)

GOSPEL QUARTET IN HARMONY

Matthew 26:17–20
Mark 14:12–17
Luke 22:7–16
John 13:1–29

The Passover Menu

Entrée	Description	In Remembrance of	Scripture
Unleavened bread	Flat, cracker-like, bakes quickly	Hasty departure from Egypt	Exodus 12:34
Lamb	Killed at the Temple, blood offered to God, roasted	Blood on doorposts, sign to death angel to *pass over*	Exodus 12:1–11; 21–23
Salt water	Bowl full set on table	Tears shed as slaves; crossing of the Red Sea	Exodus 3:7–10; 14:1–31
Bitter herbs	Mix of horseradish, chicory, endive, horehound, lettuce	Bitterness of slavery; hyssop used to smear the blood	Exodus 1:11–14; 12:22
Charosheth	Sweet mix of apples, dates, pomegranates, nuts, cinnamon sticks	Mud and straw for making bricks for Pharoah's cities	Exodus 1:11; 5:1–19
Wine	4 cups, mixed 3 parts water to one part wine	God's four liberation promises to Israel	Exodus 6:6–7

(To learn more about the events, meal, and leader of the first Passover, see GWBI, page 28; GWHN, pages 109–111; and GWMN, pages 71–90, respectively.)

Sharing meals was an important aspect of early church life (see Acts 2:42, 46; 20:7).

> **Luke 22:24** A dispute arose among [the 12] as to which of them was considered to be greatest.

The Last Rivalry

At Mid-Eastern festival meals, diners reclined on three-person couches (*triclinia*) around a square U-shaped table, their heads toward and feet away from the table. Traditionally, the host sat in the center of the closed side and guests were placed in the order of rank. The seats closest to the host were the most honored.

There's no evidence such <u>ranking</u> was observed at the Last Supper (see Luke 22:27), except in the minds of the disciples, who maintained a <u>running argument</u> about who was top banana! They brought their petty rivalry with them into the upper room. Like schoolboys they maneuvered for the best seats.

After three years observing Jesus' model of leadership, had they caught nothing of his <u>servant style</u>? And how could they have been so woefully out of touch with his pain?

> **John 13:1b–5** Having loved his own who were in the world, [Jesus] now showed them the full extent of his love. The evening meal was being served, and the devil had already prompted Judas Iscariot, son of Simon, to betray Jesus. Jesus knew that the Father had put all things under his power, and that he had come from God and was returning to God; so he got up from the meal, took off his outer clothing, and wrapped a towel around his waist. After that, he poured water into a basin and began to wash his disciples' feet, drying them with the towel that was wrapped around him.

Jesus The Slave

The roads of Israel were dusty in dry seasons and muddy when it rained. Horse, donkey, ox, and camel dung added to the filth. Shoes were leather soles tied on with straps.

Pots of water were kept in every house for the purpose of washing guests' feet—a job usually assigned to the lowest slave. If both

☞ **GO TO:**

Matthew 23:5–12; Luke 14:7–11 (ranking)

Mark 10:35–37; Luke 9:46 (running argument)

Matthew 20:25–28 (servant style)

☞ **Check It Out:**

John 13:1–20

Jewish and Gentile servants were present, the Gentile did the foot washing; if no servant was there, women or children did it.

There were no slaves in the upper room. The disciples were too taken up with <u>competition</u> to volunteer to wash each other's feet.

So Jesus got up from the table and stripped off his robe. He tied a towel around his waist, filled a basin with water (see illustration below), got on his knees, **removed** each man's sandals, and poured water on their feet, gently washing away the road filth, and wiping them with the towel.

He would be their slave. In a few hours his slavery would climax on the cross!

☞ **GO TO:**

Luke 22:24–30
(competition)

removed: Passover is eaten with shoes on (Exodus 12:11)

Merril C. Tenney: The disciples' minds were preoccupied with dreams of elevation to office in the coming kingdom. They were jealous lest one of their fellows should have the best place. Consequently, no one of them was likely to abase himself by volunteering to wash the feet of the others. They were ready to fight for a throne, but not for a towel![1]

What Others are Saying:

KEY Outline:

Jesus' Mindset
God's timing
Love for his men
Judas' treachery
God's power
Headed home
His servant role

> **John 13:6–8a** He came to Simon Peter, who said to him, "Lord, are you going to wash my feet?"
>
> Jesus replied, "You do not realize now what I am doing, but later you will understand."
>
> "No," said Peter, "you shall never wash my feet."

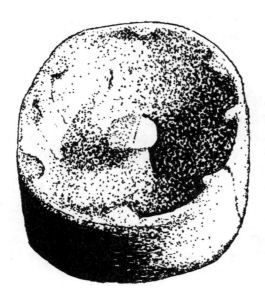

Foot Bath

Jesus may have used a clay basin or foot bath such as this to wash the disciples' feet.

☞ **Check It Out:**

John 13:6–11

☞ **GO TO:**

Mark 8:32–33
  (you shall never)

Titus 3:4–7 (from sin)

Romans 8:17;
  Ephesians 1:11–14
  (inheritance)

never: Greek: "not ever
till the end of time!"

KEY POINT

Willingness to serve
others and let them
serve us is essential to
true fellowship.

Remember
This . . .

Something
to Ponder

☞ **GO TO:**

1 John 1:7–2:2
  (continuing service)

"To Be Or Not To Be . . . Clean?"

Peter was stunned by Jesus' action: *"No, <u>you shall **never**</u> wash my feet."*

Jesus responded, *"Unless I wash you, you have no part with me"* (John 13:8). In the simplest sense, he meant they couldn't eat together unless Peter let him wash his feet.

There were also clear spiritual connotations:

1. Peter's dirty feet symbolized the necessity to be cleansed <u>from sin</u> in order to experience fellowship with Christ.
2. Unless Peter allowed Jesus to serve his needs the two could not enjoy fellowship—unwillingness to let Christ (and others) serve us is a barrier to intimacy.
3. The Jewish expression, "to have a part in me," often meant to share an inheritance. If Peter refused to be washed *spiritually,* he would lose his share in Jesus' <u>inheritance</u>.

Peter was sure he wanted to be friends with Jesus! He blurted out his feelings: If washing made him Christ's partner, then *"wash not just my feet but my hands and my head as well"* (John 13:9)!

Jesus responded, *"A person who has had a bath needs only to wash his feet; his whole body is clean"* (verse 10). Banquet guests bathed before coming to dinner. Upon arrival all they needed was foot washing. Practically speaking, Peter didn't need his hands and head washed, only his feet.

Literal foot washing is not a requirement for being a Christian; but cleansing from sin is essential. Only Jesus can do this—and only if we put our faith in him.

Spiritually speaking, if people sin after they've been cleansed from sin through faith in Christ, it is not necessary to start all over again. What is needed is to be honest about their sins and accept his <u>continuing service</u> of forgiveness and cleansing.

"You are clean," Jesus assured his men. Then he added, *"'Though not every one of you.' For he knew who was going to betray him"* (John 13:10–11).

Jesus had washed Judas' feet with the others. Could Judas have averted personal disaster by owning up to his treason and seeking forgiveness?

Revell Bible Dictionary: [Christ] was teaching two lessons through this [foot washing]. First, the washing of the disciples' feet symbolized the continual cleansing that would be available to them through his death. . . . Second, [it] provided an example for Christian leaders, who are to see themselves as servants to God's people. . . . Some Christian groups observe a ritual of foot washing, taking literally Jesus' words, "I have set you an example that you should do as I have done for you" (John 13:15). This practice, however, has never been widely adopted by the church. In fact, the only reference to foot washing in an **epistle** is an example of hospitality (1 Timothy 5:10).[2]

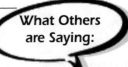
What Others are Saying:

epistle: *a letter, such as Romans, 1 and 2 Corinthians, 1 Timothy, etc.*

> **John 13:21–27** Jesus was troubled in spirit and testified, "I tell you the truth, one of you is going to betray me."
>
> His disciples stared at one another, at a loss to know which of them he meant. One of them, **the disciple whom Jesus loved**, was reclining next to him. Simon Peter motioned to this disciple and said, "Ask him which one he means."
>
> Leaning back against Jesus, he asked him, "Lord, who is it?"
>
> Jesus answered, "It is the one to whom I will give this piece of bread when I have dipped it into the dish." Then, dipping the piece of bread, he gave it to Judas Iscariot, son of Simon. As soon as Judas took the bread, Satan entered him.

the disciple whom Jesus loved: *John, writer of the fourth gospel*

The Last Appeal To A Lost Amigo

Separation between the traitor and the other disciples became increasingly apparent during the meal. Jesus had known the betrayer's identity and prophesied the betrayal since the <u>early days</u>. His treatment of the insider enemy was wonderful and heartbreaking.

- Jesus <u>handpicked</u> Judas to be his ambassador. There was no hint of treachery in the beginning—he was not chosen to be a traitor, he *became* one.

- Judas experienced the special privileges that went with being in Jesus' <u>inner circle</u>.

- Judas was given a place of honor and trust on the apostolic team, as <u>treasurer</u>.

- When others turned away from Jesus, Judas and the other 11 disciples remained <u>loyal</u>.

☞ **GO TO:**

John 6:70–71 (early days)

Luke 6:13–16 (handpicked)

Luke 6:16 (became)

Matthew 10:1–10; Luke 10:16–24 (inner circle)

John 12:4–6; 13:29 (treasurer)

John 6:68–71; 11:16 (loyal)

Dipped Bread
Honor
Friendship
Invitation
Identity

morsel: *probably a bit of the* Charosheth, *sweet fruit sauce*

After Judas contracted to sell Jesus out, the door remained open for him to reverse his decision. At the meal, Jesus offered his enemy one more invitation to be his friend.

The participants at the meal reclined on their left sides, supporting themselves on their left elbows, right hands free for feeding themselves. Food was served in large common bowls from which diners helped themselves.

John must have been on Jesus' right. When Peter asked him to find out the betrayer's identity, John leaned back and laid his head against Jesus' chest to speak to him.

Jesus told John to watch what he did with a piece of bread. A host would sometimes scoop a choice **morsel** from the dish with a piece of bread and hand it to a special guest, as an expression of honor or friendship. Jesus' action identified the betrayer and, at the same time, reminded Judas he was an especially beloved friend.

When Judas took the bread from Jesus' hand, he made the final decision that sealed his destiny. Jesus urged him to *"do quickly"* what he intended to do (John 13:27). We know the choice Judas made.

What Others are Saying:

F. L. Godet: As a sign of communion, it was a last appeal to the conscience of Judas. If, in receiving it, his heart had been broken, he still could have received pardon.[3]

George R. Beasley-Murray: [Jesus'] statement, "What you are about to do, do quickly," has the effect of setting Judas in the place of decision: he must make up his mind either to respond to Jesus' goodwill, and so repent of his plan to betray him, or to spurn it and carry out his intentions. If this be a correct reading of the situation, no man in all history was more truly "put on the spot" than Judas in that moment.[4]

Something to Ponder

When Judas walked out of the gathering, ironically, he walked into the dark of his soul's night as the full moon, which sets the date of Passover, shone brightly. Judas was not chosen for treason; he was chosen for apostleship. He chose treason.

What Others are Saying:

Michael Card:
Now, Judas, don't you come too close.
I fear that I might see.
The traitor's look upon your face
Might look too much like me.[5]

> **John 13:31–33** When [Judas] was gone, Jesus said, "Now is the Son of Man **glorified** and God is glorified in him. If God is glorified in him, God will glorify the Son in himself, and will glorify him at once.
>
> "**My children**, I will be with you only a little longer. You will look for me, and just as I told the Jews, so I tell you now: Where I am going, you cannot come."

Last Will And Testament

Eleven faithful members of Jesus' <u>spiritual family</u> shared the last meal with him.

The double-crosser was gone.

What Jesus said that night was for believers' ears only. Without commitment to follow Jesus as Lord, it is virtually impossible to comprehend the nature of the spiritual relationships he unveils to his friends. It was like the reading of his last <u>will and testament</u> . . . *before* he died.

> **John 13:34–35** "A new commandment I give you: Love one another. As I have loved you, so you must love one another. By this all men will know that you are my disciples, if you love one another."

The Last Commandment

In a few hours the relationship they'd begun three years earlier would enter a new stage.

Life under law would give way to life in the guidance and energy of the Holy Spirit. A superior, more comprehensive commandment would now rule their lives.

The command to love was not new; it was as old as the book of Leviticus. The word Jesus used for *new* doesn't mean "recent"; it means "superior, better in quality."

What makes this commandment superior?

- It establishes a family style of relationship among Christ's followers, identified throughout the New Testament by the phrase *"one another"* (John 13:34). Followers of Jesus are *brothers and sisters* in a way possible only to those who share his Spirit.

- It raises the standard for love (verse 34). The <u>Old Testament</u> called for loving one's neighbor *as oneself*. Jesus calls

☞ **GO TO:**

John 7:39; 12:16, 23, 28; 17:1, 5 (glorified)

glorified: *Christ's death and resurrection; completion of the Father's saving plan*

my children: *"little children"; expression of affection rabbis used with students*

☞ **GO TO:**

Mark 3:31–35 (spiritual family)

Hebrews 9:15–22 (will and testament)

KEY POINT

Last Supper teachings are primarily for believers.

☞ **GO TO:**

Leviticus 19:18, 34 (Old Testament)

☞ **GO TO:**

Romans 15:7; Galatians
6:1–2 (offering grace)

Mark 10:28–31;
Romans 13:8–10
(sums up)

Covenants: Testaments,
commitments, promises
governing relationship
(with God)

**What Others
are Saying:**

ACT OF THE HOLY SPIRIT

Enables Christians to
love as Christ loved

**GOSPEL QUARTET
IN HARMONY**

Luke 22:31–38
John 13:36–38

☞ **GO TO:**

James 1:13
(does not tempt)

us to love *as he loves*—putting others' welfare above our own, <u>offering grace</u>, laying our lives on the line for one another.

- It has a new impact (verse 35). Nothing demonstrates the reality of Jesus Christ more clearly to the world than Christians visibly loving each other in word and action.
- It <u>sums up</u> the moral demands of Old and New **Covenants** in a single principle.

EARLY CHURCH LIFE: Early Christians literally laid down their lives for one another. They knew the church to be a community of love.

John Powell: Going out to another in love means risk—the risks of self-disclosure, rejection, misunderstanding. It means grief, too, from the temporary separations, psychological or physical, to the final separation of death. Whoever insists on personal security and safety as the nonnegotiable conditions of life will not be willing to pay love's price or find love's enrichments. Whoever shuts himself or herself in the cocoon of self-protective defenses, keeping others always at a safe distance and holding on tightly to personal possessions and privacy, will find the price of love far too high and will remain forever a prisoner of fear.[6]

> **Luke 22:31–34** "Simon, Simon, Satan has asked to sift you as wheat. But I have prayed for you, Simon, that your faith may not fail. And when you have turned back, strengthen your brothers."
>
> But [Peter] replied, "Lord, I am ready to go with you to prison and to death."
>
> Jesus answered, "I tell you, Peter, before the rooster crows today, you will deny three times that you know me."

Damage Control

Peter was still hung up on Jesus' statement (John 13:33) that he was leaving. Jesus gave his well-intentioned friend four things to remember as the dust settled after the spiritual crash for which he was headed:

1. He must remember that the source of temptation is Satan (Luke 22:31). God <u>does not tempt</u> people to sin.

2. Because of <u>Jesus' prayers</u>, Peter's faith would survive (Luke 22:32).

3. Peter would bounce back after his spiritual lapse (Luke 22:32).

4. His failure would <u>equip</u> him to *strengthen* his fellow believers (Luke 22:32).

That night and in the days ahead, all the apostles would be at risk. And they would be without Jesus.

When he sent them to preach in <u>Galilee</u> and <u>Perea</u> they took no moneybag, knapsack, or extra shoes. Every need was supplied by people to whom they ministered.

But now the situation was different. They must be prepared to take care of themselves. "If you don't have a sword, sell the shirt off your back and get one!" he said (verse 36). **Two of them** happened to be carrying **swords**! (If taken literally, Jesus' statement here <u>contradicted</u> his other teachings. It's best to take it as a strong metaphor to emphasize the danger ahead.)

Larry (Lawrence O.) Richards: It is best to take Jesus' words as sad irony. . . . his followers will soon find only hostility and rejection in their homeland. It is interesting that the disciples were able to produce "two swords." Apparently they were intensely aware of the growing hostility to Jesus and were fearful. Significantly, when they tried to use these weapons later, Jesus rebuked them (Luke 22:49–51). For this reason some take Christ's words about buying swords as an oblique reference to the time of crisis the disciples were about to face.[7]

> **Luke 22:17–20** After taking the cup, he gave thanks and said, "Take this and divide it among you. For I tell you I will not drink again of the fruit of the vine until the kingdom of God comes."
>
> And he took bread, gave thanks and broke it, and gave it to them, saying, "This is my body given for you; do this in remembrance of me."
>
> In the same way, after the supper he took the cup, saying, "This cup is the new covenant in my blood, which is poured out for you."

"Remember Me"

As the Passover meal progressed Jesus used its most common elements—bread and wine—to introduce his friends to a new way

☞ **GO TO:**

Hebrews 7:25; 1 John 2:1 (Jesus' prayers)

2 Corinthians 1:3–7; Hebrews 2:18 (equip)

Matthew 10; Luke 9 (Galilee)

Luke 10 (Perea)

Matthew 5:38–42; Luke 6:29; 22:51 (contradicted)

What Others are Saying:

two of them: probably Simon Peter (later cut off a man's ear) and Simon the Zealot (right-wing revolutionary)

swords: Greek: short swords, like long hunting knives

GOSPEL QUARTET IN HARMONY

Matthew 26:26–29
Mark 14:22–25
Luke 22:17–20

☞ **GO TO:**

1 Corinthians 11:23–26
(to remember)

Acts 2:42, 46
(meal together)

KEY Outline:

Lord's Supper
Bread: Christ's body
- death

Wine: Christ's blood
- forgiveness

Common meal
- whosoever

Faith
- personal decision

What Others are Saying:

to remember him. Christians call it "Holy Communion" or "The Lord's Supper."

Bread and wine (see GWHN, pages 146–147) were common fare at everyday meals. This memory meal was not introduced in church. It was designed for family and friends eating an ordinary meal together in someone's home.

It's appropriate for Christians to remember Jesus at every meal, not just special "communion services."

1 *Broken bread* (Matthew 26:26; Mark 14:22; Luke 22:19). Breaking and sharing the flat Passover bread, Jesus asked them to remember his humanness and his mortal body, which in a few hours would be broken on the cross.

2 *Wine* (Matthew 26:27–28; Mark 14:23–24; Luke 22:20). Sharing the final cup of Passover wine with them, Jesus announced the end of the old system, the Old Covenant or Old Testament way of relating to God through animal sacrifices. A new system, New Covenant, or New Testament way of relating to God was being inaugurated by means of Christ's sacrifice (see Isaiah 53). Until his return (1 Corinthians 11:26), his followers would share wine together and remember his blood (Romans 5:8–9) poured out to pay the price for their *forgiveness*.

EARLY CHURCH LIFE: Early Christians shared the Lord's Supper whenever they got together, at church meetings or meals shared in their homes.

William Barclay: When two people enter into a covenant (Luke 22:20), they enter into a relationship with each other. But the covenant of which Jesus spoke was not a covenant between man and man; it was a covenant between God and man. . . . a new relationship between God and man. What Jesus was saying at the Last Supper was this: "Because of my life, and above all because of my death, a new relationship has become possible between you and God.". . . Because of what Jesus did for men, the way for men is open to all the loveliness of this new relationship with God.[8]

John R. W. Stott: Here then are the lessons of the upper room about the death of Christ. First, [his death] was central to his own thinking about himself and his mission, and he desired it to be central to ours. Secondly, [his death] took place in order to establish the <u>new covenant</u> and procure its promised forgiveness. Thirdly, [his death] needs to be appropriated individually if its benefits (the covenant and the forgiveness) are to be enjoyed. The Lord's Supper which Jesus instituted was not meant to be a slightly sentimental "forget-me-not," but rather a service rich in spiritual significance.[9]

☞ **GO TO:**

Jeremiah 31:31–34; Hebrews 8:7–13 (new covenant)

> **John 14:1–6** "Do not let your hearts be troubled. Trust in God; trust also in me. In my Father's house are many rooms; if it were not so, I would have told you. I am going to prepare a place for you. And if I go and prepare a place for you, I will come back and take you to be with me that you also may be where I am. You know the way to the place where I am going."
>
> Thomas said to him, "Lord, we don't know where you are going, so how can we know the way?"
>
> Jesus answered, "I am the way and the truth and the life. No one comes to the Father except through me."

Power Secrets

There were at least three reasons for Jesus' disciples to shake in their boots that night:

☞ **Check It Out:**

John 14:1–11

1. Jesus, on whom they depended for everything, was leaving them (John 13:33).
2. Peter, the "Rock," strongman of faith (Matthew 16:16; John 6:68–69), would deny the Lord before sunup (John 13:38).
3. Deadly danger was around the corner and they'd face it alone (Luke 22:36).

Reining In Galloping Fears

For these fears Jesus had one answer: "Believe God. Believe me" (John 14:1). Believing in Jesus when they saw him arrested, condemned, and crucified would not be a piece of cake! So Jesus gave them reasons to believe.

1 *You've got a home* (14:2–3). Peter asked, "Where are you going?" (13:36). Jesus answered, "I'm going to get your room ready in my Father's house." God's "house" illustrates two "places" Christians call home: (1) heaven, God's <u>eternal home</u>; and (2) the

☞ **GO TO:**

Hebrews 11:14–16; 12:22; Revelation 21:9–22:5 (eternal home)

☞ **GO TO:**

1 Corinthians 3:16–17;
Ephesians 2:20–22;
1 Peter 2:5
(earthly home)

What Others are Saying:

☞ **GO TO:**

Hebrews 10:20 (access)

Colossians 2:3 (truth)

John 5:57; 14:19;
Galatians 2:20 (life)

Acts 4:12 (only way)

John 1:18; John 5:17–
23; 12:44–45
(visible in Jesus)

KEY POINT

When we see Jesus,
we see the Father; we
know the way, the
truth, and the life.

greater: not greater in
power, but in scope and
number, touching more
people

---

church, God's <u>earthly home</u>, the believer's spiritual family. Jesus' death and resurrection prepared the way to both places.

2 *You know the way to God* (14:4–6). Jesus is our <u>access</u> to fellowship with God, the <u>truth</u> about what God is like, and the giver of <u>life</u> from God. When we know Jesus we've found the <u>only way</u> to God.

F. F. Bruce: All truth is God's truth, as all life is God's life; but God's truth and God's life are incarnate in Jesus.[10]

Larry (Lawrence O.) Richards: No one can deny others the right to attempt to approach God in their own way. But Jesus insisted that the only way to reach God was through faith in him. Christians simply agree . . . by saying that today's Jews, Muslims, Hindus, Buddhists, or cult members cannot be saved apart from personal faith in Jesus as God's son and their Savior. . . . The notion that all religions worship the same God is flatly contradicted by the Bible, as is the popular view that all religions lead to God.[11]

3 *You've seen the Father* (14:7–11). To know Jesus is to know the Father. Philip exclaimed, *"Show us the Father!"* (verse 8). Jesus answered, "For three years you have been looking into the face of God—haven't you seen him, Philip?" (verse 9). The invisible God is <u>visible in Jesus</u>! He and God are part of each other. Jesus speaks God's words, does God's miracles (verses 10–11).

> **John 14:12–14** "I tell you the truth, anyone who has faith in me will do what I have been doing. He will do even greater things than these, because I am going to the Father. And I will do whatever you ask in my name, so that the Son may bring glory to the Father. You may ask me for anything in my name, and I will do it."

The Show Must Go On!

God's revelation of himself among us began in Jesus. It would continue in his followers. They would do the things he had done—even **greater** things! Jesus would do for them anything they asked. This would require fundamental changes in their relationship.

1. Jesus must return to his Father so his Spirit could come to live in them (verses 12, 16).

2. They must trust in Jesus even though he would not be physically present (verse 12).

3. Their works must continue to be what Jesus would do (verse 12).

4. Their requests must be **in Jesus' name** and must bring **glory** to the Father (verses 13–14).

These qualifiers ruled out selfish whims and motives and pointed up the need for Christ's followers to understand God's purposes and the acts and attitudes that glorify God.

in Jesus' name: *consistent with his character, values, purposes*

glory: *praise, honor, revelation of his nature and redemptive plan*

John Charles Ryle: "Greater works" mean more conversions. There is no greater work possible than the conversion of a soul."[12]

What Others are Saying:

Leon Morris: What Jesus means we may see in the narratives of the Acts. There are a few miracles of healing, but the emphasis is on the mighty works of conversion. On the Day of Pentecost alone more believers were added to the little band of believers than throughout Christ's entire earthly life.[13]

KEY POINT

Through the Holy Spirit, Jesus' followers can do greater works than he did, not in power, but in scope, number, and amount of lives touched.

> **John 14:15–17** "If you love me, you will obey what I command. And I will ask the Father, and he will give you another Counselor to be with you forever—the Spirit of truth. The world cannot accept him, because it neither sees him nor knows him, for he lives with you and will be in you."

The New, Improved Relationship With Christ

Jesus unveiled the exciting adventure into which the pain of the coming hours was the gateway. When he was dead and buried, they might doubt it. But when he walked with them again in his resurrection body, these teachings would roar back to mind and set them on a course to share his glory. Following Jesus' instructions would lead to an intimacy with him beyond their wildest dreams!

☞ **Check It Out:**

John 14:15–26

Tim Stafford: Though the disciples had lived with Jesus, they had not understood him. Though they had felt compelled by him, had tried to obey him, they had been confused by him. They had had only fragmentary, momentary flashes of insight. They had hoped, wildly perhaps, that he was taking them somewhere, but

What Others are Saying:

where they had not a clue. But when the Holy Spirit came, all this was changed—transformed. They began to understand what Jesus' life meant and how he loved them and how their futures were bound up in his.[14]

Something to Ponder

Jesus promised his disciples *"another Counselor"* (John 14:16). The Greek word for *another* means "another of the same kind." When the Holy Spirit came to the first disciples in Acts 2:1–4, he was no stranger. He was the same kind of Counselor-Friend Jesus was. The Counselor-Spirit continued Jesus' work. In fact, 2 Corinthians 3:18 says the Spirit is Jesus Christ living in believers.

Remember This . . .

When anyone receives Jesus Christ and obeys his teachings, Jesus comes, in the person of his Holy Spirit and *"makes his home"* (John 14:23) in that person. Belief in Christ and willingness to live by what Jesus teaches is the opening (John 7:37–39) through which the Spirit enters.

Dig Deeper

Jesus' Teaching about the Holy Spirit

Teaching	Scripture from John
The Holy Spirit is promised to those who obey Jesus' instructions	14:15, 22–24
The Holy Spirit is given by the Father at Jesus' request	14:16
The Holy Spirit is the Christian's *Counselor* (legal friend, advocate, defender)	14:16
The Holy Spirit will be with the Christian *forever*	14:16
The Holy Spirit is *the Spirit of Truth*	14:17; 16:13
The Holy Spirit is a person, not an impersonal force or influence (*him* not "it")	14:17
The Holy Spirit lives with believers and in them	14:17
The Holy Spirit is Jesus' Spirit, coming to his followers	14:18
Through the Holy Spirit Christians can "see" Jesus with the eyes of faith	14:19
The Holy Spirit makes Christians alive with Christ's resurrection life	14:19
The Holy Spirit brings awareness of Jesus' relationship to God and ours to Christ	14:20
Through the Holy Spirit believers know and experience God's love	14:21
Through the Holy Spirit Jesus communicates his love and reveals himself	14:21–22
The Holy Spirit comes *in Jesus' name*, and teaches what Jesus taught	14:26; 16:14, 15
The Holy Spirit stirs Christians' memories to recall what Jesus said	14:26
The Holy Spirit brings us Christ's peace	14:27

Tim Stafford: In *All Things Made New* Lewis Smedes writes that Jesus "is present as the Spirit. There is no touch of the Spirit that is not the touch of the Master's hand." Is this not what Jesus implied when he said of the Holy Spirit, "You know him, for he lives with you and will be in you. I will not leave you as orphans; I will come to you" (John 14:17–18)? Jesus did not say, "I will send the Spirit to you," but "*I* will come to you." And when Jesus says, "You know him, for he lives with you," may we not see in this a reasonably clear suggestion that his disciples would recognize the Spirit as the Jesus they had been living with all along?

At **Pentecost** the Holy Spirit transformed the disciples' thinking. They could no longer see Jesus, but through the Holy Spirit they became able to understand him personally.[15]

> **John 14:31–15:5** "Come now; let us leave.
>
> "I am the true vine, and my Father is the gardener. He **cuts off** every branch in me that bears no fruit, while every branch that does bear fruit he prunes so that it will be even more fruitful. You are already clean because of the word I have spoken to you. Remain in me, and I will remain in you. No branch can bear fruit by itself; it must remain in the vine. Neither can you bear fruit unless you remain in me.
>
> "I am the vine; you are the branches. If a man remains in me and I in him, he will bear much fruit; apart from me you can do nothing."

Let's Get To Work!

When Jesus said "Let's go!" (John 14:31), he was not suggesting they leave the upper room. He was the Coach punctuating his pregame pep talk with a rallying cry: "Since we know what's coming and the exciting new power relationship it leads to, let's lift our draggin' chins off our chests and march out to meet the challenge!"

By now his men knew they were going to fail Jesus before morning (Matthew 26:31; Mark 14:27; John 13:38). His response to their fears was a model for all good leaders. Calling himself "the grapevine" and his disciples "the branches," he encouraged them by telling them the following six things.

1 *God would meet their failure by lifting them up.* John 15:2 should read, "Every branch that does not bear fruit, he *raises up*" (to

What Others are Saying:

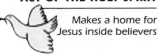

ACT OF THE HOLY SPIRIT
Makes a home for Jesus inside believers

Pentecost: the descent of the Holy Spirit on the 12 apostles

☞ **GO TO:**

John 6:35; 8:12; 8:58; 9:5; 10:7, 9, 11; 14; 11:25; 14:6 (I am)

cuts off: not a good translation; read it, "lifts up" or "picks up"

☞ **Check It Out:**

John 15:1–17

keep it from trailing on the ground). Israeli farmers lift young vines out of the dirt and prop them up so sun and air can get to them.

James M. Boice: First the believer is lifted up, encouraged, and given time to grow in his relationship with Jesus Christ and to begin to be productive.[16]

prune: trimming that ensures large, luscious grapes rather than tiny ones

2 *God would use their failures to **prune** and cleanse away spiritual hindrances to fruitfulness (John 15:2). In fact, the process of cleansing had already been happening as they listened to his words (verse 3).*

James M. Boice: Then, the Lord works to remove unproductive elements from the Christian's life. If pruning comes before lifting and establishing close relationship with Christ, what is often produced is hypocrisy. The believer confuses do's and don'ts with true devotion to the Lord and may develop spiritual pride and a critical spirit toward those he sees as "less spiritual."[17]

3 *If they'd hang on to him and let him hang on to them, they would be more fruitful than they'd ever been (John 15:4–5). They'd learn a vital principle of Christian living: "Apart from [Christ] you can do nothing."*

☞ **GO TO:**

Acts 1:8; Philippians 4:13 (can do)

John 4:35–36; Romans 8:4–6; Galatians 5:22–24; Colossians 1:10–12; James 3:17 (fruit)

4 *What happened to Judas (John 15:6) would not happen to them if they'd keep connected to Jesus (verse 7).*

5 *They would be fruitful branches. God would be glorified in all the spiritual fruit they would bear (John 15:8–17).*

6 *Jesus gave them promises to fall back on. Promises of love, joy, friendship, and usefulness were piled like sandbags (John 15:8–17) to keep them from being washed away in the flood of failure and grief about to wash over them.*

> **John 15:18** "If the world hates you, keep in mind that it hated me first."

☞ **Check It Out:**

John 15:18–16:4

No Rose Garden

Partnership with Jesus is the most exciting adventure and most costly commitment in which anyone can be involved.

Jesus promised he would be with us in the person of the Holy Spirit, empowering us, guiding us, enhancing our witness. He promised peace, joy, love, and usefulness to God.

He also told us to <u>expect to suffer</u> and be hated by the **world**, just as he was (and is), for no better reason than our association with him.

EARLY CHURCH LIFE: By the time John wrote, the Roman government had begun to persecute the church.

The Book of Acts reports the persecution of the early Christians. Before the end of the first century, synagogue congregations had begun reciting a benediction asking God to blot the names of the Christians out of the Book of Life (see GWRV, pages 302–303).

Roman writers fanned the hate-flames. Tacitus identified Christians as people "hated for their crimes." Seutonius called them "a race of men who belong to a new and evil superstition."

The world cannot tolerate Christ or righteousness. Everyone who gets serious about following Jesus should expect the world to be intolerant of him or her. In every generation, including our own, many are convinced when they kill Christians or make Christians suffer, they are *offering a service to God*" (John 16:2). The truth is, they don't have the faintest idea who God is, or they wouldn't do it (15:21)!

An unknown pagan: Through trusting [in resurrection], they have brought in this strange and new worship and despised terrors, going readily and with joy to death. Now let us see if they will rise again, and if their god be able to help them and take them out of our hands.[18]

Tertullian: The blood of Christians is seed. [It is] the bait that wins men to our school. We multiply whenever we are mown down by you. . . . For who that beholds [martyrdom] is not stirred to inquire what lies indeed within it?[19]

☞ **GO TO:**

Mark 13:9–13;
Matthew 10:17–29;
Luke 12:2–9, 51–53
(expect to suffer)

Ephesians 6:12;
Colossians 1:13–14;
2:20; 1 John 2:16;
5:19 (world)

world: *human society as a system opposed to God*

Remember This . . .

What Others are Saying:

KEY POINT

Christians were often slandered and persecuted for their identification with Jesus.

> **John 16:5–11** Because I have said these things, you are filled with grief. But I tell you the truth: It is for your good that I am going away. Unless I go away, the Counselor will not come to you; but if I go, I will send him to you. When he comes, he will convict the world of guilt in regard to sin and righteousness and judgment. In regard to sin, because men do not believe in me; in regard to righteousness, because I am going to the Father, where you can see me no longer; and in regard to judgment, because the prince of this world now stands condemned.

Face To Face Versus Spirit To Spirit

Jesus gave his followers reasons for his leaving and sending the Counselor.

1 *It is better for Jesus' followers not to be dependent on his visible, physical presence.* The physical Jesus was bound by human limitations that would have hindered the spread of the Gospel to <u>all nations</u>; in human form it was impossible for him to live in and be with all his followers wherever they were at all times. Through his Holy Spirit Jesus is **omnipresent**.

2 *The Holy Spirit could not come into the disciples until Jesus had finished his redeeming mission.* For people to be filled with God's Spirit, the estrangement between them and God must be healed. Sin must be **atoned for**. The price of forgiveness must be paid. Christ had to die and rise again.

3 *In Spirit, Jesus can get inside his people's heads and <u>write his teachings</u> on their hearts and minds, <u>changing</u> them from inside.* The Holy Spirit prepares people's hearts for hearing the bad news about their sins and the Good News about Jesus Christ. He can **convict** not just one person or a crowd, but the whole world (John 16:8–11). That is, he is able to expose hidden sin and unbelief, show where God's righteous standard has been violated, and convince people of impending judgment. When witnesses share their faith in Christ, they can be sure the Holy Spirit is already speaking to their listeners' hearts.

4 *Living in them, the Spirit teaches Christ's followers things they never understood while face to face with him* (John 16:12–15).

☞ **Check It Out:**

John 16:5–15

☞ **GO TO:**

Matthew 28:19–20 (all nations)

omnipresent: *present everywhere at all times*

atoned for: *covered, paid for, pardoned*

☞ **GO TO:**

Hebrews 10:16; 1 John 2:20–21, 26–27 (write his teachings)

2 Corinthians 3:18 (changing)

convict: *Greek legal term for investigation or cross-examination*

He gives disclosures about the future, insights into current situations, and enlightenment about his teachings, person, and relationship to God.

- The Holy Spirit does not draw attention to himself (verse 13).
- The Holy Spirit reveals only what he hears from Christ (verse 13).
- The Holy Spirit glorifies Jesus, making him the center of attention (verse 14).
- The Holy Spirit concentrates on Jesus as the ultimate Revealer of God (verse 15).

Jesus said his leaving was a **good** thing for his followers (John 16:7). Unless he left, the Counselor-Spirit could not come. I always thought it would be wonderful to know Jesus in the flesh. He insists knowing him in the Holy Spirit is better! How can that be?

Something to Ponder

What Others are Saying:

good: Greek: advantageous, beneficial, profitable, useful, better

Larry (Lawrence O.) Richards: The New Testament reveals the Spirit to be a person, one with the Father and Son (Matthew 28:19; John 15:26). . . . While the Spirit is mentioned in the Old Testament, the full revelation of his personality comes in the New. Three New Testament lines of teaching about the Spirit are important to us. First, the Spirit is seen in the gospels as the one who oversees the birth of Christ, and who is the source of Jesus' strength and power in ministry (Matthew 12:28; Luke 4:18; John 3:34). Second, the Spirit is promised to Jesus' followers and spoken of as the source of our power (John 14:16, 17; 16:5–15; Acts 1:8). Third, the epistles go into great detail about the role of the Spirit in the life of the individual believer and the Christian community. It is the Spirit who empowers individuals for ministry today. The vitality of our personal Christian life depends on the person and work of the Spirit, whom God has given to be with us, and filling our lives with his power.[20]

KEY Outline:

Quiet Spirit
No self-attention
Reveals Christ
Glorifies Christ
Concentrates on Christ

Study Questions

1. When did Judas conspire with Jesus' enemies to sell him out? What was his price? What could a person buy with that amount?
2. What three factors may have contributed to Judas becoming a traitor?

3. Identify at least five menu items for the Passover supper.
4. What "shocking" thing did Jesus do to begin the supper? How did Peter feel about it? How would you have felt? What reason did Jesus give Peter to let him do it?
5. What is the "new commandment"? Name three reasons it's "new."
6. What did Jesus mean when he called the Holy Spirit "another" Counselor (John 14:16)?
7. In Jesus' picture of the vine and branches, what does the Father do if a branch does not bear fruit?
8. What is the main reason Jesus tells his disciples he must leave them? What role of the Holy Spirit have you come to appreciate most?

CHAPTER WRAP-UP

- Judas contracted with the chief priests to turn Jesus over to them for 30 pieces of silver. (Matthew 26:14–16)

- The night before he died, Jesus met the 12 in an upper room to celebrate Passover and share many things with them. He washed their feet. He gave them his New Commandment: Love one another as I have loved you. (Matthew 26:17–35; John 13:1–38)

- Jesus told them he was going to his Father to prepare a place for them. Meanwhile, they would do the works he had done through the Holy Spirit living in them, empowering them, and revealing him to them. (John 14)

- He told them he was the vine and they the branches: they were destined to bear much fruit with the help of the Father's lifting and pruning. If they'd stay connected with him, they would have fruitful lives and ministries. (John 15:1–17)

- He warned them to expect the world to hate them as it hated him. The world would hate them because it does not know God. Many will think they are doing God a service by persecuting Christians. (John 15:18–16:4)

- He said it was good for him to leave, because the Holy Spirit could come. When the Spirit came he would convict the world of sin and teach Jesus' followers. (John 16:5–11)

Part Three

THE PRICE OF REDEMPTION

REVEREND FUN

So, Jesus, have you made any plans for Easter yet?

12 THE GREAT SURRENDER

Let's Get Started

Around the Last Supper table in the <u>upper room</u>, Jesus told his friends they would very shortly be ripped by separation and a grief made more bitter because the world would be holding a victory dance around his crucified corpse. Then he left them with this bittersweet assurance: Eventually their weeping would give birth to joy so real they would forget the pain (John 16:16–28).

In a burst of "<u>insight</u>" the disciples were sure they understood everything. At last they were certain: Jesus was the Messiah (John 16:29–30)!

While they sat there with their freshly washed feet (he'd washed them) in their collective mouths, Jesus, maybe unable to resist a bit of sarcasm, said, *"You believe at last!"* (verse 31), then burst their bubble of bogus bliss with the forecast they would all soon leave him to face death alone.

"But take heart!" he urged, as if playing their emotions like a yo-yo, *"In this world you will have trouble. But . . . I have overcome the world"* (verses 32–33). They would ultimately overcome through **his victory**.

The pain of Jesus' death "gave birth" to sextuplets of joy: Jesus' presence, answered questions, answered prayer, access to the Father, God's love, and Christ's completed work.

> **John 17:1–5** After Jesus said this, he looked toward heaven and prayed: "Father, the time has come. Glorify your Son, that your Son may glorify you. For you

---

CHAPTER HIGHLIGHTS

- The Insider Petitions
- The Great Surrender
- Night Trials
- Roman Justice

GOSPEL QUARTET IN HARMONY

Matthew 26:30–27:30
Mark 14:26–15:19
Luke 22:39–23:25
John 16:16–19:16

☞ **GO TO:**

John 13–16
(upper room)

1 Corinthians 8:1–3
(insight)

his victory: resurrection

Remember This . . .

> granted him authority over all people that he might give eternal life to all those you have given him. Now this is eternal life: that they may know you, the only true God, and Jesus Christ, whom you have sent. I have brought you glory on earth by completing the work you gave me to do. And now, Father, glorify me in your presence with the glory I had with you before the world began."

The Insider Petitions

How could these mere earthlings access the resources to deal with the responsibilities with which this night left them? Jesus mentioned the means of access several times that very evening. He taught them and made promises to them about prayer.

After teaching about prayer, Jesus modeled the principles he'd been teaching.

Sometimes John 17 is called Jesus' "High Priestly Prayer." (Sixteenth-century Lutheran theologian David Chytraeus called it that because it follows the pattern of the high **priest** on the Day of Atonement, or Yom Kippur).

It's a prayer of **intercession**. That makes it sound "religious" and formal, but this was no mere formality. Jesus and his men had not moved to some "holy place"—they were lounging around a table cluttered with dirty dishes!

Jesus *"looked toward heaven"* and talked to his Father. If prayer is a conversation with God, we obviously only have Jesus' side of the conversation. He talked from his heart in everyday language about real life issues. It came out of how he was feeling and how he knew his men were feeling.

It's a perfect example of what it means to pray "in the name" of the Lord—because this prayer was in harmony with who God is and what his purposes are. It was sure to be answered.

☞ **GO TO:**

Hebrews 4:14–16;
7:22–28
(High Priestly)

John 14:13–14; 15:16;
16:23–24
(in the name)

priest: *mediator, spiritual bridge between people and God,*

intercession: *talking to God on behalf of others*

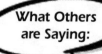

What Others are Saying:

Leon Morris: Asking in [Jesus'] name is not a way of enlisting his support. It is rather a pleading of his person and of His work for men. It is praying on the basis of all that he is and has done for our salvation.[1]

A Request For Restored Glory

First, Jesus prayed for himself. He had one request: that the Father would glorify him so he could glorify the Father. All Jesus ever wanted was to honor his heavenly Father. God is honored

Jesus' Last Supper Teachings on Prayer

Reference	Promise	Principle
John 14:13–14	"I will do whatever you ask in my name" so the son may bring glory to the Father. If you ask Me anything in my name, I will do it."	Whenever our prayers are *in Jesus'* name—that is, in harmony with his character, values and purpose to glorify God, he will do what we ask.
John 15:7–8	"If you remain in me and my words remain in you, ask whatever you wish, and it will be given you. This is to my Father's glory that you bear much fruit, showing yourselves to be my disciples."	The more closely connected we are to Christ and the more his teachings shape our desires, the more of what we ask will be given. Clue: His desires are for us to be fruitful and that the world see us as his followers.
John 15:16	"You did not choose me, but I chose you and appointed you to go and bear fruit—fruit that will last. Then the Father will give you whatever you ask in my name."	When the purpose of our prayers is to produce and harvest lasting (eternal) fruit—love, obedience, joy, knowing God's "business," friendship with him instead of slavery—the Father will give whatever we ask.
John 16:23	"In that day you will no longer ask me anything. . . . my Father will give you whatever you ask in my name."	Since Jesus' death and resurrection, believers may take their requests directly to the Father without asking Jesus to talk to God for them.
John 16:24	"Until now you have not asked for anything in my name. Ask and you will receive, and your joy will be complete."	The process of asking and receiving from the Lord is a source of joy.
John 16:26–27	"In that day you will ask in my name. I am not saying I will ask the Father on your behalf. No, the Father himself loves you because you have loved me and have believed that I came from God."	God loves people who love his Son Jesus—he is eager to answer their prayers.
John 17:9; Luke 22:31	"I pray for them. I am not praying for the world, but for those you have given me, for they are yours."	Jesus prays for us—for our protection from the devil, for our purity, unity, and effective witness in the world.

when his true nature is revealed and people see who he really is. This involves three aspects.

1 God is glorified when people know him and are **given** eternal life (John 17:2–3). **Eternal life** is a synonym for **knowing** God through receiving Jesus by faith and experiencing God (1 Corinthians 2:9–16) in daily life through his Spirit. It can't be bought or earned. It's a gift.

2 God is glorified by Jesus completing his work (verse 4). His assignment was to reveal God's love by saying farewell to heaven

given: a synonym for grace—God's kindness

eternal life: quality of life, not just duration

knowing: personal knowledge gained by experience

☞ **GO TO:**

John 1:14
(living among us)

Romans 5:6–11
(giving his life)

Philippians 2:5–11
(laid aside)

Matthew 28; Mark 16;
Luke 24; John 20;
1 Corinthians 15:1–
11 (rose)

Luke 24:50–52; Acts
1:9–11; 1 Timothy
3:16 (ascended)

Acts 2:31–36
(right hand)

☞ **Check It Out:**

John 17:6–19

☞ **GO TO:**

Luke 23:34
(on the cross)

and <u>living among us</u> as a human being, then <u>giving his life</u> to redeem us from the mess our sins have gotten us into.

3 *God is glorified by the restoration of Christ to his original splendor* (verse 5). As God's Son he <u>laid aside</u> his heavenly glory to come to earth to redeem us. His prayer was answered when he <u>rose</u> from the dead and <u>ascended</u> back to his place of honor at the Father's <u>right hand</u>.

> **John 17:9–12** "I pray for them. I am not praying for the world, but for those you have given me, for they are yours. All I have is yours, and all you have is mine. And glory has come to me through them. I will remain in the world no longer, but they are still in the world, and I am coming to you. Holy Father, protect them by the power of your name—the name you gave me—so that they may be one as we are one. While I was with them, I protected them and kept them safe by that name you gave me. None has been lost except the one doomed to destruction so that Scripture would be fulfilled."

Prayer For The Magnificent 11

Jesus did not pray for the world. He'd do that later, <u>on the cross</u>. Here he prayed for his friends, the insiders, his scouts, to blaze a trail for the kingdom of God deep into the wild, wicked, untamed territory of the world.

He prayed for them because (1) God had chosen them and they had obeyed (John 17:6); (2) they were convinced Jesus was the Messiah (verses 7–8); (3) they belonged to God (verse 9); (4) Jesus got glory from them (verse 10); and (5) they would soon be left without his physical presence in a threatening world (verses 11–12).

If anybody needed prayer, these men did! And, in spite of their imperfections, Jesus had amazing confidence in his disciples!

Jesus prayed for his kingdom pioneers (John 17:11–17)

- that they'd have God's personal protection (verse 11),
- that they'd have solidarity like Jesus and his Father share (verse 11),
- that they'd be protected from the devil while living in this hostile world (verse 15), and

- that they'd be **sanctified** by their commitment to the truth of God's word (verse 17).

sanctified: set apart, purified, distinguished from the world around them

> **John 17:20–21** "My prayer is not for them alone. I pray also for those who will believe in me through their message, that all of them may be one, Father, just as you are in me and I am in you."

A Vision Of The Future

The night before he died, Jesus prayed for you and me—people who would believe in him as the result of the message of the apostles, in their preaching and writing of the New Testament.

1 *He prayed that believers might be one* (John 17:21–23). Jesus knew Christians would come in all colors and temperaments, and from potentially divisive ethnic and social backgrounds. The model for the unity he envisioned is the relationship between himself and his Father (verses 21–22). Real spiritual oneness is based on a right relationship with God through Jesus (verses 22–23)—it is impossible for people who don't know God. Unity among believers is essential if the world is to believe that the Father sent the Son, and that God loves people (verses 21, 23).

2 *He prayed that believers might see his glory* (verses 24–26), that they might ultimately be with him in heaven (verse 24), that their knowledge of God might grow (verse 26), and that God's love and Christ's likeness would be increasingly visible in them (verse 26).

William Barclay: If we really loved each other and really loved Christ, no church would exclude any man who was Christ's disciple. Only love implanted in men's hearts by God can tear down the barriers which they have erected between each other and between their churches.[2]

> **Mark 14:32–34** They went to a place called Gethsemane, and Jesus said to his disciples, "Sit here while I pray." He took Peter, James and John along with him, and he began to be deeply distressed and troubled. "My soul is overwhelmed with sorrow to the point of death," he said to them. "Stay here and keep watch."

☞ **Check It Out:**

John 17:20–26

☞ **GO TO:**

John 5:19–20; 6:38; 8:28–29; 12:44–45; 14:9–11 (relationship)

John 14:2–3; 1 John 3:2 (with him)

John 14:26; 16:12–15 (knowledge of God)

Romans 8:28; 2 Corinthians 3:18 (increasingly visible)

What Others are Saying:

GOSPEL QUARTET IN HARMONY

Matthew 26:30–46
Mark 14:26–42
Luke 22:39–46
John 18:1

Gethsemane: *means "place of crushing" or "olive press"*

The Great Surrender

It was late when the streets of Jerusalem heard the sound of 12 lusty voices in an upstairs room singing the *Hallel*, the traditional collection of hymns sung to conclude the Passover dinner (Matthew 26:30; Mark 14:26).

The door opened and Jesus led his team down the outside stairs, through streets and along trails lit by the full Passover moon, out of the city, across the Brook Kedron, and up into the olive trees that gave Mt. Olivet its name.

Among the groves was an old olive press surrounded by a garden, a place Jesus loved to go to spend the night or pray. Mark and Matthew identify the place as **Gethsemane** (see appendix B). John tells us it was a garden.

For Jesus, the fiercest battleground was not Mount Calvary but Mount Olivet. This is not to minimize what he suffered on the cross—it was horrible. But in this olive garden Jesus recommitted himself to carry through God's plan involving suffering and death for our sins.

He confided in Peter, James, and John that he was on the verge of dying of grief! Luke uses the Greek word *agonia*, a word for intense emotion, violent inner struggle, emotional strain, "anguish" (Luke 22:44).

The gospel writers bring us deep into the garden to witness a struggle most of the disciples who were there did not see. They were asleep.

What Others are Saying:

Something to Ponder

Abba: *"Daddy" in Aramaic, the language Jesus spoke*

John R. W. Stott: Was he to become so identified with sinners as to bear their judgment? From this contact with human sin his sinless soul recoiled. From the experience of alienation from his Father which the judgment on sin would involve, he hung back in horror.[3]

Today, in that garden, there are some olive trees that are 2,000 years old—perhaps the very ones beneath which Jesus prayed.

> **Mark 14:35–36** Going a little further, he fell to the ground and prayed that if possible the hour might pass from him. "**Abba,** Father," he said, "everything is possible for you. Take this cup from me. Yet not what I will, but what you will."

---

218   GOD'S WORD FOR THE BIBLICALLY-INEPT

"Daddy, Must I?"

At no time in Jesus' story is his humanity more visible and his commitment to the Father's will clearer. He had faced death before, while shaking his finger in its face. Now he confronted it with no less courage. The physical horror of crucifixion was not the major reason he dreaded the cross. He knew that as he took the <u>punishment</u> for our sin his Father would turn away from him! That separation was the focus of his grief.

The outcome was never in doubt. But he was <u>tempted</u> to turn from the cross. Luke 22:43 reports that an angel came and strengthened him. Without that special help he might have <u>died there</u> in the garden. Even with it, his struggle was so intense Luke says he sweated blood.

Three times, face down on the ground, Jesus expressed his human wish that his Father might find some way for him to avoid the ordeal ahead. *"If it is possible, may this **cup** be taken from me"* (Matthew 26:39). Three times Jesus affirmed his uninterrupted commitment to God's plan: *"Yet not as I will, but as you will."*

After each prayer Jesus came back to the disciples and found them asleep. The first time he woke Peter (Matthew 26:41) and reminded him to pray to keep from falling into temptation. The second time he left them sleeping. The third time he woke them up because the arresting force led by Judas had entered the garden (verses 45–46).

Michael Card: Jesus cried out, "Abba." Never let anyone clothe that word in theological sophistication. It is not a sophisticated word! It is baby talk. Papa, Daddy, Abba—they are all the same thing: the first stutterings of an infant, not to be categorized in some systematic theological structure, but to be cried out from the heart of a child, a heart of faith. . . . The agony of the cross, the crushing torment of it, was the separation Jesus experienced from the Father, the result of his obedience. That painful crushing began, appropriately enough, in the garden called Gethsemane [the place of crushing].[4]

> **Mark 14:44–46** Now the betrayer had arranged a signal with them: "The one I kiss is the man; arrest him and lead him away under guard." Going at once to Jesus, Judas said, "Rabbi!" and kissed him. The men seized Jesus and arrested him.

☞ **GO TO:**

Isaiah 53:4–6, 8, 10; 2 Corinthians 5:21; 1 Peter 2:24 (punishment)

Matthew 4:5–10; 16:21–23; Hebrews 4:15 (tempted)

Matthew 26:38; Mark 14:35 (died there)

Job 21:20; Psalm 60:3; Isaiah 51:19, 22; Ezekiel 23:32–34 (cup)

cup: expression for the experience of suffering or judgment

What Others are Saying:

Matthew 26:47–56
Mark 14:43–52
Luke 22:47–53
John 18:2–12

place: *Gethsemane*

detachment: *cohort, Roman army unit of at least 200*

☞ **GO TO:**

Colossians 1:13 (dominion)

dominion: *Satan's evil empire*

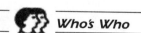

Who's Who

Something to Ponder

Capture Of The Desperado

Jesus could have been beyond the reach of the high priest's men. Instead he waited in a familiar rendezvous where the traitor could lead them to him.

When a disciple greeted a beloved rabbi, he put his hands on his mentor's shoulders and kissed him. That Judas chose this as the signal to identify Jesus deepens the sense of betrayal.

John records the same scene this way: *"Now Judas, who betrayed him, knew the* **place***, because Jesus had often met there with his disciples. So Judas came to the grove guiding a* **detachment** *of soldiers and some officials from the chief priests and Pharisees. They were carrying torches, lanterns and weapons"* (John 18:2–3). As if expecting a fight, the arresting party came with weapons poised.

"Am I leading a rebellion, that you have come with swords and clubs?" Jesus asked. *"Every day I was with you in the temple courts, and you did not lay a hand on me. But this is your hour when darkness reigns!"* (Luke 22:52–53). The dead of night was strangely appropriate for nabbing the young Messiah. After all, the real power behind the raid was the **dominion** of darkness!

Peter leaped to Jesus' defense. His blade flashed in the torchlight as it swung in a huge arc aimed at splitting the high priest's slave in two! Fortunately, it missed its mark and lopped off the man's right ear (John 18:10)! (Whew! Good thing Peter was better at casting a net than swinging a sword!)

"No more of this!" Jesus said, reattaching the severed ear (Luke 22:51). *"Shall I not drink the cup the Father has given me?"*

At that point, the disciples ran for their lives. Mark adds, a boy with *"nothing on but a linen garment"* was grabbed by the officers. Leaving his shirt, he "streaked" into the night. Mark is telling us he was there (Mark 14:51–52).

HIGH PRIEST'S SLAVE: Named Malchus. Peter cut off his ear, and Jesus reattached it. Malchus is mentioned in John 18:10, and was familiar to early Christians probably because he became a Christian as a result of Jesus' miracle.

Enough Guilt to Go Around

Putting together the four accounts of Jesus' arrest, we know the posse included temple police (Luke 22:52); religious and civil leaders (Luke 22:52; John 18:3); Roman soldiers (John 18:3); and an armed crowd of rank-and-file (nonmilitary) Jews (Matthew 26:47; Mark 14:43).

All these to arrest one unarmed Galilean carpenter!

It's a familiar list. They were the dark backdrop against which even the most beautiful things in the life of Christ took place. They represent the broad spectrum of humanity. Just as God's offer of salvation is extended to all (John 3:16), the responsibility for Jesus' death also includes us all.

> **John 18:12–13** Then the detachment of soldiers with its commander and the Jewish officials arrested Jesus. They bound him and brought him first to Annas, who was the father-in-law of Caiaphas, the high priest that year.

Night Trials

At last it was time for the enemies of Jesus to do with him what they wished. It was the moment for the world's power structures— religious and secular—to take their turns on center stage, showing what they were capable of doing to preserve their positions of power and protect their sacred institutions and traditions.

In the drama that unfolded that night we may observe the lengths to which darkness will go to <u>extinguish the light</u> that exposes inner rottenness just by shining.

By prearrangement Jesus was taken first to the palace of <u>Annas</u>, father-in-law of Caiaphas, the current high priest. Annas had once been high priest. Roman prefect Valerius Gratus fired him in 15 A.D., but Annas continued to be the power behind the throne. Many Jews considered this appropriate because the high priest was supposed to be appointed for life.

> **John 18:19–21** Meanwhile the high priest questioned Jesus about his disciples and his teaching.
> "I have spoken openly . . . I always taught in synagogues and at the temple, where all the Jews come together. I said nothing in secret. Why question me? Ask those who heard me. Surely they know what I said."

Trial Of The Deposed "Patriarch"

Annas interrogated Jesus. The bitter old Sadducee tried to get Jesus to incriminate himself as a false prophet, a crime punishable by <u>death</u>.

GOSPEL QUARTET IN HARMONY

Matthew 26:57–27:10
Mark 14:53–15:1
Luke 22:54–71
John 18:12–27

☞ **GO TO:**

John 1:5; 3:19–20
(extinguish the light)

GOSPEL QUARTET IN HARMONY

Luke 22:54
John 18:12–24

☞ **GO TO:**

John 18:24; Acts 4:6
(Annas)

Deuteronomy 13:1–10
(death)

Jewish law prescribed the procedure for such inquiries. And this wasn't it! The accused was not to be questioned by the judge.

Everything in a legitimate trial depended on the testimony of witnesses testifying under oath in open court. No witnesses were present. It was the middle of the night. Anyone who might have been called to testify in Jesus' favor was asleep.

Jesus was within his legal rights to object to Annas' illegal interrogation. But when he spoke, an officer doubled his fist and hit Jesus in the face! "Is this any way to talk to the high priest?" the official demanded. Striking an uncondemned prisoner was also illegal! Jesus demanded witnesses be produced to testify he had said something wrong.

> **Mark 14:61–62** Again the high priest asked him, "Are you the Christ, the Son of the Blessed One?"
>
> "I am," said Jesus. "And you will see the Son of Man sitting at the **right hand** of the Mighty One and coming on the clouds of heaven."

Trial Of The Puppet Priest

Annas ended his interrogation. Jesus, bound like a dangerous outlaw, was taken across the courtyard to the adjoining palace of Caiaphas, the reigning high priest (see appendix B). In phase two of this kangaroo court scenario, Caiaphas' judgment was anything but impartial. He had already made up his mind that Jesus should *"die for the people."*

Joining Caiaphas were Sanhedrin members *"looking for evidence against Jesus so that they could put him to death"* (Mark 14:55). Many witnesses perjured themselves. Their "testimony" was useless because they *"did not agree"* (verses 56–59). Jesus refused to answer their lies. But when Caiaphas asked him directly if he was the Christ, Jesus answered.

In a melodramatic gesture of outrage, Caiaphas tore his robe and shouted **"Blasphemy**!" He called for a verdict (Mark 14:63–64). The unanimous judgment was "Guilty!" (Surprise! Surprise!) The sentence: Jesus of Nazareth is *"worthy of death."*

Since legal jurisprudence had nothing whatever to do with these hate-driven proceedings, what happened next was revolting but predictable. Powerful men, prominent leaders of Israel's religion and life, teachers, lawyers, and clergy, model citizens, and police, all drunk with the taste for Jesus' blood, became a mob of hooligans. They blindfolded, mocked, spit, slapped, and **beat** him, strik-

---

right hand: place of ultimate authority at God's "right hand," judging his accusers

☞ **GO TO:**

John 11:50 (for the people)

Matthew 26:67–68; Mark 14:65; Luke 22:63–65 (striking)

blasphemy: treat God with contempt by reducing him to mere human level

beat: with skin-flaying scourge (Luke 22:63); with fist or flat side of sword (verse 64)

ing him in the face with their fists. Again! And again! And again! And those who did not participate stood with folded arms, approving.

> **John 18:15** Simon Peter and another disciple were following Jesus. Because this disciple was known to the high priest, he went with Jesus into the high priest's courtyard.

Trial Beside The Enemies' Fire

Peter and another disciple, assumed to be John, had followed the arresting force to the high priest's palace. John was **known** to the gatekeeper, so when the officers, with Jesus in chains, entered the palace grounds, John was allowed to enter with them. When he found out where the interrogation was taking place, he returned to convince the gatekeeper to let Peter in. As he came through the gate, the keeper, a young woman, asked, *"You are not one of his disciples, are you?"* (John 18:17).

"I am not," Peter lied. (That's once.)

The guardsmen and servants had built a fire in the courtyard to take the chill off the night. Peter joined them.

A little time passed. Another person said to him, *"You are not one of his disciples, are you?"* (John 18:25).

"Man, I am not!" Peter lied. (That's twice.)

An hour passed. A third person, a relative of Malchus, whose ear Peter had lopped off, identified Peter as one of Jesus' men, *"Didn't I see you with him in the olive grove?"* (John 18:26). Mark's report adds: *"You are a Galilean"* (Mark 14:70). Matthew 26:73 says Peter's accent gave him away.

> **Luke 22:60–62** Peter replied, "Man, I don't know what you're talking about! Just as he was speaking, the rooster crowed. The Lord turned and looked straight at Peter. Then Peter remembered the words the Lord had spoken to him: "Before the rooster crows today, you will disown me <u>three</u> times." And [Peter] went outside and <u>wept bitterly</u>.

That's Three!

Matthew and Mark say that this third time, Peter backed his reply with a string of oaths.

GOSPEL QUARTET IN HARMONY

Matthew 26:69–75
Mark 14:66–72
Luke 22:54–62
John 18:15–18, 25–27

known: *"familiar friend"; "kinsman"*

☞ **GO TO:**

Luke 22:34 (three)

John 21:15–23 (wept bitterly)

His denial was a crushing failure and showed, not only Peter but all of us, how weak humans are.

When in friendly company, we confidently identify with Jesus. But when in the presence of unsympathetic people, we deny knowing him (or at least keep discreetly silent).

By failing to speak the truth and by doing nothing, Peter helped to crucify Christ as surely as the priests and the soldiers who drove the nails.[5]

Although Jesus was being moved across the courtyard to another trial, he knew what Peter had done. Jesus looked at him with sorrow and love. And take-charge, rush-ahead, self-confident Peter was reduced to a heap of sobbing flesh.

While all four New Testament historians report this episode, none presents Peter in more unfavorable detail than Mark. Scholars think Peter's preaching and teaching were the main source of information for Mark's writing. Likely Peter himself wanted this story told "as an example of the readiness of the crucified and risen Lord to forgive sinners, even when they are as unworthy as the man who denied his Master."[6]

> **Luke 22:63–65** The men who were guarding Jesus began mocking and beating him. They blindfolded him and demanded, "Prophesy! Who hit you?" And they said many other insulting things to him.

Jesus Of Nazareth Versus The Sanhedrin

GOSPEL QUARTET IN HARMONY

Matthew 27:1

Mark 15:1

Luke 22:66–71

Sanhedrin: highest Jewish ruling council

tribunal: court of justice

The **Sanhedrin** (see illustration, page 225) met at dawn. As supreme court they had complete and final jurisdiction over religious and theological issues. They were bound by Jewish law to follow rules of procedure designed to give defendants the advantage.

In the case of Jesus of Nazareth versus the Sanhedrin, most of the rules were broken.

Into this **tribunal**, Jesus was dragged, dripping with spittle, his face bruised from blows by many fists. "Are you the Messiah?" they demanded. *"Tell us"* (Luke 22:67).

"You will not believe me if I tell you," he replied.

Their understanding of messiahship was a million miles from his. He wished he could ask some questions (verse 68) to try to correct their misconceptions. Rational discussion was impossible.

They would never accept as Messiah a man who questioned their right to rule.

"Are you the Son of God?" they demanded noisily.

"You are right in saying I am," he replied. He spoke with the confidence with which he had emerged from Gethsemane. He knew his answer would bring a sentence of death.

The assembly rose to its feet, declared him guilty, and dragged him off to the Roman governor to demand the death penalty. If there were <u>dissenters</u> present, they were never given a chance to speak. No witnesses for the defense were called. No poll of individual members was conducted. A lynch-mob mentality prevailed.

☞ **GO TO:**

Luke 23:50–51
(dissenters)

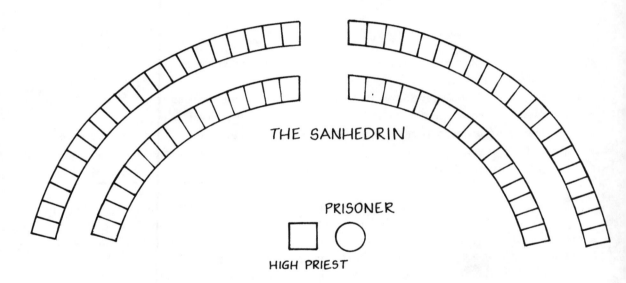

THE SANHEDRIN

PRISONER

HIGH PRIEST

GALLERY

The Sanhedrin

The sketch shows the physical arrangement of the Jewish Sanhedrin with 71 members: elders, priests, teachers of the Law, Sadducees, and Pharisees.

Trial before the Sanhedrin

Courtroom Arrangements

- Meeting place: Hall of Hewn Stone in the temple area.
- Presiding officer: High Priest.
- Members sat in a semicircle so every man could see the faces of the others.
- Rabbinical students—disciples of the scribes—sat facing the members.
- Prisoner dressed in a mourning robe.

Rules of Procedure	Broken in Jesus' trials
No trial could be held at night or at a major feast.	John 18:19–23
No decision was valid unless arrived at in the Hall of Hewn Stone.	John 18:13, 24; Luke 22:54
The accused must be treated with mercy.	John 18:22–23; Mark 14:65
Charges must be supported by evidence and testimony of at least two witnesses.	John 18:20–23
Testimony of witnesses must agree.	Mark 14:56, 59
A member could speak against the accused, then change his mind and speak for him.	No record
A rabbinical student could speak on behalf of, but never against, the accused.	No record
Each member must be polled for his verdict, from the youngest to the eldest.	Matthew 6:66
A majority of one vote was required to acquit; a majority of two votes to convict.	No poll taken
Death penalty must be considered overnight before condemning the accused.	Matthew 27:1–2

Something to Ponder

Jeshu: *Jewish name for Jesus*

sorcery: *witchcraft*

apostasy: *rejection of former beliefs about God*

☞ GO TO:

Deuteronomy 13:1–5 (enticed)

The Jewish Talmud, a collection of the insights of Jewish rabbis from 200 B.C. to 500 A.D., includes this note giving the official spin on the trial of *Jesus v. The Sanhedrin*: "On the eve of the Passover **Jeshu** was hanged. For 40 days before the execution took place a herald went forth and cried, 'He is going forth to be stoned because he has practiced **sorcery** and <u>enticed</u> Israel to **apostasy**. Anyone who can say anything in his favor, let him come forward and plead on his behalf.' But since nothing was brought forward in his favor he was hanged on the eve of the Passover."[7]

> **Matthew 27:3–4** When Judas, who had betrayed him, saw that Jesus was condemned, he was seized with remorse and returned the thirty silver coins to the chief priests and elders. "I have sinned," he said, "for I have betrayed innocent blood."

Betrayer's Remorse

The tragic end of Judas Iscariot came when the Sanhedrin condemned Jesus. Putting together the facts reported by Matthew and Peter (Acts 1:18–19) it happened like this:

"Seized with remorse," Judas brought the 30 pieces of silver to the Temple and tried to return them to the officials who hired him.

They refused to take the money, so he threw it at them (Matthew 27:5). As the coins clattered across the temple pavement, he left.

The next news of Judas came when his mangled body was found at the foot of a cliff owned by a local pottery maker. From the evidence it appeared Judas hung himself from a tree at the edge of the precipice, the limb broke, and his body plunged onto the rocks below.

The priests bought the land where he died for a pauper's burial ground using the returned silver. People called it *Akeldama*, Field of Blood (Acts 1:19).

Oswald Chambers: Never mistake remorse for repentance; remorse simply puts a man in hell while he is on earth, it carries no remedial quality with it at all, nothing that betters a man. An unawakened sinner has no remorse, but immediately a man recognizes his sin he experiences the pain of being gnawed by a sense of guilt, for which punishment would be a heaven of relief, but no punishment can touch it.[8]

> **John 18:28–32** Then the Jews led Jesus from Caiaphas to the **palace** of the Roman **governor**. By now it was early morning, and to avoid ceremonial uncleanness the Jews did not enter the palace; they wanted to be able to eat the Passover.

Roman Justice

The delegation of religious leaders stopped outside the palace gate (see appendix B). They meticulously avoided entering the governor's palace, because entering a Gentile's house would defile them ceremonially, disqualifying them from eating the Passover meal that evening (John 18:28–29).

There were three reasons for doing this at the crack of dawn: (1) Roman officials began work before sunup; (2) Sanhedrin lead-

What Others are Saying:

palace: Praetorium, Roman military headquarters near the Temple

governor: appointed by the Emperor to administer the province

GOSPEL QUARTET IN HARMONY

Matthew 27:2, 11–30
Mark 15:1–19
Luke 23:1–25
John 18:28–19:16

ers wanted Jesus to be executed before the Passover; and (3) at daylight worshipers filled the Temple and the potential for an uprising of support for Jesus increased.

What Others are Saying:

George R. Beasley-Murray: No more eloquent example than this can be found of the ability of religious people to be meticulous about external regulations of religion while being wholly at variance with God.[9]

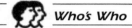

Who's Who

PONTIUS PILATE: Roman governor of Judea from 26–36 A.D., appointed by Caesar Tiberius. As governor he commanded the occupation army. He alone had power to order death sentences. Historians picture him as hostile and insensitive, corrupt, insolent, insulting, cruel, and inhumane. He was known to have condemned many to death without trial, including hundreds of Galileans murdered at a feast (Luke 13:1–3).

> **John 18:29–31** So Pilate came out to them and asked, "What charges are you bringing against this man?"
> "If he were not a criminal," they replied, "we would not have handed him over to you."
> Pilate said, "Take him yourselves and judge him by your own law."
> "But we have no right to execute anyone," the Jews objected.

GOSPEL QUARTET IN HARMONY

Matthew 27:2, 11
Mark 15:1–2
Luke 23:1–3
John 18:28–38

☞ **GO TO:**

John 18:3, 12 (soldiers)

Trial Of The Ruthless Judge

Pilate was expecting them (he would have ordered the detachment of soldiers to aid in Jesus' midnight arrest). He came out onto the platform overlooking the pavement in front of the palace.

He asked the question with which all Roman trials began: *"What charges are you bringing against this man?"*

Their sassy answer (verse 30) indicates they hoped Pilate would simply rubber-stamp their verdict and ratify the death sentence without further investigation.

After the initial retort, they brought charges against Jesus crafted to grab the Roman's attention (Luke 23:2):

1. He is the leader of a political insurrection.

2. He opposes payment of taxes.

3. He claims to be king in competition with Caesar.

"Okay," he responded (John 18:31), "you have my permission to inflict the death penalty prescribed by your law" (that is, stoning).

But that wasn't their scheme. They wanted to transfer responsibility to the Romans for the popular young prophet's execution. And they wanted Jesus to die on a cross so they could tag him with the ancient **curse** of hanging.

They most certainly did not want him to be seen as a martyr, giving his life for God, but as a false prophet, dying under God's curse. So they protested. Only Pilate had the right to execute criminals.

Little did they know they were assuring the fulfillment of Jesus' own prophecies, that he would die on a Roman cross (John 18:32)!

☞ **GO TO:**

Leviticus 20:2, 27; 24:16; Numbers 15:32–36; Deuteronomy 13:6–10 (stoning)

Deuteronomy 21:23; Galatians 3:13 (curse of hanging)

Luke 18:32; John 12:31–33 (prophecies)

curse: "Cursed is anyone who is hung on a tree."

> **John 18:33–34** Pilate then went back inside the palace, summoned Jesus and asked him, "Are you the king of the Jews?"
>
> "Is that your own idea," Jesus asked, "or did others talk to you about me?"

"Who's On Trial Here?"

Pilate went back inside the judgment hall to cross-examine the prisoner. He confronted him with the most serious charge first: *"Are you the king of the Jews?"*

Jesus asked a question of his own: whether this was Pilate's own idea, or whether he was parroting what others had said. The accused was cross-examining the judge!

Incensed, Pilate said, *"Am I a Jew?"* (In other words, I have no personal interest in your peculiar Jewish notions. So how could I know?) *"It is your people and your chief priests who handed you over to me. What is it you have done?"*

KINGDOM OF GOD

Jesus' response was to define what his kingdom *was not*. *"My kingdom is not of this world"* (John 18:36).

His servants were not trained for military action. If they had been they'd have fought the arresting force in the garden. They weren't fighting because the kingdom Jesus leads is a different kind of kingdom and it comes from a place other than this world.

Caesar can have his empire. Jesus isn't interested in it!

> **John 18:37–38** "You are a king then!" said Pilate.
> Jesus answered, "You are right in saying I am a king. In fact, for this reason I was born, and for this I came into the world, to testify to the truth. Everyone on the side of truth listens to me."
> "What is truth?" Pilate asked.

"Truth? What's That?"

Having told him what his kingdom was not, Jesus proceeded to explain to the governor what his kingdom *was*: It is the kingdom of *truth*—the <u>truth</u> about God, his sovereignty, love, and redeeming purpose to rescue human beings from the kingdom of **<u>untruth</u>**.

"Truth? What is that?" retorted the governor. He did not wait for an answer. Cynical minds ridicule the idea there is absolute truth. Pontius Pilate had just been given his best chance to embrace the truth and the life truth opens up to the believing mind.

He knew one thing for sure; however, this man was not the threat to Roman authority that the religious establishment tried to make him seem.

Cal Thomas: True believers—including me—are beginning to sense that the kingdom of this world, which regularly demands compromise, cannot be reconciled to a kingdom not of this world that allows for no compromise. Consider John 18:36, when Jesus tells Pilate: *"My kingdom is not of this world . . . my kingdom is from another place."* His is not a realm that needs soldiers to establish or defend it. . . . For Christians, the vision of worldly power is not a calling, but a distraction. It is a temptation Jesus rejected not because it was dangerous, but because it was trivial compared with his mission.[10]

C. S. Lewis: If you read history you will find that the Christians who did the most for this present world were just those who thought most of the next.[11]

> **Luke 23:4–5** Then Pilate announced to the chief priests and the crowd, "I find no basis for a charge against this man."
> But they insisted, "He stirs up the people all over Judea by his teaching. He started in Galilee and has come all the way here."

GO TO:

John 1:14–18; 8:31–32; 14:6–11 (truth)

John 8:44–45 (untruth)

untruth: *darkness, hypocrisy, dishonesty, false promises*

What Others are Saying:

Trial Of The Petty Potentate

"Is the accused Galilean?" asked Pilate (Luke 23:6). Galileans were under the jurisdiction of Herod Antipas (see appendix B), who happened to be in Jerusalem at the time.

Roman law permitted Pilate to transfer jurisdiction to the home province of the accused. Relations between Pilate and Herod were strained. Herod would see this transfer as a compliment.

Herod was pleased, and the transfer led to friendship between the two political enemies (Luke 23:12).

Herod was a shallow man who tried to get Jesus to do something sensational. Jesus treated him as his insignificance deserved. He refused to answer any questions and was returned to Pilate (see appendix B), with his herd of accusers.

Knowing he had a political hot potato on his hands, Herod didn't pronounce Jesus guilty or innocent.

> **Luke 23:13–16** Pilate called together the chief priests, the rulers and the people, and said to them, "You brought me this man as one who was inciting the people to rebellion. I have examined him in your presence and have found no basis for your charges against him. Neither has Herod, for he sent him back to us; as you can see, he has done nothing to deserve death. Therefore, I will punish him and then release him."

Litany Of Rejection

Three times Pilate pronounced Jesus innocent (Luke 23:4, 14–15, 22). Five times he tried to let him go:

1 *He told the Jews to punish Jesus themselves* (John 9:6–7). They demanded he do it.

2 *He tried to get the Sanhedrin-led mob to accept Jesus' release as the governor's traditional Passover pardon* (Mark 15:6–11; John 18:39–40). As a gesture of goodwill one prisoner was released each year at Passover. A man named Barabbas was in Roman custody awaiting execution as a violent revolutionary, assassin, rabble-rouser, and robber (Mark 15:7; Luke 23:18, 24; John 18:40). Pilate gave the mob a choice—should he release Barabbas the killer or Jesus the Christ? They chose Barabbas and screamed for Jesus' death.

GOSPEL QUARTET IN HARMONY

Matthew 27:15–26
Mark 15:6–15
Luke 23:13–25
John 18:39–19:16

Revell Bible Dictionary: The one who deserved execution was freed, and the innocent took his place. In this sense, the incident of Barabbas' release is a vivid image of redemption itself. Christ's death was, from the standpoint of human responsibility, a supreme injustice; nevertheless it proved to be the central element in the grand plan of God to release those who deserve punishment by taking on himself the stroke that justice decrees. In his death Jesus was not simply a substitute for Barabbas, but for all who receive him by faith.[12]

3 Pilate tried to get Jesus' accusers to accept a compromise punishment: He **flogged** Jesus, *intending to release him* (Luke 23:16, 22; John 19:1). When Pilate brought him out after the scourge had torn his skin to ribbons, they screamed again: *"Crucify him! Crucify him!"*

4 In disgust Pilate dared religious leaders to crucify Jesus themselves, repeating his not-guilty verdict. They let the cat out of the bag revealing their real beef against Jesus: *"We have a law, and according to that law he must die, because he claimed to be the Son of God"* (John 19:7). Like most Romans Pilate was superstitious. Ingrained in the culture were stories of children of the gods visiting earth. If Jesus was one, it could mean bad luck for Pilate. His wife added fuel to the fires of superstition by sending him a message telling of a nightmare she'd had about the prisoner. "Get off the case!" she warned (Matthew 27:19).

flogged: 39 lashes with a multi-strand leather whip with bits of bone or metal tied in the ends

KINGDOM
OF GOD

"Where do you come from?" Pilate asked Jesus (John 19:9). When Jesus did not answer his questions, Pilate demanded, "Talk to me! Don't you know I have the power to free you or kill you?" The *power* of which Pilate spoke was from the most powerful politician on earth, the Roman Emperor. Jesus told Pilate he really had no power at all that wasn't granted by God (verse 11).

5 Pilate tried one last time to free Jesus (John 19:12). So the Jews threw in a final zinger—the one accusation his instinct for survival could not ignore: *"If you let this man go, you are no friend of Caesar. Anyone who claims to be a king opposes Caesar"* (John 19:12).

Coinciding with these events in Jerusalem were history-making developments in Rome. Sejanus, commander of the **Praetorian Guard**, had been executed by the Caesar. This put fear in every provincial leader Sejanus had recommended for appointment. Pilate was one of these.

Remember This . . .

Larry (Lawrence O.) Richards: Later in a sermon the Apostle Peter would say, "*this is how God fulfilled what he had foretold through all the prophets, saying that his Christ would suffer*" (Acts 3:18). God providentially arranged distant events to bring about what he had foretold through the prophets.[13]

What Others are Saying:

> **Matthew 27:24–25** When Pilate saw that he was getting nowhere, but that instead an uproar was starting, he took water and washed his hands in front of the crowd. "I am innocent of this man's blood," he said. "It is your responsibility!"
>
> All the **people** answered, "Let his blood be on us and on our children!"

Praetorian Guard: bodyguards of the Roman Emperor

people: priests and people in the crowd, not whole city or nation

The Unwashable Stain

With his political back against the wall, faced with the inferred threat to report him to the emperor, unable (unwilling) to silence the screaming demands for Jesus' crucifixion, and fearing breakdown of order in the city, Pilate "*surrendered Jesus to their will*" (Luke 23:25), and set Barabbas free.

Pilate lied to himself and the crowd. Blame for failure to do what Roman justice, his own conscience, and human decency demanded rested squarely on his shoulders. The only right thing was to bite the bullet and face the fallout. In the Passion Play, Pilate plays the part of the coward.

☞ GO TO:

Exodus 20:5–6 (on our children)

Something to Ponder

John R. W. Stott: It is easy to condemn Pilate and overlook our own equally devious behaviour. Anxious to avoid the pain of a wholehearted commitment to Christ, we too search for convenient **subterfuges**. We either leave the decision to somebody else, or opt for a half-hearted compromise, or seek to honour Jesus for the wrong reason (*e.g.* as teacher instead of Lord), or even make a public affirmation of loyalty while at the same time denying him in our hearts.[14]

What Others are Saying:

subterfuges: deceptive ploys

Coptic: north African

Revell Bible Dictionary: One early Christian historian, Eusebius, reports that Pilate committed suicide in Gaul several years after Christ's death. Other Christian legends suggest that he and his wife became Christians. The **Coptic** Church honors Pilate on June 25th as a saint and maintains that he was ultimately converted and died as a martyr for his faith in Jesus.[15]

Dig
Deeper

Jesus' Last Day on Earth[16]

Events	Matthew	Mark	Luke	John
Jesus prays in Gethsemane	26:36–46	14:32–42	22:39–46	18:1
Jesus is arrested there	26:47–56	14:43–52	22:47–53	18:2–12
Jesus is tried before Annas				18:12–23
Jesus is tried before Caiaphas	26:57–68	14:53–65	22:54–65	18:24
Peter denies Jesus	26:69–75	14:66–72	22:54–62	18:15–27
Jesus is condemned by Sanhedrin	27:1	15:1	22:66–71	
Judas commits suicide	27:3–10			
Jesus is tried by Pilate	27:11–14	15:2–5	23:1–5	18:28–38
Jesus is tried by Herod			23:6–12	
Jesus is condemned by Pilate	27:15–26	15:6–15	23:13–25	18:39–19:16
Jesus is mocked and scourged	27:27–30	15:16–19		19:2–3
Jesus is led to Calvary	27:31–34	15:20–23	23:26–33	19:16–17

Study Questions

1. In the opening sentences of Jesus' "High Priestly Prayer" he talks about eternal life. What *is* eternal life, according to what he says there?
2. Identify the three religious (Jewish) trials of Jesus and their locales.
3. What did Peter do after his third denial of Jesus and the rooster crowed?
4. What three charges did the Jewish religious leaders bring against Jesus when they took him to Pilate? What was the real charge—the one he was accused of by the Sanhedrin?
5. What was the "Passover Pardon?" How did Pilate use it to try to free Jesus? Who was the man freed instead of Jesus, and what kind of man was he?

6. What was the final thing Pilate did to claim that he was not responsible for Jesus' death? On a scale of 1 to 10 (1 is easiest, 10 is toughest), how difficult is it for you to accept responsibility for your own decisions and actions?

CHAPTER WRAP-UP

- Jesus' disciples were saddened by the news that he would be leaving. He assured them their grief would soon be turned to joy when he rose from the dead. At that point, a new, more wonderful way of relating to him and his Father would begin. (John 16:5–24)

- The final supper with his friends ended with Jesus praying his "High Priestly Prayer" for his restoration to glory, their protection against a hostile world, their unity, and for those who would believe on him through their witness. (John 17)

- In Gethsemane, Jesus struggled with the prospect of separation from his Father that would occur when he bore God's judgment for sinners on the cross. He committed himself to do God's will. Judas led Jesus' enemies to the garden, and Jesus was arrested. (Luke 22:39–53)

- In the middle of the night Jesus was interrogated by the deposed high priest and the reigning high priest. Three times Peter denied knowing Jesus. At dawn the Sanhedrin pronounced Jesus guilty of blasphemy and condemned him to die. (John 18:12–27; Matthew 26:57–68)

- The religious leaders took Jesus to Pilate, demanding crucifixion on trumped up charges. Pilate declared him not guilty and tried five times to release Jesus. Each time Jesus' enemies resisted. In an act of cowardice, Pilate gave in to their demands. (Luke 23:1–25; John 18:28–19:16)

13 THE ULTIMATE SACRIFICE

CHAPTER HIGHLIGHTS

- Man in Purple
- Street of Sorrow
- Father, Forgive Them
- The Day the Sun Refused to Shine
- What Is the Significance of Jesus' Death on the Cross?

GOSPEL QUARTET IN HARMONY

Matthew 27:27–58
Mark 15:16–45
Luke 23:26–52
John 19:2–3, 17–37

Let's Get Started

The crucifixion of Jesus Christ in 30 A.D. was everybody's business.

It was not just a Jewish problem or a Roman problem. It was not just a religious problem or a secular problem. Church and state were both to blame. The rejection and condemnation of Christ was and is a universal problem.

The Bible teaches that Jesus' death provided forgiveness for all sinners. And—hang on to your hat—all of us are sinners! Romans 3:10–12, 23 says, *"There is no one righteous, not even one; there is no one who understands, no one who seeks God. . . . there is no one who does good, not even one. . . . for all have sinned and fall short of the glory of God."*

<u>Foolish</u> as it may seem, the Bible teaches that Christ's death on the cross was God's great *power* play. It was based on the divine rationale that people can be changed from rebellious delinquents to obedient children of God if they know they are forgiven!

So that is what God was doing in the events that led up to and through the crucifixion. Jesus did not die as a martyr for a lost cause. He died in a powerful move to solve the problem of humanity's wickedness and violence, and the estrangement from God caused by it.

How can this be?

☞ **GO TO:**

1 Corinthians 1:18–25;
1 John 1:9–2:2
(foolish)

> **Mark 15:20** And when they had mocked him, they took off the purple robe and put his own clothes on him. Then they led him out to crucify him.

GOSPEL QUARTET IN HARMONY

Matthew 27:27–30

Mark 15:16–19

John 19:2–3

☞ **GO TO:**

Luke 23:63–65 (Jews)

Romans 16:13 (Rufus)

GOSPEL QUARTET IN HARMONY

Matthew 27:31–32

Mark 15:20–21

Luke 23:26–32

John 19:17

---

cross: the crossbeam (similar to a railroad tie)

 Who's Who

Cyrene: modern Tripoli

forced: anyone could be forced to serve the Roman occupation army

---

☞ **GO TO:**

Matthew 5:41 (forced)

Mark 8:34 (take up)

Man In Purple

After the sentencing, Roman soldiers stripped Jesus and threw a purple robe over his bleeding shoulders. They twisted a crown of thorns and put it on his head, put a reed "scepter" in his right hand, and took turns kneeling before him in mock reverence, hailing him as "king of the Jews," spitting on him, and hitting him in the face. This was the second time in the hours before his crucifixion Jesus was treated like this. The Romans carried the derision and abuse to even greater extremes than the Jews. In addition to their contempt for the man himself, they poured all their anti-Jewish hatred on this lone, defenseless prisoner.

> **Mark 15:21** A certain man from Cyrene, Simon, the father of Alexander and Rufus, was passing by on his way in from the country, and they forced him to carry the cross.

Street Of Sorrow

Surrounded by four soldiers, one carrying a placard announcing his crime—his alleged claim to be "King of the Jews"—Jesus emerged from the judgment hall, carrying his **cross** (John 19:17). Hours of physical abuse, including blood loss from the 39 lashes, had left him physically exhausted; his strength gave out, and he fell beneath the weight of the heavy beam. A traveler from **Cyrene** named Simon, just entering the city, was **forced** to carry Jesus' cross to the place of crucifixion.

SIMON: Father of Alexander and Rufus—names familiar to early Christians. Sources outside the Bible say Simon became a believer and his family was prominent in the early church. He carried the cross for Jesus. Simon probably had no idea he would become a living symbol of the millions who would take up the cross and follow Christ.

> **Luke 23:27–28** A large number of people followed him, including women who mourned and wailed for him. Jesus turned and said to them, "Daughters of Jerusalem, do not weep for me; weep for yourselves and for your children."

Minority Opinion

The crowd lining the road was not entirely hostile. A group of women filled the air with wails of grief.

Jesus urged them not to grieve for him but <u>for themselves</u> and their children, because great suffering was ahead for them, too. He said, *"For if men do these things when the tree is green, what will happen when it is dry?"* (Luke 23:31).

This was a Jewish proverb meaning "If today God pours his wrath on his Son—an innocent 'green tree'—what will conditions be when he pours his wrath on the world that spurned his love and rejected his Son?"

> **Luke 23:32** Two other men, both criminals, were also led out with him to be executed.

Parade Of The Doomed

Jesus was not the only one carrying a cross that day. Two criminals walked the death road with him.

Some wonder if a trio of felons had been originally scheduled to die this day—including the **nefarious** Barabbas. When Barabbas was released, Jesus merely replaced the pardoned bad guy on the execution calendar. Jesus had come to die <u>in place of</u> sinners.

☞ **GO TO:**

Hosea 10:8; Luke 21:20–24; Revelation 6:15–17 (for themselves)

nefarious: vicious, glaringly wicked

☞ **GO TO:**

Romans 5:6–8 (in place of)

Dig Deeper

Crucifixion Events at Calvary[1]

Events	Matthew	Mark	Luke	John
Jesus refuses drugs	27:34	15:23		
Jesus is crucified	27:35	15:24	23:33	19:18
"Father, forgive them"			23:34	
Soldiers gamble for Jesus' clothes	27:35	15:24	23:34	19:23–24
Jesus is mocked by observers	27:39–44	15:29–32	23:35–36	
Jesus is ridiculed by the thieves	27:44			
One thief believes			23:39–43	
"Today you will be with me"			23:43	
To Mary: "Behold your son"				19:26–27
Darkness falls	27:45	15:33	23:44	
"My God, my God . . ."	27:46–47	15:34–36		
"I thirst"				19:28–29
"It is finished"				19:30
"Father, into your hands . . ."			23:46	
Jesus releases his spirit	27:50	15:37	23:46	19:30

☞ **GO TO:**

Luke 3:21; 7:34; 15:2
(made his life)

Luke 5:27–31; 15:1
(flocked)

KEY POINT

How appropriate for
the one about to
"become sin for us" to
die in the company of
dying criminals!

**GOSPEL QUARTET
IN HARMONY**

Matthew 27:33–44
Mark 15:22–34
Luke 23:33–43
John 19:17–27

nine o'clock: *the third
hour*

they: *soldiers, Jewish
people and leaders, all
unbelievers*

☞ **GO TO:**

Luke 23:33–34; Acts
3:17; 2 Corinthians
3:13–16; (not know)

*Remember
This . . .*

The prophet Isaiah had predicted Messiah would be *"assigned
a grave with the wicked"* (Isaiah 53:9). Why not? He had <u>made his
life</u> with them! He was baptized with repentant sinners. They
<u>flocked</u> to him like moths to a light. He spent so much time with
them it destroyed his reputation.

> **Luke 23:33–34** When they came to the place called
> the Skull, there they crucified him, along with the crimi-
> nals—one on his right, the other on his left. Jesus said,
> "Father, forgive them, for they do not know what they
> are doing." And they divided up his clothes by casting
> lots.

Father, Forgive Them

New Testament authors give no space whatsoever to details about
crucifixion itself. None mentions the hammer or nails. None describes the pain or the precise cause of death. They simply say, as
Luke does, *"they crucified him."* The soldiers carried out their grue-
some task as ordered by their commander, Pontius Pilate. They
were professionals, and this was part of their job. Before they began driving the nails, they offered Jesus wine mixed with myrrh, a
sedative to ease the pain (Mark 15:23). He refused it.

About **nine o'clock** in the morning, they drove the spikes
through his wrists. Jesus kept praying out loud, *"Father, forgive
them, for **they** do <u>not know</u> what they are doing."*

As they lifted the cross bar into place with Jesus nailed to it,
and as they drove the final supporting nail through his feet, he
continued to pray, *"Father, forgive them, for they do not know what
they are doing."*

Crucifixion originated with the Medes and Persians in the
fifth century B.C. After the Greek conquest of Persia,
Alexander the Great brought it to Greece as capital punishment for slaves. The Romans adopted it from the Greeks. In
Italy crucifixion was reserved for slaves, and thousands were
crucified after the slaves' revolt led by Spartacus was crushed.
In the Roman provinces, governors often crucified nonslaves,
especially rebels. The Jews also used crucifixion, though it
was not the preferred method of execution. Jewish Maccabean
King Alexander 1 once crucified 800 men at Jerusalem.

The Place Of The Skull

Historians say 2,000 people were crucified at Jerusalem the year Jesus died, many on the same hill, an elevated place called Golgotha (see appendix B).

Golgotha (an Aramaic name meaning "the place of the Skull" or "the **Skull**") overlooked an ancient stone quarry north of the city, clearly visible from some of the main roads into Jerusalem. It may have been named for the shape of the quarry wall at that point.

Facing Golgotha across the quarry were tombs cut into the cliff side. These are still there today. The Church of the Holy Sepulchre is located on this site.

Crucified!

The HarperCollins *Atlas of the Bible* describes death by crucifixion: "Death would occur quickly if the body were allowed to hang without support. This would be through **asphyxiation**, as the weight of the unsupported body would lead to the shutting off of the breathing passage. To prolong the agony the victim was provided with support for the feet and, at times, a seat peg as well (see illustration, page 242).

"A wooden pole was thrust into the ground, and the condemned man was then compelled to carry the top crosspiece which would then be fixed to the piece in the ground. When there were numerous victims, their arms would be simply roped to the crosspiece. In the case of the crucifixion of Jesus, our sources refer to only three being crucified at the same time. In that case, the victims were nailed both at the wrists—the nails passing between the radius and ulna—and at their feet."[2]

> **Matthew 27:39–43** Those who passed by hurled insults at him, shaking their heads and saying, "You who are going to destroy the temple and build it in three days, save yourself! Come down from the cross, if you are the Son of God!
>
> In the same way the chief priests, the teachers of the law and the elders mocked him. "He saved others," they said, "but he cannot save himself! He's the King of Israel! Let him come down now from the cross, and we will believe in him. He trusts in God. Let God rescue him now if he wants him, for he said, 'I am the Son of God.'"

GOSPEL QUARTET IN HARMONY

Matthew 27:33
Mark 15:22
Luke 23:33
John 19:17

Skull: *Latin: calvaria, from which we get the English, "Calvary"*

asphyxiation: *interruption of breathing*

 **KEY Outline:**

Crucifixion Agenda
Scourging
Carry the cross
Spikes
Lifting up
Blood
Asphyxiation
Death

☞ **GO TO:**

John 2:19–21;
  Matthew 26:61;
  Mark 14:57–58
  (destroy the temple)

Psalm 22:6–8 (rescue)

The Crucifixion

Like a slave or criminal, Jesus was hung on a cross similar to this one. Crucifixion was the most painful and degrading form of capital punishment. The titulus hangs at the top of the cross. Jesus' cross may have had a small seat such as one depicted here where he could rest to catch his breath.

GOSPEL QUARTET IN HARMONY

Matthew 27:37–44
Mark 15:26–32
Luke 23:35–39
John 19:19–22

titulus: Latin: "title," here a sign

☞ **GO TO:**

John 3:16
(entire world)

Opinion Poll At Golgotha

To the crossbar above his head, the soldiers fastened Pilate's **titulus** naming Jesus' crime: "This is the King of the Jews." The sign was written in three languages (John 19:20)—Aramaic (language of the locals), Latin (language of the Romans), and Greek (the universal language).

People from all over the world would travel the nearby roads this feast day. Pilate, of course, had no idea he was symbolizing that Jesus' death was for the entire world.

When the chief priests protested the sign should be changed to read that Jesus *claimed* to be king of the Jews, Pilate responded tersely, *"What I have written, I have written"* (John 19:22).

The instigators of this death scene gave full vent to their anger and scorn. To them Jesus was a liar, a blasphemer, worthy only of mockery.

Louis A. Barbieri Jr.: The irony of this scene was that Jesus could have done the things the crowd was shouting for him to do. He could have come down from the cross and physically saved himself. He did not lack the power to accomplish his deliverance. But it was not the Father's will to do that. It was necessary that the Son of God die for others.[3]

William Barclay: The Jews could only see God in power; but Jesus showed them that God is sacrificial love.[4]

> **Luke 23:39–43** One of the criminals who hung there hurled insults at him: "Aren't you the Christ? Save yourself and us!"
>
> But the other criminal rebuked him, "Don't you fear God," he said, "since you are under the same sentence? We are punished justly, for we are getting what our deeds deserve. But this man has done nothing wrong."
>
> Then he said, "Jesus, remember me when you come into your kingdom." Jesus answered him, "I tell you the truth, today, you will be with me in paradise."

KEY Outline:

Opinions about Jesus
King
Liar
Blasphemer
Savior

Sinners In Paradise

The two other men, presumably Barabbas' partners in crime, were crucified with Jesus—one on his right, the other on his left, with Jesus in the middle.

Both watched him as he suffered the same calamity they were going through. Both were there to hear his prayer for his enemies' forgiveness.

At first both joined the sneering detractors, refusing to believe anything but what Jesus' enemies said about him, and refusing to accept responsibility for their own situation (Matthew 27:44).

One continued to spew his bitterness until the very end. The other, however, began to see with different eyes.

Staring death in the face, the repentant criminal admitted five things:

1. He was afraid to face God alone.
2. He was guilty and deserved to be punished for his sins.
3. Jesus was innocent and not dying for his own sins.
4. Jesus was king.
5. His only hope was to be remembered by Jesus.

GOSPEL QUARTET IN HARMONY

Matthew 27:38, 44
Mark 15:27
Luke 23:32–33, 39–43
John 19:18

Jesus interpreted his attitudes and words as expressions of faith and promised that he and the dying rebel would be together that very day in **paradise**.

Something to Ponder

☞ **GO TO:**

John 8:11; Romans 5:8; Revelation 13:8 (nobody's asking)

The grace of this man Jesus is amazing! While nails tore his flesh and he fought for breath, his concern was not for himself but for the forgiveness of those who caused his suffering, and assurance of eternal life for a dying man at the end of a useless life! Yet, when you stop to consider the life Jesus lived, what could be more consistent? In fact, this is precisely the picture of God Jesus was sent to reveal: The Bible's God is the God who forgives sin, even when <u>nobody's asking</u> for it!

> **John 19:26–27** When Jesus saw his mother there, and the disciple whom he loved standing nearby, he said to his mother, "Dear woman, here is your son," and to the disciple, "Here is your mother." From that time on, this disciple took her into his home.

"Take My Mother Home"

Relatives and friends of the crucified often came to be with them and were allowed to gather near the cross.[5]

A group of women stood near Jesus' cross, along with John, Jesus' dear friend and confidant, and others, including his enemies. In the group was his mother. What he said to her and John was no mere suggestion. He used the terminology of legal adoption proceedings.

What Others are Saying:

GOSPEL QUARTET IN HARMONY

Matthew 27:45–56
Mark 15:33–41
Luke 23:44–49
John 19:28–30
sixth hour: noon

E. Stauffer: A crucified man has the right to make testamentary dispositions, even from the cross. Jesus now makes use of this right, and with the official formula of the old Jewish family law he places his mother under the protection of the apostle John.[6]

> **Luke 23:44–45a** It was now about the sixth hour, and darkness came over the whole land until the ninth hour, for the sun stopped shining.

The Day The Sun Refused To Shine

About midday (the **sixth hour**) the land of Israel became shrouded in darkness for three hours.

We do not know how dark it was or what caused it. It could not have been an eclipse of the sun, because an eclipse is impossible at full moon (by which the Passover date is determined).

New Testament writers don't connect the darkness with astronomical events but with the event taking place on Golgotha—the death of God's Son.

What Others are Saying:

Douglas Webster: At the birth of the Son of God there was brightness at midnight; at the death of the Son of God there was darkness at noon.[7]

John R. W. Stott: Gradually, the crowd thinned out, their curiosity glutted. At last silence fell and darkness came—darkness perhaps because no eye should see . . . the anguish of soul which the sinless Saviour now endured.[8]

> **Mark 15:34–35** And at the **ninth hour** Jesus cried out in a loud voice, "Eloi, Eloi, lama sabachthani?"—which means, "My God, my God, why have you forsaken me?"
>
> When some of those standing near heard this, they said, "Listen, he's calling Elijah."

ninth hour: three o'clock in the afternoon

Cry Of The Forsaken

A cry pierced the air. In that day, before the constant hum of machinery which today muffles such cries, such a cry would have been heard even in the heart of the city of Jerusalem. It came from the edge of the old quarry. The groans of the dying had often been heard from that place, but this was a cry of pain that went deeper than the physical suffering inflicted by nails and cross. It was in Aramaic, the language of the street.

*"My God, my God, why have you **forsaken** me?"*

The Greek speakers near the cross misunderstood the words (Mark 15:35–36). We still struggle to understand them. It's not that we've never heard them before . . . or said them.

They are very human words, expressing a very human feeling.

They are first found in Scripture in Psalm 22. Jewish Bible interpreters attached **messianic** significance to that ancient poem. There King David wailed his sense of abandonment in the midst of some excruciating struggle.

We know the feeling. At times, all hell is breaking loose in our lives, and we feel like God isn't listening and doesn't care! That's

GOSPEL QUARTET IN HARMONY

Matthew 27:46–49
Mark 15:34–36
John 19:28–29

forsaken: expression of emotional anguish caused by abandonment

messianic: concerning the coming Messiah, Christ

☞ **GO TO:**

Luke 22:41–44
(Gethsemane)

Isaiah 53:9; John 8:29,
46; Acts 3:14;
2 Corinthians 5:21
(without sin)

Genesis 3:8;
Deuteronomy 31:16–
18; Isaiah 59:1–2;
Ezekiel 14:7–8
(separation)

Romans 5:12–21;
Hebrews 2:9, 14–15;
Colossians 2:13–14
(necessary)

**What Others
are Saying:**

sin: *rebellion against and
independence toward
God*

separation from God:
*the Bible uses "death" as a
picture of this separation*

how Christ felt on the cross. Only with him there was much more to it.

The pain the cry expressed was exactly what Jesus had struggled with in the garden of <u>Gethsemane</u>: the prospect of experiencing separation from his Father in heaven.

Why the separation? Old and New Testament writers and Christ himself insist he was <u>without sin</u>. From eternity past he had never known anything but unbroken intimacy with God. Even when he spoke of being forsaken by his closest friends (John 16:32), Jesus confidently affirmed, *"I am not alone, for my Father is with me."*

Until he was on the cross, bearing the brunt of righteous judgment for human sin, Jesus had never experienced the spiritual consequences of **sin**, the most devastating of which is **separation from God**. Sin puts up a wall between the person and God that makes the Berlin Wall look like a crack in the sidewalk. It's a barrier no man or woman can cross without the grace of God.

In order to take the full punishment for human sin so God could justly accept forgiven sinners as friends, it was <u>necessary</u> for Jesus to bear all of sin's consequences, including separation from God.

William Barclay: In this terrible, grim, bleak moment Jesus really and truly identified himself with the sin of man. Here we have the divine paradox—Jesus knew what it was to be a sinner. . . . This experience must have been doubly agonizing for Jesus, because he had never known what it was to be separated by this barrier from God.[9]

John R. W. Stott: An actual and dreadful separation took place between the Father and the Son; it was voluntarily accepted by both the Father and the Son; it was due to our sins and their just reward; and Jesus expressed this horror of great darkness, this God-forsakenness, by quoting the only verse of Scripture which accurately described it, and which he perfectly fulfilled, namely, *"My God, My God, why have you forsaken me?"*[10]

Oswald Chambers: The cross is the crystalized point in history where eternity merges with time. The cry on the cross, *"My God, My God, why have you forsaken me?"* is not the desolation of an isolated individual: it is the revelation of the heart of God face to face with the sin of man, and going deeper down than man's sin can ever go in inconceivable heartbreak in order that every sin-stained, hell-deserving sinner might be absolutely redeemed.[11]

> **John 19:28** Later, knowing that all was now completed, and so that the Scripture would be fulfilled, Jesus said, "I am thirsty."

Pardon's Price Paid In Full

The darkness began to lift. The task he'd been <u>sent</u> to do was done. He had taken on himself the full judgment God's Law demanded for human sin.

He could go home now.

He needed strength for a final proclamation. *"I am thirsty,"* he said softly. Of the writers only John heard it.

Someone dipped a sponge in wine vinegar and held it to his lips (John 19:29). Then reaching deep inside for strength, Jesus let out a <u>loud yell</u>: *"It is finished!"* (John 19:30).

The original word John uses for what Jesus shouted means "it has been and will forever remain finished!" Archeologists have discovered papyrus tax receipts with this same word written across them, meaning "paid in full."

John R. W. Stott: It is not men who have finished their brutal deed; it is [Jesus] who has accomplished what he came into the world to do. He has borne the sins of the world. Deliberately, freely and in perfect love he has endured the judgment in our place. He has procured salvation for us, established a new **covenant** between God and humankind, and made available the chief covenant blessing, the forgiveness of sins.[12]

> **Luke 23:46** Jesus called out with a loud voice, "Father, <u>into your hands</u> I commit my spirit." When he had said this, he **breathed his last**.

In Good Hands

The death of Jesus was no ordinary death, because Jesus was no ordinary man.

1. Jesus' death was voluntary. No one could *take* his life from him: *"I lay [my life] down of my own accord,"* he said (John 10:18). He consciously yielded his spirit to God. John 19:30 describes it this way: *"He bowed his head and gave up his spirit."* He literally sent away his spirit.

☞ **GO TO:**

Philippians 2:5–11 (sent)

Matthew 27:50; Mark 15:37 (loud yell)

Something to Ponder

What Others are Saying:

covenant: *contract, terms of relationship*

☞ **GO TO:**

Psalm 31:5 (into your hands)

breathed his last: *literally, "breathed out"*

GOSPEL QUARTET IN HARMONY

Matthew 27:50–56
Mark 15:37–41
Luke 23:46–49
John 19:30b

☞ GO TO:

Hebrews 2:14–18 (die)

Exodus 12:3–11;
1 Corinthians 5:7
(paschal lambs)

Hebrews 9:26; 10:1–
18; Romans 3:25;
5:8–9
(once-and-for-all)

holy of holies: the
temple inner sanctum,
only the high priest
entered once a year on
the Day of Atonement

GOSPEL QUARTET
IN HARMONY

Matthew 27:54–56
Mark 15:39–41
Luke 23:47–49

centurion: Roman
commander of a "century"
(100 troops)

2. Jesus' death was his destiny. He'd left his Father's side 33 years earlier, to become mortal so it was possible to <u>die</u>, a substitute taking the death sentence for human sin.

3. Jesus' death was the ultimate sacrifice. As he died, <u>paschal lambs</u> were being sacrificed at the Temple. Every bleeding lamb throughout the 1,500 year history of Passovers pointed to Jesus' sacrifice. He was the last—the Lamb of God taking away the world's sin (John 1:29, 35), the <u>once-and-for-all</u> sacrifice to end all sacrifices. God brought a perfect Lamb to the altar and sacrificed him there.

4. When Jesus died an earthquake generally shook things up (Matthew 27:51)! Two amazing things accompanied the quake: (1) The heavy embroidered veil, symbolizing separation from God, in the Temple tore in two from top to bottom as if Jesus' death had ripped open access to the **holy of holies** to let ordinary sinners barge into the presence of God for grace and mercy (Matthew 27:51; Luke 23:45; Hebrews 4:16); and (2) Tombs, perhaps across the quarry from Golgotha, *"broke open."* Deceased Jews, known for righteousness, were seen alive in the city (Matthew 27:52–53).

They Saw Him Die

Scripture mentions several people who watched Jesus die and were affected by what they saw.

1. *The* **centurion** *in charge of the crucifixion.* He was a professional soldier, a Roman and a pagan. During the course of Jesus' crucifixion, the centurion's men heard him comment that Jesus was no criminal (Luke 23:47). After watching Jesus die, he exclaimed: *"Surely this man was a Son of God!"* (Mark 15:39).

2. *The sympathizers.* Jesus' enemies apparently headed into the city when the sky darkened, but sympathizers stayed to the bitter end. When he died the immenseness of the tragedy gripped these observers and they *"beat their breasts"* in an expression of grief (Luke 23:48). Some Bible scholars think the experience at Golgotha was preparation for the day of Pentecost, six weeks away, when 3,000 would turn to Christ (Acts 2:41).

3. *Jesus' friends and relatives.* The people who knew Jesus best watched at a discreet distance—his disciples and that

cluster of women who had followed him from Galilee and given him spiritual and financial support (Mark 15:40–41).

> **John 19:31–34** Now it was the day of Preparation, and the next day was to be a special Sabbath. Because the Jews did not want the bodies left on the crosses during the Sabbath, they asked Pilate to have the legs broken and the bodies taken down. The soldiers therefore came and broke the legs of the first man who had been crucified with Jesus, and then those of the other. But when they came to Jesus and found he was already dead, they did not break his legs. Instead, one of the soldiers pierced Jesus' side with a spear, bringing a sudden flow of blood and water.

Death Certificate

Jesus died about 3 P.M. Preparations for the Sabbath, which began at sundown, were underway.

Because it was a **special Sabbath**, a feast day, Jewish leaders did not want dying bodies hanging around out on Skull Hill. Romans left the bodies of the crucified on the cross as a warning to others; Jews preferred to bury them so as not to <u>defile</u> the land.

Death by crucifixion could take several days. In cases where a speedier demise was to the advantage of the powers that be, legs of victims were broken. This made it impossible for them to push themselves up against the spikes in their feet. In the crucified position this movement was absolutely necessary in order to breathe. This brought a quick death by asphyxiation (a strange mercy).

Hard blows with a heavy mallet broke the legs of the other victims, but when they came to Jesus the soldiers discovered he was already dead. No need to break his legs. (God had instructed Moses that none of the Passover lamb's <u>bones</u> must ever be broken.) To be sure he was dead, one soldier drove his <u>spear</u> into Jesus' torso. A gush of blood and water confirmed his death. The spear pierced Jesus' chest, releasing blood from the heart and water from the **pericardial sac** around the heart.

KEY Outline:

Reactions to Jesus' Death
Worship
Beaten breasts
Broken dreams

special Sabbath: *first day of the Feast of Unleavened Bread*

☞ **GO TO:**

Deuteronomy 21:23 (defile)

Exodus 12:46; Numbers 9:12; Psalm 34:20; John 19:36 (bones)

Zechariah 12:10 (spear)

pericardial sac: *membranes enclosing the heart and large blood vessels*

Proof of Death
 Dismissal cry
 Soldier's exam
 Water and blood

☞ **GO TO:**

Matthew 26:53–54
(angel armies)

*infirmities: moral
weaknesses*

*transgressions: violations
of God's Law; sin*

*iniquities: wicked actions
and attitudes*

KEY POINT

People, like sheep, are
wayward. We are
stubborn and stupid.
Yet the Lord has taken
all our sin and put it
on Jesus Christ.

*justified: pronounced,
"not guilty"*

*wrath: natural
consequences of breaking
moral laws*

What Others
are Saying:

What Is The Significance Of Jesus' Death On The Cross?

The Bible clearly reveals that the death of God's Son was always an essential part of God's plan.

The crucifixion was prophesied in the Old Testament. A dozen times before it happened, Jesus told his followers it was coming.

As God's Son, he could have summoned <u>angel armies</u> to rescue him. Instead he voluntarily surrendered to enemies he knew would not rest till he was dead.

Here are four key passages—one from the Old Testament and three from the New Testament—that explain the meaning of Jesus' death:[13]

1 *He was pierced for our transgressions (Isaiah 53:4–6).* Seven hundred years before Jesus was born, God announced through the prophet Isaiah that the Messiah would come, take our **infirmities** on himself, be pierced with our **transgressions**, and be crushed for our **iniquities**:

> *Surely he took up our infirmities*
>   *and carried our sorrows,*
> *yet we considered him stricken of God,*
>   *smitten by him, and afflicted.*
> *But he was pierced for our transgressions,*
>   *he was crushed for our iniquities;*
> *the punishment that brought us peace was upon him,*
>   *and by his wounds we are healed.*
> *We all, like sheep, have gone astray,*
>   *each of us has turned to his own way;*
> *and the Lord has laid on him*
>   *the iniquity of us all. (Isaiah 53:4–6)*

2 *Christ died for us (Romans 5:8–9).* The apostle Paul wrote a letter to the Roman Christians in which he explained the reason for Jesus' death: *"God demonstrates his own love for us in this: While we were still sinners, Christ died for us. Since we have now been justified by his blood, how much more shall we be saved from wrath through him?"* (Romans 5:8–9).

Charles E. B. Cranfield: God, because in his mercy he willed to forgive sinful men, and, being truly merciful, willed to forgive them righteously, that is, without in any way condoning their sin, purposed to direct against his own very self in the person of his Son the full weight of that righteous wrath which they deserved.[14]

3 *God made him . . . sin for us* (2 Corinthians 5:21). In his second letter to the Corinthians, Paul described an amazing transaction which took place on the cross: *"God made [Christ] who had no sin to be sin for us, so that in him we might become the righteousness of God"* (2 Corinthians 5:21).

Larry (Lawrence O.) Richards: Jesus took our sins on himself; his death took the penalty that our sins deserved. And, wonder of wonders, God then credited the righteousness of Jesus to us! With sin paid for, there was no longer a barrier between human beings and God. With Jesus' own righteousness credited to our account, we are welcome to enter God's presence.[15]

Max Lucado: The cross did what sacrificial lambs could not do. It erased our sins not for a year, but for eternity. The cross did what man cannot do. It granted us the right to talk with, love, and even live with God.[16]

4 *God . . . loved the world* (John 3:16–18). Early in his ministry in a conversation with the Pharisee Nicodemus, Jesus summed up the meaning of his life and death: *"God so loved the **world** that he gave his one and only Son, that whoever believes in him shall not perish but have eternal life. For God did not send his Son into the world to condemn the world, but to save the world through him. Whoever believes in him is not condemned, but whoever does not believe stands condemned already because he has not believed on the name of God's one and only Son"* (John 3:16–18).

Jesus' death was payment for our sins. God, because he loved all people, worked out this plan for bringing them home to him. Anyone, anywhere, who takes God at his word and puts their trust in God's Son Jesus is promised forgiveness and eternal life.

F. F. Bruce: The love of God is limitless; it embraces all mankind. No sacrifice was too great to bring its unmeasured intensity home to men and women; the best that God had to give—his only son, his well-beloved. The gospel of salvation and life has its source in the love of God.[17]

KEY POINT

The penalty of sin is death, and Jesus paid the penalty.

What Others are Saying:

KEY Outline:

Old Testament
Sacrificial lambs
- temporary forgiveness

New Testament
Jesus' sacrifice
- Lamb of God
- eternal forgiveness

world: *people*

KEY POINT

The love of God is limitless; it embraces all mankind.

What Others are Saying:

Study Questions

1. For what three groups of people was Jesus praying when he said, "Father, forgive them for they do not know what they are doing"?
2. What did the sign read that Pilate put over Jesus' head? How did the Jewish leaders react to it? How did the repentant thief react to the idea it presented?
3. From what Psalm was Jesus quoting when he cried, *"My God, My God, why have you forsaken me?"* What was Jesus experiencing at the time?
4. Identify three ways in which Christ's death was out of the ordinary.
5. What did the centurion at the cross think of Jesus after watching how he died?
6. When did the meaning of the death of Christ begin to make sense to you? How would you explain it to a friend who does not understand?

CHAPTER WRAP-UP

- The Praetorium Guards mocked and beat Jesus, calling him "King of the Jews." (John 19:23)

- Jesus was unable to carry his cross all the way to Calvary. Simon of Cyrene was forced to carry it for him. Along the way Jesus told some weeping women to weep for themselves because disaster was coming. (Luke 23:26–31)

- At a place called "the Skull" Jesus was crucified. As the nails were driven into his wrists and feet, he prayed, "Father, forgive them." His enemies milled around the cross insulting him. One of the thieves crucified with him believed in him. He gave his mother into the care of his closest disciple, John. (Luke 23:32–43; John 19:25–27)

- At noon it became dark. Jesus cried out because he was forsaken by God as he bore the guilt and condemnation for the world's sins. At the end of six hours on the cross, he shouted, "It is finished!" and sent his spirit to God's control. His redeeming work was done. (Matthew 27:45–54; John 19:28–30)

Part Four

SONRISE

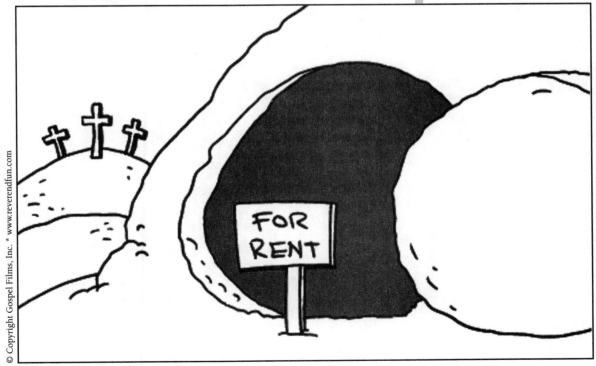

14 HE'S ALIVE!

Let's Get Started

The young Messiah, Jesus of Nazareth, was dead. He died on the eve of Passover, Friday, April 7, 30 A.D., about 3 P.M.,[1] on a Roman cross on a hill overlooking an old stone quarry just north of Jerusalem—a place called the Skull.

Most biographies end with the person's death. Not this one.

Jesus' followers intended to give him a decent burial, but they got the surprise of their lives. His enemies got the mother of all headaches. Sin's case against believing sinners was <u>thrown out</u> of court.

And the living church was born.

> **Mark 15:42–43** It was Preparation Day (that is, the day before the Sabbath). So as evening approached, Joseph of Arimathea, a prominent member of the Council, who was himself waiting for the kingdom of God, went boldly to Pilate and asked for Jesus' body.

A Decent Burial

In an unexpected twist in the story, a member of the Sanhedrin, who dissented against the decision to condemn Jesus, appeared at Pilate's offices to ask that the body of Jesus be released to him.

The man's name was Joseph, from the town of Arimathea, a

GOSPEL QUARTET IN HARMONY

Matthew 27:57–28:20
Mark 15:42–16:18
Luke 23:50–24:49
John 19:38–21:25

☞ GO TO:

Romans 4:25; 5:1, 6–11 (thrown out)

GOSPEL QUARTET IN HARMONY

Matthew 27:57–61
Mark 15:42–47
Luke 23:50–56
John 19:38–42

☞ **GO TO:**

Isaiah 53:9 (rich man)

John 3:1–2; 7:50–51
(Nicodemus)

John 12:42–43
(feared the Jews)

rich man (Matthew 27:57). He was joined by another dissenting Council member, the Pharisee Nicodemus (John 19:39).

These two had apparently been absent when the Sanhedrin handed down its verdict on Jesus—perhaps they were purposely not informed of the early morning meeting. Nicodemus had given hints of pro-Jesus sympathies; Joseph is described as *"a disciple of Jesus, but secretly because he feared the Jews"* (John 19:38).

> **Mark 15:44–47** Pilate was surprised to hear that he was already dead. Summoning the centurion, he asked him if Jesus had already died. When he learned from the centurion that it was so, he gave the body to Joseph. So Joseph bought some linen cloth, took down the body, wrapped it in the linen, and placed it in a tomb cut out of rock. Then he rolled a stone against the entrance of the tomb.

Sad Acts Of Service

When Jesus died, three hours of daylight remained before the Sabbath when no work could be done. Preparing a coffin or even moving a corpse's arm or leg was specifically forbidden on the seventh day. So Joseph, a strict Jew, had to act quickly.

When Pilate heard Jesus was dead after only six hours, he was surprised. Crucifixion victims often hung on the cross for days waiting to die. Pilate quizzed the centurion in charge of the crucifixion, who confirmed Jesus' death and released the body to Joseph.

Across the quarry from Skull Hill, Joseph had prepared a tomb for his own burial (Matthew 27:60). It was cut into the soft limestone of a craggy hillside and surrounded by a garden (John 19:41). Some tombs of the wealthy were set in private, walled gardens, with caretaker-guards to tend and watch them. This tomb had never been used (John 19:41).

While Joseph secured release of the body, Nicodemus gathered 75 pounds of burial spices—*"a mixture of myrrh and aloes"*—to pack around the body along with *"strips of linen . . . in accordance with Jewish burial customs"* (John 19:40). Egyptian burial was designed to preserve the body from decay; Jewish burial was designed to inhibit odors during decay.

JOSEPH OF ARIMATHEA: A rich man, member of the Sanhedrin, who took Jesus' body and buried it in the new tomb he had prepared for his own death.

☞ **GO TO:**

John 20:15 (caretaker)

strips of linen: strips of cloth or a single grave cloth

Who's Who

Byron R. McCane: The eyes of the deceased were closed, the corpse was washed with perfumes and ointments, its bodily orifices were stopped, and strips of cloth were wrapped tightly around the body—binding the jaw closed, fixing arms to the sides, and trying the feet together. Once prepared, the corpse was placed on a bier or in a coffin and carried out of town in a procession to the family tomb.[2]

Decency And Disgrace

Customary Jewish burials took place immediately, in the family tomb. The burial was followed by a week of intense grieving, called *shiv'ah* ("seven"), then a month of less intense mourning, called *shloshim* ("thirty"). The family continued to mourn for a year.

But Jesus died as a criminal. Different rules applied.

First, an executed criminal could not be buried in his family's tomb until a year after death. Many were buried in common graves, or even thrown on the city garbage dump to burn with the trash.

Second, no public mourning was allowed for an executed criminal. While Joseph and Nicodemus honored Jesus by caring for his body, in actuality, his burial conformed to the prohibitions: He was never buried in his family tomb, nor were any of the rituals of mourning conducted for him. He was buried in disgrace like any condemned criminal.

The final task in the burial was to roll a large **stone** over the opening to the cave (Mark 15:46). As the sun was setting, the two Johnny-come-lately disciples completed their sad work and trudged home. Following Joseph and Nicodemus to the tomb and last to leave the burial site were Mary Magdalene and Mary the mother of **Joses** (Mark 15:47).

KEY POINT

Jesus' burial conformed to the rules for burial of a criminal: no family tomb and no public mourning.

stone: large, flat cartwheel-like stone; some weighing more than a ton still seen in Israel

Joses: brother of disciple James the Younger

next day: after sunset— on the Sabbath—probably shortly after Jesus' burial

Matthew 27:61–66 The **next day**, the one after Preparation Day, the chief priests and the Pharisees went to Pilate. "Sir," they said, "we remember that while he was still alive that deceiver said, 'After three days I will rise again.' So give the order for the tomb to be made secure until the third day. Otherwise, his disciples may come and steal the body and tell the people that he has been raised from the dead. This last deception will be worse than the first."

"Take a guard," Pilate answered, "Go, make the tomb as secure as you know how." So they went and made the tomb secure by putting a seal on the stone and posting the guard."

Jesus' Tomb

Jesus was buried in a tomb similar to this one. Notice the large stone that could be rolled to cover the entrance.

KEY POINT

Jesus' enemies thought the tomb was secured with an Imperial seal and a 24-hour watch.

☞ **GO TO:**

Matthew 16:23; Luke 18:32–34 (promised)

Matthew 12:38–40; John 2:19–22 (figurative)

Don't Let That Dead Man Out Of Your Sight!

This incident is interesting for several reasons:

1. The Sadducees and Pharisees showed their desperation by breaking their cherished Sabbath rules in order to secure the tomb.

2. Even though Jesus clearly <u>promised</u> his disciples he would rise again, it seemed to have gone in one ear and out the other without disturbing the cobwebs in between! His enemies, however, clearly understood what he was saying even though he only said it to them in <u>figurative</u> language!

3. Pilate's answer is tinged with ridicule, like saying, "Keep him in the tomb if you think you can!"

4. Two things were done to secure the tomb and scare away body snatchers: (1) the stone was sealed with the

governor's **seal**, the seal of Imperial Rome; and (2) a squad of Roman soldiers was posted to stand 24-hour watch. Breaking an official seal without authorization brought a death sentence.

seal: cord and wax imprinted with official insignia

Bill Bright: [Jesus'] little band of followers was now terror-stricken and scattered. His enemies were celebrating their victory.[3]

What Others are Saying:

> **Matthew 28:1–4** After the Sabbath, at dawn on the first day of the week, Mary Magdalene and the other Mary went to look at the tomb. There was a violent earthquake, for an <u>angel</u> of the Lord came down from heaven and, going to the tomb, rolled back the stone and sat on it. His appearance was like lightning, and his clothes were white as snow. The guards were so afraid of him that they shook and became like dead men.

☞ **GO TO:**

Mark 16:6–7; Luke 24:5–7; John 20:12 (angel)

Bustin' Out!

At the crack of dawn Sunday, a group of women headed for Joseph's tomb with spices to offset the stench of the decaying body. Either Joseph and Nicodemus were unable to finish the job before Sabbath or the women simply wanted to do *something* to honor Jesus' memory.

The number of women is uncertain. Several are named. All four historians mention Mary Magdalene (Matthew 28:1; Mark 16:1; Luke 24:10; John 20:1). Others who came were Mary the mother of James, called *"the other Mary"* (Matthew 28:1; Mark 16:1; Luke 24:10); Salome (Mark 16:1), Joanna (Luke 24:10); and unnamed *"others with them"* (Luke 24:10).

On the way, they wondered who was going to roll that humongous stone from the entrance of the tomb (Mark 16:3). Not to worry!

Before they got there, the grave guards suddenly got all shook up by a violent earthquake. While they were looking around for something to hang on to, a dazzling personage appeared from nowhere, and with a flick of his little finger rolled the boulder away from the cave opening and sat on it! The knees of battle-toughened legionnaires turned to Jell-O, and they keeled over from sheer terror.

By the time the women arrived, the guards had left for the city—there was nothing for them to guard!

GOSPEL QUARTET IN HARMONY

Matthew 28:1–8
Mark 16:1–8
Luke 24:1–12
John 20:1–10

KEY Outline:

Angel at the Tomb
Like lightning
White clothes
Rolled the rock
Terrified guards
Heaven's involved

KEY POINT

Don't be alarmed!
Christ is alive!

☞ **GO TO:**

Compare Matthew
28:2; Mark 16:5;
John 20:12; Luke
25:23 (two . . . one)

*Remember
This . . .*

George R. Beasley-Murray: The presence of angels is a witness that the powers of heaven have been at work here.[4]

> **Mark 16:4–6** When [the women] looked up, they saw that the stone, which was very large, had been rolled away. As they entered the tomb, they saw a young man dressed in a white robe sitting on the right side, and they were alarmed.
>
> "Don't be alarmed," he said. "You are looking for Jesus the Nazarene, who was crucified. He has risen! He is not here."

"He's Gone!"

Finding the grave open, they went in, expecting to find the body—but the corpse was gone! Luke says they were utterly at a loss (Luke 24:4), wondering what was going on.

Suddenly a figure in bright garments stood beside them: an angel (Matthew 28:2)! Some of the women, telling this incident, said there were <u>two</u> angels, others said <u>one</u>. However many, the women were terrified.

"See the place were they laid him," the angel said (Mark 16:6).

Examination of the open tomb by the women confirmed that the body of Jesus, so carefully placed there by Joseph and Nicodemus on Friday afternoon, was no longer there.

The women were so rattled by what they'd seen and heard—the deserted grave, the vision of angels, the announcement that Jesus had risen from the dead—they were speechless at first (Mark 16:8). But by the time they got to where the disciples were hiding out in Jerusalem, they found the story impossible to keep (Luke 24:9).

To see spirit beings requires spiritual perception; not all the women perceived the "vision of angels" the same way.

> **Luke 24:9, 11** When they came back from the tomb, they told all these things to the Eleven and to all the others. . . . But they did not believe the women, because their words seemed to them like nonsense.

The Mystery Of The Missing Corpse

The response of the apostles and other followers of Jesus was less than enthusiastic. The Greek term translated *nonsense* (Luke 24:11) is a medical term for "the babbling of a fevered and insane mind."[5]

The apostles and others were sure that the women's grief had driven them off the deep end! "Risen from the dead? Bah Humbug!"

Mary Magdalene proposed the theory that someone had moved the body without letting them know (John 20:2). She'd seen the angels, but she was apparently having trouble believing her eyes!

Peter and John decided to go see for themselves (Luke 24:12; John 20:3–10). Sure enough, the grave clothes, with the spices still in them, were there, along with the cloth that covered the corpse's face. But the grave clothes were empty. After seeing the empty tomb for himself, "*the other disciple* [John] ***believed***" (John 20:8). To John empty grave clothes proved something wonderful had happened. Maybe Jesus had risen.

But "*they still did not understand from Scripture that Jesus had to rise from the dead*" (John 20:9). Peter and John returned from the grave scratching their heads. But they would soon be convinced beyond all doubt that what the angels said to the women was a fact: Jesus Christ, crucified, dead, and buried, had risen from the dead and was alive!

> **Matthew 28:11–15** While the women were on their way, some of the guards went into the city and reported to the chief priests everything that had happened. When the chief priests had met with the elders and devised a plan, they gave the soldiers a large sum of money, telling them, "You are to say, 'His disciples came during the night and stole him away while we were asleep.' If this report gets to the governor, we will satisfy him and keep you out of trouble." So the soldiers took the money and did as they were instructed. And this story has been widely circulated among the Jews to this very day.

Hush Money

The sum of money offered the Roman guardsmen to spread this cock-and-bull story must have been significant considering the risk. A soldier who fell asleep on guard duty faced execution (Acts 12:19). If Pilate had to be paid off to protect the soldiers, it would be a royal pain in the priestly pocketbook!

GOSPEL QUARTET IN HARMONY

Luke 24:12
John 20:1–10

☞ **GO TO:**

John 5:44; 6:47; 19:35; 20:29 (believed)

believed: *In John, indicates real faith*

KEY POINT

They didn't believe because they didn't understand the Scriptures.

William Barclay: The Jewish authorities . . . had used treachery to lay hold on [Jesus]. They had used illegality to try him. They had used slander to charge him to Pilate. And now they were using bribery to silence the truth about him. *And they failed. Magna est veritas et praevalebit,* ran the Roman proverb: great is the truth and it will prevail. It is a fact of history that not all men's evil machinations can in the end stop the truth. The gospel of goodness is greater than the plots of wickedness.[6]

Thomas Arnold: The evidence for our Lord's life and death and resurrection may be, and often has been, shown to be satisfactory; it is good according to the common rules for distinguishing good evidence from bad. Thousands and tens of thousands of persons have gone through it piece by piece, as carefully as every judge summing up on a most important case. I have myself done it many times over, not to persuade others but to satisfy myself. I have been used for many years to study the histories of other times, and to examine and weigh the evidence of those who have written about them, and I know of no one fact in the history of mankind which is proved by better and fuller evidence of every sort, to the understanding of a fair inquirer, than the great sign which God has given us that Christ died and rose again from the dead.[7]

Last Seen . . . Alive!

The most powerful evidence of the resurrection comes from the testimony of eyewitnesses who saw Jesus alive after he rose from the dead. The New Testament mentions more than 500, many by name.

**GOSPEL QUARTET
IN HARMONY**

Matthew 28:9–20
Mark 16:9–18
Luke 24:1–12
John 20:1–10

A few of these—Matthew, Mark, John, Paul, James, Peter, and Jude wrote as eyewitnesses. And in their books and letters they quote others who saw him alive.

When these things were written, many named as eyewitnesses were still living. Their testimony could have been checked out for accuracy by simply talking to them. Now, they form powerful links in the chain of historical evidence.

> **John 20:14–16** At this, she turned around and saw Jesus standing there, but she did not realize it was Jesus.
> "Woman," he said, "why are you crying? Who is it you are looking for?"
> Thinking he was the gardener, she said, "Sir, if you

> have carried him away, tell me where you have put him, and I will get him."
>
> Jesus said to her, "Mary."
>
> She turned toward him and cried out in Aramaic, "Rabboni!" (which means Teacher).

The Magdalene Mourner

Jerusalem, Easter Sunday morning, April 9, 30 A.D. Mary Magdalene was at the tomb again. She had shown Peter and John the way and then stayed when they left.

She was crying.

Robbed of the chance to honor the body of her dead Master, she ignored the ban on public mourning for executed criminals and set up a **funereal** wail that could be heard inside the walls of Jerusalem.

Angels appeared again inside the tomb, asking why she was wailing. As she turned from the cave, someone was standing there. The gardener, she thought. She did <u>not recognize</u> Jesus.

"Mary," he said. The familiar voice, the special way he said her name rang a bell.

"Teacher!" she cried in Aramaic. As she realized it was Jesus, she threw herself down and hugged his feet in a spontaneous and appropriate expression of affection.

But he had a job for her to do. "Don't cling to me, for I am on my way to my Father. *Go instead to my **brothers** and tell them*" (John 20:17).

She obeyed. *"I've seen the Lord!"* she told his disciples (John 20:18). She was the first.

> **Matthew 28:9–10** Suddenly Jesus met them. "Greetings," he said. They came to him, clasped his feet and worshiped him. Then Jesus said to them, "Do not be afraid. Go and tell my brothers to go to Galilee; there they will see me."

The Ladies' Embalming Committee Meeting Is Cancelled

Jerusalem, Easter Sunday morning, April 9, 30 A.D. Finding the tomb empty and having seen and heard angels, the women who came to complete the embalming process were in a hurry back into the city to report the mysterious happenings to the disciples.

They were a giddy mix of wide-eyed bewilderment and joy.

GOSPEL QUARTET IN HARMONY

Mark 16:9–11
John 20:11–18

funereal: fit for a funeral

☞ **GO TO:**

Luke 24:16, 31; John 21:4 (not recognize)

brothers: Jesus' unbelieving biological brothers or the disciples or both

Their joy hit a crescendo when Jesus suddenly met them. They dropped their spices on the road, hugged his feet, and worshiped him right there in front of God and everybody!

Emmaus Encounter

Emmaus Road, Easter afternoon, April 9, 30 A.D. On a seven-mile hike from Jerusalem to Emmaus (see appendix A), a disciple named Cleopas and another, whose name isn't given, found themselves sharing the road with a knowledgeable stranger.

The stranger engaged them in conversation for two hours about the Old Testament's teaching concerning the necessity of Christ's death and resurrection.

Their hearts were warmed as the stranger explained the Scriptures to them (Luke 24:32). But they recognized it was Jesus only after they got to Emmaus and were sharing a meal with him. As soon as they knew who he was, he vanished!

Even though it was after dark, the two hurried back to Jerusalem to share the news with **the 11** and others huddling with them in the upper room.

> **Luke 24:33b–34** There they found the Eleven and those with them, assembled together and saying, "It is true! The Lord has risen and has appeared to Simon."

The Rock Sees The Risen Redeemer

Jerusalem, Easter day, April 9, 30 A.D. When the two from Emmaus arrived, they found a group of almost-believers, ready to listen to their tale. The risen Jesus had also appeared to **Peter** that day (see 1 Corinthians 15:5). They'd thought the women were hallucinating, but when Peter reported his encounter, they began to let a little hope trickle in.

Was it male chauvinism that made them believe Peter but not the women to whom Christ first appeared, or were they just spiritually dull?

Reveille For The Revived Redeemer's Routed Regiment

Jerusalem, Easter evening, April 9, 30 A.D. Unexpectedly, while Cleopas related the Emmaus incident to the jaundiced-eyed collection of apostles and disciples, Jesus himself stood in the midst of the gathering! Even then most of the people there couldn't believe it was really Jesus. He did four things to convince them:

GOSPEL QUARTET IN HARMONY

Mark 16:12–13
Luke 24:13–35

the 11: *the 12 apostles minus Judas*

Peter: *"Simon" or "Cephas"*

Something to Ponder

- Jesus dragged their nagging doubts and fears out in the open and dealt with them (Mark 16:14; Luke 24:38).

- Jesus showed them his nail-scarred hands and feet and the wound in his side, to verify he was the crucified one (Luke 24:39, 40; John 20:20).

- Jesus invited them to touch him, and ate a piece of broiled fish so they would understand that his resurrection was complete—he was not a disembodied spirit, but spirit *and* *body* (Luke 24:39, 41–43).

- Jesus reminded them of his predictions that he would rise from the dead, and that his rising fulfilled Old Testament prophecy (Luke 24:44).

John remembers the trickle of hope turning into a river of joy (John 20:20). Before he left them that night, Jesus gave his apostles and other disciples four extremely important things:

1 *He gave them his* **Shalom***! "Peace be with you"* (John 20:21). He had greeted them this way when he first appeared in the room (verse 19); now he repeated it. In his Last Supper talks Jesus promised them <u>peace</u> more real than the world could ever give. He assured them he would keep that promise as they went out to face the world in his name.

2 *He gave them authorization to continue Christ's ministry: "As the Father has sent me, I am sending you"* (John 20:21). Christian disciples are sent to do Jesus' thing, not their own. The mission of Jesus' followers in the world is not a different mission than his. It's in a different form—through men and women who share his resurrection life through the Holy Spirit, his corporate <u>body</u>—but it's his <u>work</u> they are being sent to do.

3 *"He <u>breathed</u> on them" and urged them to "receive the <u>Holy Spirit</u>" to enable them to carry on his ministry* (John 20:22). The actual invasion of their lives by the Spirit was a few weeks away (**Pentecost**, see Acts 2), but in the context of being told their work was cut out for them, they needed assurance that they were not being sent out without the spiritual resources needed to do the job.

4 *Jesus gave the apostles and all Christians authority to deal with other people's sins* (John 20:23). The *New American Standard Bible* gives a more accurate translation of Jesus' statement here: *"If you forgive the sins of any, their sins have been forgiven; if you*

GOSPEL QUARTET IN HARMONY

Mark 16:14
Luke 24:33, 36–43
John 20:19–25

shalom: wholeness; fulfillment; inner harmony, peace with others

☞ **GO TO:**

John 14:27 (peace)

1 Corinthians 12:12–27 (body)

Matthew 28:20; Mark 15:15–16; Luke 24:46–48; John 14:12–14 (work)

Genesis 2:7; Ezekiel 37:9–10 (breathed)

Luke 24:48–49; John 7:37–39; Acts 1:8 (Holy Spirit)

Pentecost: Jewish Spring harvest festival, 50 days after Passover, when the Holy Spirit filled the disciples

retain: Greek: "hold,
carry"

retain *the sins of any, they have been retained"* (John 20:23). Jesus teaches that we are always to forgive (Matthew 18:21–22); the apostle Paul writes that when someone is *"caught in a sin"* Christ's followers are to *"carry"* the burden of the sinning person in an effort to *"restore"* him or her (Galatians 6:1–2). We have Jesus' assurance that God forgives sinners, and that he is bearing their sin as we are.

What Others are Saying:

Dietrich Bonhoeffer: As Christ bears our burdens, so ought we to bear the burdens of our fellowmen. The law of Christ, which it is our duty to fulfill, is the bearing of the cross (Galatians 6:2). My brother's burden which I must bear is not only his outward lot, his natural characteristics and gifts, but quite literally his sin. And the only way to bear that sin is by forgiving it in the power of the cross of Christ which I now share. Thus the call to follow Christ always means a call to share the work of forgiving men their sins.[8]

"Rats! I Missed It!"

It was a rock-'em-sock-'em power-packed night with the risen Lord Jesus—and Thomas missed the whole shebang (John 20:24)!

When the others told him about it, he sounded for all the world like Eyore, the sad-sack donkey of the Winnie the Pooh stories: *"Unless I see the nail prints in his hands and put my finger where the nails were, and put my hand into his side, I will not believe it"* (John 20:25).

Don't be too hard on old Tom. The other guys didn't believe it when they first heard it from the women!

☞ **GO TO:**

John 11:16; 14:5
(Thomas)

ACT OF THE HOLY SPIRIT

Prepared the disciples' minds and hearts to receive God's Spirit

> **John 20:26–28** A week later his disciples were in the house again, and Thomas was with them. Though the doors were locked, Jesus came and stood among them and said, "Peace be with you!" Then he said to Thomas, "Put your finger here; see my hands. Reach out your hand and put it into my side. Stop doubting and believe."
> Thomas said to him, "My Lord and my God!"

Seeing Is Believing, But . . .

Jerusalem, Sunday, April 16, 30 A.D. A week after the missed meeting, Jesus came again for a second visit with the disciples.

He offered his nail-scarred hands for Thomas to touch, and opened his shirt for Thomas to feel the wound in his side.

Tom didn't need to touch Jesus. Overwhelmed at the sight of him, he blurted out his confession: *"My Lord and my God!"*

Thomas did not simply mean he was convinced Jesus was alive. He understood the *meaning* of the resurrection. The <u>resurrection reveals</u> who Jesus is—*Lord* and *God*. For Thomas that was no abstract theological proposition. With the words, "My Lord and my God," Thomas pledged his personal allegiance to Jesus as the master he would serve and the God he would <u>honor</u>.

> **John 20:29** Then Jesus told him, "Because you have seen me, you have believed; **blessed** are those who have not seen and yet have believed."

Believing Without Seeing

John the writer reminds his readers that the faith of those who did not see Jesus alive after his resurrection is as solidly based as the faith of people like Thomas who did see. The written record of Jesus' life and works is in the New Testament. *"These are written that you may believe that Jesus is the Christ, the Son of God, and that by believing you may have life in his name"* (John 20:31).

George R. Beasley-Murray: They have not had the privilege of the disciples in seeing Jesus alive from the dead, nor of having their faith quickened in the extraordinary manner granted to Thomas. Theirs is a faith called forth by the word of the Gospel; but it is none the worse for that, for their trust in the Lord revealed through the Word is of special worth in his eyes.[9]

Fishing With The Good Ol' Boys

Galilee, sunrise, 30 A.D. The third time Jesus appeared to his friends after his resurrection happened like this: Passover and the Feast of Unleavened Bread were over. The disciples returned to Galilee, but stayed close to each other. Seven were together near the **Sea of Tiberias**—Peter, Thomas, **Nathanael, James, and John**, and two other guys.

One day Peter said, *"I'm going fishing."*

"We'll go with you," chimed the others. So they went fishing while it was still dark (every good fisherman knows the fish are biting best before dawn).

Scholars have read all sorts of terrible things into this deci-

Something to Ponder

☞ **GO TO:**

Romans 1:4 (resurrection reveals)

John 1:1; 5:23; 14:7–11 (honor)

blessed: *happy, fortunate, successful*

KEY POINT

Believing even when you can't see is an act of faith, and God will bless you for it.

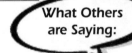

What Others are Saying:

☞ **Check It Out:**

John 21:1–25

Sea of Tiberias: *Sea of Galilee*

Nathanael: *Bartholomew*

James and John: *sons of Zebedee; John avoids giving his name, as usual*

apostasy: falling away
from the faith

sion—everything from aimlessness, to quitting the ministry, to out-and-out **apostasy**! But, hey! Even if Jesus had been crucified and risen from the dead, a guy's gotta eat and feed his family. Or, maybe, out on the lake as the sun is coming up is just a good place to sort things out.

The fishing was lousy. As the sun cast light over the eastern hills, the boat was about 100 yards out (John 21:8), and Jesus was standing on the shore (only they didn't realize it was Jesus). "Haven't caught anything, have you?" he called over the water.

"Nope," they answered.

"He said, 'Throw your net on the right side of the boat and you will find some'" (John 21:6). Maybe the guy on the shore could see something they couldn't. They had nothing to lose. So they did what he said, and suddenly their net was full!

"It's the Lord!" John told Peter. Peter jumped into the water and swam for shore. The others brought the boat in with the net full of fish. Breakfast was ready. Bread and broiled fish cooked on a little fire the Lord had kindled. They counted the fish they'd caught—153 big ones—what a great "fish story"!

And Jesus was in his old, familiar role, breaking bread and fish and sharing a meal with his friends (John 21:13). It doesn't get any better than this!

☞ **GO TO:**

John 6; Luke 22:19;
24:30
(breaking bread)

> **John 21:15–16** When they had finished eating, Jesus said to Simon Peter, "Simon son of John, do you truly love me more than these?"
>
> "Yes, Lord," he said, "you know that I love you."
>
> Jesus said, "Feed my lambs."
>
> Again Jesus said, "Simon son of John, do you truly love me?"
>
> He answered, "Yes, Lord, you know that I love you."
>
> Jesus said, "Take care of my sheep."

The Rehabilitation Of Simon Peter

But Jesus wasn't out there for a fishing trip.

In addition to reaffirming the reality of his resurrection for the seven (and us), this appearance had a highly personal purpose: to rehabilitate Peter after his dismal spiritual failure.

After breakfast, in the presence of the others, Jesus asked, *"Simon son of John, do you truly love me more than these* [others do]*?"* Ouch! Just hours before denying Jesus to protect his own skin, Peter had

☞ **GO TO:**

Luke 23:57–60; John
18:15–16, 25–26
(spiritual failure)

brashly compared his loyalty with that of the other eleven. *"Even if all fall away on account of you, I never will"* (Matthew 26:33).

Now the swagger was gone. No more comparing. No more bragging. No more overblown self-confidence. Peter answered simply, *"Yes, Lord, you know that I love you."*

Jesus asked the same question three times, not to "rub it in," but to give Peter a chance to wipe away the memory of his three-fold denial by a threefold affirmation of his love. Understandably, the third time the question stung deep (John 21:17).

All Peter could do was appeal to the Lord's knowledge of his heart: *"Lord, you know all things; you know that I love you."*

Jesus then reminded Peter of his call to **shepherd** Christ's sheep and prophesied that Peter would die when he was old, with **hands outstretched**, and his death would *"glorify God"* (verses 18–19).

In 1 Corinthians 8:1–2, Paul warns against thinking we know a lot of things when the only things we really know are that we love God and he knows us. Do you love Jesus? Feed his lambs! Give him your life!

Forty Amazing Days

Jesus showed up at many gatherings of his friends during the 40 days between discovery of the empty tomb and his ascension. The disintegrating nucleus of the church was being irresistibly <u>drawn together</u> around his living presence. If you were a disciple, the best place to be was with other disciples—I mean, suppose you skipped church and Jesus showed up!

During those 40 awesome days Jesus did the following:

1 *Jesus made more post-resurrection appearances:*

- The 11 saw Jesus on a mountain in Galilee (Matthew 28:16–20; Mark 16:15–18).
- More than 500 saw Jesus at a single gathering (1 Corinthians 15:6).
- In Jerusalem, Jesus made a special post-resurrection visit to his biological half-brother James (1 Corinthians 15:7) which turned his skeptical sibling's life around.
- Several times, in Jerusalem, Jesus met with his disciples and apostles (Luke 24:44–49; Acts 1:3–8).
- Many followed him outside Jerusalem to witness his **ascension** (Acts 1:9–12).

☞ **GO TO:**

John 10:2–16; 1 Peter 5:2 (shepherd)

shepherd: *pastor, lead*

hands outstretched: *crucifixion*

Something to Ponder

GOSPEL QUARTET IN HARMONY

Matthew 28:16–20
Mark 16:15–18
Luke 24:44–49

☞ **GO TO:**

Matthew 18:19–20 (drawn together)

ascension: *act of rising upward into heaven*

KEY Outline:

Appearances of Risen Jesus

Mary Magdalene
Women disciples
Emmaus walkers
Peter
The 10
11 with Thomas
Fishin' buddies
11 on a mountain
500 at once
Brother James
Disciples in Jerusalem
Ascension witnesses

three-dimensional:
length, mass, and time

☞ GO TO:

1 Corinthians 15:50–
57; 1 Thessalonians
3:13–18
(raises believers)

Philippians 3:20–21
(like his)

Philippians 2:5–11
(laid aside)

EARLY CHURCH LIFE: Whenever early church people got together, they expected Jesus to meet with them.

2 *Jesus did humanlike things.* What was Jesus' body like? A ghost? He emphatically answered "No!" He said, *"Look at my hands and my feet. It is I myself! Touch me and see; a ghost does not have flesh and bones, as you see I have"* (Luke 24:39).

- They recognized his face and voice (Matthew 28:9; Luke 24:31; John 20:16, 19, 20; 21:2).
- His body was recognizable by its identifying marks (Luke 24:39; John 20:27).
- They touched his body (Matthew 28:9; Luke 24:39; John 20:17, 27).
- He ate with them (Luke 24:30, 42, 43; John 21:12, 13).

The Second Coming

In his resurrection body Jesus had unusual freedom from limitations placed on us who live in a **three-dimensional** world. He could appear in a locked room (John 20:19). He vanished at will (Luke 24:31). Although his resurrected body consisted of flesh and bone, Paul calls it a *spiritual* body, which he describes as imperishable, glorious, powerful, incapable of decay, immortal, and victorious (1 Corinthians 15:42–44). When Christ <u>raises believers</u> from the dead, our bodies will be <u>like his</u>.

3 *Jesus made additional post-resurrection teachings:* The things he said were vital to the work he was leaving in their hands. Face to face with the resurrected Jesus his disciples understood like never before.

Jesus made two important points about power. First, all the earthly and heavenly power and authority he had <u>laid aside</u> in order to take on humanity and mortality were now being given back to him after successful completion of his redeeming mission. He said, *"All authority in heaven and on earth has been given to me"* (Matthew 28:18).

Second, spiritual power and authority would soon energize those who believed in Jesus, through the Holy Spirit who would soon invade their lives. Jesus said, *"Do not leave Jerusalem, but wait for the gift my Father promised, which you have heard me speak about. For John baptized with water, but in a few days you will be baptized with the Holy Spirit. . . . you will receive power when the Holy Spirit comes on you"* (Acts 1:4b–8a). The Spirit's presence would give them power to confront evil spirits, speak new languages, risk danger, heal the sick, and boldly carry his message to the world. Jesus said, *"And these signs will accompany those who believe: In my name they will drive out demons; they will speak in new tongues; they will pick up snakes with their hands; and when they drink deadly poison, it will not hurt them at all; they will place their hands on sick people, and they will get well"* (Mark 16:17–18).

Jesus also gave them the promise of his personal presence. Jesus said, *"Surely I am with you always, to the very end to the age"* (Matthew 28:20).

EARLY CHURCH LIFE: Jesus talked about the church's mission. He issued official marching orders. In what is known as the Great Commission, Jesus instructed his followers to go to all the world's peoples—*"to the ends of the earth"*—beginning in Jerusalem and Judea, introducing them to personal relationship with him, making disciples for him, teaching them to live by his teachings. People everywhere who believe and **declare** their faith and are willing to **change** will experience God's forgiveness and salvation from sin's consequences (Matthew 28:19–20a; Mark 16:15–16; Luke 24:46–48; Acts 1:8).

> **1 Corinthians 15:14–15, 17–19** If Christ has not been raised our preaching is useless and so is your faith. More than that, we are then found to be false witnesses about God, for we have testified about God that he raised Christ from the dead. . . . And if Christ has not been raised, your faith is futile; you are still in your sins. Then those who have fallen asleep in Christ are lost. If only for this life we have hope in Christ, we are to be pitied more than all men.

KEY Outline:

Resurrection Body

Recognizable

Touchable

Human

Spiritual

Free

Immortal

Victorious

ACT OF THE HOLY SPIRIT

Enables Jesus to be with believers everywhere in every situation

☞ **GO TO:**

Romans 10:9–10 (declare)

declare: literally, are baptized

change: literally, repent

KEY POINT

Jesus is with his children always, to the very end of the age.

KEY Outline:

Equipped to "Go!"
Christ's authority
Holy Spirit's energy
Spiritual gifts
Story to tell
Teaching to share
Jesus with us

What Others are Saying:

atonement: restoration of relationship with God

justification: right legal standing with God

salvation: rescue from sin's guilt and consequences

unredeemed: without the price of forgiveness having been paid

The Final Test

Paul wrote those words in about 56 A.D. In this same passage he says 500 people at the same time saw Jesus after his resurrection, *"most of whom are still living"* (1 Corinthians 15:6). If any of his readers wished to do so at that time, there were eyewitnesses alive and kicking who could be interviewed about it!

The Christian faith rises or falls on the reality that Jesus Christ is alive. If Christ is not alive, the New Testament historians, Matthew, Mark, Luke, John, and all the apostles, upon whose testimony the Christian faith is based, are liars!

They and all the witnesses whose Risen-Jesus sightings are reported in Scripture insist that Jesus is alive and that they have seen him, touched him, talked, ate—even gone fishing—with him.

If that's not true, everyone who trusts in Jesus to rescue him from sin's consequences is a fool. There is no forgiveness of sins, no assurance of life after death, no freedom from guilt, no heaven, no sense to faith, no reason to be a Christian! Christianity is a useless machine with no power to make it work![10]

The resurrection of Jesus Christ is the test question on which the truth or falsehood of the Christian Gospel turns. Either it is the greatest miracle that ever happened in the history of the world or the biggest lie ever told.

Philip Schaff: The miracle of the Resurrection and the existence of Christianity are so closely connected that they must stand or fall together. If Christ was raised from the dead, then all his miracles are sure, and our faith is not in vain. It is only his resurrection that made his death available for our **atonement**, **justification**, and **salvation**. Without the Resurrection, his death would be the grave of our hopes, we should be still **unredeemed** and under the power of our sins. A gospel of a dead savior would be a contradiction and a wretched delusion.[11]

Sifting Through The Clues

It happened a couple of milleniums ago.

So it's not like you can go out to the empty tomb and look for fingerprints on the stone, or do DNA testing.

The resurrection—or, for that matter, the fact that Jesus was born, lived and died—can't be proved in a test tube. Higher mathematics or Einstein's $E = mc^2$ won't help. We are left to sift through the historical evidence, the same as if we were trying to prove that

Julius Caesar or Atilla the Hun existed and did what they are reported to have done.

People who study the available evidence with an open mind are likely to be convinced, not only that Jesus rose from the dead, but that he is who he claimed to be: the Son of God.

> **Acts 1:1–3** In **my former book**, **Theophilus**, I <u>wrote</u> about all that Jesus began to do and to teach until the day he was <u>taken up</u> to heaven, after giving instructions through the Holy Spirit to the apostles he had chosen. After his suffering, [Jesus] showed himself to these men and gave many convincing proofs that he was alive. He appeared to them over a period of forty days and spoke about the kingdom of God.

my former book: Gospel of Luke

Theophilus: person to whom both Luke and Acts is addressed

☞ **GO TO:**

Luke 1:1–5 (wrote)

Luke 24:51; Acts 1:9 (taken up)

Convincing Proofs

New Testament writers zero in on two major *"convincing proofs that [Jesus] was alive"*: (1) the people who saw him alive and the things he did and said to them (see earlier in this chapter), and (2) the things he continued to do even after he returned to his Father in heaven (these things are reported in the Book of Acts, the rest of the New Testament, and 2,000 years of Christian history right up to the present time).

The Plague Of The "Yah-Buts"

Doubters have their reasons or excuses. Here are some common ones.

Yah, but . . . maybe all those people who said they saw Jesus alive were just "seeing things"—a **hallucination**—they wanted him so badly to be alive they imagined the whole thing!

hallucination: seeing something that isn't there

Defense: It might be possible for one or two people, after a long period of sleep deprivation or exaggerated wishful thinking to imagine they saw something they didn't.

But, if we accept the report of the New Testament historians, Jesus was seen alive by not one or two, but groups of 10, 11, 120, and 500, at different times and different locations from Jerusalem to Galilee—and everyone in each group saw the same thing at once (1 Corinthians 15:3–8).

Whole crowds having the same vision or hallucination? Turn

bodaciously: boldly

on your computer, click your mouse on that idea, and drag it **bodaciously** to the trash!

Yah, but . . . maybe it's all a hoax hatched by the apostles and early Christians made to keep their religion going; maybe they made it all up!

> **Defense:** If so, a lot of people suffered a lot of trouble and pain and a lot of them died just to keep this hoax alive!

Most of the apostles died as martyrs—their heads chopped off, crucified upside down and right side up, burned at the stake—because they refused to say it wasn't so.

Many of the eyewitnesses were driven from their homes, tortured, flogged, imprisoned, mobbed, harassed by officials and ordinary citizens, their goods confiscated—because they would not renounce their belief that Jesus rose from the dead (Acts 5:40–42; 7:54–60; 8:1–3; 12:1–5; Hebrews 10:32–34; 1 Peter 4:12–19, for example).

A hoax? Think again! That dog won't hunt.

Yah, but . . . maybe somebody snatched the corpse!

> **Defense:** Now who in the world would be dumb enough to do a thing like that? Jesus' Jewish enemies?

Wait a minute! Weren't they the guys who made sure the tomb was under 24-hour guard to make sure the body would be there Easter Sunday morning? (Matthew 27:62–66). If they moved it, why didn't they produce the corpse when people started saying Jesus was alive? (Acts 2:24).

They didn't put the corpse on display because they couldn't. The "corpse" was dancing around the country convincing people the reports of his resurrection were true.

Maybe Jesus' disciples stole the body and claimed he rose from the dead.

Those scaredy cats? They denied knowing him and failed to defend him when they had a chance while he was still alive (Matthew 26:56, 69–75). And at the time the resurrection took place they were hiding out with all the shades pulled *"for fear of the Jews"* (John 20:19).

They were now gonna screw up their courage and risk death to fight off the Roman guards, break the Roman Imperial seal on the stone, so they could snatch his corpse? To quote the stuttering Vizzini in *The Princess Bride*: "Incontheivable!"

Yah, but . . . maybe Jesus did not really die on the cross—maybe he fainted or played dead or, as a recent book suggests, there was a clever conspiracy between Jesus and an accomplice, in which Jesus was drugged. In the tomb, he regained consciousness and, at the right time (the third day) got up and walked out.

Defense: A magnificent deduction, my dear Watson! Except for a couple of elementary facts: (1) In the nature of Roman crucifixion unconsciousness on the cross would have caused death by lack of ability to breathe or suffocation. (2) Death was certified by (a) the soldiers who came to break his legs and found him already dead (John 19:32–33); (b) the blood and water that gushed when they stabbed him indicating rupture of the pericardial sac (John 19:34–35); (c) the centurion who saw him die and confirmed it to Pilate (Mark 15:44–45); and (d) Nicodemus and Joseph who embalmed and buried the corpse (John 19:38–42). By all reasonable indications Jesus was dead.

If he was "only unconscious" and revived in the tomb, he couldn't just "walk out." In his weakened, battered, and wounded condition, he single-handedly rolled away the humongous boulder from the entrance of the tomb, fought his way through that squad of armed Roman guards, and hid in some unknown place for 40 days, popping in on his friends from time to time, then leaving for parts unknown never to be seen again? Irrational to the max!

From Cowardice To Courage

The change in Jesus' friends may be the greatest proof of all that he rose from the dead. The death of their Leader left them depressed, disillusioned, terrified, and confused.

But turn the page in the Book of Acts and you see the same jelly-kneed crew sticking their necks way out (Acts 2, 3, 4). They have become people ready to risk everything for Jesus' name, pointing the accusing finger at Jesus' enemies—so spiritually powerful they are accused of turning the world upside down (Acts 17:6, KJV). Subsequent history records the early Christians did precisely that!

Simon Greenleaf: Their master had just perished as a malefactor by sentence of public tribunal. His religion sought to overthrow the teachings of his disciples. The interests and passions of

What Others are Saying:

all the rulers and great men of the world were against them. The fashion of the world was against them. Propagating this new faith, even in the most inoffensive and peaceful manner, they could expect nothing but contempt, opposition, revilings, bitter persecutions, stripes, imprisonments, torments, and deaths. Yet this faith they zealously did propagate; and all these miseries they endured undismayed, nay rejoicing.

As one after another was put to a miserable death, the survivors only **prosecuted** their work with increased vigor and resolution. They had every possible motive to review carefully the grounds of their faith, and the evidences of the great facts and truths which they asserted; and these motives were pressed upon their attention with the most melancholy and terrific frequency.

It was therefore impossible that they could have persisted in affirming the truths they have narrated, had not Jesus actually risen from the dead, and had they not known this fact as certainly as they knew any other fact. . . . If their testimony was not true, there was no possible motive for its fabrication.[12]

The Final Proof: Your Faith

In every generation since he lived, millions have believed and affirmed, based on research and personal experience, that Jesus, once crucified, dead and buried, is alive and personally living in his followers.

After all the reasoning, arguments, and sifting through the evidence, belief in the resurrection or miracles or Jesus Christ himself ultimately comes down to a <u>leap of faith</u>, the personal insight and decision that makes it possible for earthbound creatures like you and me to take in realities which lie "on the *other* side of reason."

If we are unwilling to accept the possibility of a miracle—"I'll only believe it if I see it with my own eyes! Or if it can be proved scientifically!"—no amount of argumentation or historical evidence will ever convince us that Jesus rose from the dead.

Madeleine L'Engle: If it can be verified, we don't need faith. I don't need faith to know that if a poem has fourteen lines, a specific rhyme scheme, and is in iambic pentameter, it is a sonnet. I don't need faith to know that if I take flour and butter and milk and seasonings and heat them in a double boiler, the mix will thicken and become white sauce. Faith is for that which lies on the *other* side of reason. Faith is what makes life bearable, with all

prosecuted: pursued

Something to Ponder

☞ **GO TO:**

Hebrews 11:1 (leap of faith)

What Others are Saying:

its tragedies and ambiguities and sudden, startling joys. Surely it wasn't reasonable of the Lord of the Universe to come and walk this earth with us and love us enough to die for us and then show us everlasting life? We will all grow old, and sooner or later we will die, like the old trees in the orchard. But we have been promised that this is not the end. We have been promised life.[13]

Study Questions

1. Who were the secret disciples who came forward after Jesus' death to bury him? Who confirmed his death? Where did they bury his body?

2. In what two ways was the burial of a criminal different from the usual Jewish burial?

3. Who was the first person to whom Jesus appeared after his resurrection? How did she recognize him? When and how has Jesus spoken your name in a time of grief?

4. What did Thomas think he needed in order to believe Jesus had risen from the dead? When he saw Jesus, what did he discover he really believed about him? When you have doubts, what do you find helps you overcome them? (a) Bible study, (b) others' faith, (c) remembering past miracles, (d) historical evidence, and/or (e) return to the basics.

5. Identify four characteristics of the resurrected body, as seen in Jesus after he rose from the dead.

CHAPTER WRAP-UP

- A rich, secret disciple named Joseph of Arimathea and the Pharisee Nicodemus got permission from Pilate to bury Jesus' body. It was placed in Joseph's new tomb in a garden near the crucifixion site. A huge stone was rolled over the opening of the tomb. (Mark 15:42–47)

- The chief priests and Pharisees asked Pilate to seal the stone and post a guard of Roman soldiers to keep Jesus' disciples from stealing the body and claiming he'd risen from the dead. (Matthew 27:61–66)

- On Easter morning, the tomb was empty. An angel rolled the stone away. The terrified guards ran off to tell Jesus' enemies, who bribed them to lie about what they'd seen. Women disciples came to finish embalming Jesus' body and were met by angels who told them he had risen from the dead. (Luke 24:1–8)

- Examination of the empty tomb left the disciples puzzled. Mary Magdalene thought someone had stolen the body. Jesus appeared to her and sent her to his disciples with the news. (John 20:1–18)

- That day and the next 40 days Jesus appeared to his friends one at a time, by twos, and in groups, in Jerusalem, on Emmaus Road, and in Galilee, and commissioned them to continue his work. More than 500 people saw him alive after his resurrection. (Luke 24; 1 Corinthians 15:3–8)

15 LIFT OFF!

Let's Get Started

Jesus of Nazareth had spread before his little band the daunting assignment to take his story and teachings to all the nations on the face of the earth (Matthew 28:19; Mark 16:15; Acts 1:8).

This little company of campaigners had lived their entire lives inside a radius of less than a hundred miles. They could scarcely picture *"all nations,"* to say nothing of knowing what direction to go to get there!

One more event on God's calendar of redemption would cap the mission Christ had begun 33 years before in the womb of the Virgin Mary. Christians call this event "the **ascension**." Christ's ascension made it possible for the Christian faith to become an inside job.

> **Luke 24:50–52** When he had led them out to the vicinity of Bethany, he lifted his hands and blessed them. While he was blessing them, he left them and was taken up into **heaven**. Then they worshiped him and returned to Jerusalem with great joy.

Up! Up! And Away!

According to Luke's reports (Luke 24:50–51; Acts 1:9–12), 40 days after he rose from the dead, Jesus led his followers to the east side of the Mount of Olives to a spot overlooking the village of Bethany where they watched as he was lifted—up, up, up—until he vanished in a cloud.

GOSPEL QUARTET IN HARMONY

Mark 16:19–20
Luke 24:50–53
Acts 1:9–12

ascension: lifting up

heaven: the spiritual dimension; God's home

☞ **GO TO:**

Matthew 24:30 (return)

☞ **GO TO:**

Acts 1:13–14; 2:1
(upstairs room)

right hand: *beside God on his throne; place of highest authority in the universe*

To get the disciples' focus back down to earth (where the Christian action is), two angels ("men") suddenly appeared standing with them on solid terra firma. The two terminated the sky-gazing party with the announcement that Jesus would one day <u>return</u> in the clouds, just as they'd seen him leave (Acts 1:11).

The Second Coming

Amazingly, as the disciples walked back to Jerusalem after watching the departure of their dearest friend and mentor, they were not sad. Luke says *"they returned to Jerusalem with great joy"* and spent the next few days *"continually at the temple, praising God"* (Luke 24:52–53). For 10 days they hung out together in an <u>upstairs room</u> in the temple neighborhood, waiting and praying. They had hope because Jesus said he would return.

What's Special About The Ascension?

The fact that Jesus was lifted up in the sight of the disciples does not mean heaven is up in the sky or on another planet.

His upward trajectory was symbolic—a dramatized parable indicating the heavenly world to which Jesus returned is "above" this one.

Heaven is "above" not necessarily in direction, but because it is another world, completely different from and more wonderful than this earthly dimension. Jesus had prophetically referred to this upward trip as going back to "the one who sent me" (John 7:33) or "going to the Father" (John 14:12, 28).

What did Jesus' "lift off" mean for him? And what's in it for us? Why were the disciples happy? After the ascension not one of them is ever reported longing for "the good old days" with Jesus in the flesh. The Bible tells why.

1 His ascension raised Christ to *"the highest place"* in the universe (Philippians 2:9–11), often referred to as the *"**right hand**"* of God (Mark 16:19; Luke 22:69; Acts 7:55; Hebrews 1:3; 1 Peter 3:22). Jesus is God's "right hand man." God's plans are being carried out through him.

- Christ has been given all authority in heaven and earth (Matthew 28:18). All rulers, authorities, dominions, and power structures on earth and in the world of angels and devils now answer to him (Ephesians 1:9–10, 20–21; 1 Peter 3:22).

- Christ is head of the church. He personally directs its affairs through the spiritual leaders, spiritual gifts, and the spiritual discernment he provides (Romans 12:4–8; 1 Corinthians 12; Ephesians 1:22–23; 4:7–16; Colossians 1:18; 1 John 2:20, 26–27).

- Christ is under God's appointment to serve as Judge of this world and everybody in it. As Son of God and Son of man Jesus is uniquely equipped to administer fair and impartial judgment and justice (John 5:25–30; Acts 17:31; 2 Timothy 4:1; Revelation 1:18; 5:1–10).

- Christ will ultimately rule the world—all its peoples, governments and institutions will be under his direct kingship (Revelation 11:15; 19:15). Peace, justice, economic prosperity, and spiritual knowledge will reach the universal perfection for which the universe cries (Isaiah 65:17–25; Romans 8:19–21).

EARLY CHURCH LIFE: Christ equipped the church by giving believers spiritual gifts or special abilities in such areas as teaching, administering, and encouraging. These gifts helped the church grow then and help it carry out its mission today.

2 *Christ's ascension opened the way for his present ministry as our representative in the presence of God.*

- Christ **intercedes** for us, clearing the way for God to answer our prayers (Romans 8:34; Hebrews 4:14–16; 6:20).

- Christ is our **advocate** when we sin—when we drop the ball he goes to bat for us. Jesus is *our* man at the right hand of God (Hebrews 7:23–28; 1 John 2:1).

- Christ is preparing a place for us where we can be with him in his Father's home. When our place is ready, he will come for us and we will **reign** with him (John 14:1–3; 2 Timothy 2:12; Revelation 20:4; 22:3–5).

3 *Christ's ascension cleared the way for him to send his Holy Spirit to those who trust him (John 14:15–16; 15:26–16:16).*

intercedes: prays

advocate: defense attorney, one who pleads another's cause

reign: carry out God's plan in the universe

- Christ can keep his promise to be *"with you always"* because he lives in us through the Holy Spirit (Matthew 28:20).
- Christ joins with even the smallest group of Christians (*"two or three"*) whenever they are together (Matthew 18:20).
- Christ is personally with us when we're in trouble—we can count on it! (Acts 7:54–60; 23:11; 2 Timothy 4:16–18).

What Others are Saying:

Revell Bible Dictionary: All the present works of the Holy Spirit for believers thus hinge on the ascension.[1]

The Second Coming

The ascension of Christ certifies the promise of his return. *"This same Jesus, who has been taken from you into heaven, will come back in the same way you have seen him go into heaven,"* said the angels to the men and women who saw Jesus bodily lifted up (Acts 1:11).

What Others are Saying:

Oswald Chambers: By his Ascension our Lord raises himself to glory, he becomes **omnipotent**, **omniscient** and **omnipresent**. All the splendid power, so circumscribed in his earthly life, becomes omnipotence; all the wisdom and insight, so precious but so limited during his life on earth, becomes omniscience; all the unspeakable comfort of the presence of Jesus, so confined to a few in his earthly life, becomes omnipresence, he is with us all the days.

What kind of Lord Jesus have we? Is he the All-powerful God in our present circumstances, in our providential setting? Is he the All-wise God of our thinking and our planning? Is he the Ever-present God, "closer than breathing, nearer than hands or feet"? If he is, we know what it means to "abide under the shadow of the Almighty."[2]

omnipotent: *able to do anything*

omniscient: *knows everything*

omnipresent: *present everywhere*

☞ **GO TO:**

Psalm 91:1 (Almighty)

> **Mark 16:19–20** After the Lord Jesus had spoken to them, he was taken into heaven and he sat at the right hand of God. Then the disciples went out and preached everywhere, and the Lord worked with them and confirmed his word by signs that accompanied it.

Linked With The Life Of Jesus

Jesus' resurrection and ascension made all the difference in the world for his early followers.

To them, Christianity was something more than a "religion" to be performed, traditions to be memorialized, creeds to be recited, or a moral code to follow with gritted teeth.

To the people who saw Jesus alive and those who believed on him through the testimony of those who saw him, the Christian life was a personal experience with Jesus Christ, which turned everyday life into an exciting adventure!

What Others are Saying:

J. B. Phillips: We are apt to reduce the Christian religion to a code, or at best a rule of heart and life. To these men it is quite plainly the invasion of their lives by a new quality of life altogether. They do not hesitate to describe this as Christ "living in" them. Mere moral reformation will hardly explain the transformation and the exuberant vitality of these men's lives—even if we could prove a motive for such reformation, and certainly the world around offered little encouragement to the early Christians! We are practically driven to accept their own explanation, which is that their little human lives had, through Christ, been linked up with the very life of God.

Many Christians today talk about the "difficulties of our times" as though we should have to wait for better ones before the Christian religion can take root. It is heartening to remember that this faith took root and flourished amazingly in conditions that would have killed anything less vital in a matter of weeks. These early Christians were on fire with the conviction that they had become, through Christ, literally sons of God; they were pioneers of a new humanity, founders of a new Kingdom. They still speak to us across the centuries. Perhaps if we believed what they believed, we might achieve what they achieved.[3]

Study Questions

1. What is meant by the statement that Jesus is now at the "right hand" of God?
2. Over whom does the ascended Christ have authority?
3. What are three things Jesus presently does as our representative in heaven?
4. How can Christ be with us always?
5. What future event did the angels who appeared at Christ's ascension promise?

- After 40 days, Jesus led his disciples to a hill outside of Jerusalem where he ascended back to his Father's right hand in heaven, with the promise to return, and to be with them wherever they went. (Acts 1:9–12)

- The Bible teaches that his ascension raised Christ to *"the highest place"* in the universe, from which he exercises authority over the entire material and spiritual universe, serves as head of the church, judges the world, and will one day rule the world. (Philippians 2:9–11; Ephesians 1:22–23; 4:7–16; Isaiah 65:17–25)

- In his present ministry as our representative in the presence of God, Christ intercedes for us and is our defense attorney when we sin. (Romans 8:34; Hebrews 4:14–16; 6:20; 1 John 2:1)

- From his place at God's right hand Christ sends his Holy Spirit to live in people who trust him and keeps his promise to be *"with you always."* (Matthew 28:20; John 14:15–16; 15:26–16:16)

- The ascension of Christ carries with it the promise of his return, and his presence with us as we carry out his work in the world. (Acts 1:11)

APPENDIX A — MAP OF PALESTINE

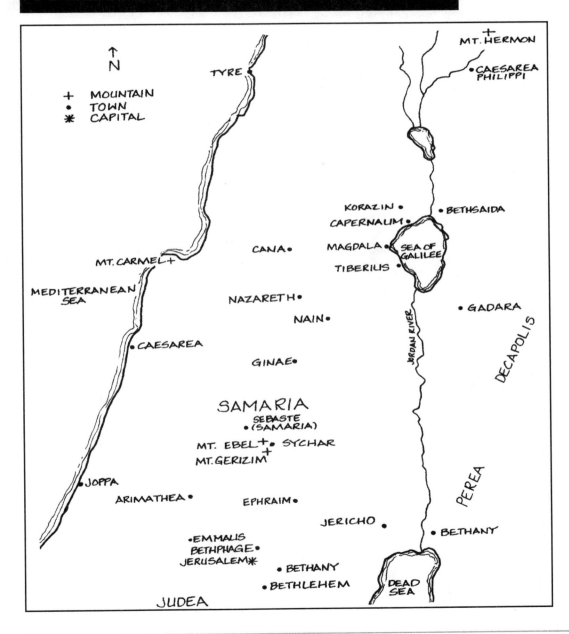

APPENDIX B — MAP OF JESUS' TRIAL AND CRUCIFIXION

The dashed lines trace the routes and order of events of Jesus' trial and crucifixion beginning at the Last Supper.

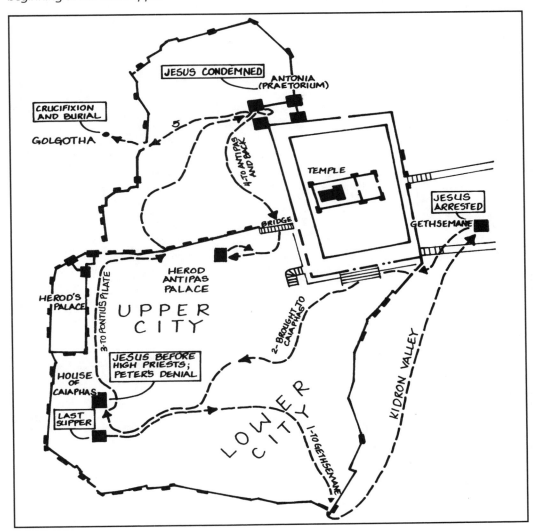

APPENDIX C — PARABLES OF JESUS

Parables of the Kingdom

Identified by "The kingdom of God is like . . ."

Category 1: The Kingdom Now

Structure, values, processes, attitudes under God's present reign

Parable	Illustrated Truth	Matthew	Mark	Luke	John
Capstone	Christ, kingdom foundation and head	21:42–44			
Growing seed	Natural process of kingdom growth		4:26–29		
Hidden treasure	The kingdom a priceless discovery	13:44			
Mustard seed	How the kingdom grows	13:31–32	4:31–32	13:18–19	
Old and new treasure	Sharing from experience	13:51–52			
Pearl of great price	Total commitment to gain the kingdom	13:45–46			
Sheep and goats	Jesus' oneness with people in trouble	25:31–46			
Sower, seed, soils	Listening, receiving the word	13:3–9, 18–23	4:3–20	8:4–15*	
Two sons	Words versus actions	21:28–32*			
Unmerciful servant	Forgiveness, torment of unforgiveness	18:23–35			
Weeds (tares)	Dealing with enemies in the church	13:24–30, 36–43			
Yeast (leaven)	Change, inner influence of the kingdom	13:33		13:20–21	

* Explained by Jesus

Parables of the Kingdom

Identified by "The kingdom of God is like . . ."

Category 2: The Kingdom Future

Last days, Christ's Second Coming, Judgment, Rewards

Parable	Illustrated Truth	Matthew	Mark	Luke	John
Alert servants	Readiness for Christ's return		13:32–37	12:35–40	
Capstone	Christ, kingdom foundation and head	21:42–44			
Fig tree, new leaves	Signs of the Christ's return	24:32–35*	13:28–31*	21:29*	
Fishing net	Separation of wicked from righteous		13:47–50*		
Great banquet	Accepting the Lord's invitation			14:16–24	
Laborers in vineyard	Fairness of God's grace, rewards	20:1–16			
Marriage (king's son)	Need to accept God's invitation	22:1–14			
Sheep and goats	Jesus' identification with people in trouble	25:31–46*			
Talents	Stewardship of gifts, opportunities	25:14–30			
Tenants	Rejection of Christ, loss of kingdom	21:33–41	12:1–9	20:9–16	
Ten minas	Wise and unwise handling of trust			19:12–27	
Ten virgins	Preparedness for Christ's coming	25:1–13			
Weeds (tares)	Dealing with enemies in the church	13:24–30, 36–43*			
Wise manager	Readiness for Christ's return			12:42–48	

* Explained by Jesus

Parables about Resources and Priorities

Parable	Illustrated Truth	Matthew	Mark	Luke	John
Rich fool	Foolish priorities, hoarding	16:19–31			
Rich man and Lazarus	Danger of indifference to the poor			12:16–21	
Sheep and goats	Jesus' identification with people in trouble	25:31–46*			
Shrewd manager	Creativity in use of worldly resources			16:1–15	
Talents	Stewardship of gifts, opportunities	25:14–30			
Ten minas	Wise and unwise handling of trust			19:12–27	
Ten virgins	Preparedness for Christ's coming	25:1–13			

* Explained by Jesus

Parables about Grace and Forgiveness

Parable	Illustrated Truth	Matthew	Mark	Luke	John
Fig tree, barren	God's patience, second chance			13:6–9	
Laborers in vineyard	Fairness of God's grace, reward	20:1–16			
Lost coin	Joy over repentant sinners			15:8–10	
Lost sheep	God's unwillingness to lose people	18:12–14		15:3–7	
Pharisee and tax collector	Spiritual pride, humility and mercy			18:9–14	
Prodigal son	Repentance, God's forgiveness			15:11–32	
Two debtors	Forgiveness, worship			7:36–50	
Unmerciful servant	Forgiveness, torment of unforgiveness	18:23–35			
Weeds (tares)	Dealing with enemies in the church	13:24–30, 36–43*			

* Explained by Jesus

Parables about Prayer

Parable	Illustrated Truth	Matthew	Mark	Luke	John
Friend at midnight	Boldness in prayer			11:5–13*	
Persistent widow	Prayer as a battle for justice			18:1–8	
Pharisee and tax collector	Spiritual pride, humility and mercy			18:9–14	

* Explained by Jesus

Parables about Various Spiritual Issues

Parable	Illustrated Truth	Matthew	Mark	Luke	John
Good Samaritan	Neighbor loving			10:25–37	
Good Shepherd	Christ's relationship to his followers				10:1–16
House on the rock	Foundation for life	7:24–27		7:48–49	
Master and servant	Servanthood and unworthiness			17:7–10*	
New patch, old shirt	Difficulty combining old and new	9:16	2:21	5:36	
New wine, wineskins	Teachability, flexibility needed	9:17	2:22	5:37–38	
Tower, warring king	Counting the cost of following Christ			14:28–33	
Vine and branches	Oneness with Christ, fruitfulness				15:1–5

* Explained by Jesus

APPENDIX D — BIOGRAPHIES OF THE DISCIPLES

Information for these biographies is taken from the New Testament, as well as from early Christian writings outside the Bible, called tradition. Some information is based on William Steuart McBirnie's book, The Search for the Twelve Apostles *(Wheaton, IL: Tyndale, 1977). Information labeled tradition is just a few of the most probable happenings of their lives.*

PETER

New Testament: He was called Simon or Cephas (meaning Rock) and was a Galilean fisherman. He was introduced to Jesus by his brother Andrew. Peter was one of the three closest to Jesus. In the early church Peter worked mainly among the Jews. He paved the way for acceptance of Gentiles by taking the Gospel to the Romans, and Cornelius (Acts 10). Peter wrote two New Testament letters—1 and 2 Peter.

Tradition: Peter influenced the writing of Mark's Gospel, which is thought to be based on his preaching and teaching. He was martyred in Rome, crucified upside down during Nero's persecution of Christians in the 60s A.D.

ANDREW

New Testament: He was Peter's brother and a Galilean fisherman. Andrew was one of the first five to follow Jesus. He had been a follower of John the Baptist.

Tradition: Andrew preached the Gospel to the Scythians (southern Russians). He was martyred by crucifixion on an X-shaped cross (now called "St. Andrew's" cross).

JAMES

New Testament: James, brother of John and son of Zebedee and Salome, was also a Galilean fisherman. Jesus called him and his brother "Sons of Thunder." James was one of the three closest to Jesus. He was also the first apostle to die for his faith when Herod Agrippa beheaded him in 44 A.D. (Acts 12:2).

Tradition: James preached the Gospel in Spain before his martyrdom in Jerusalem.

JOHN

New Testament: John was James' brother and a Galilean fisherman. He was one of the three closest to Jesus, probably *"the disciple Jesus loved"* (John 13:23). Paul called him a *"pillar of the church"* at Jerusalem (Galatians 2:6–10). John authored five New Testament books—Gospel of John, 1, 2, and 3 John, and Revelation, which was written while he was on the Isle of Patmos (Revelation 1:9).

Tradition: John ministered in Ephesus for many years. While there, he wrote his Gospel. He was exiled to prison on Patmos in a wave of persecution under Emperor Domitian. John lived to be about 98 years old, older than any of the other apostles.

PHILIP

New Testament: His name means "love of horses," which may describe him or his father. Philip was one of the first five to follow Jesus. He introduced his friend (or relative) Nathanael to Jesus.

Tradition: In later life Philip preached the Gospel in various parts of the world. He spent 20 years in Scythia and then moved to Phrygia (parts of modern Turkey). Like the evangelist Philip (Acts 8), Philip the apostle had daughters who were also effective preachers of the Gospel. He died as a martyr in Phrygia.

BARTHOLOMEW (NATHANAEL)

New Testament: His name means "son of plowman," indicating a farming background. He is probably the same person who is called Nathanael, Philip's friend from Cana in Galilee.

Tradition: Bartholomew took the Gospel to Armenia,

Mesopotamia, and Persia. He was martyred for his faith, being skinned alive and beheaded, in Armenia.

MATTHEW (LEVI)

New Testament: Matthew, called Levi, was the son of Alphaeus and probably the brother of James the Younger. A tax collector before he met Jesus, Matthew became a student of Old Testament prophecy and often cites its fulfillment in his writings. He wrote the Gospel of Matthew.

Tradition: Matthew was a literate man, perhaps the most highly educated of the original 12. He wrote his Gospel in both Hebrew and Aramaic. After spending the first years of his ministry in Israel, Matthew preached in Persia and Ethiopia, often witnessing to kings and government officials. He was martyred by fire, possibly in Egypt.

JAMES (SON OF ALPHAEUS)

New Testament: James was Matthew's brother. He was also called James the Younger or James the Less to distinguish him from John's brother James.

Tradition: Before becoming Christ's disciple, James was a Zealot committed to overthrow the Romans. This put him in direct conflict with his collaborator-tax collector brother. He renounced his political commitments to follow Christ. Because early historians often confused him with James the brother of Jesus, tracing his steps is difficult. He apparently was a key figure in the establishment of the Syrian Christian church. He was stoned to death in Jerusalem for preaching Christ.

THOMAS

New Testament: He was nicknamed Didymus, meaning "the twin." He was a committed follower of Jesus who struggled with doubt. He is sometimes called Doubting Thomas.

Tradition: Thomas took the Gospel to Babylon, Persia, and India. He was a fearless evangelist, establishing churches in both the north and south of the subcontinent. In India today, the *Mar Toma* churches trace their roots to the apostolic preaching and ministry of Thomas. He was martyred in India, run through by a lancer's spear.

SIMON

New Testament: Simon, like James the son of Alphaeus, was a rightwing revolutionary, who left the politics of violence to follow Christ. He is also called the Zealot or the Cananaean (see Mark 3:18), indicating his involvement in a movement committed to the violent overthrow of Roman rule.

Tradition: Simon preached in Egypt, North Africa, including Carthage, Spain, Britain, and Persia. He was martyred in Persia by being sawed in half.

THADDAEUS (JUDE)

New Testament: He is also called Judas the son of James or referred to as Jude. He may have been the son of James and grandson of Zebedee.

Tradition: Working with the apostle Bartholomew, and for a brief time Thomas, Jude founded the church in Armenia. He also ministered in Syria and Persia, where he teamed up with Simon. Jude and Simon were martyred in Persia along with a thousand other Christians.

JUDAS ISCARIOT

New Testament: Iscariot may mean "man of Kerioth," a town in Judea. His father's name was Simon. Judas was treasurer of the disciples. He conspired with Jesus' enemies to betray Jesus for 30 pieces of silver (Matthew 26:14–16). When Jesus was condemned, Judas regretted his deed, returned the silver, and committed suicide. The money was used to buy a burial ground for paupers—a place people called "Field of Blood." Matthias was chosen to replace him (Matthew 27:10; Acts 1:15–26).

CHAPTER 1

1. God gave Peter his revelation about who Jesus is. The gates of Hades, place of the dead, will not stand against the church founded on the conviction that Jesus is the Christ, the Son of God. (Matthew 16:18)
2. Jesus called Peter "Satan" when Peter told him to stop talking about dying (Matthew 16:23). Peter was not seeing things from God's perspective but from man's viewpoint.
3. A person who goes with Christ must expect to (1) deny himself, (2) carry his cross, and (3) follow Jesus. Answers about the effect of Jesus' companionship on lifestyle, values, priorities, and relationships will vary with each person. Some people say they have a reason for living and find they focus more on others rather than themselves.
4. Moses and Elijah appeared with Jesus on the Mount of Transfiguration (Matthew 9:2–8). Reasons for this experience for the disciples may have included: (1) visual confirmation that Jesus was what they had confessed him to be (Matthew 16:16); (2) encouragement after Jesus' disclosure of the cost of discipleship (Matthew 16:24–27); (3) to teach that cross bearing does not diminish Christ's majesty or ours; and (4) to affirm the supremacy of Christ over Old Testament Law and Prophets (Matthew 17:4–8). For Jesus, transfiguration was (1) reaffirmation of God's approval; (2) refocus on the purpose of his mission; and (3) encouragement for the ordeal ahead (Luke 9:31).
5. Jesus told Peter to forgive a person who wronged him 77 times. Some translations say "70 times seven" (Matthew 18:22). We should never stop forgiving.

CHAPTER 2

1. Differences between Jesus and his brothers: (1) They did not believe he was Messiah; he knew he was (John 7:5). (2) They were not committed to God's timing, only to what was convenient; he was committed to God's plan and timing (verse 6). (3) The world did not hate them; it hated him because he exposed wickedness (verse 7).
2. Jesus rebuked James and John, possibly saying, "You don't know what kind of spirit you are of; I did not come to destroy people but to save them." (Luke 9:55–56)
3. God gave Jesus his teaching material and authority to teach (John 7:16). The person who chooses to do God's will and practices what Jesus says comes to know Jesus' teachings are from God (John 7:17).
4. Jesus promised "streams of living water (the Holy Spirit) will flow from within" anyone who believes in him. (John 7:37–39)
5. Jesus' principles for dealing with people who fail were these: (1) Only a person who is dealing honestly with his or her own faults is in a position to judge others (Matthew 7:1–5; Luke 6:41–42); (2) The correct attitude is "no condemnation" (Luke 6:37; Romans 8:1); (3) Top priority is the person's salvation and spiritual restoration (Matthew 18:15; 1 Corinthians 5:5; Galatians 6:1); (4) Forgiveness is never withheld (Matthew 18:21–23); and (5) Forgiveness is accompanied by encouragement and confrontation to get him or her to quit the sin (Luke 17:3; Ephesians 4:15; James 5:19–20).
6. Some people are relieved that Jesus accepts them as they are. They feel encouraged and desire to please God with right behavior.

CHAPTER 3

1. What excited the returning 72 most was that demons obeyed them (Luke 10:17). Jesus suggested they should be most excited that their names were recorded in heaven (verse 20). Personally, Jesus was thrilled they were discovering the secrets of his relationship with his Father (verses 21–22).

2. Love God with your whole being and your neighbor as yourself (Luke 10:27). The Samaritan loved his neighbor by showing mercy to the robbery victim (verse 37).

3. According to Luke 11:5–13, successful praying involves (1) the brashness of the person praying (verses 5–8); and (2) the goodness of God (verses 9–13).

4. Religious sentimentality is a form of hypocrisy when it is a cover-up to keep from dealing with the realities of life and instructions of God's Word. One who hears God's Word and obeys it is more blessed than Jesus' mother (Luke 11:27–28).

5. Jesus states the calamities in Luke 11:42–52.

CHAPTER 4

1. This calls for evaluation of your personal handling of material possessions compared to Jesus' attitude and practice as revealed in Luke 12:13–34.

2. The rich farmer's choices were foolish because: (1) they were selfish; and (2) he gave no thought to eternity.

3. Jesus' investment strategy had three points: (1) Don't worry (Luke 12:22–28). (2) Seek God's kingdom (verses 29–34). (3) Use resources to move the kingdom toward its goals—that is, help needy people (verse 33).

4. To be ready for Christ's Second Coming: (1) be ready and working (Luke 12:35); (2) be faithful and filled with the Spirit (verse 35); and (3) be watching—spiritually awake, alert, attentive, vigilant (verses 37–38, 40).

5. Jesus said, "I tell you, no! But unless you repent, you too will perish" (Luke 13:3, 5). Disaster is not always the direct result of the sins of those who suffer; death is certain for everyone. The way to be ready is to turn to God and repent of sin.

6. The Pharisees cared more about their traditions than healing people. (John 9:14–16)

CHAPTER 5

1. (a) The sheepfold is the kingdom of God. (b) The sheep are God's people. (c) The shepherd is Jesus. (d) The thief is the exploitive leader. (e) The gate is Jesus, our access to God. (f) The wolf is the enemy/the devil.

2. In addition to choosing the moment to lay down his life, Jesus said he could decide when to "Take it up again" (rise from the dead). (John 10:18)

3. God rejoices when lost people are found, accepts them, and celebrates their return (Luke 15:7, 10, 20–24). The reactions of the elder brother to the prodigal's return were anger, resentment, and refusal to join the party (Luke 15:25–30).

4. Depending on your experiences you may identify with any of the three people.

5. Your upbringing may affect how you answer this question. Be honest with yourself.

CHAPTER 6

1. What is highly valued among men is "detestable in God's sight" (Luke 16:15). What the Pharisees valued most was to justify themselves in the eyes of others (verse 15). Jesus said they were serving money instead of God (verse 13).

2. These are the characteristics of hell revealed in the story of the rich man and Lazarus (Luke 16:23–31): (1) Hell is a conscious experience (verse 23); (2) a place of torment (verses 23, 27); (3) thirst (verse 24); (4) agony (verses 24, 25); (5) fire (verse 24); (6) regret (verse 28); (7) no escape (verse 26); and (8) paradise can be seen but never experienced (verses 23, 26).

3. Lazarus had been dead four days (John 11:39). Jesus told Martha, "Whoever believes in me will never die" (John 11:26). Even though a believer dies, his spirit lives on in heaven.

4. Martha believed: (1) God would give Jesus whatever he asked (John 11:22); (2) Jesus is the Messiah (Christ); (3) Jesus is the Son of God; and (4) Jesus is the Promised One—"the one who was to come into the world" (verse 27). Jesus promised if she believed Martha would see "The glory of God" (verse 40).

5. Choose the answer that best represents how you react when people cry.

CHAPTER 7

1. In the parable of the widow and judge, Jesus encouraged prayer for justice (Luke 18:1–8). In the parable of the Pharisee and tax collector, Jesus encouraged prayer for forgiveness (Luke 18:9–14). Base your last answer on your real personal desires.

2. Marriage as God designed it is: (1) for a male and a female; (2) monogamous; (3) two becoming one flesh; and (4) permanent. (Matthew 19:4–6)

3. Childlike qualities that can contribute to marriage and church life are dependence, humility, ability to play, openness, vulnerability, simplicity, trust, unworldliness, powerlessness, wonder, teachability, curiosity, joy in little things, natural obedience, easy forgiveness, etc. The hardest and easiest traits to have vary greatly according to your personality.

4. Jesus asked the man to sell all his possessions, give the money to the poor, and follow him (Luke 18:22). By giving away his wealth (1) he would demonstrate complete trust in Jesus, (2) renounce wealth as his idol, and (3) follow Jesus as an apostle.

5. Zacchaeus' story (Luke 19) reveals the following: Jesus knows where hungry hearts are (verse 5); he takes the initiative to find sinners (verse 5); he values lost people (verse 5); he refuses to let man-made proprieties and public opinion get in the way of reaching the needy (verse 7). Zacchaeus demonstrated his readiness to be saved: by acting on his desire to see Jesus; welcoming Jesus into his home; announcing his intent to live a new life; adopting a new attitude toward possessions; and making restitution for wrongs done to others (verses 4–8). Your final answer is based on personal experience.

CHAPTER 8

1. Jesus sought to correct the misconception that the kingdom would appear at once (Luke 19:11). The king represents Christ. The distant empire represents his heavenly Father. The enemies represent Christ's enemies. The servants are Christ's disciples. Your personal answer is based on consideration of your personal resources, including money, time, and abilities.

2. To Jesus, Mary's anointing was preparation for his burial. (John 12:7)

3. Jesus rode a donkey instead of a warhorse in the Triumphal Entry (1) to fulfill Zechariah's prophecy (John 12:14–15; Zechariah 9:9); and (2) to show he is the king of peace, not war (Zechariah 9:10; Luke 19:38).

4. The temple market represented (1) misuse of religious commitments for profit; (2) exploitation of people, especially the poor; (3) exclusion of Gentiles; and (4) distortion of worshipers' God-concept.

5. "Lifted up" means crucifixion. When Jesus was "lifted up" (1) the world would be judged; (2) the "prince of this world" would be driven out; and (3) people would be drawn to Jesus. (John 12:31–33)

6. They were afraid they'd be put out of the synagogue (John 12:42–43). For your final answer, consider the effect of people's approval or disapproval on your willingness to express your faith.

CHAPTER 9

1. The brother who first said "no" and later changed his mind represents tax collectors and prostitutes.

The brother who said "yes" but then never did the work represents religious leaders. To answer the second part of this question, think about your own track record on obedience to God.

2. The Pharisees joined with the Herodians, supporters of Herod (Matthew 22:15–16). Jesus showed them a Roman coin. Give to Caesar what belongs to Caesar and to God what belongs to God (verse 21).

3. In the resurrection world (1) marriage isn't necessary; (2) we will be like the angels; (3) it will be impossible for us to die; and (4) we will be recognized as God's children. (Matthew 22:30; Luke 20:36)

4. Jesus grieved for Jerusalem and its leaders (Matthew 23:37). He hates hypocrisy but loves hypocrites (the people themselves) and wants them to be saved from the disaster of hypocrisy.

CHAPTER 10

1. The disciples asked: (1) When will the Temple be destroyed? (2) What will be the sign of your coming? and (3) What will be the sign of the end of the age? (Matthew 24:3)

2. Jesus told his disciples not to be afraid when they hear of disasters and wars. These things will continue all the time between his first and second coming. (Luke 21:9)

3. These are the four promises Jesus gave Christians facing persecution: (1) Persecution will give an opportunity to share your faith. (2) Jesus will be with you and give you the words to say. (3) Your enemies will hear what you say and be unable to refute it. (4) Even if you are killed for your faith, you will never perish (Luke 21:13–19). Your last answer will be based on consideration of your own experiences of persecution.

4. When you see armies surrounding Jerusalem, get out of town! (Luke 21:21)

5. "Fireworks" accompanying Jesus' return (Matthew 24:27–31) include lightning (verse 27); death, corpses (verse 28); smoke, meteors (verse 29); worldwide visibility (verse 30); shock, grief (verse 30); clouds (verse 30); power, glory (verse 30); angels (verse 31); and trumpet blasts (verse 31).

6. Six actions upon which future judgment will be based are (1) feeding the hungry, (2) giving a drink to the thirsty, (3) showing hospitality to strangers, (4) clothing the naked, (5) caring for the sick, and (6) visiting prisoners (Matthew 25:35–36). The last two questions call for personal answers based on your abilities, interests, and limitations.

CHAPTER 11

1. The conspiracy between Judas and Jesus' enemies was arranged two days before Passover. Judas betrayed Jesus for 30 pieces of silver. That was the going price for a slave. (Mark 14:1–2; Luke 22:3–6; Exodus 21:32)

2. Apparently Judas' decision to betray Jesus was based on (1) disillusionment with Jesus' idea of the kingdom (John 12:4–5); (2) greed (Matthew 26:14–15); and (3) that Satan had entered his heart (Luke 23:3–6).

3. The Passover menu is unleavened bread, roast lamb, salt water, bitter herbs, *charosheth* (sweet fruit and nut mix), and wine.

4. Jesus washed the disciples' feet—the job of the lowest household slave (John 13:2–5). Peter refused to let Jesus wash his feet (verses 6–8). You may have felt like Peter felt. Jesus and Peter could not have fellowship if Peter didn't let him wash his feet (verse 8).

5. The new commandment is "Love one another as I have loved you." (John 13:33–35). It's new because it (1) establishes a new "family" relationship, (2) calls for a higher standard for love, (3) makes a new impact on the world, and (4) sums up Old and New Testament commandments into one (Romans 13:8).

6. Jesus meant the Holy Spirit would be to his disciples what he had been. (John 14:16)

7. John 15:2, in most translations, says he "cuts off" the fruitless branch, but a better translation is he "lifts it up" (to sun and air), giving it another chance.

8. Jesus had to leave so the Counselor (Holy Spirit) could come to the disciples (John 16:7). You may appreciate the Holy Spirit's presence, the power he gives for ministry, how he convicts you of sin, and how he teaches you (John 14–16).

CHAPTER 12

1. Eternal life is knowing the true God and Jesus Christ whom he has sent. (John 17:3)

2. The three religious trials of Jesus were (1) before Annas at his house (John 18:13–15); (2) before Caiaphas at his house (Matthew 26:57–58; John 18:24); and (3) before the entire Sanhedrin at sunup (Matthew 27:1; Mark 14:53).

3. After his third denial the rooster crowed, and Peter wept bitterly. (Luke 22:60–62)

4. Before Pilate the leaders charged Jesus with (1) insurrection ("subverting the nation"); (2) opposing payment of taxes to Rome; and (3) claiming to be a king in competition with Caesar (Luke 23:2). In reality, the Sanhedrin charged him with blasphemy for claiming to be God's Son (Mark 14:64; John 19:7).

5. The Passover Pardon was a goodwill gesture in which the governor pardoned one prisoner. Pilate tried to convince the crowd to let Jesus be the pardoned prisoner, offering them a choice between Jesus and Barabbas, an assassin and robber. Instead the crowd chose Barabbas. (John 18:39–40; Luke 23:25)

6. Pilate washed his hands and declared, *"I am innocent of this man's blood. . . . It is your responsibility"* (Matthew 27:24). Your personal answer should be based on evaluation of your ability to accept responsibility for your actions.

CHAPTER 13

1. Jesus prayed for God to forgive (1) the soldiers (Luke 23:34); (2) Jewish leaders and people (Acts 3:17; 2 Corinthians 3:13–16); and (3) all unbelievers (2 Corinthians 4:4).

2. The sign read: "This is the king of the Jews" (John 19:19–20). Jewish leaders asked Pilate to change it to say he *claimed* to be king of the Jews (John 19:21). The thief asked Jesus to remember him when he came into his kingdom, recognizing that Jesus was King of heaven. (Luke 23:42)

3. Jesus was quoting from Psalm 22:1. At the time, he was bearing God's judgment on all human sin (2 Corinthians 5:21), the most painful aspect of which is separation from God (Isaiah 59:1–2).

4. Christ's death was unusual because it was (1) voluntary, (2) his destiny, (3) a sacrifice, and (4) accompanied by an earthquake, tearing of the temple veil, and raising of some dead people. (John 10:18; Hebrews 2:14–18; John 1:29; Matthew 27:51)

5. The centurion thought Jesus was the Son of God. (Mark 15:39)

6. Your answers will be based on your recollection. You might explain the crucifixion by comparing Jesus to a perfect person who offers to take your sentence on himself, freeing you from death row in prison.

CHAPTER 14

1. Joseph of Arimathea and Nicodemus buried Jesus (John 19:38–39). The Roman centurion confirmed his death (Mark 15:42–47). They buried Jesus' body in Joseph's new tomb.

2. The differences between burial of a criminal and others were (1) a criminal could not be buried in his

family tomb for a year after death; and (2) no public mourning was allowed.

3. The first person who saw Jesus alive after his resurrection was Mary Magdalene (John 20:10–18). She recognized his voice and the way he said her name (verse 16). Your personal answer will come from recalling personal experiences.

4. Thomas thought he needed to see and touch Jesus' wounds to believe he was alive (John 20:25). When he saw Jesus, Thomas confessed him as *Lord* and *God* (verse 28). One or a combination of all these things may help you overcome doubt.

5. After resurrection Jesus' body was recognizable, touchable, human, spiritual, free from physical limitations, imperishable, immortal, powerful, glorious, incapable of decay, and victorious.

CHAPTER 15

1. "At the right hand of God" means Christ occupies the highest position in the universe, and God is carrying on all his work through him.

2. Christ has power and authority over every other rule, authority, power, and dominion in the universe, and he is head of the church. (Ephesians 1:18–23)

3. As the Christian's representative in heaven, Jesus (1) intercedes for us (Hebrews 7:25), (2) is our advocate when we sin (1 John 2:1), and (3) is preparing a permanent place for us in God's heavenly home (John 14:1–3).

4. Christ is always with us in the person of his Holy Spirit who lives in us. (John 14:15–16)

5. The angels at the ascension promised that Christ would return. (Acts 1:11)

APPENDIX F — THE EXPERTS

Thomas Arnold—Headmaster of Rugby School from 1795–1842; professor of modern history at Oxford University; author of *History of Rome* (three volumes, 1838–1843) and Oxford *Lectures on Modern History* (1842).

Louis A. Barbieri Jr.—Professor of Bible at the Moody Bible Institute, Chicago; contributing author to *The Bible Knowledge Commentary*.

William Barclay—New Testament scholar and writer; professor of Divinity and Biblical Criticism at the University of Glasgow; author of many books, including the multivolume *Daily Study Bible* commentary on all the New Testament books.

Albert Barnes—Pastor, First Presbyterian Church in Philadelphia for 35 years; his multivolume *Barnes' Notes* Bible commentary series has sold two million copies.

Donald Grey Barnhouse—Founder of *Eternity* magazine and *The Bible Study Hour* radio program; pastor.

Venerable Bede—Seventh- and eighth-century Bible scholar and hymn writer.

George R. Beasley-Murray—Former principal at Spurgeon's College, London; professor of New Testament Interpretation at Southern Baptist Theological Seminary in Louisville, Kentucky; author of several Bible commentaries and other books.

Edwin A. Blum—Vice President of Management Services, Fletcher Pacific, Honolulu; formerly professor of historical theology at Dallas Theological Seminary; contributing author to *The Bible Knowledge Commentary*.

Dietrich Bonhoeffer—German theologian, co-founder of the Confessing Church in Germany, martyred by the Nazis for resistance against Nazi persecution of Jews.

James M. Boice—Pastor of Tenth Presbyterian Church, Philadelphia; radio preacher on the *Bible Study Hour*; author.

Leslie F. Brandt—Lutheran minister, evangelist, retreat leader, and author.

Bill Bright—Founder and president of Campus Crusade for Christ International.

F. F. Bruce—Scotsman, preeminent evangelical scholar of the post-World War II era, president of both the Society for Old Testament Studies and Society for New Testament Studies.

Gary M. Burge—Professor of New Testament, Wheaton College and Graduate School, Wheaton, Illinois.

John Calvin—Sixteenth-century leader in the Swiss Protestant Reformation; his *Institutes of the Christian Religion* form the basis for the theological system known as Calvinism.

Michael Card—Contemporary Christian author, composer, performer, and recording artist who lives in Nashville, Tennessee.

Oswald Chambers—Principal of Bible Training School, London; founder of two YMCA desert camps in Egypt during World War I where he ministered to British soldiers.

Charles Clayton—Executive Director of World Vision in Great Britain.

Robert E. Coleman—Professor of Evangelism at Trinity Evangelical Divinity School, Deerfield/Chicago.

John Chrysostom—Fourth-century Bible expositor and preacher (his name means "golden-mouth"); exiled for attacks against church and civil government vices.

Jim Elliot—Martyred missionary to the Auca Indians of South America in the 1950s.

Gayle Erwin—Astronaut, editor of *Servant's Quarters* magazine.

Tony Evans—Professor at Dallas Theological Seminary; inspirational author.

Harry Emerson Fosdick—Pastor of Riverside Church, New

York City; professor of Practical Theology at Union Theological Seminary; popular radio preacher; author.

Billy Graham—International crusade, radio, and TV evangelist; he has presented the Gospel face to face to more people than any other man in history; author of many inspirational classics read by millions; founder of *Christianity Today* and *Decision* magazines.

Simon Greenleaf—Nineteenth-century professor of law at Harvard University; author of *Treatise on the Law of Evidence,* which was published in 1842 and used as a reference in courts of law across America.

Manford George Gutzke—Author of two dozen books in the *Plain Talk* Bible commentary series.

Roy Irving—Bible scholar; longtime editor of the Scripture Press *Adult Teaching Guide.*

Jerome—Fourth-century Bible scholar who translated the Old Testament from Hebrew into Latin and revised the Latin New Testament translation, completing the Vulgate Bible.

Josephus—First-century Jewish historian.

Julian of Norwich—Fourteenth-century English mystic; author of *The Sixteen Revelations of Divine Love,* the first book published by a female author in English.

Phillip Keller—A shepherd who writes about the Bible's Good Shepherd from his personal understanding of shepherds and sheep.

John Killinger—Professor of preaching, worship, and literature at Vanderbilt Divinity School, Nashville; author of more than 20 books.

Richard Kyle—Professor of history and religion at Tabor College in Hillsboro, Kansas; author.

Louis Paul Lehman—Pastor of Calvary Church, Grand Rapids, Michigan; national radio preacher; also author, poet, Bible teacher, and composer of hundreds of Gospel songs.

Madeleine L'Engle—Prolific author; winner of the Newberry Award for her novel *A Wrinkle in Time*; poet; lecturer; Christian retreat leader.

C. S. Lewis—Founder of Magdalen College, Oxford University; author of books on theology and fantasy, i.e., *The Chronicles of Narnia.*

Hal Lindsey—Influential author of *The Late Great Planet Earth* as well as other books on biblical prophecy (35 million of which are in print); TV personality.

Max Lucado—Pastor of Oak Hill Church of Christ in San Antonio, Texas; poet, artist, apologist, prolific writer of inspirational books.

Peter Marshall—Chaplain of the U.S. Senate from 1947–1949; pastor of New York Avenue Presbyterian Church, Washington, D.C.; his life story is told in the popular film *A Man Called Peter.*

John A. Martin—President of Central College, McPherson, Kansas; formerly professor of Bible Exposition at Dallas Theological Seminary; contributing author to *The Bible Knowledge Commentary.*

Dan McCartney—Associate professor of New Testament at Westminster Theological Seminary.

Byron R. McCane—Professor of Religion at Converse College in Spartanburg, South Carolina.

Sallie McFague—Theologian, feminist, critic; author of books on metaphorical theology.

Methodius of Philippi—Ninth-century Greek, who, with his brother Cyrillus, took the Gospel to Moravia.

Leon Morris—Anglican priest; principal of Ridley College in Melbourne, Australia; author of numerous books, including commentaries on Luke, John, 1 Corinthians, Thessalonians, and Revelation.

Richard J. Mouw—President of Fuller Theological Seminary in Pasadena.

Henri J. M. Nouwen—Taught at University of Notre Dame, Yale, and Harvard; from 1986 till his death in 1996 associated with L'Arche Community in France and Toronto.

J. Dwight Pentecost—Professor emeritus of Biblical Exposition at Dallas Theological Seminary; author of 20 books.

J. B. Phillips—Pastor in London during World War II; Bible translator of *The New Testament in Modern English*; friend of C. S. Lewis.

Christine Poehls—Contemporary poet, composer, performer; Director of Women's Ministries at Faith Evangelical Free Church in Tempe, Arizona.

John Powell—Jesuit; associate professor at Loyola University in the classics, English, psychology, and theology; popular lecturer, counselor, and retreat director.

Larry (Lawrence O.) Richards—Theologian, Bible scholar, ecclesiologist; prolific author of more than 175 books, including Bible commentaries and reference works for pastors, church leaders, teachers, laymen, and youth.

John Charles Ryle—Nineteenth-century bishop of Liverpool, England.

Philip Schaff—Historian; author of a widely recognized eight-volume *History of the Christian Church.*

Ronald J. Sider—Professor at Eastern Baptist Seminary; president of Evangelicals for Social Action.

Howard A. Snyder—Formerly Dean of Free Methodist Seminary in Sao Paulo, Brazil; director of Light and Life Men International; author of books on church renewal.

Aleksandr Solzhenitsyn—Russian writer, imprisoned

for anti-Stalinist sentiments; author of *The Gulag Archipelago* documenting the Soviet prison system; awarded the Nobel Prize in literature in 1970; now an American citizen.

Tim Stafford—Editor of Campus Life Books; senior writer for *Christianity Today.*

John R. W. Stott—Evangelist, preacher, Bible scholar, author; pastor of All Souls Church in London; active participant in Evangelical-Roman Catholic dialogue; director of London Institute for Contemporary Christianity.

Charles Swindoll—President of Dallas Theological Seminary; popular Bible expositor, radio preacher, author.

Mother Teresa—Founder of the Missionaries of Charity in Calcutta, India and 51 other countries; Nobel Peace Prize winner in 1979.

Cal Thomas—Syndicated newspaper columnist.

C. Peter Wagner—Senior professor of church growth at Fuller Theological Seminary, Pasadena; church growth consultant.

John Wesley—Founder of Methodism; traveled 250,000 miles on horseback, preached 42,000 sermons, authored 233 books of history, Bible commentary, and medicine; did more to change English society and religion than any other person of his time.

Dallas Willard—Professor at the University of Southern California's School of Philosophy; visiting professor at the University of Colorado.

Note: To the best of our knowledge, all of the above information is accurate and up to date. In some cases we were unable to obtain biographical information.

—THE STARBURST EDITORS

ENDNOTES

Introduction

1. Papias, an early church leader, quoted in William Barclay, *Matthew* (Philadelphia: Westminster, 1975), 5.
2. Papias, quoted in Eusebius and in Thomas C. Oden and Christopher A. Hall, eds. *Ancient Christian Commentary on Scripture: New Testament II—Mark* (Downers Grove, IL: InterVarsity, 1998), xxi.
3. William Barclay, *The Gospel of Luke* (Philadelphia: Westminster, 1975), 1.
4. Clement of Alexandria, about 180 A.D., quoted in Robert C. Girard, *Adult Living Today* (Wheaton, IL: Scripture Press, 1995), 3.

Chapter 1

1. Robert E. Coleman, *The Master Plan of Evangelism* (Old Tappan, NJ: Revell, 1963), 18.
2. J. B. Phillips, *The New Testament in Modern English,* student ed. (New York: Macmillan, 1972), 34.
3. Jerome, *Cetedoc,* quoted in Thomas C. Oden and Christopher A. Hall, *Ancient Christian Commentary on Scripture: New Testament II: Mark* (Downers Grove, IL: InterVarsity, 1998), 120.
4. Oswald Chambers, *Bringing Sons into Glory* (Fort Washington, PA: Christian Literature Crusade, 1943), 39.
5. William Barclay, *The Gospel of Luke* (Philadelphia: Westminster, 1975), 127.
6. Peter Marshall, quoted in *NRSV Classics Devotional Bible* (Grand Rapids, MI: Zondervan, 1996), 1171.
7. *Revell Bible Dictionary* (Grand Rapids, MI: Revell, 1984), 909.
8. William Barclay, *The Gospel of Matthew, vol. 1* (Philadelphia: Westminster, 1975), 195.
9. John A. Martin, "Luke," *The Bible Knowledge Commentary: New Testament,* John F. Walvoord and Roy B. Zuck, eds. (Colorado Springs, CO: Cook, 1983), 231.
10. Gayle Erwin, "Forgiveness," *Servant Quarters* (Cathedral City, CA), September-November, 1994.

11. Oswald Chambers, *Disciples Indeed* (Fort Washington, PA: Christian Literature Crusade, 1955), 1.
12. Christine Poehls, from the song, "When I Forgive," © Christine Poehls, 5135 North 86th St., Scottsdale, AZ 85250.

Chapter 2

1. William Barclay, *The Gospel of John, vol. 1* (Philadelphia: Westminster, 1975), 231.
2. Leon Morris, *Luke* (Grand Rapids, MI: Eerdmans, 1988), 197.
3. Oswald Chambers, *Disciples Indeed,* 34.
4. Dan McCartney and Charles Clayton, *Let the Reader Understand* (Wheaton, IL: Victor, 1994), 254.
5. Alfred Edersheim, *The Temple* (Grand Rapids, MI: Eerdmans, 1982), 279–280.
6. Ibid., 281.
7. Billy Graham, *The Holy Spirit: Activating God's Power in Your Life* (New York: Warner, 1978), 14.
8. Edwin A. Blum, "John," in Walvoord and Zuck, *The Bible Knowledge Commentary: New Testament,* 303.
9. Barclay, *John, vol. 2,* 6.
10. Oswald Chambers, *Run Today's Race* (Fort Washington, PA: Christian Literature Crusade, 1968), 35.

Chapter 3

1. Frank R. Klassen, *The Chronology of the Bible,* (Nashville: Regal, 1975), 58.
2. Morris, *Luke,* 200.
3. John Wesley, *The Letters of the Reverend John Wesley,* ed. John Telford, vol. 6 (London: Epworth Press, 1931), 272.
4. Morris, *Luke,* 206.
5. Roy Irving, *Adult Teaching Guide* (Wheaton, IL: Scripture Press, September-November 1984).
6. Tony Evans, *A Guide to Spiritual Success* (Nashville: Nelson, 1994), 137.
7. Barclay, *Luke,* 150.
8. Albert Barnes, *Notes on the New Testament: Luke-John* (Grand Rapids, MI: Baker, 1949), 74–75.

9. Robert L. Thomas and Stanley N. Gundry, *A Harmony of the Gospels* (San Francisco: HarperCollins, 1978), 141.

10. Tim Stafford, *Knowing the Face of God* (Grand Rapids, MI: Zondervan, 1986), 229–230.

11. Julian of Norwich, *The Sixteen Revelations of Divine Love,* quoted in *NRSV Classics Devotional Bible,* 1356.

Chapter 4

1. Barclay, *Luke,* 160.

2. Aleksandr Solzhenitsyn, quoted in Stafford, *Knowing the Face of God,* 228.

3. McCartney and Clayton, *Let the Reader Understand,* 271.

4. Girard, *Adult Teaching Guide* (Wheaton, IL: Scripture Press, September-November 1995), 125.

5. Ibid., 126

6. George R. Beasley-Murray, *Word Biblical Commentary,* vol. 36: *John* (Waco, TX: Word, 1977), 159.

7. Ibid., 160.

Chapter 5

1. Phillip Keller, *A Shepherd Looks at the Good Shepherd and His Sheep,* large print ed. (Grand Rapids, MI: Zondervan, 1978), 23.

2. Ibid., 40.

3. Octavius Winslow, *No Condemnation in Christ Jesus* (1857), quoted in John Murray, *The Epistle to the Romans,* vol. 1 (n.p.: Marshall, Morgan and Scott, 1960–1965), 324.

4. Tim Stafford, *Knowing the Face of God,* 67.

5. Larry Richards, *Bible Difficulties Solved* (Grand Rapids, MI: Revell/Baker, 1993), 308.

6. Barclay, *Matthew,* vol. 1, 304.

7. Barclay, *Luke,* 185.

8. Ronald J. Sider, *Rich Christians in an Age of Hunger* (Downers Grove, IL: InterVarsity, 1977), 78–79.

9. Morris, *Luke,* 254.

10. Oswald Chambers, *Still Higher for His Highest* (Grand Rapids, MI: Zondervan, 1970), 87.

11. Donald Grey Barnhouse, quoted in Larry Richards, *Forgiveness: The Gift that Sets Free* (Nashville: Nelson, 1996), 89.

12. John Killinger, *A Devotional Guide to Luke* (Waco, TX: Word, 1980), 89.

Chapter 6

1. Chambers, *Still Higher for His Highest,* 86.

2. Killinger, *A Devotional Guide to Luke,* 91.

3. Lawrence O. Richards, *The Victor Bible Background Commentary: New Testament* (Wheaton, IL: Victor, 1994), 190.

4. Mother Teresa, *Words to Love By* (Notre Dame: Ave Maria Press, 1983), 31.

5. Charles Swindoll, *Growing Deep in the Christian Life* (Portland, OR: Multnomah, 1986), 319–320.

6. Adapted from *Revell Bible Dictionary,* 480.

7. Leon Morris, *The Gospel According to John* (Grand Rapids, MI: Eerdmans, 1971), 542.

8. Edersheim, *Sketches of Jewish Social Life,* 174.

9. Morris, *John,* 551.

10. B. B. Warfield, quoted in Morris, *John,* 556.

11. Henri J. M. Nouwen, *Seeds of Hope* (New York: Doubleday, 1989), 171.

12. Richards, *Bible Difficulties Solved,* 308.

13. *Serendipity Bible for Study Groups* (Grand Rapids, MI: Zondervan, 1989), 1413.

Chapter 7

1. Stafford, *Knowing the Face of God,* 206.

2. Harry Emerson Fosdick, *The Man from Nazareth* (New York: Pocket Books, 1953), 180.

3. Howard A. Snyder, *Community of the King* (Downers Grove, IL: InterVarsity, 1977), 133–134.

4. Barclay, *Luke,* 220.

5. Quoted in Barclay, *Luke,* 220.

6. Ibid., 225.

7. Barclay, *Matthew,* vol. 2 (Philadelphia: Westminster, 1975), 216.

8. Richards, *Background Commentary,* 71.

9. Gary M. Burge, "Directions: You're Divorced—Can You Remarry?" *Christianity Today,* October 4, 1999, 82.

10. Ibid., 83.

11. Barclay, *Matthew,* vol. 2, 227.

12. *Adult Teaching Guide,* December 1994–February 1995, 72.

13. Sider, *Rich Christians,* 174.

14. Quote attributed to Jim Elliot.

15. Manford George Gutzke, *Plain Talk on Matthew* (Grand Rapids, MI: Zondervan, 1966), 166.

16. Thomas and Gundry, *Harmony,* 168.

17. Lawrence O. Richards, *A New Face for the Church* (Grand Rapids, MI: Zondervan, 1970), 112–113.

18. Gutzke, *Matthew,* 167.

19. Richards, *Background Commentary,* 202.

Chapter 8

1. Leslie F. Brandt, *Jesus/Now* (St. Louis: Concordia, 1978), 83.

2. Morris, *Luke,* 302.

3. J. B. Phillips, *The New Testament in Modern English,* student ed., 207.

4. Sir Edwin Hoskyns, *The Fourth Gospel* (London: Faber, 1947), 416.

5. Venerable Bede, *Homilies on the Gospel,* 2:37–38, quoted in Oden and Hall, *Ancient Christian Commentary on Scripture,* 199.

6. Methodius of Philippi, "Oration on the Psalms," quoted in *Ancient Christian Commentary on Scripture*, 156.
7. Josephus, *The Works of Flavius Josephus*, trans. William Whiston (Grand Rapids, MI: Associated Publishers and Authors, n.d.).
8. Michael Card, *Immanuel: Reflections on the Life of Christ* (Nashville: Thomas Nelson, 1990), 143–144.
9. Louis Paul Lehman, *Tears of the Bible* (Grand Rapids, MI: Zondervan, 1958), 55.
10. Morris, *John,* 593.
11. John Calvin, *St. John,* 68.

Chapter 9
1. Barclay, *Matthew,* vol. 2, 285–286.
2. Richards, *Background Commentary,* 80.
3. Sallie McFague, *Metaphorical Theology: Models of God in Religious Language* (Philadelphia: Fortress, 1982), 181.
4. Richard J. Mouw, *Political Evangelism* (Grand Rapids, MI: Eerdmans, 1973), 55.
5. Pierre Teilhard De Chardin, quoted in John Powell, *Unconditional Love* (Allen, TX: Argus Communications, 1978), 97.
6. J. Dwight Pentecost, *The Words and Works of Jesus Christ* (Grand Rapids, MI: Zondervan, 1981), 391.
7. Barclay, *Matthew,* vol. 2, 310.
8. *New American Standard Bible* (Carol Stream, IL: Creation House, 1971).
9. Dallas Willard, *The Divine Conspiracy: Rediscovering Our Hidden Life in God* (San Francisco: Harper, 1998), 189.
10. John Chrysostom, quoted in *Ancient Christian Commentary: Mark,* 180.

Chapter 10
1. Josephus, *The Works of Flavius Josephus*, 555.
2. Larry Richards, *Complete Bible Handbook* (Waco, TX: Word, 1987), 488–489.
3. Chambers, *Still Higher for His Highest,* 66.
4. Barclay, *Luke,* 271.
5. C. Peter Wagner, *On the Crest of the Wave* (Ventura, CA: Regal, 1983), back cover.
6. Josephus, quoted in Morris, *Luke,* 326.
7. Richard Kyle, "Hope Beyond the Details: An Interview with Richard Kyle," *Christian History* 18, no. 1 (issue 61): 43.
8. Hal Lindsey, *The Late, Great Planet Earth* (Grand Rapids, MI: Zondervan, 1970), 171.
9. Richards, *Background Commentary,* 86.
10. Stafford, *Knowing the Face of God*, 91.
11. Adapted from Richards, *Background Commentary,* 205.
12. Oswald Chambers, *Our Portrait in Genesis* (Fort Washington, PA: Christian Literature Crusade, 1957), 23.

13. Barclay, *Matthew,* vol. 2, 355.
14. Chambers, *Still Higher for His Highest,* 88.
15. Sider, *Rich Christians,* 69.

Chapter 11
1. Merril C. Tenney, quoted in *Adult Teaching Guide*, December 1995-February 1996, 46.
2. *Revell Bible Dictionary,* 394.
3. F. L. Godet, *Commentary on the Gospel of John* (Grand Rapids, MI: Kegel, 1978).
4. Beasley-Murray, *Word Biblical Commentary, John*, 238.
5. Card, *Immanuel,* 155.
6. John Powell, S.J., *Unconditional Love* (Allen, TX: Argus Communications, 1978), 95–96.
7. Richards, *Bible Difficulties Solved,* 297.
8. Barclay, *Matthew,* vol. 2, 377–378.
9. John R. W. Stott, *The Cross of Christ* (Downers Grove, IL: InterVarsity, 1986), 71.
10. F. F. Bruce, *The Gospel of John* (Basingstoke, England: Pickering and Inglis, 1983), 298–299.
11. Richards, *Bible Difficulties Solved,* 310.
12. John Charles Ryle, *Expository Thoughts on the Gospels, St. John* (London, 1957), quoted in Morris, *John,* 646.
13. Morris, *John,* 646.
14. Stafford, *Knowing the Face of God,* 70.
15. Ibid., 68–69.
16. James M. Boice, *The Gospel of John* (Grand Rapids, MI: Zondervan, 1979), 229.
17. Ibid.
18. Quoted in William H. C. Frend, "Evangelists to the Death," *Christian History* 17, no. 1 (issue 57): 31.
19. Ibid., 31, 33.
20. Larry Richards, *The Bible: God's Word for the Biblically-Inept* (Lancaster, PA: Starburst, 1998), 215.

Chapter 12
1. Morris, *John,* 710.
2. Barclay, *John,* 218.
3. John R. W. Stott, *The Cross of Christ,* 77.
4. Card, *Immanuel,* 153.
5. Girard, *Adult Teaching Guide*, December 1994-February 1995, 108.
6. Beasley-Murray, *John,* 326.
7. *Sanhedrin 43a*, quoted in Beasley-Murray, *John,* 319.
8. Chambers, *Still Higher,* 133.
9. Beasley-Murray, *John,* 328.
10. Cal Thomas, "Not of This World," *Newsweek*, March 29, 1999, 60.
11. C. S. Lewis, quoted in Thomas, "Not of This World."
12. *Revell Bible Dictionary,* 130.
13. Richards, *The Bible,* 207.
14. Stott, *The Cross of Christ,* 51.

15. *Revell Bible Dictionary*, 793.

16. Richards, *The Bible*, 204.

Chapter 13

1. Adapted from Richards, *The Bible*, 208.

2. *Harper Collins Atlas of the Bible*, ed. James Pritchard (Phoenix: Borders/Harper-Collins, 1999), 167.

3. Louis A. Barbieri Jr., "Matthew," *The Bible Knowledge Commentary*, ed. Walvoord and Zuck, 89.

4. Barclay, *Matthew*, vol. 2, 405.

5. E. Stauffer, *Jesus and His Story*, trans. D. M. Barton (London: SCM, 1960), 111.

6. Ibid., 113.

7. Douglas Webster, *In Debt to Christ* (London, Highway Press, 1957), 46.

8. Stott, *Cross of Christ*, 78.

9. Barclay, *Mark*, 383.

10. Stott, *Cross of Christ*, 81.

11. Chambers, *Still Higher*, 50.

12. Stott, *Cross of Christ*, 82.

13. Adapted from Richards, *The Bible*, 209–210.

14. Charles E. B. Cranfield, *The Epistle to the Romans: International Critical Commentary*, vol. 1 (Edinburgh: T and T Clark, 1975), 217.

15. Richards, *The Bible*, 210.

16. Max Lucado, *No Wonder They Call Him the Savior* (Portland, OR: Multnomah, 1986), 140.

17. Bruce, *The Gospel of John*, 90.

Chapter 14

1. Ben Witherington III, "Primary Sources," *Christian History* 17, no. 3 (issue 59): 18.

2. Byron R. McCane, "The Scandal of the Grave," *Christian History* 17, no. 3 (issue 59): 41.

3. Bill Bright, *Introduction to Ten Basic Steps toward Christian Maturity: The Uniqueness of Jesus* (San Bernardino: Campus Crusade, 1964), 31.

4. Beasley-Murray, *John*, 374.

5. Barclay, *Luke*, 305.

6. Barclay, *Matthew*, 416.

7. Thomas Arnold, quoted in Bright, *Ten Steps toward Christian Maturity*, 33.

8. Dietrich Bonhoeffer, *The Cost of Discipleship* (New York: Simon and Schuster/ Touchstone, 1959), 90.

9. Beasley-Murray, *John*, 386.

10. Robert C. Girard, *Adult Teaching Guide*, March-May 1994 (Wheaton, IL: Scripture Press), 54–55.

11. Philip Schaff, *History of the Christian Church*, vol. 1 (n.p.: A.P. and A., n.d.), 81.

12. Simon Greenleaf, An Examination of the Testimony of the Four Evangelists by the Rules of Evidence Administered in Courts of Justice (1846), quoted in Bill Bright, *Teacher's Manual for the Ten Basic Steps toward Christian Maturity* (San Bernardino: Here's Life Publishers, 1982), 46.

13. Madeleine L'Engle, *Walking on Water: Reflections on Faith and Art* (Wheaton, IL: Shaw, 1980), 22.

Chapter 15

1. *Revell Bible Dictionary*, 99.

2. Chambers, *Still Higher*, 189.

3. J. B. Phillips, *Foreword to Letters to Young Churches*, quoted in Bright, *Ten Steps to Christian Maturity*, 31–32.

INDEX

Boldface numbers refer to defined (What?) terms in the sidebar.

Christ, kingdom of, xv, 146
Christian(s):
    as believers, xxii (*See also*
        Believers)
    death as experienced by,
        105–107
    early, 187, 198, 200, 283
    eternal life and, 106–107
    fear and, 54–55
    hatred of, 206–207
    Jesus, personal relationship
        with, 47, 55, 282
    last commandment and,
        197–198
    as to love one another,
        197–198
    work of, effective, 47
    (*See also* Believers; Born again;
        Eternal life; Saved)
Christian church (*see* Church)
Christian faith, 6–8
Christian ministry, 265
Christianity:
    greatness in, 15–18
    history of, 24
    inclusiveness in, 17–18
    nature of, 6–8
    priorities in, 47
    religion vs., 30
    (*See also* Church)
Christs, counterfeit, **175**
Christs, pseudo, 75–76
Church, 6, **7**, 8, 81
    Jesus as head of, 281
    leadership in, 131–132
    mission of, 271
Clayton, Charles (*see* McCartney,
    Dan, and Charles Clayton)
Clement of Alexandria, on John,
    gospel of, xix
Cleopas, 264
Coins, 170
    denarius, 129–130; illustration
        of, 130
    dowry, illustration of, 89
    lost, parable of, 88, 291
    30 silver, 190, 226–227

Coleman, Robert E., on Jesus,
    life's purpose of, 9
Colt, 146
Commandment, last, 197–198
Commandments, Ten, 127
    most important of, 165–166
Communion, Holy, 199–200
Compadres, **67**
Compassion, **76**, 86
Conversion of souls, 203
Convict, **208**
Coptic, **234**
Costly, **144**
Counselor, Holy Spirit as, 208–209
Counterfeit christs, **175**
Court, Sanhedrin as, 42 (*See also*
    Sanhedrin)
Covenant(s), **198, 247**
    the new, 199–201
Covetousness, **60**
Cranfield, Charles E. B., on God's
    mercy, 250–251
Creeds, **6**
Cross, **238**
Crucifixion, **10**
    description of, 240–241, 249,
        256
    illustration, 242
    of Jesus, 102, 112, 237–252,
        287
Crysostom, John, on the widow's
    mite, 170
Cummin tithe, illustration of, 121
Cup, **219**
The Cup, **131**
Curse, **229**
Cuts off, **205**
Cyrene, **238**

D
Daniel, 180
Darkness, at time of crucifixion,
    244–245, 248
David (King), 166, 245
Day laborers, **129**
Day of the Lord, 181
Dead Sea, 285

Dead Sea Scrolls, 75
Death:
    believers, significance to,
        105–107
    certainty of, 65
    eternal life and, 107
    fear of, 54
    first-century Jewish beliefs and
        customs, 103, 105, 110
    physical, 165
    spiritual, 119
Death of Jesus, 247–252, 275
    significance of, 237, 250–251
    (*See also* Crucifixion)
Deceives, **26**
Declare, **271**
Dedication, Feast of, **67**, 80
Deeply moved, **109**
Demon(s):
    confronting, 43
    driving out, 14–15, 17
Demons, Jesus casting out:
    of man at Capernaum, 6
    possessed boy, healing, 13–14
    mute spirit, driving out, 49–50
Denarius, **129**, 163; illustration
    of, 130
Departure, **11**
Detachment, **220**
Detestable, **97**
Devil, 49
    doom of, 152
    limitations of, 55
    (*See also* Satan)
Didymus (*see* Thomas)
The disciple whom Jesus loved,
    xviii, **195**
Disciples, **xvi**
    Apostles, the 12, 3, 293–294
    faith of, 3–6
    larger group of, 21
    real, 37
    (*See also* Apostles; The 12;
        individual names)
Discipleship:
    cost of, 25–26
    requirements of, 37

return of (*see* Second Coming)

as shepherd (*See under* Shepherd, Jesus as)

as Son of God (*see* Son of God)

as Son of Man (*see* Son of Man)

supremacy of, 12

teaching of, xv, 27–28, 37 (*See also* individual topics)

temptation of (*See under* Temptation)

understanding, 12

value of learning about, xxii

"the way and the truth and the life," 201–202

work of, 215–216

trial and crucifixion, map of, 287 (*See also* Crucifixion; Trial)

(*See also* individual topics)

Jewish Talmud, 226

Jews, **xix**

  Matthew's gospel targeting, xvii

  salvation and, 83

  and Samaritans, animosity between, 24

  uprooting of, 179

  (*See also* Israel; Israelites)

Jews (Jewish leaders), **26**

Joanna, 259

Job, 67

  book of, 65

John the Baptist, 4, **98**, 158–159

  apostles of Jesus, as source of some, 3

  as forerunner of Jesus, 4

  introducing Jesus, 76

  as prophet, xxi

John (the disciple), 3, 131, 244, 262, 267, 293

  as "disciple whom Jesus loved," xviii, 195

  at Gethsemane, 217–221

  at Jesus' resurrection, 261

  at the Transfiguration, 10–14

(*See also* Apostles; Disciples; The 12)

John, gospel of, xviii–xix, 32

  historian, John as, 102

John Mark (*see* Mark)

Jonah, sign of, 51–52

Joppa, 285

Jordan River, 4, 41,132–133, 285

Joseph (father of Jesus), xv

Joseph of Arimathea, 255–257, 285

Josephus, 64

  on the Temple, magnificence of, 174–175

Joses, **257**

Joy, 43

Judah (Southern Kingdom of Israel), 24

Judas Iscariot, 3, 144, 294

  betrayal of Jesus by, 190, 192, 194–197, 219–220

  remorse and death of, 226–227

  (*See also* Apostles; Disciples; The 12)

Jude, 262, 294 (*See also* Apostles; Disciples; The 12)

Judea, 103, 285

  Herod Archelaus and, 141

  Herod the Great as ruler of, 5

  Jesus as born in, xv

  Jesus' ministry in, 22, 41–54

  Pontius Pilate as governor of (*see* Pontius Pilate)

  (*See also* Galilee; Palestine, map of; Promised Land)

Judge:

  in parable of persistent widow, 119–120, 292

  Jesus as, 281

Judging, as hypocrisy, 53

Judgment, **42**

  of Satan, 208

  at the Second Coming, 63–64

  of the world, 152

Judgmentalism, xv

Julian of Norwich, on defending faith, 56

Justice, **120**

Justification, **272**

Justified, **120, 250**

K

Keller, Philip:

  on Jesus as the Good Shepherd, 77

  on shepherds and sheep, 78

Keys, **7**

Kilauea, **71**

Killinger, John, on the prodigal son, 92

Kindness, rewards of, 17

King(s) (*see* individual names)

King, Jesus as, 7, 76, 146–147, 229–230, 242

Kingdom of God, xv, 117–119, 229–230

  misunderstanding, 132, 139

  seeking, 129, 187

Kingdom of Jesus (Christ), xv, 146

Knowing, **215**

Korazin, 42, 285

Kyle, Richard, on the Second Coming, 182

L

L'Engle, Madeleine, on faith, 276–277

Lake of fire, 101

Lamb, lambs:

  Lamb of God, Jesus as, 248

  Passover (Jesus as), 41, 248–249

  people as, 268

  witness of, 42

  among wolves, 41–42

Lamp(s), 62

  oil, illustration of, 63

Languages (*see* individual languages)

Last Supper, 191–201, 287

Law and the Prophets, **98**

Lawyer(s), 25, 44–46

Lazarus (beggar), **99**–100

Lazarus (of Bethany), 46–47, **102**–113, 142–144
   resurrection of, 102–113
Leadership, 131–132
Leap of faith, 276
Leaven, **189**
Legalism, **xvi**
Lehman, Louis Paul, on Jesus as weeping over sin, 148
Lepers, 10, Jesus healing, 115–116
Leprosy, **116**
Levite, **35**, 45–46
Lewis, C. S., on Christians, kingdom of God and, 230
Life of Christ, Volume 1, xiv
Life, **106**
   eternal, 106–107
   Jesus as source of, 106–107
   losing in God, 151
Light of the world, Jesus as, 35–36, 67, 72
Light, 64, **153**
   in the Bible, 38
   darkness as trying to extinguish, 221
   walking in, 104
Lights, Feast of, 67
Like the angels, **165**
Lilies, **61**
Lindsey, Hal, on the Second Coming, 182
Linen, 256
Living water, 29–30
Lord:
   God as, xxi
   Jesus as, xxi, 76
   (*See also* God; Jesus)
Lord's Prayer, 47
Lord's Supper, 199–200
Lost, **83**
Lost coin, parable of, 88, 291
Lost sheep, parable of, 88, 291
Love, **102**
   among believers, 217
   loving God, 165
   God's, 251

of Jesus, for his friends, 102
last commandment, "Love one another," 197–198
in marriage, 122–124, 126
"Love your neighbor," 44–46
Peter's, for Jesus, 267–268
John Powell on, 198
Mary's (Martha's sister) for Jesus, 144
Lucado, Max, on sin, Jesus as dying for, 251
Luke, gospel of, xviii, 131, 273
Lulab, **146**

M

Magdala, 285
Malchus, 220
Mammon, 97, 127
Mark, book of, xvii, 224, 262
Marriage, 98–99
   Jesus on, 122–126
Marshall, Peter, on childlike faith, 16
Martha, 46–47, 142–144, 102, 105–113
Martin, John A., on God as inclusive, 17
Martyrdom, **xvii, 177**, 207
   of apostles, 274, 293–294
Mary of Bethany (Martha's sister), 46–47, 142–145, 170
   anointing Jesus, 143–145
   and Lazarus, resurrection of, 102, 105–113
Mary (mother of Jesus), xiv, 181
Mary (mother of Joses), 257, 259
Mary Magdalene, 257, 259–263
Master, Jesus as, 76
Materialism (*see* Money; Wealth)
Matthew (Levi), 3, 262, 294 (*See also* Apostles; Disciples; The 12)
Matthew, book of, xvii
McCane, Byron R., on burial customs, first-century Jewish, 257

McCartney, Dan, and Charles Clayton:
   on God's will, obeying, 28
   on suffering, 68
McFague, Sallie, on Jesus and friendship, 163
Mediterranean Sea, 285
Megatrends, **178**
Menorah, illustration of, 35
Mercy, 45, **121**
Messiah **xv, xvii,** 7
   Israel's rejection of, 149, 161–162
   Jesus as, 36, 81, 224–225
   (*See also* Christ; Jesus Christ; Savior)
Messianic, **245**
Methodius of Philippi, on loving Jesus, 148
Mina, **140**
Miracles of Jesus, 6, 51
Miracles of Jesus—healing:
   Bartimaeus (two blind men), restoring sight to, 133
   blind beggar, restoring sight to, 67–73
   demon cast out of man at Capernaum, 6
   high priest's slave, reattaching ear, 220
   lepers, ten, 115–116
   paralyzed man, 29
   quadriplegic, 6
Miracles of Jesus—nature:
   calming the storm, 6
   fish, big catch on Lake Galilee, 6
   walking on water, 6
Miracles of Jesus—resurrection:
   of Lazarus (*see* Resurrection of Lazarus)
   of widow's son in Nain, 6
Miracles, in Jesus' name, 17
Miracles, Jesus regarding, 82
Miracles, significance of, 80
Miscreant, **134**
Missionary, Paul as, xviii

Prosperity, true, xv (*See also* Wealth)

Prune, **206**

Pure nard, **143**

Purple, 100

Purple robe, 237–238

Put out of the synagogue, 70

Q

Quadriplegic, Jesus healing, 6

R

Rabbi, **17, 167**
  Jesus as, 76

Rage, **179**

Rapture, 181–**182**

Ravens, **61**

Reclined, **52**

Reconciliation, xv

Reign, **281**

Religion:
  Christianity as more than, 30
  first-century, 166

Religious establishment, Jesus and, xvi (*See also* Enemies of Jesus; High priests; Pharisees; Sadduccees)

Religious sentimentalism, 50

Removed, **193**

Repentance, **xv,** 65–66, 101, 227
  of thief on cross, 243–244

Repented, **160**

Response, **24**

Restitution, **135**

Resurrection, **106**
  end-time, 106–107, 164–165
  first-century Jewish belief in, 106
  of Jesus (*see* Resurrection of Jesus)
  of righteous Jews, at death of Jesus, 248

Resurrection of Jesus, 102, 213, 259–263, 272
  post-resurrection appearances, 262–273

Resurrection of Lazarus, 102–113

Resurrection and the life, Jesus as, 106–107

Resurrection miracles of Jesus (*see* Miracles of Jesus—resurrection)

Retain, **266**

Revealed, **7, 118**

Revelation, **44**

Revell Bible Dictionary:
  on the Ascension, 282
  on foot-washing, 195
  on Jesus and Barabbas, 232
  on Pontius Pilate, 234

Reverence, 144

Rich (*see* Money; Wealth)

Rich young ruler, 127–128

Richards, Larry (Lawrence O.):
  on Caiaphas, 112
  on the end time, Jesus' prophecy for, 175
  on the Holy Spirit, 209
  on hostility toward Jesus' followers, 199
  on Jesus as God, 83
  on Jesus as only way to God, 202
  on Jesus, suffering of, 233
  on leadership and servanthood, 132
  on love of money, 98
  on repentance, 160
  on the Second Coming, readiness for,183
  on sin, Jesus as dying for, 251
  on Zacchaeus, 135

Right hand, **222, 280**

Righteous, **87, 186**

Righteousness, hunger for, xv

Robber, **77**

Rock, Jesus as, 7–8

Roman Emperor, **5**

Roman Empire, **xx**

Roman government, Matthew working for, xvii

Romans, 75
  Mark's gospel targeting, xvii
  rule of, 64–65

taxation by, 134–135

Rome:
  and Jerusalem, fall of, 179
  Palestine as colony of, xx
  Paul in, xviii
  Pontius Pilate as Roman governor (*see* Pontius Pilate)

Rooster crowing, 223

Ryle, John Charles, on conversion of souls, 203

S

Sabbath 142, 255
  crucifixion and, 249
  rules of, 29, 69, 86

Sabbath, special, **249**

Sacrifice, **14**
  Jesus' death as ultimate, 152, 248
  Old and New Testament, 251

Sacrifices, at Feast of Tabernacles, 29

Sadducees, **75, 164**, 221, 258

Salome, 131, 259

Salvation, 84, **135**, 187, 221, **272**

Samaria, 115–116, 285
  Herod the Great as ruler of, 5
  Jesus in, 23–24

Samaritan(s), 24
  Good, parable of, 45–46
  leper thanking Jesus, 116
  prejudice against, 116

Samaritan woman, 81

Sanctified, **217**

Sanhedrin, **42**, 158, **224**;
  illustration of, 225
  faith of some members, 153
  Joseph of Arimathea as in, 255
  Lazarus, resurrection of, and, 111–112, 142
  Nicodemus as member of, 31
  trial of Jesus, 222–235

Satan, 152
  confronting, 43
  sin, as source of, 198
  (*See also* Devil)

Saved, **83**, 99 (*See also* Grace)
Savior, **xv**
 trusting Jesus as, xix
 (*See also* Christ; Jesus Christ;
 Messiah)
Saviorhood, 9
Schaff, Philip, on the
 Resurrection, 272
Scribe(s), **25**, 75, illustration of,
 26
Scripture(s) (*see* Bible)
Sea of Tiberias, **267**
Seal, **259**
Seas (*see* individual names)
Second Advent, **176**
Second Coming, 118–119,
 140–141
 events of, 181–182
 impossibility of predicting,
 173, 182–183
 parables regarding, 183–187
 preparation for, 62–64, 183–184
 signs of, 180
Self-aggrandizement, **132**
Self-denial, **10**
Self-righteousness, 120
Separation from God, **246**
Sermon on the Mount, 47
Serpent, 43
Servanthood, 131–132
 greatness of, 15, 17
70 A.D., **179**
70 times seven, 18
72, the sending of, 41–42
Shalom, **265**
Sheep, 76–79, 82, 88
 and goats, parable of, 186, 290
 lost, parable of, 88, 291
 people as, 268–269
Sheepfold, **76**
Shelters, **12**, **23**
Shepherd(s), 76–79, 88, **269**
 Jesus as, 76–80, 82
Shrewd manager, parable of,
 95–96, 291
Sider, Ronald J.:
 on compassion, 86

 on Jesus as identifying with
 poor, 187
 on wealth, 128
Siege works, **179**
Sign of Jonah, 52
Sign(s), **142**, **179**, 51–52, 111, 153
Siloam, 65
Siloam, Pool of, 29, 68, 143;
 illustration, 30
Silver coins, 89, **190**
Simon of Cyrene, 238
Simon Peter (*see* Peter)
Simon the leper, 143–144
Simon (the Zealot), 3, 294 (*See
 also* Apostles; Disciples;
 The 12)
Sin, 67, **246**
 believers and, 194
 Christians' authority
 regarding, 265–266
 cleansing from, 194
 forgiven as forgotten, 91
 forgiveness of, 34
 God as forgiving, xix
 Jesus' death as paying for,
 152, 237, 239, 246–247,
 250–251
 Jesus as without, 218, 246
 Satan as source of, 198
 suffering and, 64–65, 67, 71
 yeast as metaphor for, 54
Sinners:
 God's response to, 88–93, 95
 Jesus' death as paying for,
 152, 237, 239, 246–247,
 250–251
 Jesus as friend of, 33, 87, 240
Six days, **10**
Six days before, **142**
Sixth hour, **244**
Skull, the, 240–**241**
Snyder, Howard A., on God's
 kingdom, 117–118
Solomon, King, 24, 174
Solomon's Colonnade, **80**
Solzhenitsyn, Alexandr, on
 punishment, 65

Son of God, 37, 44, 166, 273,
 248, 281
Son of Man, 166, **181**, 281
Sons of Thunder, 131
Sorcery, **226**
Sparrows, **55**
Spikenard, **144**
Spirit, **14**
Spirit, Christ's, being filled with,
 62
Spirit, Holy (*see* Holy Spirit)
Spiritual conquest, **7**
Spiritual death, **119**
Spiritual infidelity, **124**
Spirituality, true, xv
Stafford, Tim:
 on God in Jesus, 82
 on the Holy Spirit coming to
 disciples, 203–204
 on Jesus and Holy Spirit as
 one, 205
 on persecution of Christians,
 55
 on praising God, 117
 on the Second Coming, 183
 on Jesus' mother, his care of
 from cross, 244
Stayed, **105**
Steward, **63**
Stone (capstone), 161–162
Stone (tomb), **257**
Stone, stoning, **32**–33, 82, 103,
 229
Storm, Jesus calming, 6
Stott, John R. W.:
 on the crucifixion, 245
 on Jesus at Gethsemane, 218
 on Jesus, life's
 accomplishment of, 247
 on Jesus, suffering on the
 cross of, 246
 on Pontius Pilate and us, 233
 on the upper room,
 lessons of, 200–201
Stranger, **186**
Streets, **87**
Strips of linen, **256**

Wealth, 59–62, 95–98 (*See also* Money)
    rich fool, parable of, 60, 291
Webster, Douglas, on Jesus, birth and death of, 245
Wept, **109, 148**
weeping, Jesus as, 109–110
Wesley, John, on believers, power of, 44
Wheat, symbolism of, 151
Who sinned, **67**
Widow's mite, the, 169–179
Widow's son, Jesus resurrecting, 6
Willard, Dallas, on religious show-offs, 168

Wine, 120
    Holy Communion, 199–200
    at the Last Supper, 191
Winslow, Octavius, on Jesus' death, 80
Woes, **52**
Wolf, wolves, 77–78
Women, rights of, 88, 124
Word (*see* Bible)
Word of God, 101 (*See also* Bible)
World, **207, 251**
Worldliness, 61
Worry, 61–62
Worship, worshiped, **72** (*See also* Praise; Prayer)
Wrath, **250**

Written in heaven, **43**
Wrote, **34**

Y
Yahweh, xxi, **35**, 127
Yeast, 53–54, 189
Yom Kippur, 120
Young ruler, **127**

Z
Zacchaeus, 1, 133–136
Zealot, Simon (*see* Simon the Zealot)
Zealots, **16**
Zebedee, 131
Zechariah, 4, 147

Books by Starburst Publishers®
(Partial listing—full list available on request)

The **God's Word for the Biblically-Inept**™ series is already a best-seller with over 100,000 books sold! Designed to make reading the Bible easy, educational, and fun! This series of verse-by-verse Bible studies, topical studies, and overviews mixes scholarly information from experts with helpful icons, illustrations, sidebars, and time lines. It's the Bible made easy!

Life of Christ, Volume 2—God's Word for the Biblically-Inept™
Robert C. Girard

Life of Christ, Volume 2, begins with events recorded in Matthew 16. Read about Jesus' transfiguration, his miracles and parables, triumphal ride through Jerusalem, capture in the Garden of Gethsemane, and his trial, crucifixion, resurrection, and ascension. Find out how to be great in the kingdom of God, what Jesus meant when he called himself the light of the world, and what makes up real worship.
(trade paper)   ISBN 1892016397   **$16.95**

Life of Christ, Volume 1—God's Word for the Biblically-Inept™
Robert C. Girard

Girard takes the reader on an easy-to-understand journey through the gospels of Matthew, Mark, Luke, and John, tracing the story of Jesus from his virgin birth to his revolutionary ministry. Learn about Jesus' baptism, the Sermon on the Mount, and his miracles and parables.
(trade paper)   ISBN 1892016230   **$16.95**

The Bible—God's Word for the Biblically-Inept™
Larry Richards

An excellent book to start learning the entire Bible. Get the basics or the in-depth information you are seeking with this user-friendly overview. From Creation to Christ to the Millennium, learning the Bible has never been easier.
(trade paper)   ISBN 0914984551   **$16.95**

Daniel—God's Word for the Biblically-Inept™
Daymond R. Duck

Daniel is a book of prophecy and the key to understanding the mysteries of the Tribulation and End-Time events. This verse-by-verse commentary combines humor and scholarship to get at the essentials of Scripture. Perfect for those who want to know the truth about the Antichrist.
(trade paper)   ISBN 0914984489   **$16.95**

Genesis—God's Word for the Biblically-Inept™
Joyce L. Gibson

Genesis is written to make understanding and learning the Word of God simple and fun! Like the other books in this series, the author breaks the Bible down into bite-sized pieces making it easy to understand and incorporate into your life. Readers will learn about Creation, Adam and Eve, the Flood, Abraham and Isaac, and more.
(trade paper)   ISBN 1892016125   **$16.95**

Health & Nutrition—God's Word for the Biblically-Inept™
Kathleen O'Bannon Baldinger

The Bible is full of God's rules for good health! Baldinger reveals scientific evidence that proves the diet and health principles outlined in the Bible are the best for total health. Learn about the Bible diet, the food pyramid, and fruits and vegetables from the Bible! Experts include Pamela Smith, Julian Whitaker, Kenneth Cooper, and T. D. Jakes.
(trade paper)   ISBN 0914984055   **$16.95**

Men of the Bible—God's Word for the Biblically-Inept™
D. Larry Miller

Benefit from the life experiences of the powerful men of the Bible! Learn how the inspirational struggles of men such as Moses, Daniel, Paul, and David parallel the struggles of men today. It will inspire and build Christian character for any reader.
(trade paper)   ISBN 1892016079   **$16.95**

Prophecies of the Bible—God's Word for the Biblically-Inept™
Daymond R. Duck

God has a plan for this crazy planet, and now understanding it is easier than ever! Best-selling author and End-Time prophecy expert Daymond R. Duck explains the complicated prophecies of the Bible in plain English. Duck shows you all there is to know about the end of the age, the New World Order, the Second Coming, and the coming world government. Find out what prophecies have already been fulfilled and what's in store for the future!
(trade paper)   ISBN 1892016222   **$16.95**

Revelation—God's Word for the Biblically-Inept™
Daymond R. Duck

End-Time Bible prophecy expert Daymond R. Duck leads us verse by verse through one of the Bible's most confusing books. Follow the experts as they forge their way through the captivating prophecies of Revelation!
(trade paper)   ISBN 0914984985   **$16.95**

Romans—God's Word for the Biblically-Inept™
Gib Martin

The best-selling *God's Word for Biblically-Inept*™ series continues to grow! Learn about the apostle Paul, living a righteous life, and more with help from graphics, icons, and chapter summaries.
(trade paper)   ISBN 1892016273 $16.95

Women of the Bible—God's Word for the Biblically-Inept™
Kathy Collard Miller

Finally, a Bible perspective just for women! Gain valuable insight from the successes and struggles of such women as Eve, Esther, Mary, Sarah, and Rebekah. Interesting icons like "Get Close to God," "Build Your Spirit," and "Grow Your Marriage" will make it easy to incorporate God's Word into your daily life.
(trade paper)   ISBN 0914984063 $16.95

The ***What's in the Bible for . . .***™ series focuses on making the Bible applicable to everyday life. Whether you're a teenager or senior citizen, this series has the book for you! Each title is equipped with the same reader-friendly icons, call-outs, tables, illustrations, questions, and chapter summaries that are used in the *God's Word for the Biblically-Inept*™ series. It's another easy way to access God's Word!

What's in the Bible for . . .™ Women
Georgia Curtis Ling

What does the Bible have to say to women? Women of all ages will find biblical insight on topics that are meaningful to them in four sections: Wisdom for the Journey; Family Ties; Bread, Breadwinners, and Bread Makers; and Fellowship and Community Involvement. This book uses illustrations, bullet points, chapter summaries, and icons to make understanding God's Word easier than ever!
(trade paper)   ISBN 1892016109 $16.95

What's in the Bible for . . .™ Mothers
Judy Bodmer

Is home schooling a good idea? Is it okay to work? At what age should I start treating my children like responsible adults? What is the most important thing I can teach my children? If you are asking these questions and need help answering them, *What's in the Bible for . . . Mothers* is especially for you! Simple and user-friendly, this motherhood manual offers hope and instruction for today's mothers by jumping into the lives of mothers in the Bible (e.g., Naomi, Elizabeth, and Mary) and by exploring biblical principles that are essential to being a nurturing mother.
(trade paper)   ISBN 1892016265 $16.95

What's in the Bible for . . .™ Teens
Mark and Jeanette Littleton

This is a book that teens will love! *What's in the Bible for. . . Teens* contains topical Bible themes that parallel the challenges and pressures of today's adolescents. Learn about Bible prophecy, God's plan for relationships, and peer pressure in a conversational and fun tone. Helpful and eye-catching "WWJD?" icons, illustrations, and sidebars included. (Available Fall 2000.)
(trade paper)   ISBN 1892016052 $16.95

(see page 326 for purchasing information)

- **Learn more at www.biblicallyinept.com** •

God Things Come in Small Packages: Celebrating the Little Things in Life
Susan Duke, LeAnn Weiss, Caron Loveless, and Judith Carden

Enjoy touching reminders of God's simple yet generous gifts to brighten our days and gladden our hearts! Treasures like a sunset over a vast sparkling ocean, a child's trust, or the crystalline dew on a spider's web come to life in this elegant compilation. Such occasions should be celebrated as if gift wrapped from God; they're his hallmarks! Personalized scripture is artfully combined with compelling stories and reflections.
(cloth)   ISBN 1892016281 $12.95

God Things Come in Small Packages for Moms: Rejoicing in the Simple Pleasures of Motherhood
Susan Duke, LeAnn Weiss, Caron Loveless, and Judith Carden

The "small" treasures God plants in a mom's day shine in this delightful book. Savor priceless stories, which encourage us to value treasures like a shapeless, ceramic bowl presented with a toothy grin; a child's hand clinging to yours on a crowded bus; or a handful of wildflowers presented on a hectic day. Each story combines personalized scripture with heartwarming vignettes and inspiring reflections.
(cloth)   ISBN 189201629X $12.95

God Things Come in Small Packages for Friends: Exploring the Freedom of Friendship
LeAnn Weiss, Susan Duke, and Judy Carden

A heartwarming combination of true stories, paraphrased Scripture, and reflections that celebrate the simple yet cherished blessings shared between true friends. A new release from the elegant *God Things Come in Small Packages* series that combines the beauty of gift books with the depth of devotionals. Includes reflective meditation, narrative vignettes detailing powerful moments of revelation, and encouraging scripture passages presented as letters to a friend.
(cloth)   ISBN 1892016346 $12.95

God Things Come in Small Packages for Women: Celebrating the Unique Gifts of Women
LeAnn Weiss, Susan Duke, and Judy Carden

Women will experience God's love like never before through powerfully translated Scripture, true stories, and reflections, which celebrate the unique character of women. A new release from the elegant *God Things Come in Small Packages* series that combines the beauty of gift books with the depth of a devotionals. Includes reflective meditation, narrative vignettes detailing powerful moments of revelation, and encouraging scripture passages presented as letters from God.
(cloth)   ISBN 1892016354   **$12.95**

The Weekly Feeder: A Revolutionary Shopping, Cooking, and Meal-Planning System
Cori Kirkpatrick

A revolutionary meal-planning system, here is a way to make preparing home-cooked dinners more convenient than ever. At the beginning of each week, simply choose one of the eight preplanned menus, tear out the corresponding grocery list, do your shopping, and whip up each fantastic meal in less than 45 minutes! The author's household management tips, equipment checklists, and nutrition information make this system a must for any busy family. Included with every recipe is a personal anecdote from the author emphasizing the importance of good food, a healthy family, and a well-balanced life.
(trade paper)   ISBN 1892016095   **$16.95**

God Stories: They're So Amazing, Only God Could Make Them Happen
Donna I. Douglas

Famous individuals share their personal, true-life experiences with God in this beautiful new book! Find out how God has touched the lives of top recording artists, professional athletes, and other newsmakers like Jessi Colter, Deana Carter, Ben Vereen, Stephanie Zimbalist, Cindy Morgan, Sheila E., Joe Jacoby, Cheryl Landon, Brett Butler, Clifton Taulbert, Babbie Mason, Michael Medved, Sandi Patty, Charlie Daniels, and more! Their stories are intimate, poignant, and sure to inspire and motivate you as you listen for God's message in your own life!
(cloth)   ISBN 1892016117   **$18.95**

God's Little Rule Book: Simple Rules to Bring Joy & Happiness to Your Life
Starburst Publishers

Let this little book of God's rules be your personal guide to a more joyful life. Brimming with easily applicable rules, this book is sure to inspire and motivate you! Each rule includes corresponding scripture and a practical tip that will help to incorporate God's rules into everyday

life. Simple enough to fit into a busy schedule, yet powerful enough to be life changing!
(trade paper)   ISBN 1892016168   **$6.95**

Life's Little Rule Book: Simple Rules to Bring Joy & Happiness to Your Life
Starburst Publishers

Let this little book inspire you to live a happier life! The pages are filled with timeless rules such as, "Learn to cook, you'll always be in demand!" and "Help something grow." Each rule is combined with a reflective quote and a simple suggestion to help the reader incorporate the rule into everyday life.
(trade paper)   ISBN 1892016176   **$6.95**

Stories of God's Abundance for a More Joyful Life
Compiled by Kathy Collard Miller

Like its successful predecessor, *God's Abundance*, this book is filled with beautiful, inspirational, real-life stories. Those telling their stories of God share scriptures and insights that readers can apply to their daily lives. Renew your faith in life's small miracles and challenge yourself to allow God to lead the way as you find the source of abundant living for all your relationships.
(trade paper)   ISBN 1892016060   **$12.95**

More God's Abundance: Joyful Devotions for Every Season
Compiled by Kathy Collard Miller

Editor Kathy Collard Miller responds to the tremendous success of *God's Abundance* with a fresh collection of stories based on God's Word for a simpler life. Includes stories from our most beloved Christian writers, such as Liz Curtis Higgs and Patsy Clairmont, that are combined with ideas, tips, quotes, and Scripture.
(cloth)   ISBN 1892016133   **$19.95**

God's Abundance for Women: Devotions for a More Meaningful Life
Compiled by Kathy Collard Miller

Following the success of *God's Abundance*, this book will touch women of all ages as they seek a more meaningful life. Essays from our most beloved Christian authors exemplify how to gain the abundant life that Jesus promised through trusting him to fulfill our every need. Each story is enhanced with Scripture, quotes, and practical tips providing brief, yet deeply spiritual reading.
(cloth)   ISBN 1892016141   **$19.95**

Treasures of a Woman's Heart: A Daybook of Stories and Inspiration
Edited by Lynn D. Morrissey

Join the best-selling editor of *Seasons of a Woman's Heart* in this touching sequel where she unlocks the treasures

of women and glorifies God with Scripture, reflections, and a compilation of stories. Explore heartfelt living with vignettes by Kay Arthur, Elisabeth Elliot, Emilie Barnes, Claire Cloninger, and more.
(cloth)   ISBN 1892016257   **$18.95**

Seasons of a Woman's Heart: A Daybook of Stories and Inspiration
Edited by Lynn D. Morrissey
A woman's heart is complex. This daybook of stories, quotes, Scriptures, and daily reflections will inspire and refresh. Christian women share their heartfelt thoughts on seasons of faith, growth, guidance, nurturing, and victory. Includes Christian writers Kay Arthur, Emilie Barnes, Luci Swindoll, Jill Briscoe, and Florence Littauer.
(cloth)   ISBN 1892016036   **$18.95**

Why Fret That God Stuff?
Edited by Kathy Collard Miller
Subtitled: *Stories of Encouragement to Help You Let Go and Let God Take Control of All Things in Your Life*. Occasionally, we all become overwhelmed by the everyday challenges of our lives: hectic schedules, our loved ones' needs, unexpected expenses, a sagging devotional life. *Why Fret That God Stuff* is the perfect beginning to finding joy and peace for the real world!
(trade paper)   ISBN 0914984-500   **$12.95**

More of Him, Less of Me
Jan Christiansen
Subtitled: *A Daybook of My Personal Insights, Inspirations & Meditations on the Weigh Down™ Diet*. The insight shared in this year long daybook of inspiration will encourage you on your weight-loss journey, bring you to a deeper relationship with God, and help you improve any facet of your life. Each page includes an essay, scripture, and a tip-of-the-day that will encourage and uplift you as you trust God to help you achieve your proper weight. Perfect companion guide for anyone on the Weigh Down™ diet!
(cloth)   ISBN 1892016001   **$17.95**

Desert Morsels: A Journal with Encouraging Tidbits from My Journey on the Weigh Down™ Diet
Jan Christiansen
When Jan Christiansen set out to lose weight on the Weigh Down™ diet she got more than she bargained for! In addition to *losing* over 35 pounds and *gaining* a closer relationship with God, Jan discovered a gift—her ability to entertain and comfort fellow dieters! Jan's inspiring website led to the release of her best-selling first book, *More of Him, Less of Me*. Now, Jan serves another helping of her wit and His wisdom in this lovely companion journal. Includes inspiring scripture, insightful comments, stories from readers, room for the reader's personal reflection, and *Plenty of Attitude* (p-attitude).
(cloth)   ISBN 1892016214   **$17.95**

Purchasing Information

www.starburstpublishers.com

Books are available from your favorite bookstore, either from current stock or special order. To assist bookstores in locating your selection, be sure to give title, author, and ISBN. If unable to purchase from a bookstore, you may order direct from STARBURST PUBLISHERS. When ordering please enclose full payment plus shipping and handling as follows:

Post Office (4th class)
$3.00 with a purchase of up to $20.00
$4.00 ($20.01–$50.00)
5% of purchase price for purchases of $50.01 and up

United Parcel Service (UPS)
$4.50 (up to $20.00)
$6.00 ($20.01–$50.00)
7% ($50.01 and up)

Canada
$5.00 (up to $35.00)
15% ($35.01 and up)

Overseas
$5.00 (up to $25.00)
20% ($25.01 and up)

Payment in U.S. funds only. Please allow two to four weeks minimum for delivery by USPS (longer for overseas and Canada). Allow two to seven working days for delivery by UPS. Make checks payable to and mail to:

Starburst Publishers® • P.O. Box 4123 • Lancaster, PA 17604

Credit card orders may be placed by calling 1-800-441-1456, Mon–Fri, 8:30 A.M. to 5:30 P.M. Eastern Standard Time. Prices are subject to change without notice. Catalogs are available for a 9 x 12 self-addressed envelope with four first-class stamps.

NOTES

NOTES